중학 영어듣기 한 방에 끝낸다

AFTER SCHOOL Listening

안천구·넥서스영어교육연구소 지음

애프터스쿨 리스닝 level 3

NEXUS Edu

애프터스쿨 리스닝 level 3

After School Listening Level 3

지은이 안천구, 넥서스영어교육연구소
펴낸이 임상진
펴낸곳 (주)넥서스

출판신고 1992년 4월 3일 제311-2002-2호 ㉿
10880 경기도 파주시 지목로 5
Tel (02)330-5500 Fax (02)330-5555

ISBN 978-89-6000-823-6 58740
         978-89-6000-820-5 (SET)

www.nexusEDU.kr

After School Listening is ...

◆ ◆ ◆ ◆ 최신 기출문제 유형을 공부합니다.

지난 5년간 출제된 〈전국 15개 시, 도교육청 공동 주관 영어듣기능력평가〉의
출제유형을 철저히 분석하여 시험에 자주 나오는 최신 문제유형을 제공합니다.
_모의고사 16회 + dictation
_실전모의고사 2회

◆ ◆ ◆ ◆ 듣기 시험에 자신감을 심어줍니다.

실제 시험보다 난이도와 속도가 향상된 모의고사를 풀어봄으로써 실전에 대한
적응력을 높이는 것은 물론 평소보다 어려운 문제가 나왔을 경우에도 당황하지
않고 문제를 해결할 수 있는 능력을 키워줍니다.

◆ ◆ ◆ ◆ 체계적으로 공부합니다.

전국 15개 시, 도교육청 공동 주관 영어듣기능력평가를 분석하여 가장 많이
출제된 유형을 정리하여 부록으로 제공합니다.
_미니북 : 유형별 학습

◆ ◆ ◆ ◆ 영어실력을 한 단계 향상시킬 수 있습니다.

유형분석뿐만 아니라 각 유형과 관련된 단어와 표현 등을 집중적으로 학습하여
듣기 능력뿐만 아니라 전체적인 영어 실력을 향상시킬 수 있습니다.

Constitution

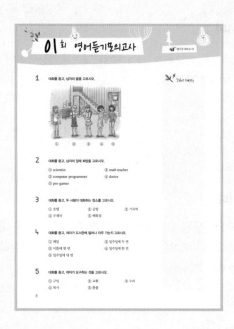

영어듣기모의고사 16회

최근 5년간 출제된 문제유형을 철저히 분석하여 출제 가능성이 높은 16회분 총 320문제의 최신 유형 문제들만 실었습니다.

Dictation

한 회가 끝날 때마다 지문을 다시 한 번 들으면서 놓치기 쉬운 주요 표현들을 받아쓰고 학습할 수 있도록 구성하였습니다.

실전모의고사 2회

영어듣기모의고사 16회를 통해서 갈고닦은 영어듣기
실력을 최종 실전모의고사 2회를 통해서 점검하고,
실전에 대비할 수 있습니다.

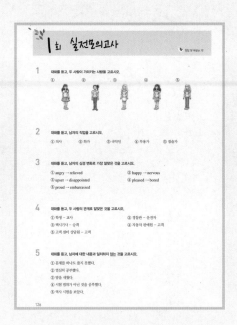

Mini book - 유형별 학습

부록으로 포함된 미니북에는 자주 출제되는
기출 유형과 이에 따른 단어, 숙어, 표현들을
정리하였습니다.
유형과 표현 학습을 끝내고 나서 기출문제를
풀어봄으로써 유형별 문제 풀이 능력을
향상시킬 수 있습니다.

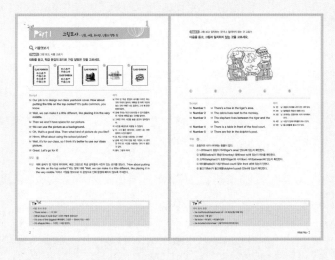

Contents

영어듣기모의고사 이~16회
실전모의고사 1~2회

01회 영어듣기모의고사

1 대화를 듣고, 남자의 딸을 고르시오.

① ② ③ ④ ⑤

Take notes

2 대화를 듣고, 남자의 장래 희망을 고르시오.

① scientist ② math teacher
③ computer programmer ④ doctor
⑤ pro-gamer

3 대화를 듣고, 두 사람이 대화하는 장소를 고르시오.

① 호텔 ② 공항 ③ 기차역
④ 우체국 ⑤ 백화점

4 대화를 듣고, 여자가 도서관에 얼마나 자주 가는지 고르시오.

① 매일 ② 일주일에 두 번
③ 이틀에 한 번 ④ 일주일에 한 번
⑤ 일주일에 네 번

5 대화를 듣고, 여자가 요구하는 것을 고르시오.

① 구입 ② 교환 ③ 수리
④ 복사 ⑤ 환불

6 다음을 듣고, 그림의 상황에 가장 잘 어울리는 대화를 고르시오.

Take notes

①   ②   ③   ④   ⑤

7 다음을 듣고, Kelly에 대한 설명으로 알맞지 <u>않은</u> 것을 고르시오.

① 한국에 온지 6개월 되었다.
② 자원봉사를 하려고 한국에 왔다.
③ 가난한 아이들을 도와준다.
④ 아이들에게 영어를 가르친다.
⑤ 그녀는 일해서 번 돈을 아이들을 위해 쓴다.

8 대화를 듣고, 여자가 휴대 전화를 새로 사려는 이유를 고르시오.

① 화면이 깨져서   ② 문자판이 닳아서
③ 오래된 모델이라서   ④ 분실해서
⑤ 작동이 되질 않아서

9 대화를 듣고, 남자가 지불해야 할 금액을 고르시오.

① $27   ② $32   ③ $36   ④ $39   ⑤ $42

10 다음 뉴스를 듣고, 알 수 <u>없는</u> 것을 고르시오.

① 뉴스 진행자   ② 뉴스 시간
③ 복구 대비책   ④ 재난 발생 원인
⑤ 재난 발생 장소

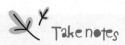

11 다음을 듣고, 메뉴의 내용과 일치하지 <u>않는</u> 것을 고르시오.

MENU

T-bone Steak: $10.00
Burger: $4.50
Ham Sandwich: $5.00
Tuna Sandwich: $6.00
Spaghetti: $6.00
Salad: $3.00
Soda: $1.50
free refill

①   ②   ③   ④   ⑤

12 다음을 듣고, 무엇에 대한 설명인지 고르시오.

① 행복   ② 시간   ③ 돈   ④ 가족   ⑤ 노력

13 다음을 듣고, 상황에 가장 잘 어울리는 속담을 고르시오.

① Don't count your chickens before they are hatched.
② Heaven helps those who help themselves.
③ Time and tide wait for no man.
④ Kill two birds with one stone.
⑤ Time heals all wounds.

14 대화를 듣고, 꽃의 가격으로 알맞은 것을 고르시오.

① $5   ② $8   ③ $10   ④ $13   ⑤ $30

15 대화를 듣고, 여자의 직업을 고르시오.

① 사진사   ② 주차 단속원   ③ 변호사
④ 운전면허 시험관   ⑤ 세관원

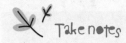

16 대화를 듣고, Ben의 현재 키로 알맞은 것을 고르시오.

① 153cm   ② 155cm   ③ 163cm

④ 165cm   ⑤ 179cm

17 대화를 듣고, 여자가 연주회에 갈 수 <u>없는</u> 이유를 고르시오.

① 파티에 가야 해서

② 시험공부를 해야 해서

③ 선생님과 약속이 있어서

④ 친구들과 과제를 해야 해서

⑤ 어머니의 일을 도와드려야 해서

18 대화를 듣고, 남자의 마지막 말에 대한 여자의 심정으로 알맞은 것을 고르시오.

① 불쌍한   ② 황당한   ③ 외로운

④ 즐거운   ⑤ 무서운

19-20 대화를 듣고, 남자의 마지막 말에 이어질 여자의 응답으로 가장 알맞은 것을 고르시오.

19

① I'm sorry to hear that.

② I'll go there by airplane.

③ I may not go traveling with you.

④ Really? You must be very excited.

⑤ That's great! How was New York?

20

① I'm not afraid that.

② Thank you. I'll pay next time.

③ I'm afraid you can't. I didn't bring it.

④ Nowadays, the price of cell phones is cheap.

⑤ Sorry to hear that you couldn't pay the phone bill.

Dictation

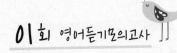

1

W Are you here with your daughter?

M Yes, I am. She's _____ _____ _____ over there.

W Which one?

M She is tall and thin.

W Most of them are tall and thin.

M That's right. But she has _____ _____ _____.

W I see. She's the one wearing glasses, right?

M No, she is _____ _____ _____.

2

W What do you want to do _____ _____ _____, John?

M I want to continue studying math.

W Do you _____ _____ _____ a math teacher?

M No, I don't.

W Then, what?

M My uncle, who is a computer programmer, told me to _____ _____ math to be a programmer like himself.

3

W Could you _____ _____ _____ _____ here, please?

M Sure, I have 3 suitcases.

W We only allow 2 pieces. You'll _____ _____ _____ an extra charge.

M Oh, _____ _____ _____, can I carry this one with me?

W No, I'm sorry. It won't fit under your seat.

M Then how much do I have to pay?

W You have to pay 25 dollars. You are good to go after I _____ _____ _____ _____ _____ and give you your baggage claim stubs.

4

W Where are you going, Mark?

M To the library.

W You seem to go to the library _____ _____.

M I do, but not as often as you do.

W How often do you go there?

M Well, I just go there when I _____ _____ it. How about you?

W As you know, I can't concentrate at all at home, so I go there _____ _____ _____.

M I see. Let's get going.

5

M What can I do for you, ma'am?

W I'm pretty _____ _____ this blender.

M What happened?

W I bought it last month, but it stopped working. So, I _____ _____ _____, but it broke again.

M I'm so sorry.

W Save your breath. I just want my money back.

M OK. Let me talk to my manager, and I'll _____ _____. Did you bring your receipt?

W Of course, I did.

6

① W It's time to go home.
  M Let's go. It's _____ _____.
② W How many times have I told you not to come late?
  M Sorry, Mom. It won't happen again.
③ W My watch is not working. Can you fix it?
  M Sure. You can _____ _____ _____ tomorrow.
④ W Where is your homework?
  M I'm sorry, Ms. Smith. I think I left it at home.
⑤ W I heard the clock strike eleven.
  M Yeah, we'd better _____ _____ _____.

7

W Kelly is from Australia. She's been in Korea for 6 months. She came here to learn Korean, but she now spends _____ _____ _____ _____ helping poor children who suffer from poverty and disease. She sometimes does English tutoring. She also works at a language institute part-time _____ _____ _____ _____ and spends a good percentage of her income on the children.

8

M Can I see your cell phone?
W Why? Do you need to _____ _____ _____ _____ _____?
M No, I just want to see your phone.
W OK. Here you go.
M Wow. The keypad is all worn out.
W I know. That's why I want to buy a new one. I've sent a lot of text messages. _____ _____ _____?
M I'm also thinking of buying a new one because I dropped it and broke the screen, but _____ _____ _____ _____.

9

[Telephone rings.]
W Hello, ticket office. _____ _____ _____ help you?
M Yes. Do you still have tickets for the Animal Show?
W Let me check. We still have tickets at 15 dollars a piece.
M Is there _____ _____ _____ _____ students?
W Yes, student tickets are 12 dollars each.
M That's good. Two student tickets and one adult, please.
W How would you like to pay for your tickets?
M I'll _____ _____ _____ at the ticket office.

10

W Hi, this is Abby Carter with the nine o'clock news from NBC radio. _____ _____ _____ is a major storm hit New Orleans today, and many houses and buildings _____ _____. People in the area are furious because the weather forecast was wrong. They _____ _____ _____ the disaster. Many volunteers have gathered to help those who have lost their house and family members.

Dictation

11

W ① You need _____ _____

_____ _____ spaghetti and salad.

② You need 11 dollars and 50 cents to have a steak and soda.

③ You can have _____ _____ for your soda.

④ You need 6 dollars to have a burger and soda.

⑤ You need 8 dollars to have _____

_____ _____ and salad.

12

W Everyone in our society _____

_____ _____, but not all of them can get the amount they want. It can make you happy or unhappy, but it _____

_____ how you feel about the amount you have. For example, some have a lot of this, but they are still not satisfied with it and look for more of this, _____

_____ _____ _____.

Others have a little, but they are happy with it. Therefore, the amount you have is not important, but rather how you use it.

13

M Mike is more popular _____

_____ _____ _____ in his school. He is handsome, tall, and smart. He is very confident about himself. One day, when he was _____ _____

_____ _____, an attractive girl looked at him and kept smiling. He thought

he had caught her eye, and she wanted to talk. He waited until she _____

_____ _____ him. Finally, up close she said, "Your fly is open." He was so embarrassed.

14

M What can I do for you?

W I like the vase _____ _____

_____ _____.

M Good choice. Many people have bought one since I put it there.

W How much are you asking for it?

M It's 13 dollars _____ _____

_____ with flowers.

W I don't want the flowers. I just want the vase.

M Then, _____ _____ _____ 8 dollars.

15

M Excuse me, what are you doing?

W Sir, you illegally parked your car.

M I _____ _____ _____

_____.

W Okay, but I still have to give you a ticket.

M Oh, no. Please _____ _____

_____ _____.

W I can't. I've already written down your license plate number.

M Come on. I wasn't even here for 5 minutes.

W Sorry, sir. But I'm just _____

_____ _____.

14

16

W   You look troubled, Ben. What's wrong?

M   I think I'm too short.

W   Don't worry. You're only 15 years old. You'll _____ _____ until you reach the age of 20.

M   I know, but I was 160cm last year, and when I checked my height this morning, there was not _____ _____.

W   Let me tell you this. Your father was 153cm when he was your age, but he is now 179cm. He grew 26cm in two years.

M   I know. He told me about that, but I have only grown 3cm _____ _____ _____.

17

M   Jenny, I got two tickets _____ _____ _____.

W   You did? I'm so sorry, but I don't think I can go if it's on Saturday.

M   Why not?

W   I have to go to Susie's house.

M   Why? Is she having a party or something?

W   No, our teacher gave us a group project to _____ _____.

M   That's too bad. Maybe _____ _____ _____.

18

W   Kevin, _____ _____ _____ _____?

M   I'm sorry. I had an accident.

W   Are you okay? What kind of accident?

M   Someone robbed me on the way over here.

W   Really? _____ _____ _____?

M   No. I'm okay.

W   That's good. By the way, _____ _____ _____ _____?

M   I did, but the thief took my notebook as well.

19

W   Hey, Sam. Are you going to _____ _____ with me this Sunday?

M   I'm sorry. I won't be able to _____ _____ _____ _____.

W   Why? Are you going somewhere?

M   Yes, my family's _____ _____ _____ _____ to New York.

W   Really? You must be very excited.

20

W   Hey, Leo. Are you _____ _____ something?

M   Is there a payphone around here? I need to call my mom to _____ _____ _____ that I'm going to be a little late.

W   I don't think there is. There is one near the main gate, but it's kind of far.

M   I see. Then, can I use your cell phone? I'll pay you for the call.

W   _____ _____ _____ _____ _____. I didn't bring it.

✗ Take notes

1 다음을 듣고, 찾고 있는 아이와 일치하는 그림을 고르시오.

①   ②   ③

④   ⑤

2 대화를 듣고, 두 사람이 대화하는 장소를 고르시오.

① 식당 ② 우체국 ③ 병원 ④ 학교 ⑤ 예식장

3 대화를 듣고, 일치하지 <u>않는</u> 것을 고르시오.

① 여자는 초보자이다.
② 일주일에 세 번 초보자를 위한 강습이 있다.
③ 한 달 수강료는 300달러이다.
④ 연습은 언제든지 할 수 있다.
⑤ 수강료는 신용카드로 낼 수 있다.

4 대화를 듣고, 여자의 직업으로 알맞은 것을 고르시오.

① 의사 ② 간호사 ③ 승무원
④ 판매원 ⑤ 호텔 직원

5 대화를 듣고, 남자가 여자에게 주어야 할 돈의 액수를 고르시오.

① $20 ② $24 ③ $30 ④ $34 ⑤ $38

6 대화를 듣고, 남자에 대한 내용과 일치하지 <u>않는</u> 것을 고르시오.

① 이곳에 온지 거의 일 년이 되었다.

② 친한 친구가 없다.

③ 수줍음을 많이 탄다.

④ 시골 출신이라고 사람들이 비웃는다고 생각한다.

⑤ 말을 할 때 억양 때문에 긴장을 한다.

Take notes

7 대화를 듣고, 두 사람이 만날 시간으로 알맞은 것을 고르시오.

① 1:00   ② 1:30   ③ 2:00   ④ 2:30   ⑤ 3:00

8 대화를 듣고, 내용과 일치하지 <u>않는</u> 것을 고르시오.

① 소년은 차와 가볍게 부딪쳤다.

② 소년은 가벼운 찰과상을 입었다.

③ 운전자는 소년을 병원에 데려가지 않았다.

④ 소년은 남자에게 명함을 받았다.

⑤ 소년은 부모에게 사고에 대해 말하지 않았다.

9 다음을 듣고, 상황에 가장 잘 어울리는 속담을 고르시오.

① Walls have ears.

② Better late than never.

③ Even a worm will turn.

④ The early bird catches the worm.

⑤ Heaven helps those who help themselves.

10 대화를 듣고, 남자가 전화를 건 목적을 고르시오.

① 책을 주문하려고

② 분실물을 찾으려고

③ 버스표를 예매하려고

④ 영어 책을 빌리려고

⑤ 버스 시간을 알아보려고

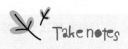

11 다음을 듣고, 광고의 내용과 일치하지 <u>않는</u> 것을 고르시오.

①   ②   ③   ④   ⑤

12 다음을 듣고, 여자가 극장에 갈 수 <u>없는</u> 이유를 고르시오.

① 숙제 때문에   ② 시험공부를 해야 해서
③ 사고로 다쳐서   ④ 기차가 연착이 되어서
⑤ 부모님이 허락하지 않아서

13 대화를 듣고, 여자가 내일 할 일로 알맞은 것을 고르시오.

① 시내 관광 안내   ② 공항에 데려다 주기
③ 식사 초대   ④ 구직 안내
⑤ 학교 안내

14 다음을 듣고, 여자가 고민하는 것을 고르시오.

① 소심한 성격   ② 말을 더듬는 것
③ 다리 흔드는 것   ④ 손톱 물어뜯는 것
⑤ 머리 긁적이는 것

15 다음을 듣고, 두 사람의 대화가 <u>어색한</u> 것을 고르시오.

①   ②   ③   ④   ⑤

16 다음을 듣고, "I"가 가리키는 것을 고르시오.

① balloon   ② fireworks   ③ airplane

④ movie star   ⑤ fire station

Take notes

17 대화를 듣고, 여자가 화가 난 이유를 고르시오.

① 남자가 숙제를 안 해서

② 남자가 시험 준비를 하지 않아서

③ 남자가 자신의 공책을 잃어버려서

④ 남자가 자신의 숙제를 그대로 베껴서

⑤ 남자가 빌려 준 공책을 가져오지 않아서

18 대화를 듣고, 여자의 심정으로 알맞은 것을 고르시오.

① angry   ② pleased   ③ scared

④ jealous   ⑤ hopeful

19-20 대화를 듣고, 여자의 마지막 말에 이어질 남자의 응답으로 가장 알맞은 것을 고르시오.

19
① Yes, I'd love to.

② No, go right ahead.

③ Wow, it's fantastic!

④ Thanks! What's that?

⑤ You're very welcome.

20
① My seat number is 12C.

② It will probably land at 3:30.

③ As soon as you get on the plane.

④ Thank you for your information.

⑤ The departure time is 10:30 P.M.

Dictation

1

W Hello, shoppers! We're looking for a boy. His name is Peter Jackson. He _____ _____ in the shoe store on the third floor. He's wearing a striped shirt and blue jeans. He's also wearing a baseball cap with number 13 on it.

_____ _____ _____ _____, please bring him to the information desk near the main exit. Thank you.

2

M Excuse me.

W Yes, do you need something?

M Yes, just _____ _____ _____ _____ this. I think it is too overcooked.

W Didn't you order it well-done?

M Yes, I did. But this is _____ _____.

W Do you want me to get you a new one?

M Yes, please.

W Okay. I'll _____ _____ _____.

3

W Excuse me, when do you offer guitar lessons?

M That _____ _____ your level. Are you a beginner?

W Yes, I am.

M Then, every Monday, Wednesday, and Friday.

W How much is the lesson fee?

M 300 dollars a month. You can also _____ _____ to practice any time.

W Okay, do you take credit cards?

M Sorry, we only _____ _____.

4

M Excuse me, someone dropped this boarding pass.

W Thank you. I'll give it to the person _____ _____ _____.

M By the way, do you have any extra blankets?

W Sure, I do. Is it cold in here?

M No, it's not. I just might feel cold while I sleep. _____ _____.

W OK. I'll bring _____ _____ _____.

M Thank you.

5

W John, pay me what you owe me.

M Of course, what do I owe you?

W _____ _____ _____, you lost the book I lent you. That's 10 dollars. Second, you borrowed 20 dollars from me last week. Do you remember?

M How can I forget? _____ _____ _____?

W No, you dropped my cell phone, and the case broke. It's 8 dollars for that.

M Come on! _____ _____ _____ _____, OK?

W OK, but you have to pay me now.

M All right.

6

M Can I talk to you for a second?

W Sure. _____ _____ _____?

M I've been here for almost a year, but I still don't have any friends. I mean a close friend.

W You must be very shy, am I right?

M No, I'm not. That's not the reason. I think some people laugh at me because I'm from the countryside and even _____ _____ _____ my accent. I get very nervous when I talk to people.

W I understand that you have a little different accent than people in Seoul, but you _____ _____ _____ _____ nervous. Be confident. OK?

7

M Amanda, you are leaving tomorrow, right?

W Yes, I am.

M If there isn't anyone to _____ _____ _____ _____, I can. What time is the train?

W The train leaves at 3, and I need to get there 30 minutes early.

M That's no problem. Then, what time do you want me _____ _____ _____ _____?

W How long does it take to get there?

M 30 minutes. Then, let's meet an hour and a half before the train leaves.

8

W William, what happened to you? Where did you get those scratches?

M I tried to avoid a car coming at me and _____ _____ this morning.

W Oh, no. Are you okay now?

M Yes, I didn't get too _____ _____.

Only these.

W Did the driver take you to the hospital?

M No, he just gave me his _____ _____.

W Did you tell your parents about it?

M No, I'm going to _____ _____ _____.

9

M Ben is in the last year of junior high, but he is very small and weak. In his class, there is one boy who keeps bothering him and sometimes _____ _____ _____ _____. Since he is tall and strong, Ben can't help doing what he is told to do. Today, at the cafeteria, the boy told Ben to bring him some water, but Ben _____ _____ _____ _____, so he refused to do so. Then, this boy came up to Ben and hit him on the back of his head. Ben got angry, turned around, and threw a punch toward his face.

10

[Telephone rings.]

W Hello.

M Hello. _____ _____ _____ you could help me.

W Yes. What's the problem?

M I left a few English books I bought on the bus.

W That's too bad. Do you remember _____ _____ _____ _____ _____ _____ and the approximate time?

M Yes, I think it was 7112, and it was around 3 o'clock.

W All right. I'll let you know right after I _____ _____ the driver.

M Thank you. My number is 010-5400-5186.

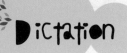

Dictation

11

W ① If a bike is 200 dollars, you just need one hundred and eighty dollars.

② You can get a 15 percent _____ _____.

③ If a necklace is 50 dollars, you just need 45 dollars.

④ The sale starts on Dec 1st and ends on _____ _____ _____ _____ _____ _____.

⑤ The shop opens for 13 hours a day.

12

W Hi, David. I'm leaving a message to let you know that I can't go to the movies with you tonight. _____ _____ _____ _____, but the train I'm on is delayed because of an unexpected accident. _____ _____ _____ I get to Seoul, I'll call you. Sorry that I can't _____ _____, but we can go to the movies some other time. Bye.

13

M This is my first time in New York. I heard there are so many skyscrapers in Manhattan.

W That's right. It's even hard to see the moon at night _____ _____ _____, but you are going to like this place.

M You think so?

W Of course. What time _____ _____ _____ _____ _____ go

for a sightseeing tour of the city?

M Anytime. I'm ready.

W OK. I guess you are pretty tired, so have a good sleep, and I'll call you tomorrow morning.

M _____ _____.

14

W I'm a sixteen-year old girl. I'm an active and outgoing person. I'm confident and _____ _____ _____ _____ in anything with boys, but I get too nervous when speaking before a group. Even though I prepare a lot for a speech, my mind _____ _____, and I even stutter. It's because my schoolteacher made fun of me when I spoke in class. Since that time, I get pale and confused when _____ _____ _____.

15

① W How was that concert?
   M It was really fantastic.
② W I'd like to buy a small lamp.
   M _____ _____ _____, please.
③ W What time shall we make it?
   M _____ _____ _____ the post office.
④ W May I speak to Mike?
   M Sorry, but there is no one here _____ _____ _____.
⑤ W _____ _____ _____ repeating that?
   M Of course not.

22

16

M I'm used at festivals, parties, or national holidays. I can make people excited and surprised. I explode _____ _____ _____ and produce colored lights, so I can beautifully color the night sky. But I also produce loud noises and _____ _____ _____ _____ _____.

17

W Did you _____ _____ _____ with the notebook I lent you? You didn't just copy it from my notebook, did you?

M Of course, I didn't.

W Let me see. Oh my God! You copied me _____ _____ _____.

M No, I changed a few things.

W Only a few. If our teacher finds out that yours is almost _____ _____ _____ _____, he'll give both of us an F.

M Don't worry. It won't happen. I don't think he's going to take a look at all of ours.

W What if he does?

18

W Excuse me?

M Me? Are you talking to me?

W Yes, you.

M What is it?

W You just spilt soda on the floor.

M So what? It's _____ _____ _____ _____.

W It's my business. I walk on this floor every day, and you made it dirty. _____ _____, someone might step on it and fall down. It's very dangerous.

M If you think it's that dangerous, you can _____ _____ _____ _____.

W So, you're saying you are not going to clean it up, and you don't care if anyone gets hurt?

M Right, I don't care!

W _____ _____ _____.

19

M Hi! Emma. Come on in. _____ _____ _____ _____ to my housewarming party.

W Hi, David. This is for you.

M Thank you. Let me put this on the table.

W It's a bit cold outside.

M I know. Please, _____ _____ _____ _____. Can I take your coat?

W Thanks. This is a great apartment! Do you mind if I _____ _____ _____ _____?

M No, go right ahead.

20

M _____ _____ _____ _____?

W I'd like to get some information on a flight.

M What flight number would that be for?

W It's OZ 201. What time is _____ _____ _____?

M The departure time is 10:30 P.M.

03회 영어듣기모의고사

정답 및 해설 p.13

1 대화를 듣고, 여자가 원하는 머리 모양을 고르시오.

①   ②   ③

④   ⑤

2 대화를 듣고, 여자가 대화 후 가장 먼저 할 일을 고르시오.

① 숙제　　　　　② 텔레비전 시청　　　③ 저녁 식사
④ 농구 연습　　　⑤ 샤워

3 대화를 듣고, 남자가 지불할 금액을 고르시오.

① $2　　② $3　　③ $5　　④ $6　　⑤ $8

4 대화를 듣고, 여자가 지금 필요로 하는 것이 무엇인지 고르시오.

① 수정액　　　　② 클립　　　　③ 스테이플러
④ 컴퓨터　　　　⑤ 압정

5 다음을 듣고, 주어진 질문에 알맞은 답을 고르시오.

① 4권　　② 5권　　③ 6권　　④ 7권　　⑤ 8권

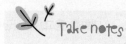
6 대화를 듣고, 여자의 심정으로 알맞은 것을 고르시오.

① 자랑스러운   ② 안도한   ③ 슬픈   ④ 당황한   ⑤ 기쁜

7 다음을 듣고, 두 사람의 대화가 <u>어색한</u> 것을 고르시오.

①   ②   ③   ④   ⑤

8 대화를 듣고, 여자가 남자에게 화가 난 이유를 고르시오.

① 사진기를 잃어버려서
② 사진기가 고장이 나서
③ MP3 재생기가 고장이 나서
④ 빌린 물건을 함부로 다루어서
⑤ 사진기를 제때 가져오지 않아서

9 대화를 듣고, 여자가 한 마지막 말의 의도를 고르시오.

① agreement   ② warning   ③ suggestion
④ praise   ⑤ advice

10 대화를 듣고, 그림의 상황에 가장 잘 어울리는 대화를 고르시오.

①   ②   ③   ④   ⑤

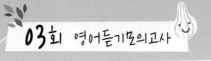

11 대화를 듣고, 두 사람이 대화하는 장소를 고르시오.

① 병원   ② 식당   ③ 회사   ④ 학교   ⑤ 공항

12 다음을 듣고, 아시아에 대한 내용으로 언급되지 <u>않은</u> 것을 고르시오.

① 문화   ② 면적   ③ 인구   ④ 기후   ⑤ 주식

13 대화를 듣고, 내용과 일치하는 것을 표에서 고르시오.

	도착지	편도 / 왕복	출발일	좌석등급
①	Seoul	one-way	Saturday	business class
②	New York	one-way	Sunday	economy class
③	Seoul	one-way	Sunday	business class
④	New York	round-trip	Saturday	business class
⑤	Seoul	round-trip	Saturday	economy class

14 다음을 듣고, 무엇에 대한 설명인지 고르시오.

① 쥐불놀이   ② 썰매타기   ③ 제기차기
④ 팽이치기   ⑤ 연날리기

15 대화를 듣고, 여자가 대화 후 가장 먼저 할 일을 고르시오.

① 배관공에게 전화하기
② 관리인에게 항의하기
③ 윗집에 알리기
④ 바닥 닦기
⑤ 수돗물 잠그기

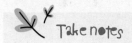

16 대화를 듣고, Susie의 생일 파티가 열리는 날짜를 고르시오.

① 6월 4일　　　② 6월 7일　　　③ 7월 1일
④ 7월 4일　　　⑤ 7월 7일

17 대화를 듣고, 남자가 세탁소에 간 이유를 고르시오.

① 항의하려고
② 옷을 맡기려고
③ 옷을 찾으려고
④ 돈을 지불하려고
⑤ 얼룩 제거법을 물어보려고

18 대화를 듣고, 여자가 대화 후 할 일을 고르시오.

① 가족과 저녁 식사
② 병원에 진료 예약하기
③ 도서관에서 공부하기
④ 상담교사에게 전화하기
⑤ 부모님과 대화하기

19-20 대화를 듣고, 남자의 마지막 말에 이어질 여자의 응답으로 가장 알맞은 것을 고르시오.

19
① Just kidding.
② There are six.
③ It's too simple and easy.
④ I don't know the answer.
⑤ You told me to repeat after you.

20
① We watched a lot of TV.
② There was nothing else to do.
③ We went shopping almost every day.
④ My father was angry with my mother.
⑤ Like I told you, we stayed in the hotel.

Dictation

1

M How would you like to _____
   _____ _____?

W I'd like a straight perm.

M OK. You want to keep your beautiful long
   hair, am I right?

W That's correct, but I'd like to cut it a little.

M Then, how about keeping it 10 centimeters
   _____ _____ _____?

W OK.

2

M Sally, let's do homework together.

W I already _____ _____
   _____.

M Really? Then, are you going to watch TV
   now?

W No. I'd rather have supper first. I'm hungry.

M Okay. I heard that you have a basketball
   game tomorrow.

W Yes, I just practiced a lot _____
   _____ _____ _____.

M You did?

W Yes. I'm going to _____ _____
   _____ after supper and go to sleep
   early for tomorrow's game.

3

M I'm here to return these three DVDs.

W Can I see your membership card?

M OK. Here you go.

W Thank you. Let me see. Peter Kim.
   _____ _____ _____ was
   yesterday, which means you have to pay a
   late charge.

M Oh, I'm sorry. How much is that?

W You pay a dollar _____ _____
   _____ _____.

M OK. And I want to rent Brave Heart.

W That one's 3 dollars.

M I only have 5 dollars. What can I do?

W Okay. I'll give you a discount since you're
   _____ _____ _____.

4

M Do you have a stapler?

W Yes, _____ _____ _____.

M Thanks. There are no staples in it.

W Don't worry. I'll get you some. _____
   _____ _____, do you have
   correction fluid?

M I think I do. It's right here.

W Thanks. I have _____ _____
   _____ _____ _____.

5

W _____ _____ it takes 20 hours
   for Alan to read 4 books. _____
   _____, it takes 5 hours
   for Alan to read one book _____
   _____. Then, how many books can
   Alan read in 30 hours?

6

W Hey, Chris. (slapping sound on his back)

M Ouch! _____ _____ _____?

W Chris, it's me. Joan.

M Do I know you?

W Of course. You and I went to Jackson Elementary School together.

M _____ _____ _____ _____, but I went to St. Mary Elementary School, and my name is not Chris.

7

① W I'm getting nervous.

　 M _____ _____ _____. It'll be over soon.

② W How long does the movie run?

　 M It runs for one hundred and twenty minutes.

③ W Can you give me _____ _____ _____ _____?

　 M How about some green tea with ice?

④ W What kind of movie is this?

　 M Yes, I like it. I'm sure you'll like it, too.

⑤ W How much do you think it's going to cost _____ _____ _____ _____ _____?

　 M Well, I guess at least 200 dollars.

8

W Julian, do you have my digital camera with you?

M No. But I can get it _____ _____.

W Please go and get it then. I need it for my mother's birthday.

M OK. But before that, I have _____ _____ _____ _____ _____.

W I'm listening.

M There are some scratches on it. The other day, I _____ _____ _____ my brother and dropped it.

W Are you serious? Last time when you borrowed my MP3 player, you scratched it, too. Remember? You're always careless. I don't think I'll lend you my stuff anymore.

M I'm really sorry, but the camera still works fine.

9

[Telephone rings.]

W Did you finish the homework?

M Almost.

W _____ _____ _____ _____ _____ _____?

M My friend called me while I was doing it.

W Do you realize that you have been doing your homework for 3 hours? I've been watching you, but you haven't been concentrating at all.

M Sorry.

W This will be _____ _____ _____ I talk to you. Do it _____ _____ _____.

10

① W _____ _____ _____ _____ _____ for a ticket?

　 M It's 5 dollars for an adult.

② W Where can I find the box office?

　 M It's right over there.

③ W Where would you like to go sightseeing?

　 M I'd like to go to N Seoul Tower.

④ W What's the purpose of your visit?

　 M I'm here _____ _____ _____ _____.

⑤ W Should I pay for it now?

　 M It's _____ _____ _____ _____.

Dictation

11

W Hey, James. What a surprise! I didn't expect to see you here.

M Hi, Sandra. My wife is in the delivery room. She's already been there _____ _____ _____ _____. Are you visiting someone here?

W No, I'm pregnant. I'm on my 4th week now.

M Congratulations!

W Thanks. I have to go now. I'll _____ _____ _____.

12

M Asia _____ _____ _____ _____ approximately 50 countries. These countries have different cultures and hardly have anything _____ _____. Asia makes up nearly one third of the Earth's land and has more people _____ _____ _____ _____. In fact, two out of every three people on Earth are Asians. For the people of this continent, rice is a very common food.

13

[Telephone rings.]

W Best Airlines. How may I help you?

M I'd like to _____ _____ _____ _____ from New York to Seoul.

W That would be a one-way ticket, right?

M Yes, and I would like to leave this Sunday.

W I'm sorry, but Sunday _____ _____ _____. There are still _____ _____ _____ on Saturday or Monday.

M Um. Then, Saturday will be fine.

W Which class would you like?

M Business class, please.

14

W This is something we usually do in winter. This is _____ _____ _____ our country. I have seen some people in other countries do this, and they have the same kind _____ _____ _____. It is a light frame covered with colored paper or plastic, and it is easy to make. The windier it is, the higher you can make it fly. A long time ago, we used it during war _____ _____ _____.

15

W Ralph, look at the floor.

M Oh, no. Where is this water _____ _____?

W I think the bathtub upstairs is leaking again.

M We need to call a plumber right now.

W I will, but before that, I need to _____ _____ this water first.

M Let me do that.

W Then, I'll call the manager and _____ _____ _____.

M Hey, honey. I think you should let the upstairs tenants know what's happening here first.

W OK. I'll do that now.

16

M Have you been invited to Susie's birthday party?

W Sure. It's on July 4th, right?

M No, that's a national holiday, so it's being held _____ _____ _____ at her house.

W How come she didn't tell me?

M Maybe she hasn't had _____ _____ _____ _____ to you.

W It's still at 6 o'clock, right?

M Right. If you need a ride, call me _____ _____ _____.

W Thank you.

17

W Are you here to _____ _____ _____ _____?

M No, I brought a dress shirt.

W Okay. Your name and phone number, please.

M John Hopkins. My phone number is 786-6131.

W Thank you.

M I have one thing to tell you. There is a stain on the left sleeve. Can you _____ _____ _____ it?

W I guess I can do it easily _____ _____ _____ _____. You can pick it up tomorrow.

18

W I think I really studied hard, but my test result was terrible. I don't know _____ _____ _____ _____.

M How about talking to the school counselor? She will _____ _____ _____ _____.

W Where is her office?

M I'll show you, but you need to _____ _____ first.

W Do you mean I have to call her?

M Yeah. Here's her phone number.

19

M Hey, Judith. Let's _____ _____ _____. I'll give you a quiz, and you give me an answer. OK?

W OK. I'll _____ _____.

M The rule is very simple. Just repeat after me.

W OK.

M One yellow ball.

W One yellow ball.

M Two white balls.

W Two white balls.

M Three black balls.

W Three black balls.

M How many are there?

W How many are there?

M You're wrong. There are six balls.

W You told me to _____ _____ _____.

20

M How was your trip to Hawaii?

W It was raining every day, so we couldn't enjoy the beach.

M _____ _____ _____ _____.

W It was nice for my father, though. He actually liked staying in the hotel.

M I see.

W _____ _____ _____ that we spent rather a lot of money.

M How so?

W We _____ _____ almost every day.

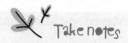
1 대화를 듣고, 두 사람이 이번 주말에 할 일을 고르시오.

① 야구 경기 관람　　② 생일 파티 참석　　③ 외식
④ 잔디 깎기　　　　⑤ 집들이

 Take notes

2 대화를 듣고, 남자가 찾는 사람을 고르시오.

①　　②　　③　

④　　⑤　

3 대화를 듣고, 여자가 지불해야 할 금액을 고르시오.

① $10　　② $15　　③ $20　　④ $25　　⑤ $45

4 대화를 듣고, 남자가 여자와 만나기로 한 시각을 고르시오.

① 3:00　　② 3:30　　③ 4:00　　④ 5:30　　⑤ 6:00

5 대화를 듣고, 남자가 전화를 건 목적을 고르시오.

① 콘서트 티켓을 팔려고
② 콘서트에 같이 가자고
③ 콘서트 시간을 알아보려고
④ 콘서트 장소를 알아보려고
⑤ 콘서트 가는 길을 물어보려고

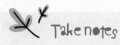

6 대화를 듣고, 남자의 마지막 말에 대한 여자의 심정으로 알맞은 것을 고르시오.

① 지루한　　② 기쁜　　③ 만족한　　④ 불쾌한　　⑤ 황당한

7 대화를 듣고, 여자의 직업으로 알맞은 것을 고르시오.

① police officer　　② clerk　　③ flight attendant
④ teller　　⑤ tour guide

8 대화를 듣고, 상황에 어울리는 속담으로 알맞은 것을 고르시오.

① No news good news.
② Still waters run deep.
③ Don't cry over spilt milk.
④ Two heads are better than one.
⑤ Too many cooks spoil the broth.

9 다음을 듣고, 무엇에 관한 설명인지 고르시오.

① 담배　　② 술　　③ 컴퓨터 게임
④ 휴대 전화　　⑤ 거짓말

10 대화를 듣고, 여자가 찾아가려는 장소를 고르시오.

11 다음을 듣고, 그림의 상황에 가장 잘 어울리는 대화를 고르시오.

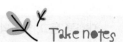

①   ②   ③   ④   ⑤

12 대화를 듣고, 두 사람의 관계로 가장 알맞은 것을 고르시오.

① 서점 직원 – 고객   ② 사서교사 – 학생

③ 백화점 직원 – 고객   ④ 주차장 직원 – 고객

⑤ 은행 직원 – 고객

13 대화를 듣고, 여자의 심경으로 알맞은 것을 고르시오.

① angry   ② depressed   ③ nervous

④ disappointed   ⑤ excited

14 대화를 듣고, 내용과 일치하지 <u>않는</u> 것을 고르시오.

① 여행하는 총 인원은 3명이다.

② 숙박료로 하루에 백 달러와 세금을 내야 한다.

③ 여자는 가격이 다소 비싸다고 생각한다.

④ 일행은 5일을 묵을 예정이다.

⑤ 여자는 숙박비를 현금으로 지불할 것이다.

15 다음을 듣고, 두 사람의 대화가 <u>어색한</u> 것을 고르시오.

①   ②   ③   ④   ⑤

16 다음을 듣고, 여자가 Charles에게 할 말로 가장 알맞은 것을 고르시오.

✗ Take notes

① Calm down!

② Be confident!

③ Have a happy life.

④ Don't be so selfish!

⑤ Don't be disappointed!

17 대화를 듣고, 두 사람이 대화하는 장소를 고르시오.

① hospital ② post office ③ bank

④ Internet cafe ⑤ library

18 다음을 듣고, 과체중의 원인으로 언급되지 <u>않은</u> 것을 고르시오.

① 과도한 패스트푸드 섭취 ② 부족한 운동

③ 불규칙적인 식사 시간 ④ 지나친 TV시청

⑤ 지나친 컴퓨터 게임

[19~20] 대화를 듣고, 남자의 마지막 말에 이어질 여자의 응답으로 가장 알맞은 것을 고르시오.

19 ① Thank you very much.

② She really wants to see you.

③ I'm sorry that you feel that way.

④ Don't worry. You will lose weight.

⑤ I understand your reasoning, but it was impolite.

20 ① She's always late and often doesn't show up.

② She wants to be the club president.

③ I think she comes too often.

④ OK. I'll call her right now.

⑤ Because it is interesting.

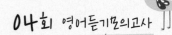
1

W Is Mike going to visit us next Friday or this Friday?

M Next Friday. He told me if we buy him dinner, he'll _____ _____ _____ _____ _____ _____.

W OK.

M So, which restaurant do you want to go?

W Let's go to a Korean restaurant.

M Sounds good. By the way, I'll _____ _____ _____ this weekend. You are going to help me, right?

W Sure.

2

M My name is Nick Campbell. _____ _____ _____ _____ Mr. Henderson.

W Do you _____ _____ _____?

M Yes. At 10 o'clock.

W Okay. We have two Hendersons in our office.

M I mean James Henderson.

W _____ _____ _____ _____ _____, but their first names are the same.

M He has a mustache, and he is bald.

W Okay. I'll contact him right away.

3

W Two tickets, please.

M _____ _____?

W Row A.

M That'll be 20 dollars each.

W That's too expensive. _____ _____ row B?

M That'll be 10 dollars each.

W Let me see. OK. I'll take those.

M All right. Is the boy your son? If he is over 5, he has to _____ _____ _____.

W I guess I _____ _____ _____. Tickets for two adults and one child in row B.

4

W Are you going to _____ _____ Mr. Kim?

M Yes. If you are too, we can go together.

W What time is his flight?

M _____ _____ _____ is 6 P.M.

W I see. What time should we meet?

M I think we should be there at 5, and _____ _____ _____ to get to the airport. So, I'll pick you up 30 minutes earlier. Is that OK?

W Yeah. I'll see you soon.

5

[Telephone rings.]

M Hey! Kelly. It's Jason. I got some tickets for a great concert.

W I'm sorry, but I'm _____ _____ busy these days.

M That's not the reason I'm calling you. I want to get rid of them. I'll let them _____ _____ _____ _____ _____.

W Okay. I'll _____ _____, but I think it's going to be hard.

M Just ask around for me, okay?

6

M Where to?

W Seoul Plaza, please.

M OK.

W Excuse me, I'm a pretty forgetful person, so _____ _____ _____ I might forget where I'm going. So, please _____ _____ if I ask, OK?

M Sure. Don't worry.

W Oh, no. Excuse me, where am I going?

M Hey! Where did you _____ _____?

7

W May I help you?

M Yes. I'd like to _____ _____ _____.

W Okay. Is this the first time with us?

M Yes, it is.

W Okay. Please _____ _____ _____ _____. Can I ask you how much you will deposit?

M 500 dollars. I'm done with the form.

W Thank you. I'll process an ATM card now.

M Thank you.

8

W Do you know Alex Smith?

M Sure, I do. He _____ _____ _____. Why?

W He's my classmate. He got a perfect score on the final, and he is the top in our school.

M I didn't know that. He doesn't _____ _____ himself much, and he is a good listener.

W And you know what? His ideas and ways of thinking are very creative. His science project _____ _____ _____ last semester. We were all amazed.

M Wow! What an intelligent boy he is! He never brags about himself.

9

M I'm _____ _____. I'm not good for one's health. People in America even call me a cancer stick, but some people still like me. These days, a lot of women and teenagers try me, so I'd like to warn you that _____ _____ _____ _____, it is almost impossible to stop. I have another warning for sellers of me. Please remember that _____ _____ _____ to sell me to teenagers.

10

W Excuse me, Mr. Can you tell me _____ _____ _____ _____ the National Bank?

M Sure. It's a little far from here, but it's _____ _____ _____ _____.

W Okay.

M Go straight for two blocks and make a left at the corner.

W Okay, and then?

M Then, go one more block and turn right at the corner. You'll see it on your left.

W That's pretty complicated. I think I should _____ _____ _____.

Dictation

11

① M May I see your driver's license?
   W What did I do wrong?

② M Your car is ready _____
       _____ _____ _____ .
   W Thank you.

③ M I really like your car.
   W Thanks. I bought it _____
       _____ _____ .

④ M Excuse me, something is burning.
   W Oh my God! I forgot to _____
       _____ _____ _____ .

⑤ M What a terrific driver you are!
   W Thank you! I learned _____
       _____ _____ from my
       father.

12

M What can I do for you?
W How many books can I _____
   _____ ?
M You can check out _____ _____
   _____ 10 items. But make sure you
   return them by the due date. Otherwise,
   you have to _____ _____
   _____ _____ .
W I understand. Can I check out weekly
   magazines, too?
M I'm afraid you can't.
W I got it. Thank you.

13

W Hey, Eric. When do we fly?
M We still got 45 minutes.
W Then, let me go to the restroom. I need to
   _____ _____ _____ .
M Sure. But don't you think you go to the
   restroom too often? You've been to it five
   times already since we came to the airport.

W I know, but my stomach is upset. It is my
   first time to _____ _____
   _____ .
M Is it? It'll be okay. Try to _____
   _____ _____ _____ and
   calm down.

14

W Excuse me, do you _____ _____
   _____ ?
M Yes, we do.
W That's great. I need one double bed for my
   parents and a single for me.
M OK.
W What's _____ _____
   _____ _____ _____ ?
M 60 and 40 plus tax.
W That's pretty reasonable. I'd like to stay for
   5 days.
M I see. _____ _____ _____
   _____ _____ _____ for
   it?
W Cash.

15

① M How would you like to get the money?
   W Please give it to me in twenty-dollar
      bills.

② M Excuse me, I'd like to _____
      _____ .
   W Can I have your passport, please?

③ M _____ _____ _____ ,
      please.
   W Absolutely.

④ M What are you majoring in?
   W Biology.

⑤ M Does Chris _____ _____ his
      grandfather?
   W Yes, he really likes his grandfather.

16

W My friend, Charles, who goes to the same school _____ _____ _____, is too shy. He never says what he needs or wants. So, people around him think he is a little dumb, but it's not true. He's just too shy and cares too much about others' opinion. He's _____ _____ _____ _____ _____.

17

W Excuse me.

M Hi, are you a member?

W No, I'm not.

M Then, _____ _____ _____. One hour is 2,000 won.

W Okay. Where should I sit?

M You can sit _____ _____ _____.

W I see. Which section is non-smoking?

M On your left.

W Okay. I'm sorry, but _____ _____ _____ _____ this.

M Okay. Please type the card number on the screen, and then you are ready to go.

W Thank you.

18

M These days, lots of teenagers _____ _____ _____. That might be because they eat too much fast food, or they get little exercise and watch TV too much. They also spend _____ _____ _____ _____ _____ playing computer games. Among them, the main problem is that they don't want to exercise. They even _____ _____ _____ or a bus when going a short distance.

19

W I heard that Mary _____ _____ _____ _____ you.

M I know. I think I made her upset.

W What did you do to her?

M I asked her about her weight.

W That's terrible. You _____ _____ _____ that kind of question.

M I know. I was just trying to help her find a way to _____ _____.

W I understand your reasoning, but it was impolite.

20

M Is everyone here?

W Except Janet.

M What happened to her?

W _____ _____.

M Can you call her cell phone?

W I already did, but her phone _____ _____ _____.

M That's strange.

W I think she's not interested in our club.

M What makes you think that?

W She's always late and often _____ _____ _____.

1 다음을 듣고, 동작의 순서가 올바른 것을 고르시오.

(A)  (B)  (C)

① (A) – (B) – (C)   ② (A) – (C) – (B)   ③ (B) – (A) – (C)
④ (B) – (C) – (A)   ⑤ (C) – (B) – (A)

2 대화를 듣고, 반에서 키가 가장 큰 사람을 고르시오.

① Jason   ② Kevin   ③ Mark   ④ Henry   ⑤ David

3 대화를 듣고, 남자가 하려고 하는 것을 고르시오.

① 야구 시합
② 농구 시합
③ 야구 경기 시청
④ 야구 경기표 예매
⑤ 야구 규칙을 설명

4 대화를 듣고, 여자가 한 마지막 말의 의도를 고르시오.

① 충고   ② 칭찬   ③ 감사   ④ 기대   ⑤ 불평

5 대화를 듣고, 여자의 심경으로 가장 알맞은 것을 고르시오.

① pleased   ② angry   ③ nervous
④ sad   ⑤ depressed

Take notes

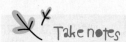

6 대화를 듣고, 언급되지 **않은** 것을 고르시오.

① James Powell은 운동선수이다.
② 곧 육상 대회가 열릴 것이다.
③ Powell은 100미터 세계 기록 보유자이다.
④ 남자는 스포츠에 관심이 없다.
⑤ 남자의 형은 스포츠에 관심이 많다.

7 다음을 듣고, 그림의 상황에 가장 잘 어울리는 대화를 고르시오.

①   ②   ③   ④   ⑤

8 다음을 듣고, 주어진 질문에 알맞은 답을 고르시오.

① $0   ② $5   ③ $10   ④ $15   ⑤ $50

9 대화를 듣고, 남자가 전화를 건 목적을 고르시오.

① 기차 예약   ② 예약 취소   ③ 연장운행 문의
④ 예약 확인   ⑤ 축제 일정 확인

10 대화를 듣고, 남자의 직업으로 알맞은 것을 고르시오.

① 페인트공   ② 경찰   ③ 배관공
④ 열쇠 수리공   ⑤ 정비공

11 대화를 듣고, 여자가 미안해하는 이유를 고르시오.

① 교과서를 다른 사람에게 빌려 줘서
② 교과서를 못 쓰게 만들어서
③ 교과서를 빌려 줄 수 없어서
④ 교과서를 가져오지 않아서
⑤ 교과서를 잃어버려서

12 다음을 듣고, 질문에 알맞은 답을 고르시오.

① 1 days   ② 2 days   ③ 3 days   ④ 4 days   ⑤ 5 days

13 대화를 듣고, 상황에 가장 잘 어울리는 속담을 고르시오.

① It's a piece of cake.
② Every dog has his day.
③ Well begun is half done.
④ Too many cooks spoil the broth.
⑤ Don't judge a book by its cover.

14 대화를 듣고, 남자가 이번 주말에 하겠다고 한 일을 고르시오.

① 미술관 관람   ② 영화 관람   ③ 도보 여행
④ 집수리   ⑤ 휴식

15 다음을 듣고, 남자가 Hoon에게 해 줄 충고로 가장 알맞은 것을 고르시오.

① Say "Hello" to your friends.
② Shake hands with your friends.
③ Stop making noise in the library.
④ Don't run away from your problems.
⑤ Look someone in the eye when you're talking.

Take notes

16 대화를 듣고, 두 사람이 대화하는 장소를 고르시오.

① 도서관   ② 병원   ③ 식당   ④ 약국   ⑤ 교실

✗ ✗ Take notes

17 다음을 듣고, 가장 많은 칼로리를 섭취한 사람을 고르시오.

Food	Calories (kcal)
Hotdog	350
Hamburger	600
A Slice of Pizza	250
Spaghetti	630

① Mike   ② John   ③ Kevin

④ Peter   ⑤ David

18 다음을 듣고, 무엇에 관한 내용인지 고르시오.

① 인내심   ② 성실성   ③ 배려심

④ 침착성   ⑤ 존경심

`19-20` 대화를 듣고, 남자의 마지막 말에 이어질 여자의 응답으로 가장 알맞은 것을 고르시오.

19
① Yeah, I got it.

② Yes, I was too busy.

③ I know. It's not easy to get muscles.

④ Yes. I really like playing badminton.

⑤ Why don't we play badminton sometime together?

20
① Sounds terrible.

② He has to stay home.

③ He tripped over a rock.

④ Let's see what happens.

⑤ Nobody knows he is sick.

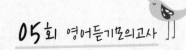
1

W   Everybody, _____ _____. Put your feet apart and place your arms at your sides. Next lift your arms _____ _____. Okay, that's it. Now put your fingers together with your palms up and push your arms up _____ _____ _____ _____. Hold this position for a second.

2

W   I think Jason is _____ _____ _____ last year.

M   I know. He was shorter than me last year, but he is far taller than me now.

W   But Kevin is taller than him, right?

M   I think so. I guess Kevin is a little over 180cm.

W   How about Mark, then?

M   In fact, _____ _____ _____ a boy taller than him.

W   Then, what about Henry?

M   He's _____ _____ _____ me.

3

M   What's your favorite sport, Susie?

W   Basketball. Do you like basketball, Andrew?

M   Yes, I do. But I like baseball better. I think baseball is _____ _____ _____ _____. What do you think?

W   Well, it is a little difficult for girls to play baseball, and most girls really don't know how to play. It is _____ _____.

M   That's true. Let me explain it to you, Susie.

W   Will you?

M   Sure, I've got _____ _____ _____ now.

W   Thanks a lot.

4

M   Have you met Shelly lately?

W   No, I haven't. Is she here?

M   Yes, she came here last night and is _____ _____ her uncle's house.

W   That's surprising news.

M   I know no one would've expected her to _____ _____ here so early.

W   That's right. How is she, anyway?

M   She looks very healthy and even more beautiful.

W   _____ _____ _____ _____ seeing her soon.

5

W   Hey, Michael. Do you know there _____ _____ _____ _____?

M   I know. It's going to be held on May 14th.

W   Can you tell me who you're voting for?

M   I can't tell you. You know that.

W   Come on! It's just _____ _____ _____ _____.

M   Still, I can't tell you.

W   Oh, come on.

M   OK. I'll _____ _____ you. Are you satisfied now?

W   I knew you would.

6

W　Mike, have you _____ _____ James Powell?

M　No. Who's that?

W　He's a famous athlete from Jamaica.

M　What else do you know about him?

W　He has a world record in the 100 and 200 meters.

M　I see.

W　Don't you ever watch any sports games?

M　No, I don't. _____ _____ _____ _____ any sports activities.

W　You are so different from your brother.

M　I know he is a real sports buff.

7

① W　Bless you. Did you _____ _____ _____?

　 M　I'm not sure, but I feel a little bit cold.

② W　Did you bring any pills for a headache?

　 M　Yes, I did. Do you want some?

③ W　How long have you had it?

　 M　I've had it for a few days.

④ W　You must be _____ _____ _____ _____ that.

　 M　How did you know?

⑤ W　What am I supposed to do?

　 M　You should _____ _____ _____ her.

8

W　Today is Christmas. Cindy bought some presents _____ _____ _____. She had 50 dollars in total. She bought a ten-dollar necktie for her father and a ten-dollar scarf for her mother. She also bought two five-dollar hairpins for her twin sisters. _____, she paid 5 dollars for her brother's pen. How much money _____ _____ _____ _____?

9

[Telephone rings.]

W　Hello, New York Metro. May I help you?

M　Hi, my name is Mike Jackson. _____ _____ _____, there will be a festival on Martin Street next week. I believe that the last train will be at 12:30 A.M., but there will still be a lot of people hanging around the festival. So, do you have any plans for them?

W　We sure do. There will be trains running until 1:30.

M　That's great. _____ _____ _____ _____.

W　You're welcome. _____ _____ _____ _____ I can help you with?

M　No, that's all.

10

W　Hey, John. Can you come over here? I _____ _____ _____ _____ the house.

M　How did that happen?

W　I heard someone _____ _____ _____ _____, so I came out, but no one was there.

M　I see. I need to get some tools to open the door.

W　Go ahead. I'll stay here. Thanks. How much is it?

M　I usually charge 5 dollars _____ _____ _____. Isn't this the third time already?

W　That's right. My carelessness is making you rich.

11

W Justin, I can't tell you _____

_____ _____ _____ .

M Why? What's wrong?

W Do you remember the textbook _____

_____ _____ _____ last week? Well, I have to buy you another one.

M Really? What happened?

W My brother spilt milk _____

_____ _____ _____ . It wasn't my fault though.

M Oh, no. I wrote all my important notes from my class on it.

W I'm terribly sorry.

12

M This is a very simple question, and I believe everyone can _____ _____

_____ _____ _____ .

Listen carefully. There are 28 days in February. Kevin's mother works every tenth day in February. Her first day of work in February is on the first of February.

_____ _____ _____

_____ _____ _____ in February?

13

M Mom, what are we going to do _____

_____ ?

W I'm not sure. Your father likes water sports, so he wanted to go to one of the islands in the Philippines.

M But you don't like water, and you don't even know _____ _____ _____ .

W Right. I _____ _____ stay home and get some sleep. I'm exhausted these days.

M Mom, but don't you think we have to do something? I can't just stay home and spend my holiday here. What about going mountain climbing?

W That doesn't sound good. It's hard to

_____ _____ _____ when everyone has a different idea.

14

W Aden, what did you do _____

_____ _____ ?

M I went to an art gallery with my sister, but the gallery was closed for renovation.

W Oh, really?

M Yes. So, we went to a movie instead. The movie was really boring. I almost

_____ _____ .

W That's too bad. I'm going hiking with my father this coming weekend. Do you want to _____ _____ ?

M Sorry. I'm going to try the gallery again. They say they're going to reopen this weekend.

15

M Hoon is my best friend from Korea. He has been here for at least 2 years. He's very active and enthusiastic, but _____

_____ _____ _____ other people, he has a problem. In America, when you have a conversation with a person, you should _____ _____

_____ , but he always avoids eye contact. The people he's talking to may get upset if they feel that he's not interested in

_____ _____ _____ .

16

W Excuse me, is everything all right?

M Yes. This is _____ _____ _____ _____ I've ever had.

W Thank you. Would you mind _____ _____ _____ _____, sir?

M What's that?

W Is the boy running around your son?

M Yes, he is.

W Would you please keep him _____ _____? Some customers are complaining about that.

M I'm terribly sorry. I'll make him stop.

17

W Mike had one hotdog and _____ _____ _____ pizza. John had spaghetti and _____ _____ _____ water. Kevin had two hotdogs. Peter had a slice of pizza and spaghetti. David had one hamburger and one hotdog.

18

W I have a close friend called David. He is very nice and generous to other people. One day, when he was _____ _____ _____ _____, one of his shoes fell to the ground. The train started to move, so he couldn't pick it up. But he didn't look sad. He quickly _____ _____ the other shoe and threw it out of the train. I asked him _____ _____ _____ _____. David told me if

a poor man finds the first shoe, he will now have _____ _____ _____ _____.

19

W Hey, Mark.
Do you _____ _____?

M Yes, I do. I do some weight training.

W I see. I work out, too. I play badminton sometimes.

M Sorry, but I think _____ _____ _____ is not a workout.

W What do you mean?

M That seems kind of _____ _____ _____, not a workout. I think a workout is something you do regularly not just sometimes. Do you know what I mean?

W Yeah, _____ _____ _____.

20

M Where is John? He's supposed to be here today.

W I don't think he's _____ _____ _____ _____.

M Why?

W I'm sure he's at home now.

M His mother won't let him go out, right?

W No, that's not it. He _____ _____ _____ yesterday, and it's in a cast.

M Do you know how it happened?

W He _____ _____ a rock.

06회 영어듣기모의고사

정답 및 해설 p.31

1 대화를 듣고, 남자가 사기로 한 물건을 고르시오.

①

②

③

④

⑤

2 대화를 듣고, 두 사람이 대화하는 장소를 고르시오.

① 호텔   ② 공항   ③ 우체국   ④ 은행   ⑤ 선물가게

3 대화를 듣고, 남자가 전화를 건 목적을 고르시오.

① 경고하려고   ② 감사하려고
③ 충고하려고   ④ 제안하려고
⑤ 위로하려고

4 대화를 듣고, 남자가 앞으로 할 일을 고르시오.

① 토론 대회 참가   ② 연설 클럽 가입
③ 언어 치료   ④ 노래 대회 참가
⑤ 운동 클럽 가입

5 대화를 듣고, 여자가 마지막에 느꼈을 심정으로 알맞은 것을 고르시오.

① upset   ② proud   ③ surprised
④ relieved   ⑤ disappointed

6 대화를 듣고, 남자의 직업을 고르시오.

① 경찰관   ② 의사   ③ 기자   ④ 교사   ⑤ 소방관

✗ Take notes

7 다음을 듣고, 무엇에 관한 내용인지 고르시오.

① 여행할 장소 설명   ② 호텔 예약하는 방법
③ 저렴하게 여행하는 방법   ④ 안전하게 여행하는 방법
⑤ 관광 안내원이 되는 방법

8 다음을 듣고, 그림의 상황에 가장 잘 어울리는 대화를 고르시오.

①   ②   ③   ④   ⑤

9 다음을 듣고, 무엇에 관한 내용인지 고르시오.

① 부정행위에 대한 벌칙
② 시험 일정에 관한 안내
③ 수학시험에서의 객관성
④ 수학시험에서 계산기의 사용
⑤ 시험 시간에 준수해야 할 규칙

10 대화를 듣고, 여자가 한 마지막 말의 의도를 고르시오.

① 허락   ② 문의   ③ 제안   ④ 충고   ⑤ 동의

Take notes

11 다음을 듣고, 녹음 내용으로 알 수 없는 것을 고르시오.

① 진료 시간   ② 병원 위치   ③ 주차 장소

④ 교통편   ⑤ 진료 과목

12 대화를 듣고, 남자가 여자에게 빌려 주겠다고 한 금액이 얼마인지 고르시오.

① $50   ② $70   ③ $80

④ $100   ⑤ $200

13 대화를 듣고, 두 사람이 출발할 시각을 고르시오.

① 5:15   ② 5:30   ③ 5:45

④ 6:00   ⑤ 6:15

14 다음을 듣고, 내용과 일치하지 않는 것을 고르시오.

① David는 반 아이들 모두를 초대하고 싶지는 않았다.

② David의 엄마는 반 아이들 모두를 초대하라고 했다.

③ Mark와 David는 몇 주 전에 싸움을 했다.

④ Mark는 David에게만 심술궂게 군다.

⑤ David는 Jason에게 질투심을 느꼈다.

15 대화를 듣고, 두 사람이 하게 될 활동을 표에서 고르시오.

	Adventure Camp	Activity Cost
①	Rock Climbing	$15
②	Rafting	$25
③	Bungee Jumping	$30
④	Paragliding	$40
⑤	Horseback Riding	$20

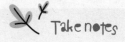

16 대화를 듣고, 일본인이 건강한 이유로 언급된 것이 <u>아닌</u> 것을 고르시오.

① 스트레스가 없어서　　② 운동 때문에

③ 식단 때문에　　④ 생활 방식 때문에

⑤ 소식해서

17 대화를 듣고, 여자가 남자에게 부탁하는 것을 고르시오.

① 쓰레기 통 비우기　　② 개 먹이 주기

③ 거실 청소하기　　④ 옷걸이 가져오기

⑤ 빨래하기

18 다음을 듣고, 두 사람의 대화가 <u>어색한</u> 것을 고르시오.

①　　②　　③　　④　　⑤

19-20 대화를 듣고, 남자의 마지막 말에 이어질 여자의 응답으로 가장 알맞은 것을 고르시오.

19　① He's just stepped out.

② I think John is coming soon.

③ Is that right? That's wonderful.

④ Sorry. I can't find him right now.

⑤ There is no one here by that name.

20　① You have to keep a diary.

② I'm sorry, but I don't know.

③ Sure, you can write about it.

④ I wrote about my summer vacation.

⑤ You can write about whatever you want.

Dictation

1

W How can I help you?

M Do you have these in size 5? It's for my daughter.

W I'm afraid we're out of size 5. How about these boots? They're very _____ _____ young girls. Why didn't you bring your daughter with you?

M This _____ _____ _____ a surprise gift for her birthday. She'll become 15 years old tomorrow.

W I understand. I'm sure she'll like those boots.

M OK. I'll take them.

2

M What can I do for you?

W I'd like to send this package to Seoul.

M May I ask _____ _____ _____?

W It's a sweat suit for my son.

M I see. How would you like to send it?

W _____ _____, _____ _____.

M OK. That'll be 5 dollars. It'll get there _____ _____ _____.

W Here you go. Thank you.

3

[Telephone rings.]

M Hello, can I speak to Andy?

W He's not in. Who's calling, please?

M This is Kelly's dad, Michael Barton.

W Hi, Mr. Barton. Andy went out _____ _____ _____ _____. What is this about?

M The reason I'm calling is to thank him for what he did for my daughter.

W _____ _____ _____ _____?

M There were a couple of boys who tried to rob her, and your son stopped them _____ _____ _____.

W He did?

M Yes. That's what I heard from my daughter.

4

M Congratulations! I heard you _____ _____ _____ in the speech contest, Kate.

W Thanks.

M I envy you. I've never heard _____ _____ _____ _____.

W It's nice of you to say so. But anyone can be a good speaker if they practice enough.

M Really? I've found it's not easy. How come you are so good at speech?

W Well, I practice speaking in the Speech Club every Saturday. _____ _____ _____ _____ join us?

M Sure. Why not?

5

M Here we are. This is the place you requested?

W Yes. Thank you. _____ _____ _____?

M It's 19 dollars.

W OK. Oh, no. Excuse me, but I'm afraid I don't have enough money. I only have 17 dollars on me. _____ _____ _____ _____?

M Isn't there anybody inside that can lend you a few dollars?

W No one. Let me call my friend next door. She is not answering. I'm sorry.

M It's okay. I'll just take _____ _____ _____.

W Thank you. You are very kind.

6

W Can you tell me why you chose this job? I know it's a very tough job.

M I saw my father saving many lives _____ _____.

W You mean your father works in this field, too?

M Yes. Well, he did. He retired last year.

W I see. Have you been injured _____ _____ _____ before?

M Of course. Once when I was trying to _____ _____ _____, my left leg got burned.

W Can you show me?

M Sure.

W Oh, that's terrible.

M It's OK now.

7

W How much you _____ _____ _____ is really up to you. Here are some tips on saving your money. Number one: Go off-season. Popular destinations are very crowded, but after the peak-season they are less crowded. Usually, hotels offer special discounts _____ _____ _____. Number two: Use coupons. From dozens of web pages you can find discount coupons for hotels and restaurants. _____ _____ _____, take them, and save money.

8

① M The weather forecast said it _____ _____.

W Sometimes the weather forecast can be wrong.

② M Do you mind getting wet?

W Yes. Let's run to the school.

③ M Would you like to _____ _____?

W Thanks. I didn't expect rain today.

④ M Is this your umbrella? Can I borrow it?

W Sure, I have two. You can use this one.

⑤ M I left my umbrella on the bus.

W Don't worry. It's _____ _____ _____.

9

W In the United States and other western countries, students are allowed to use a calculator while they take a math test. _____ _____ it sounds really strange to Korean students, it's pretty reasonable for students to use a calculator. Students can _____ _____ when they calculate in their head, even though they know how to _____ _____ _____. That's why teachers let students use a calculator. However, in Korea, calculating is also considered to be a part of a test.

10

W Is this your first time _____ _____?

M Yes, it is. But I feel right at home.

W That's good. Where have you been _____ _____?

M I don't know the exact names, but I have been to a few palaces. Those palaces were fantastic. I enjoyed seeing them a lot.

W I'm sure you had a lot of fun.

11

[Beep]

W You have reached the office of Happy Dental Clinic. Our office hours are _____ _____ _____ from 10 A.M. to 6 P.M. The office is located on Gulf Avenue. _____ _____ _____ at the rear of the building. If this is an emergency, press 1 _____ _____ _____. If you would like to make an appointment to have your teeth cleaned, press 2. If you want to talk to one of our nurses, press 0.

12

W Jake, can you _____ _____ _____ _____?

M How much do you want?

W I needed 200 dollars, but Jenny already gave me 80 dollars, and Mike gave me 50 dollars. Now I just need 70 dollars.

M Well, I have 100 dollars on me, so I can give you _____ _____ _____.

W That's great. I'll _____ _____ _____ next month. Thanks a lot.

M You're welcome.

13

M What time do you want to leave?

W I'm not sure. What time is it now?

M It's _____ _____ _____.

W Then let's make it a quarter to six.

M That early?

W Why? You've got something to do?

M Not really. I just need to check my email.

W How about _____ _____ _____ _____ then?

M OK.

14

W David was _____ _____ _____ _____. He didn't want to invite all the boys from his class, but his mom told him he had to invite them all. David didn't listen to his mom. _____ _____ _____ _____ David was inviting Mark to his party. Mark gave him a black eye a few weeks ago. Besides he was mean to everyone. David didn't invite Jason, either. He was _____ _____ _____ Jason being so smart.

15

M Today is _____ _____ _____ of camp.

W Right. What do you want to do during our free time this afternoon?

M How about rock climbing? I want to _____ _____ _____ _____.

W I'm afraid I can't. My legs are still hurting from rafting yesterday.

M Are they? Then, let's go bungee jumping.

W I'm sorry, but I'm afraid of heights. And it's 30 dollars a person. All I have is 20 dollars.

M I only have 20 bucks, too.

W In that case, there is only _____ _____ _____ _____ _____.

16

W Hey, look at this article. It's about Japanese people's health. It says their rates of heart disease and cancer are _____ _____ _____ those in other countries.

M Really? Are there any secrets behind that?

W Many scientists have tried to find the reasons, and they _____ _____ _____ three most important factors: diet, exercise, and lifestyle.

M I think I can add one more thing.

W What is that?

M _____ _____ _____.

W That's true.

17

W Did you _____ _____ _____?

M Sure, they're done. I'm going to watch TV.

W _____ _____ _____. Can you get some hangers for me?

M Where are they?

W In the closet.

M OK. Don't ask me anything else though. I'm really tired.

W _____ _____ _____! All you did was do the dishes. How about me? I cleaned the living room, _____ _____ _____, and fed the dog.

M All right.

18

① M She caught a thief, and she was awarded _____ _____ _____ _____.

W That's terrible.

② M I think we should help the poor.

W _____ _____ _____ _____ _____ _____.

③ M Why do you want to get a red one?

W Hey, people have different tastes.

④ M Can I talk to Mr. Kim?

W Sure, I'll _____ _____ _____ _____ right away.

⑤ M Would you do me a favor?

W What is it?

19

[Telephone rings.]

M Hello, may I speak to John?

W I think you've _____ _____ _____ _____.

M Isn't this 245-2451?

W Yes, the phone number is right.

M That's strange. John gave me this number last night.

W There is no one here _____ _____ _____.

20

W Today is the last day of the semester. Enjoy your vacation. You have some homework to do _____ _____ _____. It's not a lot, so don't worry.

M What do we have to do, Mrs. Smith?

W You have to _____ _____ _____ that is at least three A4-sized pages long.

M What do we have to write about?

W You can write about _____ _____ _____.

1 대화를 듣고, 여자가 사려는 강아지를 고르시오.

① ② ③ ④ ⑤

2 다음을 듣고, 무엇에 대한 설명인지 고르시오.

① 냉장고　　② 청소기　　③ 믹서　　④ 오븐　　⑤ 가습기

3 대화를 듣고, 남자가 전화를 끊고 가장 먼저 할 일을 고르시오.

① 감자 삶기　　　　② 찬물 붓기　　　　③ 감자 자르기
④ 간장 넣기　　　　⑤ 휘젓기

4 대화를 듣고, 남자의 직업을 고르시오.

① cook　　② waiter　　③ doctor　　④ counselor　　⑤ teacher

5 대화를 듣고, 여자가 한 마지막 말의 의도를 고르시오.

① 제안　　② 비판　　③ 위로　　④ 명령　　⑤ 요구

Take notes

6 대화를 듣고, 남자가 고민하는 것을 고르시오.

① 외모   ② 신장   ③ 성적

④ 이성   ⑤ 인간관계

7 대화를 듣고, 여자가 지불해야 할 금액을 고르시오.

① $2   ② $5   ③ $6

④ $7.5   ⑤ $10

8 대화를 듣고, 여자가 탈 비행기의 출발 시각을 고르시오.

① 3:00   ② 3:30   ③ 4:00

④ 4:30   ⑤ 5:00

9 대화를 듣고, 남자가 전화를 건 목적을 고르시오.

① 예약을 하려고   ② 책을 찾으려고

③ 책을 주문하려고   ④ 예약을 취소하려고

⑤ 음식에 대해 항의하려고

10 다음을 듣고, 그림의 상황에 가장 잘 어울리는 대화를 고르시오.

①   ②   ③   ④   ⑤

11 대화를 듣고, 남자가 여자에게 바라는 것을 고르시오.

① 아침에 운동을 해라.
② 아침을 거르지 마라.
③ 잠을 일찍 자라.
④ 건강한 식단을 짜라.
⑤ 과식하지 마라.

12 대화를 듣고, 두 사람이 대화하는 장소를 고르시오.

① 세탁소 ② 병원 ③ 가게 ④ 은행 ⑤ 공원

13 대화를 듣고, 남자의 심정으로 알맞은 것을 고르시오.

① happy ② disappointed ③ pleasant
④ proud ⑤ embarrassed

14 다음을 듣고, 무엇에 관한 설명인지 고르시오.

① 촉각 ② 후각 ③ 미각 ④ 시각 ⑤ 청각

15 대화를 듣고, 여자가 물어본 표지판을 고르시오.

①   ②   ③

④   ⑤

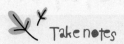

16 대화를 듣고, 벼룩시장에서 볼 수 있는 것이 <u>아닌</u> 것을 고르시오.

① 중고용품　　　　② 고가구　　　　③ 수공예품

④ 저렴한 의류　　　⑤ 마술 쇼

17 다음을 듣고, 두 사람의 대화가 <u>어색한</u> 것을 고르시오.

①　　　　②　　　　③　　　　④　　　　⑤

18 다음을 듣고, Eric이 마지막에 할 말로 알맞은 것을 고르시오.

① You are doing great.

② I appreciate your help.

③ Sorry, but this is my car.

④ You are not supposed to park here.

⑤ It's hard to find a parking space near the park.

19-20 대화를 듣고, 남자의 마지막 말에 이어질 여자의 응답으로 가장 알맞은 것을 고르시오.

19 ① But it looks very heavy.

② Sorry, but I can't walk fast.

③ I don't usually carry that bag.

④ I'm strong enough to carry you.

⑤ Thank you. I should have been more careful.

20 ① Thanks for the time.

② What's wrong with it?

③ Thanks. I appreciate it.

④ When am I supposed to come?

⑤ It's not your watch but your attitude.

Dictation

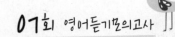

1

W Hi. I'd like to _____ _____ _____. Could you recommend a smart one?

M The white one beside the black puppy is pretty smart.

W Oh, you mean the one _____ _____ _____ _____ of the black one?

M No, the one on the right side.

W The one _____ _____ _____ in his mouth?

M Yes, that's him.

W Oh, he looks very cute. I'll take him.

2

W Everyone of us has this at home, and it is _____ _____ _____ _____ of equipment for housewives. Recently, some companies have invented a robot version, and it can do its job _____ _____ _____. Once you plug it in, it automatically _____ _____, sucking up all the dust from the floor of your house.

3

[Telephone rings.]

M Hello, Christine. I need your help. Can you help me?

W Sure, go ahead.

M I'm making potato stew, and I don't know _____ _____ _____ next.

W Tell me what you have done so far.

M I have boiled _____ _____ _____ potatoes and have rinsed them with cold water.

W And?

M And have cut the potatoes into edible sizes and have put them into a pot. This is pretty much what I've done so far.

W Okay. Add _____ _____ _____ soy sauce and sugar, and stir the potatoes. That's it.

M Thank you so much.

4

W Excuse me, could you come over here?

M Yes, ma'am. Is there something wrong?

W Yes. I _____ _____ _____ _____ peanuts. Did you make this sauce with peanuts?

M I'm not sure. I have to check with the kitchen. Could you wait for a second?

W Okay. Please check.

M Ma'am. There are a few peanuts in this sauce. I'll _____ _____ _____ with one without any sauce.

W Thank you. Could you put some olive oil _____ _____ _____?

M Okay.

5

W What's the result?

M It is _____ _____ _____ _____ I expected. It's kind of disappointing actually.

W That's too bad, but don't you have another chance?

M Yes, I do.

W Then, you don't need to be disappointed.

M Thanks, but I really worked hard this time.

W I know, but don't _____ _____ _____ _____.

6

W Hi, Henry. What's up?

M Don't ask. I have pimples _____ _____ _____. I really don't know what to do.

W Don't worry. Many people get them.

M I know, but mine are _____ _____ _____ _____ others'.

W Wash your face without using any soap in the morning and evening.

M Will that work?

W Just _____ _____ _____ _____.

M Okay. I'll try it from now on.

7

W How much are the oranges?

M They're 2 dollars each, but the more you buy, _____ _____ _____ _____ _____.

W How is that possible?

M If you buy 5, they're 1 dollar 50 cents each, but if you buy more than 10, they're a dollar each.

W _____ _____ _____ _____. But since I live alone, I don't need that many oranges. I'll just take 5.

M OK. Let me put them in a plastic bag for you.

W Thank you.

8

W _____ _____ _____ _____ _____?

M It is scheduled to leave at 3:30, but it's going to be delayed 30 minutes.

W What's the reason?

M They say the incoming flight _____ _____.

W This seems to happen a lot. Mine is delayed, too.

M Then, what time is your flight going to depart?

W 30 minutes later than yours.

M Then, let's get _____ _____ _____. I feel a little hungry.

9

W Thanks for calling Big Boy. May I help you?

M Yes, my name is Peter Brown, and I just had dinner there. I think I left my book on the table. Could you please _____ _____ _____ if it's still there?

W Sir, a waitress found a book and put it beside the cashier _____ _____ _____ _____.

M I see. The name of the book is The Old Man and The Sea.

W OK. It must be yours, then.

M I'll _____ _____ within 30 minutes and pick it up. Thank you.

10

① W Tom, take a look at this.
　 M Wow, it's wonderful.

② W Someone _____ _____ _____.
　 M That's too bad.

③ W Hey, you _____ _____ _____.
　 M I'm terribly sorry.

④ W Is this your paper?
　 M Where did you find it?

⑤ W Hey, stop cheating and bring your paper to me.
　 M Please _____ _____ _____ _____.

Dictation

11

M You don't seem to eat breakfast.

W I don't have an appetite in the morning, so I _____ _____ every day.

M That's because you get up too late, and you're always _____ _____ _____.

W I know, but whether it is good or not, it is a habit I've had for a long time.

M I understand. The reason why I'm telling you this is that once you skip your breakfast, you _____ _____ _____ _____ a lot at lunch. So, it's hard for you to _____ _____ _____.

W That's why I'm exercising these days.

12

M How much _____ _____ _____ _____?

W You owe me 40 dollars.

M Here you go. Let me see if you _____ _____ _____ _____.

W Don't worry.

M Hey, take a close look at these trousers.

W What is it?

M There are a lot of wrinkles on the back.

W That can't be. _____ _____ _____ _____? Oh, I'm terribly sorry. Could you wait a minute?

M OK.

13

W Did you get the job _____ _____ _____?

M No. I wasn't even given the chance to interview for the position.

W _____ _____ _____.

M I guess I'm not the person they are looking for.

W Don't worry. I think you have a lot of skills and experience, so you'll get a better one.

M That was what my parents told me, but now I'm starting to _____ _____.

14

M _____ _____ _____ located on your head, this sense is all over your body. _____ _____ _____, you receive an endless flow of information about the world and yourself from this sense. It tells you if something is hot or cold, hard or soft. It sends messages of pain, _____ _____ a headache or a sore throat.

15

W Look! There are _____ _____ _____ _____ over there.

M Do you know what they mean?

W No, I don't. Can you _____ _____ _____ _____?

M Sure.

W What does this sign say?

M It says it's only _____ _____ _____.

W I get it.

16

W Have you been to a flea market before?

M No, I haven't.

W I'm going to one now. Do you want to _____ _____? You'll see many interesting things at the market.

M Like what?

W Various used products from _____ _____ _____ _____.

M I see. What else?

W Antique furniture, _____ _____, and second-hand accessories. You can even see some magic shows.

17

① W How do you like these cookies?
   M They're so delicious.

② W Would you like some pizza?
   M _____ _____.

③ W What does this sign say?
   M There's _____ _____ _____.

④ W Are you interested in popular music?
   M Sure. I listen to it often.

⑤ W May I help you?
   M No, thanks. _____ _____ _____.

18

W When Eric was on his way home, he found someone illegally parked _____ _____ _____ his house. There was a parking lot near the park, but the driver wanted _____ _____ _____ parking fees. The car is blocking his driveway, so he might have a hard time getting his car _____ _____ _____ _____. In this situation, what would Eric say to the driver?

19

M Hey, Diana. _____ _____ _____!

W Ouch!

M Does it hurt?

W Yeah. I think I _____ _____ _____. I can't get up.

M You'd better go to see a doctor.

W I don't think I can walk.

M Don't worry. I can carry you on my back.

W Thank you. I _____ _____ _____ more careful.

20

W Hello, Mr. Simpson. I'd like to _____ _____ _____ _____.

M Oh, what seems to be the problem with it?

W It's running _____ _____ _____.

M I see. You can leave the watch with me, and I'll call you when it's ready, okay?

W Thanks. _____ _____ _____.

08회 영어듣기모의고사

1 다음을 듣고, 여자가 설명하는 동작으로 알맞은 것을 고르시오.

①   ②   ③

④  ⑤

2 대화를 듣고, 남자의 심경으로 가장 알맞은 것을 고르시오.

① satisfied   ② lonely   ③ upset   ④ bored   ⑤ curious

3 대화를 듣고, 남자의 문제점으로 언급된 것을 고르시오.

① 이기적이다.
② 직업이 없다.
③ 욕심이 지나치다.
④ 위생적이지 않다.
⑤ 정리정돈을 못한다.

4 대화를 듣고, 여자가 파티 준비를 위해 도착할 시각을 고르시오.

① 4:30   ② 5:00   ③ 5:30   ④ 6:00   ⑤ 7:00

5 대화를 듣고, 남자가 마지막에 가방을 놓은 곳을 고르시오.

① 체육관   ② 자동차 트렁크   ③ 자동차 앞좌석
④ 세탁소   ⑤ 사무실

6 대화를 듣고, 상황에 어울리는 속담으로 알맞은 것을 고르시오.

① No pain, no gain.

② Well begun is half done.

③ Don't cry over split milk.

④ Kill two birds with one stone.

⑤ Too many cooks spoil the broth.

Take notes

7 대화를 듣고, 여자가 남자에게 부탁하는 것을 고르시오.

① 전화기를 꺼라.

② 음식을 먹지 마라.

③ 말을 시키지 마라.

④ 전화기를 진동으로 해라.

⑤ 다리를 의자에 올리지 마라.

8 대화를 듣고, 두 사람이 대화하는 장소를 고르시오.

① 매표소   ② 박물관   ③ 도서관

④ 우체국   ⑤ 여행 안내소

9 다음을 듣고, 남자에 대한 내용과 일치하는 것을 고르시오.

① 전학을 간 학교에서 옛 친구를 만났다.

② 첫 수업이지만 긴장하지 않았다.

③ 선생님이 반 학생들에게 소개를 했다.

④ 영어를 잘 하지 못했다.

⑤ 여러 친구들이 환영해 주었다.

10 대화를 듣고, 여자가 남자와 점심을 함께 하지 못한 이유를 고르시오.

① 너무 바빠서   ② 도로가 붐벼서

③ 책을 읽느라고   ④ 급한 일이 생겨서

⑤ 약속을 잊어버려서

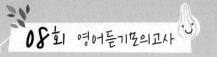

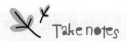 Take notes

11 대화를 듣고, 여자가 찾아갈 장소를 고르시오.

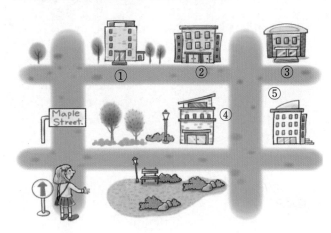

12 대화를 듣고, 여자의 직업을 고르시오.

① 관리인   ② 경찰관   ③ 교사

④ 환경미화원   ⑤ 세탁소 주인

13 대화를 듣고, 여자가 주문을 취소한 것을 고르시오.

① tuna sandwich   ② chicken salad   ③ Sprite

④ cheese burger   ⑤ Coke

14 대화를 듣고, 여자가 대화 후 할 일을 고르시오.

① 아이들 불러오기   ② 칠판 지우기   ③ 청소하기

④ 숙제하기   ⑤ 창문 열기

15 다음을 듣고, 방송을 하는 목적이 무엇인지 고르시오.

① 도서관 이용 시간 안내

② 도서 대출 기간 안내

③ 도서관 출입 통제 안내

④ 도서관 시설 보수 안내

⑤ 도서관 이전 안내

16 다음을 듣고, 표에서 글의 내용과 일치하지 <u>않는</u> 것을 고르시오.

Jazz Concert	
Who	① Stevie Wonder
When	② 7 P.M.
	③ Every Weekend
Where	④ All That Jazz Club
How much	⑤ $25

17 다음을 듣고, "I"가 가리키는 것이 무엇인지 고르시오.

① 장학금　　　　　② 성적표　　　　　③ 시간표

④ 이름표　　　　　⑤ 출석부

18 다음을 듣고, 두 사람의 대화가 <u>어색한</u> 것을 고르시오.

①　　　　②　　　　③　　　　④　　　　⑤

19-20 대화를 듣고, 여자의 마지막 말에 이어질 남자의 응답으로 가장 알맞은 것을 고르시오.

19
① Let's make dinner.

② How may I help you?

③ Yes. I'd be glad to help you.

④ Yes, next time I will put it in the garbage.

⑤ Do you want to play computer games with me?

20
① You are so lucky.

② Please, be careful.

③ You are in trouble.

④ OK, I will. Thanks.

⑤ May I order it now?

Dictation

1

W When you're sitting down, you need to do some exercises to _____ _____ _____. First, bend your upper body forward and lift your heels _____ _____ _____ _____. At the same time put your hands on your knees. If you _____ _____ _____ for 5 seconds, your muscles will feel more relaxed.

2

M Mom, you promised to buy me a suit, right?

W Well, I was going to buy you a suit, but your uncle told me that he has one that he _____ _____ _____, but looks good as new.

M I don't want to wear a used suit.

W Listen! _____ _____ _____.

M It's like a new one, but it's not a new one.

W Mark, if the suit looked old and _____ _____ _____, I would buy you a new one. But just like I told you, it looks fantastic. I'm sure you'll like it once you see it.

3

W What a mess!

M I'm sorry. I'm always like this.

W _____ _____ _____ _____ on your desk. What would you do if you needed something?

M I know. That's why every time I _____ _____ something, it takes me all day.

4

W You should _____ _____ _____ _____ _____.

M I know, but it's not easy. I'll try.

4

M I'm having a surprise party for my sister. Can you come and _____ _____ _____ _____ with the party preparations?

W Absolutely. What time?

M At 5 in the evening.

W Well, I'm afraid I may be about _____ _____ _____ _____ late. Since I haven't bought a present for her, I have to _____ _____ _____ the department store.

M That's all right. She'll probably come home around 7.

W Okay. See you then.

5

M I just can't find my gym bag anywhere.

W When was the last time you had your bag with you?

M I had it with me when I _____ _____ _____ the gym.

W Then?

M I put the bag _____ _____ _____ _____.

W And?

M I picked up my shirts at the cleaners. Until then, I was holding the bag in my hand. I think I left it _____ _____ _____.

W You'd better call them before they close.

6

W   Jimmy, I'm ready. It took almost 5 hours _____ _____ _____ , but I'm satisfied. How about you?

M   I am not ready yet, but let's go.

W   What do you mean?

M   I didn't even start, and I don't think I can do it.
I'm just going to _____ _____ .

W   Hey. _____ _____ _____ , but once you start doing it, you can finish it.

M   Do you think so?

W   Yes, just do it.

7

M   What time does the movie start?

W   In 5 minutes. _____ _____ _____ _____ _____ before the movie are pretty interesting.

M   I know, but there's a trick. They only show us interesting scenes, but when we actually watch the movie, it is sometimes _____ _____ _____ .

W   That's true. Peter, the movie is starting now. _____ _____ _____ set your cell phone to vibration? I already did mine.

M   No problem.

8

W   Welcome. What can I do for you?

M   Yes. May I have _____ _____ _____ _____ _____ ?

W   Sure. Here you are.

M   Can you recommend some interesting places around here?

W   This map helps you _____ _____ famous sights such as palaces, skyscrapers, and national museums. They are within a walking distance.

M   Thank you. It's very kind of you.

W   Not at all. That's my job, and I hope you _____ _____ _____ _____ .

9

M   It was the first class at a new school. I was very nervous because I didn't know anyone and didn't _____ _____ _____ . When the class ended, all of the students left the room. _____ _____ _____ _____ to talk to me. I felt very sad. Then, suddenly, I heard someone call my name. I turned around and saw a girl from my class. She gave me a big, friendly smile. I felt better _____ _____ .

10

W   Hello, sorry I'm late. The streets are _____ _____ .

M   That's all right. I just got here, too.

W   I'd like to tell you _____ _____ _____ _____ about the mix-up yesterday.

M   What happened to you? I thought we were going to have lunch together.

W   I really apologize. I completely _____ _____ our appointment.

M   Don't worry about it.

11

W Excuse me, could you tell me _____ _____ _____ _____ _____ _____ ?

M Let me see. Go straight along Maple Street and turn right at the second corner. Then go one more block and _____ _____ at the corner. It's on your right.

W That's not simple. Turn right at the second corner. Go one more block and turn left, and it is _____ _____ _____ .

M That's right.

W Thank you very much.

12

W Excuse me, but you are not supposed to drink here.

M Why not?

W Look at the floor. It's all carpeted. If you spill your drink, it will cost a lot _____ _____ _____ _____ .

M OK. Where is a trash can?

W There is one _____ _____ _____ the restroom.

M Thank you. By the way, I saw the sign saying you will be closed for a week.

W That's right. We'll be remodeling _____ _____ _____ .

M OK, thank you.

13

M Are you ready to order?

W Yes. I'd like to have a tuna sandwich and a chicken salad.

M _____ _____ _____ ?

W Sprite, please. And I'd like some take-out for my brother. A cheese burger and a Coke.

M OK. It'll be ready _____ _____ _____ you finish your meal.

W Thank you. Wait a minute! _____ _____ _____ the soda? I think I have some at home.

M Sure.

14

M _____ _____ _____ _____ ?

W I'm not sure, Mr. Brown.

M Who was _____ _____ _____ ?

W Jacob and Harry. When I got here, they were leaving.

M I see. Do you know where they went?

W I wish I knew, Mr. Brown.

M Could you _____ _____ _____ for me, Sally?

W Yes, sir.

15

W Attention, please. As you all know, we run two different libraries. _____ is for students, and _____ _____ is for adults. Since last week, there have been some complaints from the adults that some students are using their building and are _____ _____ _____ _____ _____ . That library is limited to adults only. Any student caught entering the library _____ _____ _____ _____ the student library. Thank you.

16

W Do you like jazz? _____ _____
_____, you're going to like the jazz
music of Stevie Wonder. You can see him
_____ _____ at 7 P.M. Stevie
Wonder is playing two concerts this Friday
and Saturday at the "All That Jazz Club."
The cover charge is 25 dollars which
includes a glass of wine served _____
_____ _____. Thank you.

17

M I'm very closely _____ _____
students. Sometimes they feel very happy,
and sometimes they feel very sad because of
me. _____ _____ _____
_____, some students are longing
to receive me, while others are not. When
students receive me, they show me to their
parents. It's _____ _____
_____ _____ the students'
grades.

18

① M How often does the bus run?
   W _____ _____ _____
      _____ _____, you can catch
      it every 15 minutes.
② M We have some guide books for tourists.
      What would you like to know?
   W We're interested in the historical sites.
③ M What's _____ _____
      _____ to explore Seoul?
   W The city tour bus is a good option.

④ M I'm planning to fly to New York. Have
      you ever been there?
   W Maybe 13 hours or so.
⑤ M I bought this CD player yesterday, but it
      doesn't work.
   W Let me see. I'm sorry _____
      _____ _____.

19

W Julian, what are you doing now?
M I'm playing computer games.
W Could you _____ _____
   _____ _____ and help me,
   please?
M OK. What do you want me to do?
W The house needs to be clean before Mom
   and Dad get home. They will be arriving
   shortly. Can you _____ _____
   _____ _____?
M Yes. I'd be glad to help you.

20

W John, what happened? Your clothes are all
   dirty.
M We _____ _____ _____
   _____ on the way here. While I was
   helping my father change the tire, I got
   _____ _____ _____
   _____ _____.
W I'm glad you didn't have an accident.
M Yeah, me too. But look at me. What am I
   supposed to do?
W Oh, don't worry. You can wear my brother's
   suit. He is _____ _____
   _____.
M OK, I will. Thanks.

정답 및 해설 p.48

09회 영어듣기모의고사

1 다음을 듣고, 여자의 설명과 일치하는 그림을 고르시오.

Take notes

①
②
③

④
⑤

2 대화를 듣고, 여자의 직업을 고르시오.

① actress   ② artist   ③ director
④ librarian   ⑤ playwright

3 대화를 듣고, 두 사람이 대화하는 장소를 고르시오.

① 공항   ② 공원   ③ 사진관   ④ 학원   ⑤ 도서관

4 대화를 듣고, 남자가 한 마지막 말의 의도를 고르시오.

① 거절   ② 동의   ③ 비판   ④ 제안   ⑤ 감사

5 대화를 듣고, 달력을 참고하여 오늘이 며칠인지 고르시오.

SUN	MON	TUE	WED	THU	FRI	SAT
				1	2	3
4	5	6	7	8	9	10
11	12	13	14	15	16	17
18	19	20	21	22	23	24
25	26	27	28	29	30	31

① 3일   ② 13일   ③ 16일   ④ 18일   ⑤ 20일

6 대화를 듣고, 여자가 남자에게 부탁하는 것을 고르시오.

① 의자 치우기　　② 숙제하기　　③ 불 *끄*기

④ 부엌 청소하기　　⑤ 전구 교체하기

Take notes

7 대화를 듣고, 남자가 세탁과 건조를 하는 데 걸리는 총 시간을 고르시오.

① 1시간 30분　　② 2시간　　③ 2시간 30분

④ 3시간 30분　　⑤ 4시간

8 대화를 듣고, 여자가 원하는 것을 고르시오.

① 보충 수업　　② 강의실 변경　　③ 과목 변경

④ 교수 연락처　　⑤ 수업 시간 변경

9 대화를 듣고, 내용과 일치하지 <u>않는</u> 것을 고르시오.

① 남자는 시를 쓰는 것에 관심이 있다.

② 남자는 학교 신문에 자신의 시를 게재하고 싶어 한다.

③ 여자는 어린이들에게 스케이트를 가르치는 데 관심이 있다.

④ 여자는 스케이트를 가르치고 있다.

⑤ 여자는 차비 이외에는 따로 돈을 받지 않는다.

10 대화를 듣고, 여자가 이번 주말에 할 일로 알맞은 그림을 고르시오.

①

②

③

④

⑤

11 다음을 듣고, 자전거에 장치되어 있지 <u>않은</u> 것을 고르시오.

① 큰 헤드라이트 ② 두 개의 로봇 팔
③ 타이어의 미끄럼 방지용 핀 ④ 도난 방지용 알람
⑤ 우산

12 대화를 듣고, 여자가 자전거 두 대를 빌리는 데 지불할 금액을 고르시오.

① $2 ② $4 ③ $6 ④ $8 ⑤ $10

13 대화를 듣고, 남자가 대화 후 가장 먼저 할 일을 고르시오.

① 약을 사온다. ② 난방기를 켠다.
③ 여자를 병원에 데려간다. ④ 물을 가져다준다.
⑤ 담요를 가져다준다.

14 대화를 듣고, Tom이 공항에 도착할 시각을 고르시오.

① 2:20 ② 3:00 ③ 3:10 ④ 3:20 ⑤ 3:30

15 다음을 듣고, 그림의 상황에 가장 잘 어울리는 대화를 고르시오.

① ② ③ ④ ⑤

16 대화를 듣고, 여자의 심정으로 알맞은 것을 고르시오.

① scared   ② curious   ③ ashamed

④ bored   ⑤ excited

17 대화를 듣고, 언급되지 않은 것을 고르시오.

① 지진   ② 태풍   ③ 홍수

④ 산사태   ⑤ 대피 장소

18 대화를 듣고, 여자가 걱정하는 이유를 고르시오.

① 졸려서

② 길을 잃어서

③ 시간이 부족해서

④ 기름이 떨어져가서

⑤ 대화할 상대가 없어서

19-20 대화를 듣고, 여자의 마지막 말에 이어질 남자의 응답으로 가장 알맞은 것을 고르시오.

19 ① Right. I can't wait.

② I'm sorry for being late.

③ Yes, I saw the Eiffel Tower.

④ Summer vacation is almost over.

⑤ Thank you. It was a great experience.

20 ① I don't like exercising.

② I hope, but I can't work.

③ I don't want to get a job.

④ It is hard to get a job these days.

⑤ Don't say that. I don't have any money.

Dictation

1

W Listen carefully. I'd like you to _____ _____ I'm going to describe now. If you do well, I'll _____ _____ _____ right away. Now draw a circle inside a triangle and draw a square _____ _____ _____.
It's a very simple drawing. Please show me what you have drawn now.

2

M Excuse me, are you Ms. Baker? I'm a huge fan of yours. It's a great pleasure meeting you here.

W Thank you. It's my pleasure, too.

M I've read every play you have written. Are you _____ _____ _____ _____?

W Yes. I'm writing a new play about my life.

M That sounds interesting.

W _____ _____ _____ _____.

M I hope your writing _____ _____.

W Thank you.

3

W Hello, Mr. Johnson.

M Hi, Kelly. What can I do for you today?

W I'd like to _____ _____ _____ _____.

M What's it for?

W It's for my passport.

M You must be going somewhere.

W Yes, _____ _____ _____ _____ and _____ a language program in the States.

M I see.

4

W Are you OK?

M Yes. Mrs. Kim told me _____ _____ _____ _____, she'll call my mother.

W Aren't you going to tell your mom about what happened?

M Are you crazy? If I do, she would kill me.

W Then, I am not supposed to tell her, right?

M That's exactly _____ _____ _____ _____ _____.

5

W My father's birthday is coming, so I'm making a card for my dad.

M That's a good idea. What are you going to _____ _____ _____ _____?

W I'm going to write, "Thank you, Dad. Be happy. I'll _____ _____ _____ to be a good daughter."

M Good. By the way, when is his birthday?

W It's the third Sunday in May. It's _____ _____ _____ _____ _____.

M I see. Your dad will be glad to know you love him so much.

6

W John, can you _____ _____ and help me?

M Sure. What is it?

W I need you to replace this light bulb for me.

M Where?

W It's the one _____ _____ _____.

M Then, I need a chair. I don't think I'm _____ _____ _____ _____ it.

W You can bring the chair from your room.

M OK, Mom.

7

W Wow! You have really a lot of _____ _____ _____.

M This is my first time to wash my clothes in this Laundromat. I'm going to wash these and dry them afterward.

W It'll take _____ _____ _____ _____ to wash and dry them all.

M How long will it take?

W It'll take one and a half hours to wash them.

M That doesn't seem so long.

W But the drying takes 30 minutes _____ _____ _____ _____.

M Yeah. That's quite a long time.

8

W Hi, Mr. Johnson. I'd like to change my class schedule.

M OK. What do you want to change?

W I want to switch my biology class to English.

M I'm sorry, but you can't do that. The English class _____ _____ _____.

W Ah, no way!

M Is there _____ _____ _____ you want to take?

W What about history?

M Let me check. Good, _____ _____.

9

W David, what are you interested in the most?

M My main interest is writing poems. I've written two poems _____ _____ _____ _____.

W That's great!

M How about you, Kathy?

W _____ _____ _____ teaching ice-skating to young children. I've taught skating for 3 years. I only get 20 dollars _____ _____ _____ for bus fare. I'm not making any money from that.

M Then, you can say it's voluntary work.

10

W What are you going to do this weekend?

M I'm not sure. I guess I'll just stay home. Maybe I'll help my father _____ _____ _____ _____. What about you? Do you have any plans?

W My parents have _____ _____ _____ at a beach resort. I plan on getting a little sun.

M Sounds fantastic!

W Why don't you join us? We have enough room.

M Great! _____ _____ _____ _____.

09회 영어듣기모의고사 · 77

Dictation

11

M It took 2 years for me to invent my Super Bike. I'll show you what's special about it. First, there's a big headlight _____ _____ _____ _____ the handlebar. Next, there are two robot arms from the main frame _____ _____ _____. The tires are also very special. There are little pins on the tires. They make your bike-riding safe when it snows. There is also a button near the seat. If you push it, an umbrella will _____ _____ to protect you from rain and sun.

12

W Excuse me, how much do you charge for _____ _____ _____?

M 4 dollars an hour.

W That's too expensive. My brother and I don't _____ _____ _____.

M How much do you have?

W We had 10 dollars, but we each ate a hotdog. The hotdogs were 2 dollars each. So, this is _____ _____ _____.

M Okay. Then, I'll just take that.

W Thank you very much.

13

W I'm very cold.

M Let me see. You've _____ _____ _____.

W How bad is it?

M I think you should _____ _____ _____ a doctor now.

W I can't even walk. Could you bring me a blanket first?

M Sure. I'll _____ _____ _____ _____ for you, OK?

W Would you give me the blanket first? My body is shaking now.

M OK. I'll be right back.

14

W What time does _____ _____ _____?

M 3:30. My boarding time is 3:10, so I have to get to the gate before 3:10.

W I see. Then, you only have _____ _____ _____ before the flight. When is Tom going to be here?

M He should be here soon. He'll probably be here 10 minutes before boarding time. He's _____ _____ _____.

W I see.

15

① **W** Sorry, but I have to leave now.
   M Then, when can I see you again?

② **W** Hey, you are not supposed to _____ _____ _____.
   M I'm sorry. I thought you were not in line.

③ **W** Watch out!
   M Thanks, I couldn't see the bike coming.

④ **W** Would you help me carry these boxes?
   M Sorry. _____ _____ _____ _____ right now.

⑤ **W** I can't _____ _____ right now.
   M That's OK. I'll call him later.

78

16

W Is anyone _____ _____?

M Yes. Who is it?

W It's Cindy. It's very dark here, and I can't see anything. Please help me.

M What are you doing there?

W The power _____ _____ _____, and the elevator has stopped.

M Why don't you push the yellow button there?

W I tried, but _____ _____ _____.

M Did you call 911 to help you?

W My cell phone doesn't work in here. Can you call them for me?

17

W _____ _____ there was a natural disaster here in your town?

M You mean like an earthquake, typhoon, or flood?

W Yes. _____ _____ _____.

M I don't know. I might get frightened. How about you?

W I would find _____ _____ _____ _____ like a basement.

M What if you are not inside a building?

W I haven't really thought about that.

18

W Hey, John. Wake up! I'm kind of sleepy. Please start talking to me.

M Okay. _____ _____ _____ _____?

W No, not yet.

M _____ _____ _____ do we still have to go?

W We have to go for 2 hours more.

M It takes longer than _____ _____.

W Yeah. We still have a long way to go. And what's more, I'm afraid we've _____ _____ _____ gas.

19

M Wow! Summer vacation is _____ _____.

W Right. Only one more week to go.

M Do you have any plans for the vacation?

W Not really. My mom told me if I don't prepare for the next semester, I'll _____ _____ _____. My grades are _____ _____ _____ _____. By the way, I heard you're going to Paris this summer vacation.

M Right. I can't wait.

20

W Have you lost some weight since you _____ _____ _____?

M Just a little.

W You told me you don't eat anything after 7, right?

M That's true, but _____ _____ _____ _____.

W Why don't you _____ _____ _____?

M I don't like exercising.

10회 영어듣기모의고사

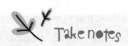
정답 및 해설 p.54

1 다음을 듣고, 그림과 일치하지 <u>않는</u> 것을 고르시오.

①   ②   ③   ④   ⑤

2 대화를 듣고, 두 사람의 관계로 가장 알맞은 것을 고르시오.

① 세입자 – 집주인   ② 부동산 중개인 – 고객

③ 호텔 직원 – 고객   ④ 교사 – 학생

⑤ 점원 – 고객

3 대화를 듣고, 여자가 지불해야 할 금액을 고르시오.

① $5   ② $60   ③ $200   ④ $65   ⑤ $205

4 대화를 듣고, 남자가 사고를 당한 요일을 고르시오.

① 화요일   ② 수요일   ③ 목요일   ④ 금요일   ⑤ 토요일

5 다음을 듣고, 두 사람의 대화가 <u>어색한</u> 것을 고르시오.

①   ②   ③   ④   ⑤

Take notes

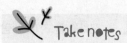

6 다음을 듣고, 무엇에 관한 내용인지 고르시오.

① 학교 구내식당의 위생 상태 개선을 촉구
② 학생들의 급식 활동에 많은 학부모의 참여를 독려
③ 학생들의 식중독 문제 해결에 학부모의 동참을 촉구
④ 새로운 구내식당 건축에 관한 학부모 의견 제시를 요청
⑤ 학생들의 식중독 예방을 위한 정부의 대책 마련을 촉구

7 대화를 듣고, 여자에 대한 내용으로 일치하지 <u>않는</u> 것을 고르시오.

① 처음으로 해외여행을 한다.
② 미국의 15개 주를 여행할 것이다.
③ 친한 친구와 함께 갈 것이다.
④ 여행 스케줄이 바쁘다.
⑤ 여행 가방을 샀다.

8 다음을 듣고, 무엇에 대한 설명인지 고르시오.

① fish   ② frogs   ③ birds
④ whales   ⑤ butterflies

9 대화를 듣고, 여자가 사려는 쿠션을 고르시오.

①    ②   ③

④    ⑤

10 대화를 듣고, 여자가 남자에게 부탁한 것이 <u>아닌</u> 것을 고르시오.

① 우유 사오기   ② 빵 사오기   ③ 빨래하기
④ 쓰레기통 비우기   ⑤ 유리창 청소

11 대화를 듣고, 두 사람이 대화하는 장소를 고르시오.

① 공항　　　② 병원　　　③ 백화점　　　④ 경찰서　　　⑤ 우체국

12 대화를 듣고, 여자가 지금 불편한 이유로 가장 알맞은 것을 고르시오.

① 피곤해서　　　　② 머리가 아파서　　　③ 돈이 없어서

④ 멀미가 나서　　　⑤ 배가 고파서

13 다음을 듣고, 무엇에 관한 내용인지 고르시오.

① 새로운 기술을 배워야 하는 이유

② 어린이들이 운동을 해야 하는 이유

③ 어린이들이 낮잠을 자야 하는 이유

④ 영양상태가 아이들의 발육에 끼치는 영향

⑤ 편식하지 않는 것이 아이들에게 중요한 이유

14 대화를 듣고, 남자의 심정으로 알맞은 것을 고르시오.

① upset　　　　② amused　　　③ frightened

④ depressed　　⑤ proud

15 다음을 듣고, 그림의 상황에 가장 잘 어울리는 대화를 고르시오.

①　　　　②　　　　③　　　　④　　　　⑤

82

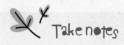

16 대화를 듣고, 두 사람이 주말에 하기로 한 일을 고르시오.

① 영화 관람　　　　　　② 자전거 타기
③ 수상스키 타기　　　　④ 수영
⑤ 놀이공원에 가기

17 대화를 듣고, 남자가 전화를 건 목적을 고르시오.

① 식사에 초대하려고　　　② 식당을 알아보려고
③ 음식 취향을 알아보려고　④ 예약을 하려고
⑤ 식사 약속을 연기하려고

18 대화를 듣고, 여자에 대해 알 수 <u>없는</u> 것을 고르시오.

① 출생지　　　　　　② 현재 거주지
③ 대학 입학 연도　　④ 직업
⑤ 대학에서의 전공

<u>19-20</u> 대화를 듣고, 여자의 마지막 말에 이어질 남자의 응답으로 가장 알맞은 것을 고르시오.

19
① Why didn't you buy it earlier?
② That's true. It's better to buy later.
③ I guess you need to save more money.
④ I can't choose either one of them now.
⑤ I think you'd better buy a used one. They're cheaper.

20
① What a mess!
② That's why it's so neat.
③ Why didn't you do that?
④ Did your mother punish you?
⑤ I'll help you clean your room.

Dictation

1

M ① The TV set is between the two windows.
② There is a bed _____ _____ _____ _____ of the room.
③ A picture frame is _____ _____ _____ _____ above the dresser.
④ There is a dresser on the other side of the bed.
⑤ The lamp stand is _____ _____ _____ the dresser.

2

M Good morning, how can I help you?
W _____ _____ _____ a house for my family.
M Okay. Tell me what type you're looking for.
W I'm looking for a three-bedroom apartment _____ _____ _____.
M We surely have a place close to the subway.
W What's the monthly rent?
M 1,800 dollars a month including water and electricity. Would you like to go and _____ _____ the apartment?
W Sure.

3

W I'd like to send this package _____ _____ to San Francisco.
M Sure. It weighs 20 pounds. That'll be 60 dollars.
W OK. I'd like to have it insured.
M Then, I need to know the exact _____ _____ _____ _____.

W It's 200 dollars.
M Then, it's 5 dollars extra _____ _____.
W Thank you. Here you are.

4

W Thank God it's Friday.
M It sure was a long week. _____ _____ _____ _____ was terrible.
W What happened?
M While walking to work, I bumped into a bike and _____ _____ _____ _____.
W Are you all right?
M Not really. I still _____ _____ _____.
W I hope you get better.
M Thank you.

5

① M What was the problem?
   W The way he did it was excellent.
② M Can I have this?
   W You can have whatever you want _____ _____.
③ M Do you have time to talk to me?
   W Sure. Will it take long?
④ M Why did she _____ _____ _____?
   W Because she can't move to another city.
⑤ M What do you think of this computer game?
   W To me, it's _____ _____ _____ _____.

6

M   There have been serious problems _____ _____ what our children eat at the school cafeteria. Every year many students become hospitalized due to food poisoning. The government keeps telling us they will _____ _____ _____ _____, but nothing has been done so far. Therefore, we parents should do something to protect our kids from food poisoning. I'd be happy to get any suggestions from parents as to _____ _____ _____ _____ with this issue.

7

M   _____ _____ _____ _____ the trip?

W   Of course, it's my first overseas trip.

M   Right. You'll have a wonderful experience in the USA.

W   I think so. I'm going to _____ _____ 15 different states.

M   That's a pretty busy schedule. By the way, do you _____ _____ _____?

W   Yes. I just bought one.

8

W   They are the most beautiful and _____ _____ _____ _____. They serve us well by destroying harmful insects, and they also give us pleasure. Their various colors, their beautiful flight, and their musical songs always delight us. And we _____ _____ _____

their mysterious migration practices. How do they find their way _____ _____ _____ _____?

9

M   Look at these cushions, Jessica. How about this one?

W   The heart-shaped one? Oh, 30 dollars is too much.

M   What about that square one?

W   20 dollars isn't bad, but the shape is _____ _____.

M   Then, how about the round one?

W   I want something more practical. I might use it _____ _____ _____.

M   Then, what do you think about this long and narrow one?

W   It _____ _____ a pillow. And the price is reasonable, only 15 dollars. Okay. I'll take that one.

10

W   Nick, did you buy the milk and bread I asked you to?

M   Yes, they are _____ _____ _____.

W   Thank you. Now go to the cleaners and pick up the laundry. And when you get back, could you _____ _____ _____ _____?

M   OK. I'll get everything done, Mom.

W   Thank you. _____ _____ _____, clean all the windows, okay?

M   Sure, I think Dad will be happy to see the house cleaned.

Dictation

11

M Can I see what you have in your bag?

W Sure. Do you want me to open it?

M Please, do. What is this?

W It's for my brother. _____ _____ only 50 dollars.

M OK. How about this?

W It's a digital camera for my sister. It's only 200 dollars.

M Do you have _____ _____ _____ to declare in that small bag?

W No, just clothes.

M OK. Thank you. _____ _____ _____.

12

W How long will it take to _____ _____ _____ _____?

M We're almost there. What's the problem? You look pale.

W I feel like I _____ _____ _____.

M Why don't you open the window and get some fresh air?

W Okay. I feel better now.

M Come on. We'll have a great time in Waikiki. It's a perfect place for surfing.

13

M Young kids' bodies are growing and changing _____ _____ _____ _____, which requires a lot of energy. In addition, the world _____ _____ _____ _____ so many interesting things to discover and so many new skills to learn, and all that stimulation can make a child pretty tired. Whether big or little, people don't perform _____ _____ _____ when they are too tired. Therefore, young kids need not only a good night's sleep but also a little nap. This extra sleep keeps them healthy.

14

W May I help you, sir?

M Yes. I bought this golf club 2 weeks ago. I have a complaint about it.

W What did you _____ _____ _____ _____?

M I found a scratch on the club. Will you _____ _____ _____ give me a new one?

W I'm not sure if I can. We can only replace goods within 10 days of purchase.

M I noticed it yesterday, and I've never used it.

W I don't think we can exchange it for you. The period has to be within _____ _____ _____ _____ as mentioned.

15

① M What is your father doing now?
     W He is fixing the roof.

② M Wow, you're wearing nice shoes!
     W Thanks. I just bought them.

③ M Do you need any help washing the dishes?
     W No, thank you. I can _____ _____ _____.

④ M Excuse me, do you know where a shoe-repair shop is?
     W Yes. There's one in the shopping mall over there.

⑤ M We've got a flat tire. I don't know _____ _____ _____ _____ _____.
     W Then, what can we do?

16

W Let's do something exciting for this weekend. Do you have _____ _____?

M How about water skiing?

W I'm not _____ _____ _____ for that. Any other suggestions?

M How about going to an amusement park?

W The closest one is too far. Let's ride a bike _____ _____ _____.

M Sounds great.

17

[Telephone rings.]

M Hey, Betty. It's Johnny.

W What's up?

M I need to find _____ _____ _____. My relatives from Japan will be here tomorrow.

W I see. Do they like Korean food? I know a good restaurant _____ _____. It's really great.

M Where is it?

W It's behind the Charles Hotel. And it's open from 11 A.M. to 11 P.M.

M Do you think I need to _____ _____ _____?

W Yes. I think so.

18

M Where were you born, Jenny?

W I was born and _____ _____ in Germany.

M Oh! So, you weren't born in the USA.

W No, I came here in 2003.

M Did you _____ _____ right away?

W No. My English wasn't very good, so I took language courses for one year and then went to college.

M I think you _____ _____ _____ now.

W Thanks. I majored in English Literature at a university in New York.

19

M What are you looking at?

W I'm thinking of buying a new computer. Mine is _____ _____ and _____ _____. The worst thing is that it breaks down too often.

M That's why you are looking at the computers.

W But my mother told me if I _____ _____ another 6 months, there will be a newer model with more powerful chips at a cheaper price.

M You know it's _____ _____ _____.

W I know, so I'm trying to decide whether to buy now or wait for another 6 months.

M I think you'd better buy a used one. They're cheaper.

20

M Can I _____ _____ your room?

W No. Please don't.

M Why not?

W It's my private space.

M Come on! _____ _____ _____ for a long time.

W Okay, come on in.

M Wow, you have _____ _____ _____ in your room.

W I spent a few hours arranging things last night.

M That's why it's so neat.

11회 영어듣기모의고사

1 대화를 듣고, 범인의 인상으로 알맞은 것을 고르시오.

①    ②   ③

④   ⑤

2 대화를 듣고, 여자의 심경을 가장 잘 나타낸 것을 고르시오.

① relieved   ② lonely   ③ exciting

④ angry   ⑤ happy

3 대화를 듣고, 여자가 선물하기로 한 것을 고르시오.

① 반지   ② 목걸이   ③ 귀고리

④ 팔찌   ⑤ 열쇠고리

4 대화를 듣고, 남자가 책값으로 지불해야 할 금액을 고르시오.

① $30   ② $35   ③ $40   ④ $45   ⑤ $50

5 다음을 듣고, 일치하지 않는 것을 고르시오.

① 등산은 다리 근육에 많은 도움이 된다.
② 나는 처음에는 정상까지 오르지 못했다.
③ 정상에 오르면 좋은 경치를 볼 수 있다.
④ 요즈음 나는 친구와 가족과 함께 등산을 한다.
⑤ 나는 등산에 익숙해져 있다.

Take notes

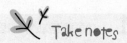

6 대화를 듣고, 남자가 전화를 건 목적을 고르시오.

① 놀러 오라고
② 물이 새어서
③ 월세를 연기하려고
④ 난방기가 고장 나서
⑤ 문이 안 열려서

7 대화를 듣고, 여행 경비로 언급되지 <u>않은</u> 것을 고르시오.

① 비행기 요금　　② 가이드 봉사료　　③ 숙박료
④ 현지 교통비　　⑤ 식비

8 대화를 듣고, 두 사람이 대화하는 장소를 고르시오.

① department store　　② gas station　　③ airport
④ grocery store　　⑤ parking lot

9 대화를 듣고, 남자의 직업을 고르시오.

① 사진관 직원　　② 영화관 직원　　③ 부동산 개발업자
④ 운동선수　　⑤ 정원사

10 다음을 듣고, 그림의 상황에 가장 잘 어울리는 대화를 고르시오.

①　　　②　　　③　　　④　　　⑤

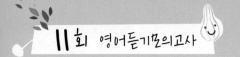

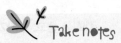

11 대화를 듣고, 두 사람이 관람할 것을 고르시오.

Entertainment Guide
① Opera *"Butterfly"* The Arts Center 6:00
② Opera *"Aria"* The Opera House 7:00
③ Ballet *"Serenade"* The American Theater 6:00
④ Ballet *"Swan Lake"* The Modern Theater 7:00
⑤ Musical *"42nd street"* The Cultural Center 8:00

12 대화를 듣고, 남자가 한 마지막 말의 의도를 고르시오.

① 거절   ② 확신   ③ 추측   ④ 제안   ⑤ 의심

13 다음을 듣고, 알맞게 그린 그림을 고르시오.

14 다음을 듣고, 두 사람의 대화가 <u>어색한</u> 것을 고르시오.

①   ②   ③   ④   ⑤

15 대화를 듣고, 여자가 혼자 여행을 가는 이유를 고르시오.

① 초청을 받아서

② 비행기 표가 없어서

③ 같이 갈 친구가 없어서

④ 혼자 다니는 데 익숙해서

⑤ 자유롭게 여행하고 싶어서

16 대화를 듣고, 여자가 오늘 하려는 것을 고르시오.

① 테니스 치기   ② 영화보기

③ 친구와 외출하기   ④ TV 시청

⑤ 독서

17 대화를 듣고, 상황에 가장 잘 어울리는 속담을 고르시오.

① No pain, no gain.

② Better late than never.

③ Don't cry over split milk.

④ Too many cooks spoil the broth.

⑤ The first step is always the hardest.

18 대화를 듣고, 두 사람이 대화 후 갈 장소를 고르시오.

① 서점   ② 안경점

③ 집   ④ 도서관

⑤ 은행

19-20 대화를 듣고, 남자의 마지막 말에 이어질 여자의 응답으로 가장 알맞은 것을 고르시오.

19

① I work hard for it.

② Thanks for your advice.

③ I'll give you an English test tomorrow.

④ OK. I'll help you find the answers.

⑤ Keep in mind what I'm telling you.

20

① He may go to the movies.

② I'm sure his girlfriend is pretty.

③ That can't be. He must have lied to me.

④ It is impossible for him to go to class.

⑤ You can see him cross the street at night.

Dictation

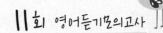

1

W Please help me. Some man snatched my bag and ran that way.

M Tell me _____ _____ _____ _____ .

W He doesn't look like one of those common criminals. He has short hair, and... I don't know.

M _____ _____ _____ .

W He just looks ordinary. He has big eyes.

M Does he _____ _____ _____ or a beard?

W No, nothing.

2

W Hey! The train is late! I've been waiting here so long.

M Which train are you _____ _____ ?

W The three thirty to San Jose.

M To San Jose? I'm afraid you've _____ _____ _____ , ma'am.

W A mistake? But I took this train last week.

M We've changed the schedule recently.

W Changed it? Why didn't you _____ _____ _____ _____ ?

M Oh, that...

W I don't believe this! You've changed the train schedule, but commuters were not notified at all. How could you do that?

3

W I'm looking for some souvenirs for my daughters.

M How about these key rings?

W _____ _____ _____ _____ .

M Oh, I see. What about those necklaces? Most girls like them.

W I'm afraid my daughters don't wear necklaces.

M How about the earrings?

W No, they don't fit their style. What about these bracelets?

M Bracelets? You _____ _____ _____ _____ . They're 18 dollars each.

W OK. I'll take them.

4

M Excuse me, I'm _____ _____ a book about the Joseon Dynasty.

W Let me find one for you. Here you go.

M Thank you. What's _____ _____ _____ _____ _____ ?

W It's 50 dollars. But if you have a membership card, you can get 20 percent off.

M Yes, I do. Here you are.

5

W I enjoy climbing mountains. I climb mountains every weekend. It helps me _____ _____ _____ _____ . When I first started climbing mountains, I couldn't climb all the way up to the peak. A few months later, I made it to the top of the mountain. These days, I climb many different mountains with my friends and family. The higher I reach, the happier I am, and the higher I reach, the fresher the air I can breathe. _____ _____ _____ _____ _____ mountains now.

6

[Telephone rings.]

W Hello?

M Hello, Ms. Benson. This is Mr. Brown in apartment 771.

W Oh, yes. _____ _____ _____ _____ _____? Is it the leaking problem again?

M No, it's not that. It's the heating system this time. I think something's wrong with the temperature control. It's too cold in here.

W Really? OK. I'll _____ _____ _____ _____ _____ it right away.

7

[Telephone rings]

W Green Tour, may I help you?

M Hi, this is Mike Cowen. I just called _____ _____ _____ that my trip is all set.

W Yes. It's all set. You paid for everything, and you are _____ _____ _____.

M Thanks. Can I check the information again?

W Yes. The package deal includes hotels, meals, local transportation, and the plane fare.

M Okay. Thanks. Then, I'll see you _____ _____ _____.

W Sure thing.

8

M Good morning, ma'am. May I help you?

W Yes, please. Would you _____ _____ _____?

M Regular or premium?

W Regular, please.

M Do you want me to check _____ _____ _____?

W Yes, please.

M Your oil is still OK. Now, just let me _____ _____ _____.

W Thank you.

9

M Hi, ma'am. What can I do for you?

W I want to print these _____ _____ _____.

M Sure.

W When can I _____ _____ _____?

M They'll be ready by tomorrow afternoon.

W Can you make it a little bit sooner than that?

M We can _____ _____ in about 40 minutes, but it'll cost more.

W All right. I'll pick them up in 40 minutes.

10

① M Which would you rather do, watch or play?

   W I can't _____ _____ _____ _____.

② M Excuse me, could you _____ _____ _____?

   W Sure. Do I just push this button?

③ M Ma'am, you dropped your handkerchief.

   W Thank you. You are so kind.

④ M I bought a round-trip ticket to Hawaii.

   W Is that right?

⑤ M Hello. I'd like to _____ _____ _____ _____.

   W Sure. It will be ready tomorrow.

Dictation

11

W Hurry up. We're late already.

M Okay, okay. What time is it now?

W It's 6 P.M.

M Then, we _____ _____ _____ _____.

W What do you mean? It starts at 7 sharp.

M I thought it starts at 8. All right, I'm coming. What theater is it?

W How many times have I told you? It's at the Modern Theater. The traffic will be terrible, so we'd better _____ _____ _____.

M That's a good idea.

12

W Let's go.

M David hasn't come yet.

W I know, but we don't need to wait for him. He has a ticket, and he knows _____ _____ _____, right?

M I know, but I want to go there with him as well.

W We don't have much time.

M Christine, _____ _____ _____. He's usually not late.

W So, do you think he'll be here in a minute?

M Yes. There's _____ _____ _____ _____.

13

W Please _____ _____ _____, 3 blocks by 3. In the center, draw a smiley face. From there, go one block to the right, and then _____ _____ _____. Draw a triangle

there. And now, put a star right next to it. Finally, put another star below the smiley face. _____ _____ _____ _____?

14

① W Hello, can I talk to Mr. Brown?
   M This is he.

② W Is Mike there?
   M He just _____ _____ _____. He'll be back in 30 minutes.

③ W Do you think it is possible?
   M No, _____ _____ _____ _____ _____.

④ W Isn't this 786-6131? I'm sure that this is the right number.
   M It can't be.

⑤ W How did he get the money?
   M He got the money yesterday.

15

M I heard you are _____ _____ _____ _____ Europe.

W That's right. I'm leaving the day after tomorrow.

M Who are you going with, anyway?

W I'm going alone.

M Alone? Isn't that a little dangerous?

W I guess so, but I prefer to go alone because I can do _____ _____ _____. If I go with my friends, we may argue a lot, especially about where to go, when to go, what to eat, and _____ _____ _____.

M That's true.

16

M Jennifer, let's play tennis this afternoon.

W Sorry, but I _____ _____ _____ _____ .

M Come on. You are looking pale because you haven't been outside for a few days.

W I know, but I really don't want to.

M Then, let's _____ _____ _____ _____ .

W I'm really sorry, John. I don't feel like going out. Today, I'd rather read a book at home than _____ _____ .

17

M What time is it now?

W It's 8:30.

M I can't find _____ _____ _____ _____ _____ .

W Do you have a flashlight?

M If I had one, I would already be using it.

W What are we supposed to do then?

M I don't know. We _____ _____ _____ to the guide.

18

W I need to get _____ _____ _____ _____ glasses.

M What's wrong?

W I left them at the bookstore, and when I went back there to get them, they had gone.

M That's too bad. Do you want to get a new pair from _____ _____ _____ _____ ?

W I don't have any money.

M That's okay. My uncle owns it, and you can pay _____ _____ _____ every month.

W That's a great idea. Thank you. Let's go.

19

W Mike, tell me how you _____ _____ _____ in your English tests all the time.

M Well, it's not as hard as you think.

W It's easy for you to say, but not me.

M You should review what you learn every day. I've never missed _____ _____ _____ .

W That's tough.

M I know, but it will _____ _____ _____ .

W Thanks for your advice.

20

W John _____ _____ _____ class today.

M Really? What's his reason?

W He said _____ _____ _____ .

M That's pretty strange.

W What do you mean?

M I saw him _____ _____ _____ with his girlfriend 10 minutes ago. He didn't look sick.

W That can't be. He must have lied to me.

정답 및 해설 p.66

1 대화를 듣고, 여자가 구입할 셔츠로 알맞은 것을 고르시오.

①   ②  ③

④   ⑤

2 대화를 듣고, 남자가 사용하려는 것을 고르시오.

① 현금 인출기   ② 음료 자판기

③ 즉석 증명 사진기   ④ 스토브

⑤ 청소기

3 대화를 듣고, 두 사람의 관계로 가장 알맞은 것을 고르시오.

① 매표소 점원 – 고객   ② 운동선수 – 심판

③ 마라톤 선수 – 코치   ④ 방송 진행자 – 배우

⑤ 가수 – 매니저

4 대화를 듣고, 남자가 항공료로 지불해야 할 금액을 고르시오.

① $950   ② $1,000   ③ $1,050   ④ $1,200   ⑤ $2,500

5 대화를 듣고, 남자의 직업으로 알맞은 것을 고르시오.

① farmer   ② soldier   ③ policeman

④ businessman   ⑤ customs officer

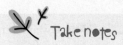

6 대화를 듣고, 일치하지 <u>않는</u> 것을 고르시오.

① Kelly는 내일 오후에 친척을 마중하러 갈 것이다.

② Mark는 Kelly와 발레를 보고 싶어 한다.

③ Kelly와 Mark는 내일 저녁에 「백조의 호수」를 볼 것이다.

④ 발레는 7시 정각에 시작한다.

⑤ Kelly와 Mark는 6시 30분에 만나기로 약속했다.

7 대화를 듣고, 남자의 장래 희망을 고르시오.

① 건축가   ② 승무원   ③ 군인

④ 사진작가   ⑤ 교사

8 다음을 듣고, 두 사람의 대화가 <u>어색한</u> 것을 고르시오.

①   ②   ③   ④   ⑤

9 대화를 듣고, 내용과 일치하는 동작을 고르시오.

①   ②   ③

④   ⑤

10 대화를 듣고, 여자가 호주에서 본 것이 <u>아닌</u> 것을 고르시오.

① 코알라   ② 캥거루   ③ 악어

④ 오페라 하우스   ⑤ 빙하

11 대화를 듣고, 여자가 버스를 타라고 추천하는 이유를 고르시오.

① 요금이 저렴해서 ② 편리해서

③ 풍경을 볼 수 있어서 ④ 거리가 짧아서

⑤ 붐비지 않아서

12 대화를 듣고, 남자가 여자에게 충고하는 것을 고르시오.

① 혼자 힘으로 해라.

② 시간을 절약해라.

③ 일찍 시작해라.

④ 좀 더 창의적이 되어라.

⑤ 남에게 도움을 주어라.

13 다음을 듣고, 그림의 상황에 가장 잘 어울리는 대화를 고르시오.

①   ②   ③   ④   ⑤

14 대화를 듣고, 남자가 앞으로 하려고 하는 것을 고르시오.

① 운동   ② 식사조절   ③ 달리기   ④ 걷기   ⑤ 테니스

15 대화를 듣고, 오늘의 날짜로 알맞은 것을 고르시오.

① 13th Friday   ② 15th Sunday   ③ 17th Tuesday

④ 18th Wednesday   ⑤ 19th Thursday

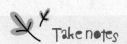

16 다음을 듣고, 무엇에 관한 내용인지 고르시오.

① 동물 실험 반대
② 애완동물 훈련 방법
③ 부모 역할의 중요성
④ 조기 학습의 중요성
⑤ 타인과의 놀이의 중요성

17 대화를 듣고, 남자가 오늘 오후에 할 일을 고르시오.

① 컴퓨터 게임 ② 보고서 작성
③ 차고 청소 ④ 생일잔치 참석
⑤ 그림 그리기

18 다음을 듣고, 무엇에 대한 설명인지 고르시오.

① 메아리 ② 화성 ③ 일식 ④ 무지개 ⑤ 운석

19-20 대화를 듣고, 여자의 마지막 말에 이어질 남자의 응답으로 가장 알맞은 것을 고르시오.

19
① You are very tired.
② I'm afraid you're wrong.
③ Why does he punish me?
④ I'll do my homework every day.
⑤ That's true. He prefers teaching girls.

20
① That will be great.
② I would feel terrible.
③ She was upset with me.
④ Thank you for the tickets.
⑤ Okay, I'll buy you dinner.

Dictation

12회 영어듣기모의고사

1

W Dad, are you going to buy me a shirt?

M Sure. Go ahead and _____ _____ anything you want.

W Okay. I like the one with the stripes.

M I don't think it _____ _____.

W How about the checkered one, then?

M _____ _____, _____.

W Okay. Then, I'll just pick the black round neck T-shirt.

M Okay.

2

M Excuse me, do you know how to use this machine?

W Sure. First, put the money _____ _____ _____. Then, choose the size and press the button.

M All right. And then, what do I do?

W _____ _____ _____ _____. Can you see the red laser point? You need to look at it and wait for a few seconds.

M Thank you.

W If you wait for two or three minutes, your pictures will be ready, but _____ _____ _____ _____ first.

3

W Good morning, Mr. Smith.

M Good morning, Ms. Anderson. _____ _____ _____ _____.

W Thank you for inviting me here. I'm so excited to be here.

M We'd like to know more about you. We

have _____ _____ _____ _____. Are you ready to answer them?

W Sure. Go ahead.

M Your new movie just came out. Could you tell us about the new release?

W Yes, I was a marathoner and _____ _____ _____.

M Really? How interesting! We'll be right back after this commercial break.

4

M I'd like to _____ _____ _____ to Sweden.

W Is that round trip?

M Yes, it is.

W When would you like to fly?

M September, 25th.

W And _____ _____?

M I'm not sure. Can I decide later?

W If you return within a month, it'll be nine hundred and fifty dollars, but after a month it would be 100 dollars more.

M I see. I don't think I can return _____ _____ _____.

W OK.

5

M Hi, do you have _____ _____ _____?

W No, nothing to declare.

M Do you have any food, agricultural products, drugs, or weapons?

W No. All I have are clothes and some souvenirs _____ _____ _____ and relatives.

M Okay. Can you open your bag, please? What are these?

100

W They are vitamin pills. I take them every day.

M All right. I think you can go now.
   _____ _____ _____
   _____ .

6

M Kelly, do you have time tomorrow?

W I'm supposed to _____ _____ a
   relative from Canada at 3 P.M. Why, Mark?

M I want to see the ballet Swan Lake with
   you. It starts at 7. Do you think you can
   _____ _____ _____ ?

W Sure.

M _____ _____ _____ since
   the ballet starts at 7 sharp. We have to be
   there at least 30 minutes early.

W Let's meet one hour before the ballet at the
   bus stop.

M Okay. See you then.

7

M Sarah, can I ask you _____
   _____ _____ _____
   _____ in the future?

W Sure. I want to be a flight attendant because
   I'd like to travel _____ _____
   _____ _____ .

M That sounds wonderful.

W How about you?

M Me? I'm interested in architecture. I'd like
   to _____ _____ _____
   that many people will remember.

8

① W What do you think of this movie?
   M I think it's very interesting.

② W _____ _____ do you think it
   is to the airport?

M I guess it's almost 5 miles.

③ W _____ _____ _____
   _____ _____ Rome before?

M No, but I want to go there someday.

④ W Where do you think you will stay in
   Paris?

M I'll stay for 3 days in Paris.

⑤ W _____ _____ _____
   _____ your coffee?

M With sugar, please.

9

W I had a chance to talk with an American, and
   he taught me a few interesting gestures.

M _____ _____ ?

W I'll teach you _____ _____
   _____ . Make a fist and lift up your
   thumb, index finger, and the little finger.

M Like this?

W Yes. It's a combination of the letters, I, L,
   and Y, and it's _____ _____
   _____ _____ .

M I see.

10

M How was your trip to Australia? Did you see
   anything particular?

W Australia _____ _____
   _____ _____ the States, but
   there are several animals you can't see there.

M Like what?

W Like koalas, kangaroos, and alligators.

M I see. Did you see _____ _____
   _____ ?

W Yeah, and the alligators were scary. I've also
   been to the opera house.

M Did you see any glaciers?

W No, but I saw them in New Zealand.

Dictation

11

W How are you going to _____ _____ _____ _____?

M I'm going to ride a bike.

W Don't do that. It's too far and very dangerous. It'll take at least 2 hours.

M OK. Then, I'll take the subway. _____ _____ _____.

W I know, but it'll be a long journey.

M Then, what should I take?

W You should take bus 3431 since _____ _____ _____ _____.

M OK. Thanks for your help.

12

W Robert, I need _____ _____ _____ _____ with my school project.

M Haven't you finished it yet?

W No, I started it last night.

M I think you will need to do it all day today.

W That's why I need some help.

M But as far as I know, everyone has done it _____ _____. Your success _____ _____ your effort not others' help.

13

① W What can I do for you, sir?
   M _____ _____ _____ _____.

② W Look! A fire in the trash can!
   M Let me _____ _____ _____ that.

③ W May I help you?
   M I'd like to have this prescription filled, please.

④ W You have a lot of packages to send! Just put them on the counter here.
   M Thanks. Most of my family _____ _____ _____.

⑤ W Would you mind closing the door?
   M Of course not.

14

M I've been _____ _____ a lot of weight recently.

W Is that right?

M Yes. I need to do something to lose weight.

W How about going to a fitness center?

M There is no fitness center _____ _____ _____.

W Then, do some simple exercises at home.

M I don't feel like exercising at home.

W Then, _____ _____ _____ _____ to go to work _____ _____.

M That's a great idea. I'll start doing that.

15

W Have you finished _____ _____ _____?

M No, I haven't. How about you?

W I've finished. As you know, I like writing.

M I know, and I think you are a talented writer. I envy you. By the way, _____ _____ _____ _____?

W It's due Tuesday, the 17th.

M Right. We still have _____ _____ time.

W I don't think two days is enough time to write an essay, but you think that way...

M Maybe that's the reason I'm not a good writer.

102

16

M Most parents in Korea want their children _____ _____ _____ _____ _____, so they make their children stay home and study. However, when we watch kittens and puppies playing, we realize that they're learning _____ _____ _____ _____. They learn not only physical skills but also social interaction. The same is true for our children. Some experts say that it's important for children _____ _____ _____ _____ for two to three hours a day.

17

W What are you going to do this afternoon?
M I'm thinking of playing computer games.
W Oh, not again. I think you are _____ _____ _____.
M No, I'm not.
W Yes, you are. You spend most of your free time doing it.
M That's not true. I'll _____ _____ _____ today.
W Will you? Then, clean the garage for your dad.
M Okay, but you _____ _____ what you just said to me.

18

M A long time ago, many scientists in Europe found _____ _____ _____, but people in Asia thought of this as a kind of disaster. This occurs when the Moon passes between the Sun and the Earth. This occurs at least twice and _____ _____ _____ _____ each year.

19

M You don't like our English teacher, do you?
W _____, _____ _____ _____.
M Why not?
W I think our English teacher likes you _____ _____ _____.
M Why are you saying that?
W When I don't do my homework, _____ _____ _____, but I've never seen him punish you.
M I'm afraid you're wrong.

20

W John, I heard that you _____ _____ Jenny.
M That's right. She _____ _____ _____ me because I didn't give her the free ticket to the concert.
W Why didn't you?
M I just don't like her.
W Hey, listen. You should _____ _____ _____ _____, and if there is something you don't like about her, you should tell her.
M Okay.
W _____ _____ _____ _____ if someone treated you that way?
M I would feel terrible.

1 대화를 듣고, 남자의 엄마를 고르시오.

① ② ③ ④ ⑤

2 대화를 듣고, 현재 남자의 직업을 고르시오.

① writer   ② teacher   ③ photographer
④ film director   ⑤ farmer

3 대화를 듣고, 여자가 필요하다고 언급한 물건이 <u>아닌</u> 것을 고르시오.

① hairpin   ② hairspray   ③ comb
④ mirror   ⑤ hairdryer

4 대화를 듣고, 여자의 심정으로 알맞은 것을 고르시오.

① surprised   ② disappointed   ③ afraid
④ pleased   ⑤ exciting

5 대화를 듣고, 남자가 하려고 하는 것을 고르시오.

① 나무 심기   ② 물주기   ③ 잡초 제거
④ 잔디 심기   ⑤ 청소하기

6 대화를 듣고, 여자가 Florence에 대해 가장 마음에 들어 하는 것을 고르시오.

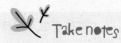 Take notes

① 역사   ② 건축물   ③ 경치

④ 친절한 사람들   ⑤ 싼 물가

7 다음을 듣고, 무엇에 대한 설명인지 고르시오.

① ambition   ② cooperation   ③ creativity

④ confidence   ⑤ challenge

8 대화를 듣고, 두 사람이 대화하는 장소를 고르시오.

① 사진관   ② 박물관   ③ 고층건물

④ 바닷가   ⑤ 병원

9 대화를 듣고, 남자가 선택한 카드를 고르시오.

①   ②   ③

④   ⑤

10 다음을 듣고, 내용과 일치하지 <u>않는</u> 것을 고르시오.

① 친구들과 놀이공원에 갔다.

② 놀이기구를 많이 탔다.

③ 돈을 계획 없이 사용했다.

④ 행인들에게 돈을 구걸했다.

⑤ 부모님이 걱정을 많이 하셨다.

11 대화를 듣고, 두 사람이 만날 요일과 시각을 고르시오.

① 월요일 5시   ② 월요일 6시   ③ 월요일 6시

④ 목요일 6시   ⑤ 목요일 7시

12 대화를 듣고, 두 사람이 지불할 금액을 고르시오.

① $50   ② $52   ③ $55   ④ $57   ⑤ $65

13 대화를 듣고, 여자가 남자에게 하는 충고로 알맞은 것을 고르시오.

① 시간을 지켜라.

② 물자를 아껴 써라.

③ 더 좋은 클럽을 찾아봐라.

④ 클럽 활동을 열심히 해라.

⑤ 남의 의사를 존중해라.

14 대화를 듣고, 두 사람의 관계로 알맞은 것을 고르시오.

① 학생 – 학생   ② 교사 – 학생   ③ 아버지 – 딸

④ 교장 – 교사   ⑤ 교사 – 학부모

15 다음을 듣고, 그림의 상황에 가장 잘 어울리는 대화를 고르시오.

①   ②   ③   ④   ⑤

Take notes

16 다음을 듣고, 교통사고에 대한 내용과 일치하지 <u>않는</u> 것을 고르시오.

① 독일의 고속도로에서 발생한 사고이다.

② 256대의 차가 충돌했다.

③ 많은 사람들이 죽거나 다쳤다.

④ 비 때문에 길이 미끄러웠다.

⑤ 일부 운전자들이 고속으로 달린 탓도 있다.

17 다음을 듣고, 무엇에 대한 설명인지 고르시오.

① 관습   ② 전통   ③ 영토   ④ 깃발   ⑤ 화폐

18 다음을 듣고, Rebecca가 Kevin에게 할 말로 가장 알맞은 것을 고르시오.

①   ②   ③   ④   ⑤

19-20 대화를 듣고, 여자의 마지막 말에 이어질 남자의 응답으로 가장 알맞은 것을 고르시오.

19 ① Yes, it is clean. Thank you.

② I'm sure you can do it alone.

③ Sorry. I'll clean it right away.

④ Now, you can push the button.

⑤ Sure, thanks. You're really helpful.

20 ① Thank you for repairing it.

② Sure, let's see how fast it is.

③ Well, I don't think it's possible.

④ No. I think you should turn it on right now.

⑤ Yes. It's old and slow, so you need a new one.

Dictation

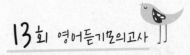

1

W Andrew, who's your mother _____ _____?

M My mother is wearing a pair of glasses.

W There are three ladies wearing glasses, but _____ _____ _____. I'll say the one with long hair in the white shirt.

M No, that's Susie's mom. My mother has short curly hair. She's _____ _____ _____ Susie's mom.

W Now, I got it.

2

W How is everything, Mike?

M I'm doing fine. How about you?

W _____ _____ _____ _____. Do you still teach kids?

M No, I _____ _____ but not anymore.

W Then, what do you do?

M I'm shooting motion pictures these days. It's mainly about life _____ _____ _____.

W Is it kind of an independent film?

M That's right.

3

W Today is the most important day of my life. I have _____ _____ _____ _____.

M I know. Just tell me what you need.

W First of all, I need some hairspray and a comb.

M OK. Let me _____ _____ _____.

W And I need a small mirror and a hairdryer.

M OK. _____ _____ do you need?

W Well, I think that's all.

4

W Mark, do you know who John picked?

M _____ _____ _____, but it wasn't you.

W How do you know?

M He told me he wouldn't pick you.

W Do you know why?

M He said he needed _____ _____ _____ _____, but your specialty is English.

W That's not fair.

5

W Did you plant all these flowers?

M I did some but _____ _____ _____ _____.

W Where did you get them?

M I bought them _____ _____ _____ _____. I also bought some grass, too.

W I see. What are these flowers?

M They are not flowers. They're weeds.

W Are they? What are you going to do with them?

M I'm about to _____ _____ _____.

108

6

M I heard that you're going to Florence.

W Yes, my aunt invited me there.

M What is _____ _____ _____ _____?

W It's known for its art and architecture. People there are very polite and kind.

M I see. I'm sure there are many famous buildings.

W Of course, but _____ _____ _____, I like its beautiful scenery.

M I really want to go there, too.

7

M I believe that this is _____ _____ _____ _____ _____ in our society. This is something you can learn when you work with others to _____ _____ _____. School is a good place to practice it. We are often given projects so that we can learn how to _____ _____. When we work in a group, we can't bring a good result without this.

8

M It looks really wonderful.

W Thank you, but please _____ _____ _____. It took me 5 hours to build this sandcastle.

M You spent so much time, but one big wave will _____ _____ _____ completely.

W I know, but I wanted to do it.

M Can I take a picture of it?

W Sure, go ahead. It'll be destroyed soon.

M Thank you. Why don't you _____ _____ _____ _____ _____? I'll take a picture of you and your wonderful work.

W Thanks.

9

M Hi, I'd like to buy a card _____ _____ _____.

W Here is a heart-shaped one. It looks really lovely.

M Yeah, but that's a card for girlfriends. I need a thank-you card.

W Okay, then. I think _____ _____ _____ _____ _____. It says "Special Thanks."

M You mean the one with no pictures or the one with flowers?

W Neither. I mean the one with the ribbon _____ _____ _____.

M That looks great! I'll take it.

10

M Hi. I'm David. I'm going to tell you _____ _____ _____ yesterday. I went to Big Mountain Amusement Park with my friends. We really _____ _____ _____ riding all kinds of roller coasters. When it was time to leave, we realized that none of us had any money to return home. My friends and I had to ask passersby for money. When we finally got home, it was nine o'clock at 9. _____ _____ _____.

Dictation

11

W Eric, do you know Monica is _____ _____ _____ next Monday?

M I know she's having a recital, but as far as I know, it's not next Monday.

W Is that right?

M She said _____ _____ _____ to Thursday.

W I see. It starts at 6, right?

M That also has been changed to 7.

W Okay. Then, we can meet at 6 to help her _____ _____ .

M OK. See you then.

12

M This was certainly a delicious meal.

W I enjoyed it, too. I think it was _____ _____ _____ _____ I've recently had. How much is it, anyway?

M Don't worry about it. I'll pay this time.

W Then, I'll take care of the tip. _____ _____ _____ _____ ?

M Let's see. The bill is 50 dollars. I think in a restaurant like this, 10 percent is usual.

W The food was good, and the waitress was kind. So, I'll tip an extra 2 dollars _____ _____ _____ .

M Okay. Sounds great.

13

W Mike said he would not join the club.

M Why not?

W He said he found _____ _____ _____ .

M He will regret it. Our club is the best.

W I understand you _____ _____ _____ your club, but not everyone

has to join your club. And you should _____ _____ _____ _____ , too.

M Okay. I see what you mean.

14

M Jenny, what's wrong?

W I'm so depressed, and I _____ _____ _____ , too.

M Why did you lose your appetite? Did the test result come back already?

W No, not yet. But I'm sure I didn't _____ _____ _____ .

M Why do you think that?

W The test was very difficult for me. How about you?

M Me? I'm not sure. I even don't remember the questions anyway. _____ _____ _____ _____ .

15

① M Would you like to take a picture with me?

W Sure. I want to _____ _____ _____ _____ _____ with my camera, too.

② M _____ _____ _____ your digital camera?

W No problem.

③ M Excuse me, how much is this paint?

W The pink paint is 10 dollars.

④ M These are real masterpieces.

W That's right. I like paintings by Pablo Picasso.

⑤ M Wow! _____ _____ this many _____ _____ people here before?

W Never. This is going to be a very exciting game.

110

16

M A huge car accident happened on the Autobahn in Germany. It involved 256 cars. Miraculously, _____ _____ _____, although 66 people were injured. It is believed that the accident _____ _____ _____ slippery road conditions as it was raining heavily at that time. Some motorists who were driving _____ _____ _____ on the Autobahn might also be to blame.

17

M This is _____ _____ _____ _____ with a special colored pattern or picture on it that is the symbol of a particular country or organization, or has a particular meaning. It's also used in some sports _____ _____ _____ or as a sign showing the position of something. This can be attached to a pole or _____ _____ _____ _____.

18

W Kevin meets Rebecca on the way to school. Kevin tells her he _____ _____ _____ _____ _____ last night. All the other students in his English class went to a party at their teacher's house, but Kevin couldn't get there. From their school, he took the subway, but he took the one _____ _____ _____ _____ and got completely lost. He really wanted to go to the party last night, but he missed it _____ _____ _____ _____. In this situation, what would Rebecca most probably say to him?

① I'm sorry to hear that.
② We're going to miss you.
③ Why didn't you come to the party?
④ It's a pity that you weren't invited.
⑤ That's okay. You can do better next time.

19

M Can you tell me _____ _____ _____ this machine?
W Don't you have instructions for this?
M Yes, I do. But I don't quite understand them.
W Well. Can you see that red button? It's the start button.
M I know.
W Push that button first and _____ _____ _____ _____ and pull it when it moves. _____ _____ _____?
M Sure, thanks. You're really helpful.

20

W Jake, my computer won't work again.
M What happened?
W I don't know. I just turned it on, and _____ _____ _____.
M Let me see it. I think there is some problem with the hardware.
W Do you think you can _____ _____ _____ right now?
M Well, I don't think it's possible.

Take notes

1 다음을 듣고, 여자가 설명하는 동물로 알맞은 것을 고르시오.

①

②

③

④

⑤

2 대화를 듣고, 여자의 장래 희망을 고르시오.

① 교사   ② 의사   ③ 변호사
④ 판사   ⑤ 사회복지사

3 대화를 듣고, 남자가 내일 할 일로 알맞은 것을 고르시오.

① 파티 가기   ② 가구 폐기하기   ③ 청소하기
④ 단어 외우기   ⑤ 숙제하기

4 대화를 듣고, 여자가 한 마지막 말의 의도를 고르시오.

① 제안   ② 변명   ③ 초대   ④ 사과   ⑤ 격려

5 대화를 듣고, 두 사람의 관계로 가장 알맞은 것을 고르시오.

① 학생 – 교사   ② 점원 – 손님   ③ 교사 – 학부모
④ 의사 – 환자   ⑤ 승객 – 승무원

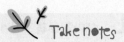

6 대화를 듣고, 여자가 받을 거스름돈을 고르시오.

① $4   ② $4.75   ③ $5   ④ $5.75   ⑤ $6.25

7 대화를 듣고, 현재 연료통에 남아있는 기름의 양을 고르시오.

① 3 *l*   ② 5 *l*   ③ 7 *l*   ④ 10 *l*   ⑤ 25 *l*

8 대화를 듣고, 남자가 부탁하는 것을 고르시오.

① 친구를 데려오라고
② 시간을 지켜 달라고
③ 음식 준비를 해 달라고
④ 파티 준비물을 가져오라고
⑤ 파티 하는 것을 비밀로 해 달라고

9 대화를 듣고, 두 사람이 대화하는 장소를 고르시오.

① museum   ② movie theater
③ shopping mall   ④ amusement park
⑤ baseball stadium

10 대화를 듣고, 여자가 사려고 하는 물건을 고르시오.

①   ②   ③

④   ⑤

11 대화를 듣고, 여자가 어젯밤에 전화를 끊은 이유를 고르시오.

① 집에 가야 해서　　　　② 어머니에게 혼이 나서
③ 화가 나서　　　　④ 배터리가 다 되어서
⑤ 숙제를 하려고

12 다음을 듣고, 두 사람의 대화가 <u>어색한</u> 것을 고르시오.

①　　　　②　　　　③　　　　④　　　　⑤

13 대화를 듣고, 남자가 해본 것이 <u>아닌</u> 것을 고르시오.

① 요트 타기　　　　② 수산 시장 구경
③ 뷔페식당에서 식사　　　　④ 국제 영화 축제에서 영화 관람
⑤ 시내 관광

14 다음을 듣고, 그림의 상황에 가장 잘 어울리는 대화를 고르시오.

①　　　　②　　　　③　　　　④　　　　⑤

15 대화를 듣고, 남자의 심정으로 가장 알맞은 것을 고르시오.

① happy　　　　② frustrated　　　　③ jealous
④ proud　　　　⑤ pleasant

16 대화를 듣고, 남자에 관한 사실과 일치하지 <u>않는</u> 것을 고르시오.

Take notes

① 유명한 축구 선수이다.

② 뉴 헤이븐에 자주 방문했다.

③ 현재 샌프란시스코에서 살고 있다.

④ 열두 살에 뉴욕으로 이사했다.

⑤ 뉴욕에서 대학을 다녔다.

17 다음을 듣고, 무엇에 대한 설명인지 고르시오.

① medal   ② flag   ③ map   ④ currency   ⑤ stamp

18 대화를 듣고, 여자가 <u>잘못</u> 메모한 것을 고르시오.

number of people	① 4 people
name	② John Cooper
date	③ July 15th
time	④ 7 P.M.
phone number	⑤ 212-223-5186

19-20 대화를 듣고, 여자의 마지막 말에 이어질 남자의 응답으로 가장 알맞은 것을 고르시오.

19
① Isn't that normal for everyone?

② I can do that for you if you want.

③ You have a natural talent for that.

④ Get some books and keep practicing.

⑤ I understand that. Try to use a microphone.

20
① I think we can reach a conclusion.

② I think you can stay in my house.

③ We can't touch that any more.

④ That's what I was thinking.

⑤ How will you get that?

Dictation

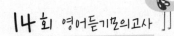

1

W This is an animal that mainly lives in water and has a soft body _____ _____ a hard shell. It cannot breathe underwater, but it can _____ _____ _____ for various lengths of time. In fact, it breathes air. Although many of them live in or around water, they don't _____ _____ underwater. They can also spend much of their lives on dry land. Surprisingly, they are commonly kept _____ _____.

2

W What do you want to be in the future, Henry?

M _____ _____ _____ studying law, but my parents want me to be a doctor.

W I see.

M _____ _____ _____ _____ _____ _____?

W I think your opinion is more important.

M Thanks. How about you, Sarah?

W I'm thinking of becoming a social worker.

M _____ _____ _____ _____ because you always like to help others.

3

M Do you have any plans for tomorrow?

W I'm going to study English. I really hate to memorize English vocabulary, but I have _____ _____ _____. How about you?

M My mom has bought some furniture, and I have to get rid of the old stuff with my father.

W I see. If you need any help, just let me know. I can _____ _____ _____ _____.

M Thanks.

4

W Hi, Tom. You don't look happy. Is there _____ _____?

M I have a final exam tomorrow.

W Don't worry too much. You will _____ _____.

M I don't think I'm ready yet.

W I don't think you need to feel so anxious because I've seen you _____ _____ _____.

5

W Hi, Mr. Adams. I dropped by to say goodbye.

M _____ _____ _____ your country? When are you leaving?

W This coming Friday. My flight is at 7 P.M.

M I really enjoyed having you here.

W I just want to thank you and _____ _____ _____ _____.

M We're going to miss you. Did you say goodbye to your classmates?

W Sure, I did. And some of them are going to _____ _____ _____ at the airport.

M Then, have a good trip. Goodbye.

116

6

M May I _____ _____ _____?

W Yes, I'd like two slices of pizza and a large Coke.

M _____ _____ _____ _____?

W Here, please.

M That comes to 5 dollars and 25 cents.

W Here's 10 dollars.

M Thanks.

W Just a moment. I have a quarter.

M Okay. _____ _____ _____.

7

W Can you check the fuel tank, please?

M I'm sure _____ _____ _____.

W I want to know the exact amount.

M OK. There was 25 liters when I first checked the fuel tank this morning. After that, John took 5 liters, and then Kevin took 10 liters. _____ _____ _____ _____.

W OK. Mike also used 3 liters.

M Is that right?

W Yes. _____ _____ no one has used it.

8

W Ken, I'll be there around 6. Do you want me to _____ _____?

M Nothing. My mother has already prepared everything, but I have _____ _____ _____ _____ you.

W What is it?

M I invited Harry _____ _____ _____, but he doesn't want to come.

W Why not?

M Since he _____ _____ Kate, he doesn't want to see her anymore.

W I see. So, you want me to bring Harry to the party?

M That's right.

9

W Excuse me, can you help me?

M Sure. What do you need?

W I've _____ _____ _____, and I can't find them. What should I do?

M Where did you last see them?

W I think it was at the roller coaster. I _____ _____ _____ when we bought the tickets.

M _____ _____ _____ _____, I would ask the main office to page them.

W I think I will. Thank you for your advice.

10

M Can I help you?

W Yes. I need to get something for my brother.

M Pen sets are always _____ _____ _____. We have a set with 3 pencils and an eraser, and another with 3 ballpoint pens and correction fluid. _____ _____ _____ _____ colored pencils, there are 12 different colored pencils in a set.

W But I don't think he needs colored pencils. He is a middle school student.

M I see. Then choose this set. It has a pencil, a ballpoint pen, and an eraser.

W I'll take that. _____ _____ _____, please?

M No problem. Wait a second, please.

Dictation

11

W Hi, Daniel. I'm sorry _____

_____ _____ _____

_____ last night.

M Oh, that! Actually I was wondering why.

W I'm really sorry. My mother scolded me for _____ _____ _____

_____ too long.

M I see. I thought you _____

_____ _____ me.

W No, not at all.

M OK. Then, are we still doing our homework together tonight?

W Sure. I'll see you at 6.

12

① W Where do you want me to place this vase?
   M Please put it on the table.

② W She seems _____ _____

_____ _____.

   M Yeah. She looks depressed.

③ W Don't forget to _____ _____

_____.

   M Don't worry. I already returned the books.

④ W What's tomorrow's schedule?
   M _____ _____ _____

_____ _____.

⑤ W Did you attend the English class?
   M Sure. I never miss any English classes.

13

W Hi, Eden! How was your trip to Bangkok?

M Great! I enjoyed _____ _____

_____ _____.

W Did you visit the famous fish market?

M No, I didn't have enough time. I just went to a buffet restaurant. It was so huge that the waiters and waitresses use roller skates _____ _____ _____.

W That's great. Did you also go to the International Movie Festival?

M Sure. The movies were fantastic!

_____ _____ _____

_____ _____ _____ was

fun, too.

14

① W You are not supposed to litter.
   M I'm sorry. I'll pick it up.

② W Stop bothering your sister.
   M She _____ _____

_____.

③ W Do not _____ _____

_____ _____ on the street.

   M I'm sorry. I won't do it again.

④ W I hope that it stops pouring.
   M Me, too. I want to _____

_____ _____ _____.

⑤ W It looks really dirty.
   M No, it's not. I cleaned it this morning.

15

M Hi, Cindy. Would you do me a favor?

W What is it?

M I need to call Mrs. Adams, so can you give me her phone number? And _____

_____ _____ your cell phone,

too?

W My cell phone is here, and Mrs. Adams's phone number is... I need to check my phonebook.

M Could you _____ _____

_____? It's urgent.

W Oh my God! I've just erased all of the phone numbers in my phonebook. I think I pushed the wrong button _____ _____.
This is terrible.

M I've lost my cell phone. You've erased all of your phone numbers. Now, what can we do?

118

16

W　We're talking today with Mike, a famous soccer player. Good evening, Mike.

M　Good evening. Thank you for inviting me.

W　Is this _____ _____ _____ _____ New Haven?

M　No. I've been here before many times for games.

W　Oh, really? Where's your hometown?

M　San Francisco. I moved to New York when I was 12. _____ _____, I've lived in here.

W　And you went to university in New York?

M　That's right.

W　Thanks. _____ _____ _____ _____. We'll be right back. Stay tuned!

17

M　This is the system or type of money that a country uses. Each country has _____ _____ _____ for this and its famous people or symbol on this. This has _____ _____ _____ different values and types. Mainly there are coins and bills. The most common one is the US dollar, which can be used _____ _____ _____ _____.

18

W　Secret Garden, may I help you?

M　Hi, I'd like to make a reservation for 4 people. My name is John Cooper.

W　Okay. _____ _____ _____ _____ _____?

M　On the fifth of July

W　Okay, _____ _____ _____?

M　7 P.M.

W　Okay. Can I have your phone number, please?

M　It's 212-223-5186.

W　I see. If there is any change, please let us know _____ _____.

M　Okay. Thank you.

19

M　What are you doing?

W　I'm trying to _____ _____ _____.

M　What for?

W　I'm supposed to make a five-minute speech _____ _____.

M　It must be very difficult.

W　No, not at all. But the problem is that I _____ _____ _____ when I speak in front of other people.

M　Isn't that normal for everyone?

20

M　Kelly, is that you?

W　Mike! _____ _____ _____ _____. I haven't seen you for a long time.

M　Yeah, but look at you! You haven't changed at all.

W　Thank you for saying so. I think we should _____ _____ _____ _____ _____ more often.

M　That's what I was thinking.

15회 영어듣기모의고사

정답 및 해설 p.83

1 대화를 듣고, 여자가 원하는 스티커 모양으로 알맞은 것을 고르시오.

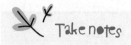

①

②

③

④

⑤

2 대화를 듣고, 남자가 체중을 줄이기 위해 하고 있는 것을 고르시오.

① 식이요법　　② 조깅　　③ 등산　　④ 수영　　⑤ 농구

3 다음을 듣고, 무엇에 관한 설명인지 고르시오.

① 자　　② 저울　　③ 온도계　　④ 벽시계　　⑤ 건전지

4 대화를 듣고, 남자가 여자에게 부탁하는 일을 고르시오.

① 짝을 바꾸어 달라고　　　　② 시험을 미뤄달라고

③ 대회에 참여하게 해 달라고　　④ 숙제를 줄여 달라고

⑤ 대회를 관람하게 해달라고

5 대화를 듣고, 여자가 내일 아침에 할 일을 고르시오.

① 영화를 본다.

② 수영장에 간다.

③ 동생을 돌본다.

④ 백화점에 간다.

⑤ 롤러블레이드를 타러 간다.

6 다음을 듣고, 두 사람의 대화가 <u>어색한</u> 것을 고르시오.

① ② ③ ④ ⑤

✗ ✗ Take notes

7 다음을 듣고, 표의 내용과 일치하는 것을 고르시오.

What do Korean Jr. High School students do in free time?

rank	activity	%
1	playing computer games	68
2	watching TV	54
3	spending time with friends	48
4	reading	35
5	exercising	18

① ② ③ ④ ⑤

8 다음을 듣고, 무엇에 관한 내용인지 고르시오.

① 기차 이용을 권유
② 교통규칙 준수를 권고
③ 중고 자동차 구입을 제안
④ 환경 친화적인 차의 구입을 제안
⑤ 차 운전 시 경비 절감 방안을 소개

9 대화를 듣고, Hyde Park까지 걸리는 시간과 지하철 요금이 바르게 짝지어진 것을 고르시오.

	시간	요금
①	약 30분	$1.50
②	약 45분	$1.00
③	약 45분	$1.50
④	약 1시간	$1.00
⑤	약 1시간	$1.50

10 대화를 듣고, 두 사람이 영화를 볼 시각을 고르시오.

① 6:30   ② 7:00   ③ 7:30   ④ 8:30   ⑤ 9:30

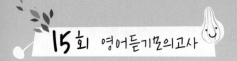

11 대화를 듣고, 두 사람의 관계로 가장 알맞은 것을 고르시오.

① 어머니 – 아들　　② 의사 – 환자　　③ 점원 – 고객

④ 운전사 – 승객　　⑤ 교사 – 학생

Take notes

12 대화를 듣고, 여자가 남자의 의견에 대해 조언하는 내용을 고르시오.

① 사실대로 쓸 것　　　　② 간결하게 쓸 것

③ 충분한 예를 들 것　　　④ 창의적으로 쓸 것

⑤ 제출 기한을 지킬 것

13 다음을 듣고, 내용과 일치하는 것을 고르시오.

① David는 이탈리아의 유적지를 여행했다.

② David는 독일에 자전거를 타고 갔다.

③ David는 베를린 장벽을 보았다.

④ David는 독일에 거주한다.

⑤ David는 기념품을 사지 못 했다.

14 다음을 듣고, 그림의 상황에 가장 잘 어울리는 대화를 고르시오.

①　　　　②　　　　③　　　　④　　　　⑤

15 대화를 듣고, 두 사람이 대화하는 장소를 고르시오.

① police station　　② bank　　③ school

④ airplane　　⑤ restaurant

16 대화를 듣고, 두 사람의 심정으로 가장 알맞은 것을 고르시오.

① excited   ② scared   ③ depressed

④ disappointed   ⑤ nervous

Take notes

17 대화를 듣고, 여자의 문제점이 무엇인지 고르시오.

① 허약한 체력   ② 편식   ③ 수면 부족

④ 집중력 부족   ⑤ 인내심 결여

18 대화를 듣고, 상황에 어울리는 속담으로 알맞은 것을 고르시오.

① 티끌모아 태산

② 피는 물보다 진하다.

③ 공든 탑이 무너지랴.

④ 소 잃고 외양간 고친다.

⑤ 자기 꾀에 자기가 넘어간다.

19-20 대화를 듣고, 남자의 마지막 말에 이어질 여자의 응답으로 가장 알맞은 것을 고르시오.

19
① They are angry at you.

② They need to buy a new phone.

③ You'd better go and look for them.

④ Library is a good place to study.

⑤ Don't use a phone at the library.

20
① Can you help me find her?

② There is nothing like a ghost.

③ She must be surprised at you.

④ That's okay. She was my mother.

⑤ I won't be able to sleep alone tonight.

Dictation

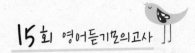

1

W Hello, I'd like to make some stickers
_____ _____.

M Okay. Can you _____ _____
what you want on the sticker?

W Sure. "A Lovely Girl"

M That's it?

W Please make each word _____
_____ a capital and put a rose
_____ _____ _____.

M Okay.

2

W You look like you've _____
_____ _____ _____.

M Yes, I know. I haven't exercised at all lately.

W If I were you, I would start dieting or
jogging.

M I'm already on a diet, but I don't like
jogging.

W Why don't you _____ _____
_____ _____?

M I don't like to sweat, and my left elbow isn't
good.

W _____ _____ _____ then?

M Swimming? Well, I can't swim.

3

M This is an instrument used for _____
_____. To use it properly, you have to
put it _____ _____ _____
_____. Older versions have a pointer
on the scale that indicates how much
a certain item weighs. But these days
_____ _____ _____ are

digitalized. However, you can still see the
old ones in a market or you might even have
one at home.

4

M Can I talk to you for a second?

W Sure, come on in and _____
_____ _____. What can I do for
you, Edward?

M I was wondering who you're going to select
for the contest.

W Why do you want to know about that?

M Because I would like to _____
_____ the contest.

W I'm sorry, but I don't think you will be
chosen.

M I think I have pretty good skills. I should
_____ _____ _____
_____.

W I understand, but I'll choose the most
competitive applicant.

5

W What are you doing tomorrow afternoon?

M I have to take care of my brother since my
parents are _____ _____.
Why? Do you have any plans?

W I was thinking of asking you to the
movies, but you _____ _____
_____ _____...

M Yeah, _____ _____ _____.

W OK. But you'll still go rollerblading with
me tomorrow morning, right?

M Yes.

6

① W How was the exhibition?

    M There weren't _____ _____

        _____ _____.

② W _____ _____ _____

        _____ _____ _____?

    M How about 7:30?

③ W What is Seoul like?

    M It's so crowded, and traffic is terrible.

④ W Where did you get that bike?

    M It's my birthday present from my dad.

⑤ W _____ _____ _____

        _____ your ID, please?

    M I'm sorry, but I sold it yesterday.

7

W ① Playing computer games is the students'

        _____ _____ _____.

② Students like watching TV more than

    reading _____ _____

    _____ _____.

③ Few students like spending time with

    their friends.

④ Students like exercising more than

    reading.

⑤ _____ _____ _____

    _____ the students like exercising.

8

M I know you want to go _____

_____ when you go to your hometown
this New Year's Day. However, I think
taking a train is faster, especially on days
like New Year's, and more convenient than
taking a car. It's _____

_____ _____. If you go by
train, you won't have to worry about traffic
jams. And you won't have to worry about
parking when you arrive there. Nowadays,

it's really difficult to find a parking space
even _____ _____ _____

_____. Moreover, you can save money
since you don't have to spend money on fuel
and toll fees.

9

W Excuse me, _____ _____

_____ _____ how to get to
Hyde Park?

M Sure. You should take the subway.

W I see. Which line should I take?

M Take the yellow line and _____

_____ the green line at City Hall.

W I got it. How long does it take?

M It takes a little _____ _____

_____ _____ _____ to
City Hall, and about 15 minutes to the park.

W Do you happen to know the fare?

M Yes. It's 1 dollar 50 cents. You'll just need a
dollar if you are a student.

W No, I'm not. Thanks.

10

M Erica invited us over for dinner tomorrow.

W We were planning to go _____

_____ _____ at 7:30, right?

M You're right. I forgot.

W Why don't we have lunch with her?

M Well, she said she _____ _____

_____ _____ at 1. What should
we do?

W How about going to the next movie after
dinner?

M What time does the next movie begin?

W It begins _____ _____

_____.

M Okay.

Dictation

11

[Telephone rings.]

M Hello?

W Hi, Jake! _____ _____

_____ _____ _____

Linda? What are you doing now?

M We're playing a board game.

W Sounds fun. What time are you going to visit grandma?

M As soon as I finish playing.

W She misses you a lot, so _____ _____ you drop by today.

M Don't worry. I miss her, too.

W Tell Grandma _____ _____ _____ on Sunday.

M Okay.

12

W Could I _____ _____ _____ with you?

M Yes, sure.

W Well, it's about the idea you suggested.

M Yes, what about it?

W Thank you for your ideas, but they are a little _____ _____ _____. I saw the same thing on other internet sites.

M Oh, right. Okay.

W I know you _____ _____ _____, but next time you should be more creative, OK?

M Okay. Thank you.

13

M David _____ _____ _____ in Germany after leaving Italy. He wanted to see historic sites in Germany. It's not good

to _____ _____ or ride a bike in Germany. He took the bus to explore the sites, and he joined a tour group. He met many tourists _____ _____ _____. When he visited the Berlin Wall, he bought some souvenirs.

14

① W John, wake up. It's _____ _____ _____ _____ _____.

M 5 more minutes, please.

② W Open your eyes to the new world.

M Thank you for your advice.

③ W William, this is not a place for a nap.

M Sorry. I _____ _____ last night.

④ W Get up and _____ _____ _____ _____.

M Okay. I will go right now.

⑤ W Is this your classmate?

M Yes, he is very kind and smart.

15

M Good morning, ma'am. May I help you?

W Good morning, I want to buy some US dollars.

M How much _____ _____ _____?

W 200 dollars.

M Sure. Please _____ _____ _____ _____, and I need your passport.

W OK. Here it is.

M Thank you. How would you like them?

W Ten twenties.

M OK. Here you go.

W Thank you.

16

M I finally _____ _____ for Beyonce's concert!

W No way! They are so expensive!

M Well, it's my birthday tomorrow, so my dad gave me some money for the tickets!

W That's fantastic!

M Let's _____ _____ early in the afternoon and have dinner before the concert.

W That's terrific.

17

M Did you _____ _____ _____ _____?

W Yes, I did. I've got my mother's signature.

M Okay. What did she say?

W She said I should study harder.

M I see. Do you know what your problem is?

W Yes, I do. _____ _____ _____.

M Now that you know that, you need to fix it. Okay? _____ _____ _____ _____ _____.

W Thank you.

18

W What is _____ _____ _____ of studying English?

M It's memorizing words. There are too many words to memorize.

W I see. Let me give you _____ _____ _____ _____. If there is little snow, it melts quickly, but if there is a lot of snow, it doesn't melt easily. Likewise, if you keep memorizing words, they will _____ _____ in your brain.

M I see.

W Just do it little by little every day, and you'll end up with _____ _____ _____ memorized in your head.

M OK. I'll do that from now on.

19

M Hey, Mary. Have you seen Kate?

W Yes. I saw her at the library.

M Was she with Mark?

W No. I didn't see Mark there. Why are you _____ _____ them?

M We're doing a school project together, and we were supposed to meet this morning, but I forgot. I just called them, but _____ _____ answered my phone.

W Maybe they didn't notice their phone ringing.

M Yeah, maybe you are right.

W _____ _____ _____ and look for them.

20

W Mike, I'm so tired. I _____ _____ _____ _____ last night.

M Why?

W I saw a ghost. It was terrible.

M Really? I can't believe it.

W It's true. I left my room to use the bathroom. There was a woman outside the window in the living room.

M What did she do? _____ _____ _____ _____?

W No. As soon as I saw her, I shouted and _____ _____ my parents' room.

M Well, forget it. It'll never happen again.

W I won't be able to sleep alone tonight.

16회 영어듣기모의고사

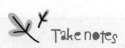

1 다음을 듣고, 그림의 상황에 가장 잘 어울리는 대화를 고르시오.

①   ②   ③   ④   ⑤

Take notes

2 다음을 듣고, 오늘로 예상되는 요일을 고르시오.

① Tuesday   ② Wednesday   ③ Thursday
④ Friday   ⑤ Saturday

3 대화를 듣고, 남자의 심정으로 가장 알맞은 것을 고르시오.

① relieved   ② excited   ③ frustrated
④ bored   ⑤ tired

4 대화를 듣고, 두 사람이 대화하는 장소를 고르시오.

① 비행기   ② 가게   ③ 영화관   ④ 서점   ⑤ 도서관

5 대화를 듣고, 예일 대학에서의 교수 한 명당 학생 수를 고르시오.

① 4   ② 5   ③ 6   ④ 7   ⑤ 8

6 대화를 듣고, 내용과 일치하지 <u>않는</u> 것을 고르시오.

① 백화점에서 판매직을 구하고 있다.

② 신문에 백화점 구직 광고가 났다.

③ 백화점은 20명을 고용할 예정이다.

④ 지원자는 일어와 영어를 할 줄 알아야 한다.

⑤ 지원자는 최소한 2년의 경험이 있어야 한다.

✗✗ Take notes

7 대화를 듣고, 두 사람이 어제 저녁에 한 일을 고르시오.

① 파티 참석   ② 동네 청소   ③ 리포트 작성

④ 강의 참석   ⑤ 영화 관람

8 다음을 듣고, 여자의 직업을 고르시오.

① police officer   ② clerk   ③ teller

④ tour guide   ⑤ counselor

9 대화를 듣고, 메모 내용 중 <u>잘못된</u> 것을 고르시오.

From	① Cathy
To	② Peter
Message	③ Regarding: history homework
	④ Due Date: 14th Wednesday
	⑤ Pages: 128 to 140

10 대화를 듣고, 남자가 공항에 몇 시까지 도착해야 하는지 고르시오.

① 8:00   ② 8:30   ③ 9:00

④ 10:00   ⑤ 10:30

11 대화를 듣고, 문제점으로 지적된 사항으로 알맞은 것을 고르시오.

① 학생 간의 실력 격차
② 초등학생들의 폭력성
③ 어린 시절 학습의 중요성
④ 초등학교의 남학생 과잉 현상
⑤ 초등학생을 가르치는 것의 어려움

Take notes

12 대화를 듣고, 여자가 텔레비전의 값으로 지불할 금액을 고르시오.

① $1,600 ② $1,650 ③ $1,800
④ $1,850 ⑤ $2,000

13 대화를 듣고, 여자가 전화를 건 목적을 고르시오.

① 여행을 예약하려고
② 비행기 표를 찾아가라고
③ 여행 계획을 상의하려고
④ 변경된 일정을 알려주려고
⑤ 여행이 어땠는지 물어보려고

14 대화를 듣고, Richard가 이사한 이유로 가장 알맞은 것을 고르시오.

① 시끄러워서
② 방이 작아서
③ 집세가 비싸서
④ 직장을 옮겨서
⑤ 교통이 불편해서

15 다음을 듣고, Neverland에서 체험 할 수 없는 것을 고르시오.

① 동물원 ② 쇼핑몰 ③ 백사장
④ 이국풍의 요리 ⑤ 놀이기구

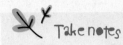

16 다음을 듣고, 남자가 한 마지막 말의 의도를 고르시오.

① 경고　　　② 제안　　　③ 동의　　　④ 칭찬　　　⑤ 감사

17 다음을 듣고, 두 사람의 대화가 <u>어색한</u> 것을 고르시오.

①　　　　②　　　　③　　　　④　　　　⑤

18 다음을 듣고, 남자에 대해 알 수 <u>없는</u> 것을 고르시오.

① 어렸을 적에 늦잠을 자본 적이 없다.
② 아버지가 암으로 돌아 가셨다.
③ 16년 동안 아침에 일찍 일어났다.
④ 아침에 일찍 일어나는 것에 익숙하다.
⑤ 육군으로 입대를 했었다.

19-20 대화를 듣고, 남자의 마지막 말에 이어질 여자의 응답으로 가장 알맞은 것을 고르시오.

19
① Sounds great!
② I'm with them now.
③ That's fine with me.
④ My father didn't allow me.
⑤ They will invite me to Paris.

20
① He studies hard by himself.
② He is really friendly and active.
③ No. I don't know him very well.
④ Yes. He is good at playing table tennis.
⑤ Yes. I would like to make friends with him.

Dictation

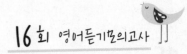

1

① M I came to pick up my wallet.
  W What does it _____ _____, and what's inside?

② M Who is the lady in this picture?
  W She is my grandmother when she was young.

③ M Could you take a picture for us?
  W Sure. Where would you like to stand?

④ M I'd like to _____ _____ _____.
  W May I have your name?

⑤ M Where are the books on driving?
  W They're _____ _____ _____ _____ on your right.

2

W Here is our five-day forecast. Tomorrow should be sunny and slightly warmer with temperatures around twenty. On Thursday and Friday, things _____ _____ _____ again, with temperatures in the low teens. Unfortunately the weekend _____ _____ _____, but hopefully a little warmer with temperatures _____ _____ _____ _____. Now you will be watching our headline news in a second. Thank you.

3

W _____ _____ _____ _____, George. What's wrong?

M I dropped my cell phone into the toilet, and I picked it up very quickly, but…

W Oh, dear. So, what did you do?

M I _____ _____ _____ and dried it.

W Is it okay?

M No. I tried to turn my phone on several times. It's not working. _____ _____ _____ _____ that I bought it yesterday.

4

M Can you bring me a blanket?

W Sure, anything else?

M Yes, can you _____ _____ _____ _____ _____?

W Sure, I'll bring you a weekly magazine. Is that all right?

M Thanks. It's _____ _____ _____ _____ that I have already read a couple of books _____ _____ _____.

W I'm sure you like reading. I'll be right back.

5

M Have you _____ _____ the University of Yale?

W Sure, it's _____ _____ _____ _____ in the world.

M It was founded in 1701 and has almost 2,000 professors now.

W That's an incredible number. What is the student population?

M There are 6,000 undergraduate students at the university, and another 6,000 in graduate courses.

W I guess there aren't many students compared to the number of professors.

6

M How did you know about _____ _____ _____ in the sales department at Wise Department Store?

W I _____ _____ _____ in the paper.

M How many employees are they hiring?

W It says that they are hiring about 20 people.

M Does one have to speak any foreign languages?

W Yes, it says applicants need to speak _____ _____ _____ _____.

M How about job experience? Do we need any?

W It says a minimum of two years.

7

M What did you think about the boy you met last night?

W He was very friendly, but talked too much.

M Oh, I thought _____ _____ _____.

W He _____ _____ _____ _____. I felt like he was a lecturer.

M I know. He was the only one that asked many questions about the environment.

W Anyway, the lecture was good.

M That's right. I learned a lot _____ _____ _____.

8

M I'd like to buy a bottle of whisky.

W Do you have any ID?

M I have my passport. Is that good enough?

W Sure, _____ _____ _____ _____?

M Here it is.

W Thank you. I see you're _____ _____ _____ _____.

alcohol. How would you like to pay?

M By credit card.

9

[Telephone rings.]

M Hello.

W Hello. _____ _____ _____ _____ Peter?

M Sorry, but he's not here. He went to the library.

W Oh, did he? Then, when will he be back?

M I'm not sure. Would you like to _____ _____ _____?

W Yes. This is Cathy. I'm his classmate. I'm calling to tell him that our history homework is due on the 13th, Tuesday, not the 14th, Wednesday. And the pages are from 128 to 140.

M OK. I'll pass it on to him him.

W Thank you.

10

W World Airlines. How may I help you?

M I'd like to make a reservation. Are there any flights to New York on October 25th?

W There is a flight at 10 in the morning. Is that all right?

M Yes. I'd like to _____ _____ _____.

W May I have your name and phone number, please?

M My name is Jake Smith, and my phone number is 786-6131.

W OK. You're booked on Flight 201 leaving San Francisco International Airport on the 25th. And you should arrive at the airport one and a half hours _____ _____ the departure time.

M I see. Thank you.

Dictation

11

W What are you reading?

M An article on elementary school.

W _____ _____ _____
   _____ ?

M It says boys _____ _____ 70
   percent of all elementary school students.

W I see. I also heard that there are _____
   _____ _____ , so some boys
   don't have an opportunity to sit next to a girl.

M You _____ _____ _____ .

W But I think it can't be helped.

M I know.

12

W How much is this TV?

M It's 2,000 dollars, but it's _____
   _____ for 10 percent off.

W Can you give me a bigger discount?

M How much are you _____ _____ ?

W How about a 20 percent discount?

M That much? Sorry, but I can't. _____
   _____ _____ _____
   _____ is 10 percent.

13

[Telephone rings.]

W Hello, this is Cathy from Top Travel. May I
   speak to Mr. Smith, please?

M _____ .

W I have a new schedule for your trip to
   Rome. You leave Seoul this coming Friday
   _____ _____ Thursday at 10
   A.M. and you arrive in Rome the next day
   _____ _____ .

M I see. I'll _____ _____ your
   office to pick up my flight ticket this
   afternoon.

W That's fine with me.

14

M Richard _____ _____ last
   weekend. I was there with Robert to help
   him.

W Were you?

M Yes, he's now living in a very nice quiet
   neighborhood _____ _____
   _____ _____ .

W Do you know why he moved to the new
   apartment?

M He couldn't sleep at night because of
   the noises _____ _____
   _____ .

W Really? I didn't know about that.

15

M Now wonderful Neverland finally opens
   on the first of March. We have everything
   _____ _____ _____
   _____ . This exciting tourist spot
   provides an Animal Park where children
   can touch and _____ _____
   _____ . We also have world-class
   shopping malls, white sand beaches, and
   restaurants serving exotic international
   dishes. We will _____ _____
   _____ _____ .

16

W I'm too cold. Please tell the driver to _____ _____ the air conditioner.

M I don't think he will _____ _____ me.

W Why not?

M See, there are more than 30 passengers on this bus, but you are probably the only one that feels cold.

W How do you know that?

M As you can see, no one has complained yet.

W Then what should I do?

M _____ _____ _____ _____ my jacket?

17

① W Do you know what she _____ _____ _____ _____?

  M I think she is a firefighter.

② W Do you think you can finish it today?

  M _____ _____ _____ _____, I don't think so.

③ W What brought you here?

  M I'm here to meet Mr. Kim.

④ W Can you buy me a snack?

  M Sorry, I left my wallet in the car.

⑤ W What makes you really happy?

  M I was scolded for _____ _____ _____.

18

M When I was young, my father always _____ _____ _____ around 6 o'clock in the morning. He never skipped a day until he _____ _____. He died of cancer when I was

16 years old. After that, I thought I could sleep longer, but I _____ _____ _____ _____ _____ early in the morning. It was really helpful when I joined the army.

19

M Hi, Susie! What a surprise! It's _____ _____ _____ _____.

W Hi, Mark! How are you?

M Pretty good. I thought you went to Paris with Jenny and Susan.

W Well, Jenny and Susan did go to Paris _____ _____ _____, but not me.

M Why didn't you go with them?

W My father _____ _____ _____.

20

W Do you know the guy who _____ _____ _____ with us?

M Yes, he is my classmate.

W Is he a new student?

M Yes, he _____ _____ New York. I think his father is a lawyer, and his mother is a doctor.

W I see.

M Do you want me to _____ _____?

W Yes. I would like to _____ _____ him.

1   대화를 듣고, 두 사람이 가리키는 사람을 고르시오.

①    ②    ③    ④    ⑤

2   대화를 듣고, 남자의 직업을 고르시오.

① 의사   ② 화가   ③ 국악인   ④ 무용가   ⑤ 점술가

3   대화를 듣고, 남자의 심경 변화로 가장 알맞은 것을 고르시오.

① angry → relieved   ② happy → nervous

③ upset → disappointed   ④ pleased → bored

⑤ proud → embarrassed

4   대화를 듣고, 두 사람의 관계로 알맞은 것을 고르시오.

① 학생 – 교사   ② 경찰관 – 운전자

③ 택시기사 – 승객   ④ 자동차 판매원 – 고객

⑤ 고객 센터 상담원 – 고객

5   대화를 듣고, 남자에 대한 내용과 일치하지 않는 것을 고르시오.

① 문제를 하나도 풀지 못했다.

② 열심히 공부했다.

③ 밤을 새웠다.

④ 시험 범위가 아닌 것을 공부했다.

⑤ 역사 시험을 보았다.

6 대화를 듣고, 두 사람이 대화를 마친 후 할 일을 고르시오.

① 환전   ② 박물관 견학   ③ 점심
④ 특별 전시회 관람   ⑤ 자유의 여신상 방문

7 다음을 듣고, 자동 응답기에 남겨진 내용과 <u>다른</u> 것을 고르시오.

Telephone Message	
To	Lucy
From	Rebecca
Message	① Rebecca invites Lucy.
	② It's Rebecca's fifteenth birthday.
	③ The party is at six o'clock this Friday evening.
	④ Rebecca invited Susie, Richard, and Ray.
	⑤ No need for a return-call

8 대화를 듣고, 여자가 책을 교환하려는 이유를 고르시오.

① 벌써 읽은 책이라서   ② 책이 파본이라서   ③ 책이 지저분해서
④ 책을 잘못 골라서   ⑤ 책 초반 내용이 지루해서

9 대화를 듣고, 두 사람이 대화하는 장소를 고르시오.

① 고아원   ② 학교   ③ 장례식   ④ 결혼식   ⑤ 은행

10 다음을 듣고, 피해야 하는 질문이 <u>아닌</u> 것을 고르시오.

① How old are you?
② Are you married?
③ Do you believe in God?
④ Do you have any siblings?
⑤ How much money do you earn?

11 대화를 듣고, 어머니가 아들에게 조언하는 바를 고르시오.

① 돈을 낭비하지 마라.
② 공부를 게을리하지 마라.
③ 광고에 현혹되지 마라.
④ 옷을 아껴 입어라.
⑤ 자신을 잘 돌봐라.

12 대화를 듣고, 남자가 사무실에 돌아 올 시각을 고르시오.

① 12:00   ② 1:00   ③ 3:00   ④ 4:00   ⑤ 5:00

13 다음을 듣고, 올림픽에 대한 설명으로 알맞지 <u>않은</u> 것을 고르시오.

① 첫 번째 근대 올림픽은 그리스에서 열렸다.
② 처음에는 남자들만 참여했다.
③ 처음 열렸던 근대 올림픽에서는 금메달이 없었다.
④ 초창기 올림픽은 대륙별로 열렸었다.
⑤ 최근에는 점점 더 많은 여성들이 올림픽에 참여한다.

14 다음을 듣고, 내용이 가리키는 표지판을 고르시오.

①   ②   ③   ④   ⑤

15 대화를 듣고, 남자가 한 마지막 말의 의도를 고르시오.

① 비판   ② 동의   ③ 제안   ④ 충고   ⑤ 칭찬

16 다음을 듣고, 두 사람의 대화가 <u>어색한</u> 것을 고르시오.

①   ②   ③   ④   ⑤

17 대화를 듣고, 여자가 받을 거스름돈을 고르시오.

① $20   ② $32   ③ $36   ④ $40   ⑤ $60

18 다음을 듣고, 그림의 상황에 가장 잘 어울리는 대화를 고르시오.

①   ②   ③   ④   ⑤

19- 20 대화를 듣고, 여자의 마지막 말에 이어질 남자의 응답으로 가장 알맞은 것을 고르시오.

19
① What a shame!
② I'm afraid I've lost both of them.
③ Don't worry. I think that's enough.
④ I have some cash but not the student ID card.
⑤ It's lucky that you found them in Lost and Found.

20
① No. I can help you study.
② Isn't it too early to do that?
③ Okay, I'll accept your advice.
④ Yes. You have to prepare for the test.
⑤ Yes. Can you lend me your notebook?

1 대화를 듣고, 남자가 사려고 하는 것을 고르시오.

①   ②   ③   ④   ⑤

2 대화를 듣고, 영어 선생님이 취한 행동으로 알맞은 것을 고르시오.

①   ②   ③   ④  ⑤

3 대화를 듣고, 두 사람의 관계로 가장 알맞은 것을 고르시오.

① 교사 – 학생 ② 가이드 – 관광객 ③ 종업원 – 손님
④ 면접관 – 지원자 ⑤ 경찰관 – 운전자

4 대화를 듣고, 여자가 부탁하는 것을 고르시오.

① 병원에 함께 가기 ② 숙제 알려 주기 ③ 과제물 제출하기
④ 진도 알려 주기 ⑤ 학교에 데려다 주기

5 대화를 듣고, 여자의 심경을 가장 잘 나타낸 것을 고르시오.

① scared ② excited ③ surprised ④ satisfied ⑤ disappointed

6   대화를 듣고, 남자가 도서관에 온 목적을 고르시오.

① 책을 빌리려고   ② 공부를 하려고   ③ 보고서 자료를 찾으려고

④ 엄마를 도와주려고   ⑤ 잡지를 읽으려고

7   대화를 듣고, 여자가 한 마지막 말의 의도를 고르시오.

① 거절   ② 비판   ③ 동의   ④ 제안   ⑤ 감사

8   대화를 듣고, 내용과 일치하지 <u>않는</u> 것을 고르시오.

① 여자가 승객들에게 음료를 제공하고 있다.

② 남자가 찬물을 달라고 요청했다.

③ 남자가 자는 것을 여자가 깨웠다.

④ 남자는 곧 식사를 제공 받을 것이다.

⑤ 오늘의 식사메뉴는 쇠고기와 닭고기이다.

9   대화를 듣고, 상황에 어울리는 속담으로 알맞은 것을 고르시오.

① Like father, like son.

② Look before you leap.

③ No news is good news.

④ Well begun is half done.

⑤ Don't judge a book by its cover.

10   다음을 듣고, 그림의 상황에 가장 잘 어울리는 대화를 고르시오.

①   ②   ③   ④   ⑤

11 대화를 듣고, 두 사람이 대화하는 장소를 고르시오.

① 병원   ② 건설 현장   ③ 경찰서   ④ 놀이 공원   ⑤ 자전거 경주

12 대화를 듣고, 여자가 휴가를 낼 수 있는 최장 기간을 고르시오.

① 3일   ② 5일   ③ 1주일   ④ 2주일   ⑤ 한 달

13 다음 안내정보를 보면서 대화를 듣고, 두 사람이 참여할 수 있는 것을 고르시오.

> ### Amusement Park Information
> • Dance Party ------------------------ 2:00 P.M.
> • Character Parade -------------------- 3:00 P.M.
> • Acrobatic ---------------------------- 4:00 P.M.
> • Lighting Celebration -------------- 6:00 P.M.
> • Fireworks --------------------------- 7:00 P.M.

① Character Parade, Fireworks

② Dance Party, Acrobatic

③ Acrobatic, Character Parade

④ Acrobatic, Lighting Celebration

⑤ Character Parade, Lighting Celebration

14 대화를 듣고, 남자가 전화를 건 목적을 고르시오.

① 예약하기 위해   ② 일자리를 알아보려고   ③ 계산이 잘못 되어서

④ 영업시간을 알아보려고   ⑤ 예약 확인을 하기 위해

15 다음을 듣고, 일치하지 않는 것을 고르시오.

① 오늘 200미터 자유형 수영경기가 있었다.

② Mike Phelphs가 금메달을 땄다.

③ Mike Phelphs가 세계 신기록을 수립했다.

④ 오늘로 올림픽이 3일째 진행 중이다.

⑤ 미국 팀은 총 8개의 금메달을 획득했다.

16 대화를 듣고, 여자가 남동생에게 화가 난 이유를 고르시오.

① 귀찮게 해서 　　　　② 숙제를 베껴서 　　　　③ 공책에 낙서를 해서

④ 공책을 잃어버려서 　　⑤ 공책을 찢어서

17 대화를 듣고, 남자가 빌리려고 하는 것을 고르시오.

① 백과사전 　　② 영어사전 　　③ 컴퓨터 　　④ 휴대전화 　　⑤ 시집

18 다음을 듣고, Jake가 Jessica에게 할 말로 가장 알맞은 것을 고르시오.

① It's a piece of cake.

② It's okay. That was old anyway.

③ I found my camera at the Lost and Found.

④ Thank you for looking for my camera with me.

⑤ That camera was really expensive. I don't know what I can do.

19- 20 대화를 듣고, 남자의 마지막 말에 이어질 여자의 응답으로 가장 알맞은 것을 고르시오.

19
① Sounds great!

② This is unacceptable.

③ That's okay. I'll wait.

④ Of course, I'll calm down.

⑤ Thank you for your concern.

20
① That's wonderful. Thank you.

② It is nice of you to recognize me.

③ Sorry, I don't have any money now.

④ Thank you. I can give you my signature.

⑤ Try to practice every day as much as possible.

이것이 THIS IS 시리즈다!

THIS IS GRAMMAR 시리즈
▷ 중·고등 내신에 꼭 등장하는 어법 포인트 분석 및 총정리

강남인강
강의교재

THIS IS READING 시리즈
▷ 다양한 소재의 지문으로 내신 및 수능 완벽 대비

강남인강
강의교재

THIS IS VOCABULARY 시리즈
▷ 주제별로 분류한 교육부 권장 어휘

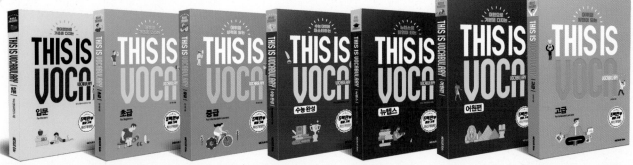

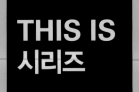

THIS IS 시리즈

무료 MP3 및 부가자료 다운로드
www.nexusbook.com
www.nexusEDU.kr

THIS IS GRAMMAR 시리즈
Starter 1~3   영어교육연구소 지음 | 205×265 | 144쪽 | 각 권 12,000원
초·중·고급 1·2   넥서스영어교육연구소 지음 | 205×265 | 250쪽 내외 | 각 권 12,000원

THIS IS READING 시리즈
Starter 1~3   김태연 지음 | 205×265 | 156쪽 | 각 권 12,000원
1·2·3·4   넥서스영어교육연구소 지음 | 205×265 | 192쪽 내외 | 각 권 10,000원

THIS IS VOCABULARY 시리즈
입문   넥서스영어교육연구소 지음 | 152×225 | 224쪽 | 10,000원
초·중·고급·어원편 권기하 지음 | 152×225 | 180×257 | 344쪽~444쪽 | 10,000원~12,000원
수능 완성   넥서스영어교육연구소 지음 | 152×225 | 280쪽 | 12,000원
뉴텝스   넥서스 TEPS연구소 지음 | 152×225 | 452쪽 | 13,800원

LEVEL CHART

	초1	초2	초3	초4	초5	초6	중1	중2	중3	고1	고2	고3
VOCA	초등필수 영단어 1-2 · 3-4 · 5-6학년용											
				The VOCA + (플러스) 1~7								
			THIS IS VOCABULARY 입문 · 초급 · 중급						고급 · 어원 · 수능 완성 · 뉴텝스			
						WORD FOCUS 중등 종합 5000 · 고등 필수 5000 · 고등 종합 9500						
Grammar			초등필수 영문법 + 쓰기 1~2									
			OK Grammar 1~4									
			This Is Grammar Starter 1~3									
				This Is Grammar 초급~고급 (각 2권: 총 6권)							
					Grammar 공감 1~3							
					Grammar 101 1~3							
					Grammar Bridge 1~3							
					The Grammar Starter, 1~3							
						한 권으로 끝내는 필수 구문 1000제						
						구사일생 (구문독해 Basic) 1~2						
							구문독해 204 1~2					
							그래머 캡처 1~2					
							[특급 단기 특강] 어법어휘 모의고사					

중학 영어듣기
한 방에 끝낸다

AFTER
SCHOOL
Listening
애프터스쿨
리스닝
level 3

정답 및 해설

NEXUS Edu

중학 영어듣기
한 방에 끝낸다

AFTER SCHOOL Listening

애프터스쿨
리스닝
level 3

정답 및 해설

NEXUS Edu

01회 영어듣기모의고사

01 ⑤	02 ③	03 ②	04 ③	05 ⑤
06 ②	07 ②	08 ②	09 ④	10 ③
11 ⑤	12 ③	13 ①	14 ①	15 ②
16 ③	17 ④	18 ②	19 ④	20 ③

01 ⑤

Script

W Are you here with your daughter?

M Yes, I am. She's with her friends over there.

W Which one?

M She is tall and thin.

W Most of them are tall and thin.

M That's right. But she has dark curly hair.

W I see. She's the one wearing glasses, right?

M No, she is next to her.

해석

여 여기에 딸과 함께 오셨나요?

남 네, 그래요. 그 애는 저기에 친구들과 함께 있어요.

여 어떤 아이인가요?

남 그 아이는 키가 크고 말랐어요.

여 아이들 대부분이 키가 크고 말랐어요.

남 그렇군요. 하지만, 제 딸은 검정 곱슬머리예요.

여 알았어요. 안경을 낀 아이군요, 그렇죠?

남 아니요, 그 애 옆에 있는 애예요.

해설

남자의 딸은 키가 크고 말랐으며, 검정 곱슬머리에 안경을 끼지 않은 아이이다.

어휘

thin[θin] 마른, 여윈 / wear[wɛər] ~을 쓰다, 입다, 신다 / next to ~의 옆에

02 ③

Script

W What do you want to do in the future, John?

M I want to continue studying math.

W Do you want to be a math teacher?

M No, I don't.

W Then, what?

M My uncle, who is a computer programmer, told me to major in math to be a programmer like himself.

해석

여 John, 너는 장차 무엇을 하고 싶니?

남 나는 수학 공부를 계속하고 싶어.

여 수학 선생님이 되고 싶니?

남 아니.

여 그러면, 뭐?

남 우리 삼촌이 컴퓨터 프로그래머인데, 자기처럼 프로그래머가 되려면 수학을 전공해야 한다고 했어.

해설

남자가 수학 공부를 계속하려는 이유는 삼촌과 같은 컴퓨터 프로그래머가 되고 싶어서이다.

어휘

in the future 장차, 미래에 / continue[kəntínju:] ~을 계속하다 / programmer[próugræmər] 프로그래머 / major in ~을 전공하다

03 ②

Script

W Could you put your luggage up here, please?

M Sure, I have 3 suitcases.

W We only allow 2 pieces. You'll have to pay an extra charge.

M Oh, in that case, can I carry this one with me?

W No, I'm sorry. It won't fit under your seat.

M Then how much do I have to pay?

W You have to pay 25 dollars. You are good to go after I put the bag tags on and give you your baggage claim stubs.

해석

여 여기에 짐을 좀 올려 주시겠습니까?

남 네, 저는 가방이 세 개 있습니다.

여 가방은 두 개만 허용됩니다. 추가 비용을 내셔야 합니다.

남 아, 그렇다면 이것은 가지고 타도 될까요?

여 안 됩니다. 죄송합니다. 그것은 좌석 아래에 들어가지 않을 겁니다.

남 그러면 얼마를 내야 하죠?

여 25달러를 내셔야 해요. 제가 짐표를 부착하고 수화물 확인증을 드리면 가져도 됩니다.

해설

공항에서 짐을 부칠 때 하는 대화이다.

어휘

luggage[lʌ́gidʒ] 수하물, 짐 / suitcase[súːtkèis] 여행 가방 / allow[əláu] ~을 허용하다 / extra charge 추가 요금 / in that case 그렇다면, 그 경우는 / carry[kǽri] ~을 들고가다, 운반하다 / fit[fit] 맞다 / bag tag 짐표 / baggage claim 수화물 확인증 / stub[stʌb] (입장권이나 확인증 등의) 떼어 주고 남은 쪽

04 ③

Script

W Where are you going, Mark?

M To the library.

W You seem to go to the library quite often.

M I do, but not as often as you do.

W How often do you go there?

M Well, I just go there when I feel like it. How about you?

W As you know, I can't concentrate at all at home, so I go there every other day.

M I see. Let's get going.

해석

여 Mark야, 너 어디 가니?

남 도서관에.

여 너는 도서관에 꽤 자주 가는 것 같구나.

남 자주 가지만, 너만큼 자주는 아니야.

여 도서관에 얼마나 자주 가니?

남 글쎄, 나는 그냥 가고 싶을 때 가. 너는?

여 너도 알다시피, 나는 집에서는 전혀 집중을 할 수가 없어서, 이틀에 한 번씩 도서관에 가.

남 그렇구나. 자, 가자.

해설

여자는 이틀에 한 번씩(every other day) 도서관에 간다.

어휘

seem[siːm] ~인 것 같다 / feel like ~을 하고 싶다 / concentrate[kánsəntrèit] 집중하다 / every other day 이틀에 한 번 / get going ~하기 시작하다, 출발하다, 서두르다

05 ⑤

Script

M What can I do for you, ma'am?

W I'm pretty upset with this blender.

M What happened?

W I bought it last month, but it stopped working. So, I had it fixed, but it broke again.

M I'm so sorry.

W Save your breath. I just want my money back.

M OK. Let me talk to my manager, and I'll get back to you. Did you bring your receipt?

W Of course, I did.

해석

남 무엇을 도와드릴까요, 손님?

여 이 믹서 때문에 정말 화가 나네요.

남 무슨 일이신데요?

여 제가 지난달에 이것을 샀는데 작동을 멈췄어요. 그래서 고쳤는데, 다시 고장이 났어요.

남 정말 죄송합니다.

여 쓸데없는 이야긴 접어두죠. 그냥 제 돈이나 돌려주세요.

남 알았습니다. 매니저에게 얘기해 보고 바로 오겠습니다. 영수증은 가져오셨나요?

여 물론 가져왔어요.

해설

여자는 믹서 값을 되돌려 받기를 원하므로 환불을 요구하는 것이다.

어휘

upset[ʌpsét] 화가 난 / blender[bléndər] 믹서 / save your breath 잠자코 있다, 쓸데없는 논쟁을 피하다 / get back to ~에게 되돌아오다 / receipt[risíːt] 영수증

06 ②

Script

① **W** It's time to go home.

　 M Let's go. It's getting late.

② **W** How many times have I told you not to come late?

　 M Sorry, Mom. It won't happen again.

③ **W** My watch is not working. Can you fix it?

　 M Sure. You can pick it up tomorrow.

④ **W** Where is your homework?

　 M I'm sorry, Ms. Smith. I think I left it at home.

⑤ **W** I heard the clock strike eleven.

　 M Yeah, we'd better go to sleep.

해석

① 여 집에 갈 시간이야.

　 남 가자. 늦어지고 있어.

② 여 내가 늦게 오지 말라고 몇 번이나 말을 했니?

　 남 죄송해요, 엄마. 다시는 그러지 않을게요.

③ 여 제 시계가 가질 않아요. 좀 고쳐 주실래요?

　 남 그러죠. 내일 찾으러 오세요.

④ 여 네 숙제는 어디에 있니?

　 남 죄송해요, Smith 선생님. 집에 놓고 왔나 봐요.

⑤ 여 시계가 열한 시를 치는 소리를 들었어.

　 남 응, 잠을 자러 가는 게 좋겠어.

해설

아들이 집에 늦게 와서 엄마가 아들을 꾸짖는 상황이다.

어휘

happen[hǽpən] 일어나다, 발생하다 / fix[fiks] ~을 수리하다 / strike[straik] (시계, 종 등이 시각을) 치다, 쳐서 알리다 / had better ~해야 하다, ~하는 편이 낫다

07 ②

Script

W Kelly is from Australia. She's been in Korea for 6 months. She came here to learn Korean, but she now spends most of her time helping poor children who suffer from poverty and disease. She sometimes does English tutoring. She also works at a language institute part-time as an English teacher and spends a good percentage of her income on the children.

해석

여 Kelly는 호주 출신이다. 그녀는 한국에 온 지 여섯 달이 되었다. 그녀는 한국어를 배우러 여기에 왔지만, 이제는 자신의 시간 대부분을 가난과 질병으로 고통받는 불쌍한 아이들을 돕는 데 쓴다. 그녀는 가끔 개별적으로 영어를 가르쳐 준다. 그녀는 영어 학원 선생님으로 아르바이트하기도 하고, 자기 수입의 상당량을 아이들을 돕는 데 사용한다.

Kelly는 한국에 자원봉사를 하려고 온 것이 아니라 한국어를 배우려고 왔다.

어휘

suffer from ~으로 고통받다 / poverty[pávərti] 가난 /
disease[dizíːz] 질병 / tutor[tjúːtər] 개인 교사로서 가르치다; 가정교사 /
language institute 어학원 / part-time 시간제로, 파트타임으로 /
good[gud] (수량, 정도가) 충분한 / percentage[pərséntidʒ] 비율 /
income[ínkʌm] 수입

08 ②

Script

M Can I see your cell phone?

W Why? Do you need to make a phone call?

M No, I just want to see your phone.

W OK. Here you go.

M Wow. The keypad is all worn out.

W I know. That's why I want to buy a new one. I've sent a lot of text messages. What about yours?

M I'm also thinking of buying a new one because I dropped it and broke the screen, but it still works.

해석

남 너의 휴대 전화를 좀 보여 줄래?

여 왜? 전화를 해야 하니?

남 아니, 그냥 네 전화기를 좀 보고 싶어서.

여 알았어. 여기 있어.

남 와. 문자판이 다 닳았네.

여 알아. 그래서 하나 새로 사려고. 나는 문자 메시지를 많이 보냈거든. 네 것은 어때?

남 나도 새것을 사려고 생각 중이야. 떨어뜨려서 화면이 깨졌거든. 하지만, 아직 전화는 할 수 있어.

해설

여자는 문자 메시지를 많이 보내서 문자판이 닳았기 때문에 휴대 전화를 새로 사려고 한다.

어휘

make a phone call 전화를 걸다 / worn out 낡은, 닳은 /
drop[drɑp] ~을 떨어뜨리다

09 ④

Script

[Telephone rings.]

W Hello, ticket office. How can I help you?

M Yes. Do you still have tickets for the Animal Show?

W Let me check. We still have tickets at 15 dollars a piece.

M Is there a special price for students?

W Yes, student tickets are 12 dollars each.

M That's good. Two student tickets and one adult, please.

W How would you like to pay for your tickets?

M I'll pay in cash at the ticket office.

해석

여 여보세요, 매표소입니다. 어떻게 도와드릴까요?

남 네. 동물 공연 표가 아직 있나요?

여 확인해보죠. 한 장에 15달러하는 표가 아직 있습니다.

남 학생 할인이 되나요?

여 네, 학생 표는 한 장에 12달러입니다.

남 잘 됐네요. 학생 표 두 장하고, 성인 표 한 장 주세요.

여 지불은 어떻게 하시겠어요?

남 매표소에서 현금으로 하겠습니다.

해설

학생 둘은 24달러, 성인은 15달러이므로 총 39달러를 지불해야 한다.

어휘

ticket office 매표소 / special[spéʃəl] 특별한, 전용의 / adult[ədʌ́lt] 성인 /
pay in cash 현금으로 지불하다

10 ③

Script

W Hi, this is Abby Carter with the nine o'clock news from NBC radio. Our headline news is a major storm hit New Orleans today, and many houses and buildings are flooded. People in the area are furious because the weather forecast was wrong. They weren't prepared for the disaster. Many volunteers have gathered to help those who have lost their house and family members.

해석

여 안녕하세요. 저는 엔비시 라디오 아홉 시 뉴스의 Abby Carter입니다. 주요 뉴스입니다. 오늘 거대한 폭풍이 뉴올리언스를 강타해서 많은 집과 건물이 범람했습니다. 이 지역 시민은 일기 예보가 빗나가서 매우 화가 나 있습니다. 사람들은 그 재난에 대비되어 있지 않았습니다. 많은 자원봉사자가 집과 가족을 잃은 사람들을 도우려고 모였습니다.

해설

뉴스 진행자는 Abby Carter, 뉴스 시간은 아홉 시, 재난 발생 원인은 태풍, 재난 발생 장소는 뉴올리언스이고, 복구 대비책은 알 수 없다.

어휘

headline[hédlàin] 주요 뉴스 / major[méidʒər] 주요한 /
storm[stɔːrm] 폭풍 / hit[hit] (폭풍 등이 어떤 곳을) 덮치다, 엄습하다 /
flood[flʌd] 범람시키다, 물에 잠기게 하다 / furious[fjúəriəs] 성난, 화난 /
weather forecast 일기 예보 / prepare for ~을 준비하다 /
disaster[dizǽstər] 재해, 재난 / volunteer[vàləntíər] 자원봉사자 /
gather[gǽðər] 모이다

11 ⑤

Script

W ① You need 9 dollars to have spaghetti and salad.

② You need 11 dollars and 50 cents to have a steak and soda.

③ You can have free refills for your soda.

④ You need 6 dollars to have a burger and soda.

⑤ You need 8 dollars to have a tuna sandwich and

salad.

해석

여 ① 스파게티와 샐러드를 다 먹으려면 9달러가 필요하다.

② 스테이크를 먹고, 음료수를 마시려면 11달러 50센트가 필요하다.

③ 음료수는 무료로 다시 채울 수 있다.

④ 버거를 먹고, 음료수를 마시려면 6달러가 필요하다.

⑤ 참치 샌드위치와 샐러드를 먹으려면 8달러가 필요하다.

해설

참치 샌드위치와 샐러드를 먹으려면 8달러가 아니라 9달러가 필요하다.

어휘

need[niːd] 필요하다 / spaghetti[spəgéti] 스파게티 / free[friː] 무료의 / refill[riːfíl] (음식의) 다시 채운 것 / tuna[tjúːnə] 참치

12 ③

Script

W Everyone in our society seeks out this, but not all of them can get the amount they want. It can make you happy or unhappy, but it depends on how you feel about the amount you have. For example, some have a lot of this, but they are still not satisfied with it and look for more of this, ending up in disaster. Others have a little, but they are happy with it. Therefore, the amount you have is not important, but rather how you use it.

해석

여 우리 사회의 모든 사람이 이것을 얻으려고 애를 쓰지만, 그들 모두가 자신이 원하는 양을 얻을 수 있는 것은 아니다. 그것이 당신을 행복하게 하거나 불행하게 할 수도 있지만, 그것은 당신이 가진 양에 대해 당신이 어떻게 느끼느냐에 달렸다. 예를 들어, 어떤 사람들은 이것을 많이 가지고 있지만, 여전히 만족하지 않고 이것을 더 많이 찾다가 결국 재앙으로 끝을 맺는다. 또 다른 사람들은 조금 가지고 있지만, 그것에 만족한다. 그러므로 당신이 가진 양이 중요한 것이 아니라, 오히려 그것을 어떻게 사용하느냐가 중요한 것이다.

해설

모든 사람이 다른 양을 가지고 있으며, 많이 가지고 있느냐 아니냐가 중요한 것이 아니라 어떻게 쓰느냐가 중요한 것은 돈이다.

어휘

society[səsáiəti] 사회 / seek out ~을 찾아내다 / amount[əmáunt] 양, 액 / depend on ~에 달려있다 / be satisfied with ~에 만족하다 / end up 결국 ~이 되다 / disaster[dizǽstər] 재앙 / therefore[ðɛ́ərfɔ̀ːr] 그러므로 / rather[rǽðər] 오히려

13 ①

Script

M Mike is more popular than any other boy in his school. He is handsome, tall, and smart. He is very confident about himself. One day, when he was walking on the street, an attractive girl looked at him and kept smiling. He thought he had caught her eye, and she wanted to talk. He waited until she walked up to him. Finally, up close she said, "Your fly is open." He was so

embarrassed.

해석

남 Mike는 학교에서 가장 인기 있는 소년이다. 그는 잘생기고, 키도 크고, 똑똑하다. 그는 스스로 자신에게 매우 자신이 있다. 어느 날 그가 길을 걷고 있는데 매력적인 한 소녀가 그를 쳐다보며 계속 미소를 지었다. 그는 자신이 그녀의 시선을 사로잡았고, 그녀가 자신에게 말을 하고 싶어 한다고 생각했다. 그는 그녀가 자기에게 다가올 때까지 기다렸다. 마침내 그녀가 바로 가까이에 다가와서 이렇게 말했다. "바지 지퍼가 열려 있어요." 그는 너무 부끄러웠다.

해설

바지 지퍼가 열려 있는 것을 모르고 소녀가 자기를 좋아하는 것으로 오해했으므로 "떡 줄 사람은 생각도 안 하는데 김칫국부터 마신다."라는 속담이 가장 적절하다.

② 하늘은 스스로 돕는 자를 돕는다.

③ 세월(시간과 파도는)은 사람을 기다려주지 않는다.

④ 일석이조

⑤ 시간이 약이다.

어휘

confident[kánfidənt] 자신 있는 / attractive[ətrǽktiv] 매력적인 / keep[kiːp] 계속 ~하다 / catch one's eye 관심을 끌다, 눈에 띄다 / up close 바로 가까이에, 접근하여 / fly[flai] 바지 지퍼 / embarrassed[imbǽrəst] 부끄러운, 당황한

14 ①

Script

M What can I do for you?

W I like the vase in the display section.

M Good choice. Many people have bought one since I put it there.

W How much are you asking for it?

M It's 13 dollars for the vase with flowers.

W I don't want the flowers. I just want the vase.

M Then, just pay me 8 dollars.

해석

남 무엇을 도와 드릴까요?

여 전시되어 있는 화병이 마음에 들어서요.

남 잘 고르셨습니다. 제가 그것을 거기에 놓은 이후로 많은 사람이 사갔어요.

여 얼마인가요?

남 꽃병과 꽃까지 해서 13달러입니다.

여 저는 꽃은 원하지 않아요. 저는 그냥 꽃병만 원해요.

남 그러면 8달러만 내세요.

해설

꽃병과 꽃을 합한 가격이 13달러이고, 그 중 꽃병 가격이 8달러이므로 꽃은 5달러이다.

어휘

vase[veis] 꽃병 / display[displéi] 전시, 진열 / pay[pei] 지불하다, 내다

15 ②

Script

M	Excuse me, what are you doing?
W	Sir, you illegally parked your car.
M	I was about to leave.
W	Okay, but I still have to give you a ticket.
M	Oh, no. Please forgive me this time.
W	I can't. I've already written down your license plate number.
M	Come on. I wasn't even here for 5 minutes.
W	Sorry, sir. But I'm just doing my job.

해석

남	실례합니다만 뭘 하고 계시죠?
여	선생님, 불법으로 주차하셨습니다.
남	막 떠나려고 했습니다.
여	알았습니다만, 그래도 티켓을 발부해야 합니다.
남	아, 안 돼요. 이번만 봐주세요.
여	그럴 수 없습니다. 저는 이미 당신의 자동차 번호를 적었어요.
남	제발요. 저는 여기에 채 5분도 있지 않았어요.
여	미안합니다만, 선생님. 저는 제 일을 할 뿐이에요.

해설

여자는 불법으로 주차된 차량에 과태료를 부과하고 있으므로 주차 단속원이다.

어휘

illegally[ilíːgəli] 불법으로 / be about to+동사원형 막 ~하려던 참이다 / license plate 자동차 번호판

16 ③
Script

W	You look troubled, Ben. What's wrong?
M	I think I'm too short.
W	Don't worry. You're only 15 years old. You'll keep growing until you reach the age of 20.
M	I know, but I was 160cm last year, and when I checked my height this morning, there was not much difference.
W	Let me tell you this. Your father was 153cm when he was your age, but he is now 179cm. He grew 26cm in two years.
M	I know. He told me about that, but I have only grown 3cm this past year.

해석

여	Ben, 너 근심이 있는 것 같구나. 무슨 일이니?
남	저는 너무 작은 것 같아요.
여	걱정하지 마. 너는 이제 겨우 열다섯 살이잖니. 스무 살이 될 때까지 계속 자랄 거란다.
남	알아요. 하지만 작년에 160cm이었는데, 오늘 아침에 키를 확인해 보니 별 차이가 없었어요.
여	내 이야기를 들어 봐라. 너의 아버지는 네 나이였을 때 153cm이었는데 지금은 179cm잖니. 아버지는 2년 동안에 26cm나 자라셨단다.
남	알아요. 아버지가 말씀해 주셨어요. 하지만 저는 작년에 겨우 3센티미터 자란걸요.

해설

Ben은 작년에 160센티미터였고, 지난 1년 동안 3센티미터 자랐으므로 지금은 163센티미터이다.

어휘

troubled[trʌ́bld] 근심스러운 / reach[riːtʃ] ~에 도달하다 / height[hait] 높이, 키 / difference[dífərəns] 차이

17 ④
Script

M	Jenny, I got two tickets for the concert.
W	You did? I'm so sorry, but I don't think I can go if it's on Saturday.
M	Why not?
W	I have to go to Susie's house.
M	Why? Is she having a party or something?
W	No, our teacher gave us a group project to work on.
M	That's too bad. Maybe some other time.

해석

남	Jenny, 나 연주회 표 두 장이 생겼어.
여	그래? 정말 미안하지만, 연주회가 토요일이면 못 갈 것 같아.
남	왜 못 가?
여	Susie의 집에 가야 해.
남	왜? 무슨 파티라도 하는 거야?
여	아니, 우리 선생님이 같이해야 하는 그룹 숙제를 내 주셨어.
남	저런 안 됐다. 다음에 기회에 가자.

해설

여자는 Susie네 집에 가서 친구들과 과제를 해야 하므로 연주회에 갈 수 없다.

어휘

work on ~에 착수하다, 일을 하다 / some other time 언젠가, 조만간

18 ②
Script

W	Kevin, why are you late?
M	I'm sorry. I had an accident.
W	Are you okay? What kind of accident?
M	Someone robbed me on the way over here.
W	Really? Are you hurt?
M	No. I'm okay.
W	That's good. By the way, did you do your homework?
M	I did, but the thief took my notebook as well.

해석

여	Kevin, 너 왜 늦었니?
남	죄송해요. 사고가 있었어요.
여	괜찮니? 무슨 사고였어?
남	여기로 오는 길에 강도를 만났어요.
여	정말? 다쳤니?
남	아니요. 괜찮아요.

여　다행이다. 그런데, 숙제는 했니?

남　했는데요. 도둑이 공책도 가져갔어요.

해설

도둑이 숙제를 가져갔다는 남자의 말을 듣고, 여자는 황당할 것이다.

어휘

accident[ǽksidənt] 사고 / rob[rάb] ~을 강탈하다, 빼앗다 / hurt[həːrt] ~을 다치게 하다 / thief[θiːf] 도둑 / as well 게다가, 그 위에

19 ④

Script

W Hey, Sam. Are you going to play tennis with me this Sunday?

M I'm sorry. I won't be able to join you this weekend.

W Why? Are you going somewhere?

M Yes, my family's going on a trip to New York.

W Really? You must be very excited.

해석

여　안녕, Sam. 이번 일요일에 나랑 테니스 칠 거야?

남　미안해. 이번 주말에는 너와 같이하지 못할 거야.

여　왜? 어디 가니?

남　응, 우리 가족이 뉴욕으로 여행을 가.

여　정말? 너 정말 신나겠구나.

해설

남자가 가족과 뉴욕으로 여행을 간다고 했으므로 "정말? 너 정말 신나겠구나." 라는 응답이 가장 적절하다.

① 그랬다니 안 됐다.

② 나는 거기에 비행기를 타고 갈 거야.

③ 나는 너랑 같이 여행을 못 갈지도 몰라.

⑤ 그거 멋진데! 뉴욕은 어땠어?

어휘

join[dʒɔin] (기다리는 사람과) 만나다, 합류하다 / somewhere[sʌ́mhwὲər] 어떤 장소 / go on a trip 여행을 가다

20 ③

Script

W Hey, Leo. Are you looking for something?

M Is there a payphone around here? I need to call my mom to let her know that I'm going to be a little late.

W I don't think there is. There is one near the main gate, but it's kind of far.

M I see. Then, can I use your cell phone? I'll pay you for the call.

W I'm afraid you can't. I didn't bring it.

해석

여　안녕, Leo. 뭔가를 찾고 있니?

남　이 주변에 공중전화가 있니? 엄마에게 약간 늦을 것이라고 알려주려고 전화를 해야 해서.

여　이 주위에는 없는 것 같은데. 정문 근처에 하나 있는데 그건 좀 멀어.

남　그렇구나. 그러면 너의 휴대 전화를 써도 될까? 전화 요금은 줄게.

여　미안하지만 그럴 수 없어. 전화기를 안 가져왔어.

해설

남자가 전화기를 사용해도 되느냐고 물었으므로 "미안하지만 그럴 수 없어. 전화기를 안 가져왔어."라는 응답이 가장 적절하다.

① 나는 그런 것은 두렵지 않아.

② 고마워. 다음엔 내가 낼게.

④ 요즈음은 휴대 전화기의 가격이 싸다.

⑤ 전화요금을 못 냈다니 안 됐다.

어휘

look for ~을 찾다 / payphone[peifoun] 공중전화 / main gate 정문 / far[fɑːr] 먼

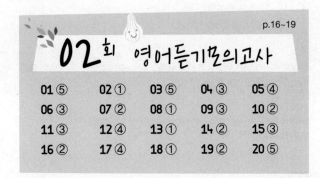

p.16~19

02회 영어듣기모의고사

01 ⑤	02 ①	03 ⑤	04 ③	05 ④
06 ③	07 ②	08 ①	09 ③	10 ②
11 ③	12 ④	13 ①	14 ②	15 ③
16 ②	17 ④	18 ①	19 ②	20 ⑤

01 ⑤

Script

W Hello, shoppers! We're looking for a boy. His name is Peter Jackson. He was last seen in the shoe store on the third floor. He's wearing a striped shirt and blue jeans. He's also wearing a baseball cap with number 13 on it. If you see him, please bring him to the information desk near the main exit. Thank you.

해석

여　안녕하세요, 고객 여러분! 소년을 찾고 있습니다. 이름은 Peter Jackson입니다. 3층에 있는 신발 가게에서 마지막으로 목격되었습니다. 소년은 줄무늬 셔츠와 청바지를 입고 있으며, 13이라는 숫자가 쓰인 야구 모자를 쓰고 있습니다. 여러분이 이 소년을 발견하시면, 정문 근처의 안내소로 데려와 주십시오. 감사합니다.

해설

소년은 줄무늬 셔츠와 청바지를 입고 있고, 13이라는 숫자가 적힌 야구 모자를 쓰고 있다.

어휘

last[lɑst] 마지막에 / striped[straipt] 줄무늬가 있는 / exit[éksit] 출구

02 ①

Script

M Excuse me.

W Yes, do you need something?

M Yes, just take a look at this. I think it is too overcooked.

W Didn't you order it well-done?

M Yes, I did. But this is too much.

W Do you want me to get you a new one?

M Yes, please.

W Okay. I'll be right back.

해석

남 실례합니다.

여 네, 필요하신 것이 있으신가요?

남 네, 이것 좀 보세요. 제 생각에는 너무 익은 것 같아요.

여 완전히 익혀 달라고 하지 않으셨나요?

남 네, 그랬어요. 하지만 이것은 너무 심하네요.

여 새것으로 하나 가져다 드릴까요?

남 네, 그렇게 해 주세요.

여 알았습니다. 곧 돌아오겠습니다.

해설

손님이 고기가 너무 익었다며 바꿔 달라고 하는 것으로 보아 두 사람이 대화하는 장소는 식당임을 알 수 있다.

어휘

take a look at ~을 보다 / overcooked[òuvərkúkt] 너무 익은 / order[ɔ́:rdər] 주문하다

03 ⑤

Script

W Excuse me, when do you offer guitar lessons?

M That depends on your level. Are you a beginner?

W Yes, I am.

M Then, every Monday, Wednesday, and Friday.

W How much is the lesson fee?

M 300 dollars a month. You can also drop by to practice any time.

W Okay, do you take credit cards?

M Sorry, we only take cash.

해석

여 실례합니다, 기타 수업이 언제 있나요?

남 수준에 따라서 다릅니다. 초보자이신가요?

여 네, 처음입니다.

남 그러면, 매주 월요일, 수요일, 금요일에 있습니다.

여 수강료는 얼마인가요?

남 한 달에 300달러입니다. 언제라도 오셔서 연습하실 수도 있습니다.

여 알았어요, 신용카드로 지불해도 되나요?

남 죄송하지만, 현금만 받습니다.

해설

수강료는 신용카드로 낼 수 없고 현금으로만 받는다.

어휘

offer[ɔ́(:)fər] ~을 제공하다 / depend on ~에 따라 결정되다, ~에 달려있다 / fee[fi:] 수업료, 요금 / drop by ~에 들르다 / practice[prǽktis] 연습하다

04 ③

Script

M Excuse me, someone dropped this boarding pass.

W Thank you. I'll give it to the person it belongs to.

M By the way, do you have any extra blankets?

W Sure, I do. Is it cold in here?

M No, it's not. I just might feel cold while I sleep. That's why.

W OK. I'll bring one for you.

M Thank you.

해석

남 실례합니다. 누군가 이 탑승권을 떨어뜨렸네요.

여 감사합니다. 제가 주인을 찾아 드리겠습니다.

남 그런데, 여분의 담요가 있나요?

여 네, 있습니다. 추우신가요?

남 아니요, 그렇지 않습니다. 잘 때 추울 것 같아서요. 그래서요.

여 알았습니다. 하나 가져다 드릴게요.

남 감사합니다.

해설

탑승권 이야기가 나오고, 여분의 담요를 가져다준다는 것으로 보아 여자는 승무원임을 알 수 있다.

어휘

drop[drɑp] ~을 떨어뜨리다 / boarding pass 탑승권 / belong to ~에게 속하다 / blanket[blǽŋkit] 담요

05 ④

Script

W John, pay me what you owe me.

M Of course, what do I owe you?

W First of all, you lost the book I lent you. That's 10 dollars. Second, you borrowed 20 dollars from me last week. Do you remember?

M How can I forget? Is that all?

W No, you dropped my cell phone, and the case broke. It's 8 dollars for that.

M Come on! Let me pay half, OK?

W OK, but you have to pay me now.

M All right.

해석

여 John, 나에게 빚진 것 좀 갚아.

남 그래, 내가 너에게 빚진 것이 뭐지?

여 우선, 너는 내가 너에게 빌려 준 책을 잃어버렸지. 그 책은 10달러야. 두 번째, 지난주에 너는 나에게 20달러를 빌렸어. 기억나니?

남 어떻게 잊겠니? 그게 다야?

여 아니, 네가 내 휴대 전화를 떨어뜨려서 케이스가 부서졌잖아. 그것은 8달러야.

남 너무 한다! 반만 내게 해 줘, 응?

여 알았어. 하지만 지금 갚아야 해.
남 알았어.

해설
남자는 잃어버린 책값 10달러, 지난주에 빌린 돈 20달러, 휴대 전화 케이스 가격의 반인 4달러, 모두 합해서 34달러를 여자에게 갚아야 한다.

어휘
owe[ou] 빚지고 있다 / first of all 우선 / lend[lend] ~을 빌려 주다 / borrow[bɔ́(ː)rou] ~을 빌리다 / drop[drɑp] 떨어뜨리다 / break[breik] 부서지다 / come on 제발, 왜 이래(상대방에 대한 가벼운 항의 표현)

06 ③
Script

M Can I talk to you for a second?

W Sure. What is it?

M I've been here for almost a year, but I still don't have any friends. I mean a close friend.

W You must be very shy, am I right?

M No, I'm not. That's not the reason. I think some people laugh at me because I'm from the countryside and even make fun of my accent. I get very nervous when I talk to people.

W I understand that you have a little different accent than people in Seoul, but you don't have to be nervous. Be confident. OK?

해석
남 잠시 얘기를 좀 나눌 수 있을까요?
여 물론이죠, 무엇이지요?
남 저는 여기에 거의 1년을 있었는데, 아직도 친구가 없어요. 제 말은 친한 친구 말이에요.
여 수줍음을 많이 타는군요. 맞지요?
남 아니요, 그렇지 않아요. 그것 때문이 아니에요. 저는 일부 사람들이 제가 시골 출신이라고 비웃는 것 같고, 심지어 제 발음을 가지고 놀리는 것 같은 생각이 들어요. 사람들에게 말할 때 매우 긴장을 하게 돼요.
여 당신의 발음이 서울 사람들하고 약간 다르다는 건 알지만, 긴장할 필요 없어요. 자신감을 가져요. 알았죠?

해설
남자는 수줍음을 많이 타는 사람이 아니다.

어휘
close[klous] 친한, 가까운 / shy[ʃai] 수줍어하는, 소심한 / laugh at ~을 비웃다 / countryside[kʌ́ntrisàid] 시골, 지방 / make fun of ~을 놀리다, 조롱하다 / accent[ǽksent] 억양 / nervous[nə́ːrvəs] 긴장한 / confident[kɑ́nfidənt] 자신 있는

07 ②
Script

M Amanda, you are leaving tomorrow, right?

W Yes, I am.

M If there isn't anyone to give you a ride, I can. What time is the train?

W The train leaves at 3, and I need to get there 30 minutes early.

M That's no problem. Then, what time do you want me to pick you up?

W How long does it take to get there?

M 30 minutes. Then, let's meet an hour and a half before the train leaves.

해석
남 Amanda, 너 내일 떠날 거지, 맞지?
여 응.
남 태워 줄 사람이 없으면 내가 태워 줄게. 기차가 몇 시에 떠나니?
여 기차는 세 시에 출발하고, 나는 기차역에 30분 일찍 도착해야 해.
남 문제없어. 그러면 내가 너를 몇 시에 데리러 갈까?
여 거기까지 얼마나 걸리는데?
남 30분. 그러면, 기차가 출발하기 한 시간 반 전에 만나자.

해설
기차 출발 시각은 3시이고 한 시간 반 전에 만나자고 했으니까, 두 사람은 1시 30분에 만날 것이다.

어휘
give a person a ride ~을 태워 주다 / pick up ~을 태우러 가다

08 ①
Script

W William, what happened to you? Where did you get those scratches?

M I tried to avoid a car coming at me and fell down this morning.

W Oh, no. Are you okay now?

M Yes, I didn't get too badly hurt. Only these.

W Did the driver take you to the hospital?

M No, he just gave me his business card.

W Did you tell your parents about it?

M No, I'm going to tell them later.

해석
여 William, 무슨 일이니? 그 상처는 어떻게 생긴 거야?
남 오늘 아침에 나에게 달려오는 차를 피하려다가 넘어졌어.
여 저런. 지금은 괜찮니?
남 응. 심하게 다치지는 않았어. 이 상처뿐이야.
여 그 운전자가 너를 병원에 데려갔니?
남 아니, 그냥 자기 명함만 줬어.
여 부모님께 그것에 대해 말했니?
남 아니, 나중에 말할 거야.

해설
소년은 차와 부딪친 것이 아니라 차를 피하다가 넘어졌다.

어휘
scratch[skrætʃ] 긁힌 상처 / avoid[əvɔ́id] ~을 피하다 / fall down 넘어지다 / get hurt 다치다 / badly[bǽdli] 심하게, 몹시 / business card 명함

09 ③

Script

M Ben is in the last year of junior high, but he is very small and weak. In his class, there is one boy who keeps bothering him and sometimes makes him run errands. Since he is tall and strong, Ben can't help doing what he is told to do. Today, at the cafeteria, the boy told Ben to bring him some water, but Ben couldn't stand it anymore, so he refused to do so. Then, this boy came up to Ben and hit him on the back of his head. Ben got angry, turned around, and threw a punch toward his face.

해석

남 Ben은 중학교에서 최고 학년이지만, 매우 작고 약하다. 그의 반에 그를 계속 괴롭히고 때로는 그에게 심부름을 시키는 소년이 있다. 그는 키가 크고 강해서 Ben은 그가 시키는 일을 하지 않을 수 없다. 오늘, 식당에서 그 소년이 Ben에게 물을 가져오라고 했는데 Ben은 더는 참을 수 없어서 그 일을 거절했다. 그러자 이 소년이 Ben에게 다가와서 뒤통수를 때렸다. Ben은 화가 나서, 뒤를 돌아 그의 얼굴을 향해 주먹을 날렸다.

해설

작고 약한 Ben이 크고 힘센 아이에게 괴롭힘을 당하다가 참지 못하게 되는 상황이므로, 아무리 미천한 사람도 지나치게 업신여기면 성을 내게 된다는 의미의 "지렁이도 밟으면 꿈틀한다."라는 속담이 가장 적절하다.

① 벽에도 귀가 있다. (낮말은 새가 듣고, 밤말은 쥐가 듣는다.)

② 아예 안 오는 것보다 늦게라도 오는 것이 낫다.

④ 일찍 일어나는 새가 먹이를 잡는다.

⑤ 하늘은 스스로 돕는 자를 돕는다.

어휘

bother[báðər] 괴롭히다 / run a errand 심부름하다 / cannot help -ing ~하지 않을 수 없다 / stand[stænd] ~을 참다, 견디다 / refuse[rifjúːz] ~을 거절하다 / come up to ~에게 다가오다 / turn around 뒤돌아보다 / throw a punch 주먹을 날리다

10 ②

Script

[Telephone rings.]

W Hello.

M Hello. I'm wondering if you could help me.

W Yes. What's the problem?

M I left a few English books I bought on the bus.

W That's too bad. Do you remember the license plate of the bus and the approximate time?

M Yes, I think it was 7112, and it was around 3 o'clock.

W All right. I'll let you know right after I talk to the driver.

M Thank you. My number is 010-5400-5186.

해석

여 여보세요.

남 여보세요. 저를 좀 도와주실 수 있는지 궁금해서요.

여 네, 무엇이 문제입니까?

남 제가 산 영어책 몇 권을 버스에 두고 내렸습니다.

여 저런 안 됐네요. 버스 번호하고 대략적인 시간을 기억하세요?

남 네, 번호는 7112번이고, 시간은 대략 3시였던 거 같아요.

여 알았습니다. 운전사와 이야기를 한 후에 바로 알려 드리겠습니다.

남 감사합니다. 제 번호는 010-5400-5186입니다.

해설

남자는 놓고 내린 영어책, 즉 분실물을 찾으려고 전화했다.

어휘

wonder[wʌ́ndər] ~을 궁금해하다 / license plate (자동차의) 번호판 / approximate[əpráksəmèit] 대략의

11 ③

Script

W ① If a bike is 200 dollars, you just need one hundred and eighty dollars.

② You can get a 15 percent discount on toys.

③ If a necklace is 50 dollars, you just need 45 dollars.

④ The sale starts on Dec 1st and ends on the last day of the month.

⑤ The shop opens for 13 hours a day.

해석

여 ① 자전거가 200달러이면, 180달러만 있으면 된다.

② 장난감은 15% 할인을 받을 수 있다.

③ 목걸이가 50달러이면, 45달러만 있으면 된다.

④ 할인판매는 12월 1일에 시작해서 그달의 마지막 날에 끝난다.

⑤ 가게는 하루에 13시간 동안 문을 연다.

해설

목걸이는 액세서리이므로 20% 할인을 받을 수 있다. 목걸이가 50달러이면 45달러가 아니라 40달러만 있으면 된다.

어휘

discount[dískaunt] 할인 / necklace[néklis] 목걸이 / end[end] 끝나다

12 ④

Script

W Hi, David. I'm leaving a message to let you know that I can't go to the movies with you tonight. I wish I could, but the train I'm on is delayed because of an unexpected accident. As soon as I get to Seoul, I'll call you. Sorry that I can't make it, but we can go to the movies some other time. Bye.

해석

여 안녕, David. 나는 오늘 밤에 너와 함께 영화를 보러 갈 수 없다는 것을 알리려고 메시지를 남기고 있어. 나도 가고 싶지만, 내가 탄 기차가 예기치 않은 사고로 연착되고 있어. 서울에 도착하자마자, 너에게 전화할게. 시간을 못 맞추어 미안하지만, 다음에 같이 영화를 보러 갈 수 있을 거야. 안녕.

해설

기차가 예기치 않은 사고로 연착해서 늦어지고 있기 때문에 극장에 갈 수 없다.

어휘
delay[diléi] 늦추다, 지체시키다 / unexpected[ʌ̀nikspéktid] 예기치 않은 /
make it 제시간에 도착하다

13 ①
Script

M This is my first time in New York. I heard there are so
    many skyscrapers in Manhattan.

W That's right. It's even hard to see the moon at night
    because of them, but you are going to like this place.

M You think so?

W Of course. What time would you like to go for a
    sightseeing tour of the city?

M Anytime. I'm ready.

W OK. I guess you are pretty tired, so have a good sleep,
    and I'll call you tomorrow morning.

M Sounds great.

해석
남 뉴욕은 이번이 처음이에요. 맨해튼에는 고층빌딩이 많이 있다고 들었어요.

여 맞습니다. 고층빌딩 때문에 밤에 달을 보기가 어렵기도 하지요. 하지만,
    이곳을 좋아하시게 될 거예요.

남 그렇게 생각하세요?

여 물론이죠. 몇 시에 시내 관광을 가고 싶으세요?

남 언제든지요. 저는 준비가 되어 있어요.

여 알았어요. 제 생각에 꽤 피곤하실 것 같으니, 푹 주무세요. 내일 아침에
    전화 드릴게요.

남 좋아요.

해설
여자는 뉴욕에 처음 온 남자에게 뉴욕 시내 관광을 시켜 줄 것이다.

어휘
skyscraper[skáiskrèipər] 마천루, 고층빌딩 / sightseeing[sáitsì:iŋ] 관광

14 ②
Script

W I'm a sixteen-year old girl. I'm an active and outgoing
    person. I'm confident and strong enough to compete
    in anything with boys, but I get too nervous when
    speaking before a group. Even though I prepare a
    lot for a speech, my mind goes blank, and I even
    stutter. It's because my schoolteacher made fun of me
    when I spoke in class. Since that time, I get pale and
    confused when making a speech.

해석
여 나는 16세 소녀입니다. 나는 매우 활동적이고 외향적인 사람입니다. 나
    는 어떤 것이든 소년들과 겨룰 정도로 강하고 자신감이 있지만, 사람들
    앞에서 말을 할 때는 너무 긴장을 합니다. 연설을 위해 준비를 많이 하
    더라도 정신이 멍해지고, 말을 더듬기까지 합니다. 왜냐하면 내가 수업
    시간에 말을 할 때 우리 학교 선생님이 나를 놀렸기 때문입니다. 그때
    이후로 나는 발표를 할 때면 창백해지고 혼란스러워합니다.

해설
여자는 발표하거나 사람들 앞에서 말할 때 긴장을 해서 말을 더듬는 것이 고
민이다.

어휘
active[ǽktiv] 활동적인 / outgoing[áutgòuiŋ] 외향적인 /
confident[kánfidənt] 자신 있는 / compete sth with sb
~으로 …와 경쟁하다 / nervous[nə́:rvəs] 긴장한 / go blank 멍해지다 /
stutter[stʌ́tər] 말을 더듬다 / schoolteacher[skú:ltì:tʃər]
(초 · 중 · 고등학교의) 교사 / make fun of ~을 놀리다 / pale[peil] 창백한 /
confused[kənfjú:zd] 혼란스러운 / make a speech 연설하다, 발표하다

15 ③
Script

① **W** How was that concert?

    M It was really fantastic.

② **W** I'd like to buy a small lamp.

    M Come this way, please.

③ **W** What time shall we make it?

    M In front of the post office.

④ **W** May I speak to Mike?

    M Sorry, but there is no one here by that name.

⑤ **W** Would you mind repeating that?

    M Of course not.

해석
① 여 그 콘서트는 어땠어?

    남 정말로 좋았어.

② 여 작은 전등을 사고 싶습니다.

    남 이쪽으로 오세요.

③ 여 몇 시로 정할까요?

    남 우체국 앞에서요.

④ 여 Mike 좀 바꿔 주실래요?

    남 미안하지만, 여기에는 그런 이름의 사람이 없습니다.

⑤ 여 다시 말씀해 주시겠어요?

    남 물론이죠.

해설
③ 몇 시로 정할까를 물었는데 장소로 대답하고 있으므로 대화가 어색하다.

어휘
fantastic[fæntǽstik] 환상적인, 멋진 / would like to ~하고 싶다 /
lamp[læmp] 전등 / make it (서로) 만나기로 하다 / post office 우체국

16 ②
Script

M I'm used at festivals, parties, or national holidays. I can
    make people excited and surprised. I explode in the air
    and produce colored lights, so I can beautifully color
    the night sky. But I also produce loud noises and can
    be a little dangerous.

해석
남 나는 페스티벌이나 파티, 국경일에 사용된다. 나는 사람들을 신나게 하
    고, 놀라게 할 수 있다. 나는 공중에서 폭발하고 색이 있는 불빛을 만들

어내서 밤하늘을 아름답게 색칠할 수 있다. 하지만, 나는 큰 소리를 내고 약간 위험하기도 하다.

해설
파티에 쓰이며, 공중에서 폭발하고, 밤하늘을 아름답게 색칠하지만, 위험하기도 한 것은 폭죽이다.

어휘
national holiday 국경일 / explode[iksplóud] 폭발하다 / produce[prədjúːs] 생산하다, 만들어 내다 / color[kʌ́lər] ~을 색칠하다; 색 / loud[laud] 큰

17 ④
Script

W Did you <u>do the homework</u> with the notebook I lent you? You didn't just copy it from my notebook, did you?

M Of course, I didn't.

W Let me see. Oh my God! You copied me <u>word for word</u>.

M No, I changed a few things.

W Only a few. If our teacher finds out that yours is almost <u>the same as mine</u>, he'll give both of us an F.

M Don't worry. It won't happen. I don't think he's going to take a look at all of ours.

W What if he does?

해석
여 너 내가 빌려 준 공책을 가지고 숙제했니? 내 공책을 그대로 베껴 쓰지는 않았겠지, 그렇지?

남 물론, 안 그랬어.

여 어디 보자. 맙소사! 내 것을 글자 그대로 베꼈잖아.

남 아니야, 약간 바꿨어.

여 겨우 몇 개잖아. 우리 선생님이 네 것과 내 것이 거의 같다는 것을 알아내시면, 우리 둘 모두에게 F를 주실 거야.

남 걱정하지 마. 그런 일은 없을 거야. 내 생각에 선생님이 우리 모두의 숙제를 보시지는 않을 거야.

여 만약 그렇게 하시면?

해설
남자가 여자의 숙제를 거의 그대로 베껴 써서 여자가 화가 났다.

어휘
lend[lend] 빌려 주다 / copy[kápi] ~을 베끼다 / word for word 글자 그대로 / find out 찾아내다, 발견하다

18 ①
Script

W Excuse me?

M Me? Are you talking to me?

W Yes, you.

M What is it?

W You just spilt soda on the floor.

M So what? It's <u>none of your business</u>.

W It's my business. I walk on this floor every day, and you made it dirty. <u>In</u> addition, someone might step on it and fall down. It's very dangerous.

M If you think it's that dangerous, you can <u>clean it up yourself</u>.

W So, you're saying you are not going to clean it up, and you don't care if anyone gets hurt?

M Right, I don't care!

W <u>You are hopeless</u>.

해석
여 저기요?

남 저요? 저에게 말씀하시는 건가요?

여 네, 당신이요.

남 무슨 일이죠?

여 지금 바닥에 음료수를 흘리셨어요.

남 그래서 뭐요? 당신이 상관할 일이 아니잖아요.

여 나의 일이지요. 저는 매일 이 바닥을 걸어 다녀요. 당신이 그것을 더럽게 만들고 있잖아요. 게다가 누군가 그것을 밟고 넘어질 수 있어요. 매우 위험해요.

남 그것이 그렇게 위험하다고 생각되시면 직접 치우시죠.

여 그러면 당신은 음료수를 치우지 않을 것이고, 누군가 다치든지 말든지 상관없다는 말인가요?

남 맞아요, 상관없어요!

여 당신은 정말 구제불능이군요.

해설
여자는 음료수를 흘리고 치우지도 않으며, 다른 사람을 배려하지 않는 남자 때문에 화가 났다.

어휘
spill[spil] 흘리다, 엎지르다 / It's none of your business. 상관 마. / in addition 게다가, 더욱이 / step on ~을 밟다 / fall down 넘어지다 / clean up ~을 청소하다, 깨끗이 하다 / hopeless[hóuplis] 희망이 없는, 절망적인

19 ②
Script

M Hi! Emma. Come on in. <u>Thank you for coming</u> to my housewarming party.

W Hi, David. This is for you.

M Thank you. Let me put this on the table.

W It's a bit cold outside.

M I know. Please, <u>make yourself at home</u>. Can I take your coat?

W Thanks. This is a great apartment! Do you mind if I <u>take a look around</u>?

M No, go right ahead.

해석
남 안녕! Emma. 들어 와. 집들이에 와 줘서 고마워.

여 안녕, David. 이건 네 거야.

남 고마워. 테이블 위에 올려놓을게.

여　밖이 약간 춥다.

남　그러게. 편안히 쉬어. 코트를 받아 줄까?

여　고마워. 아파트가 참 좋구나! 내가 좀 둘러봐도 될까?

남　<u>응, 둘러봐.</u>

해설

집을 둘러봐도 되느냐고 물었으므로 "응, 둘러봐."라는 말이 가장 알맞은 응답이 된다. mind는 '~을 꺼려하다'라는 의미이므로 의미 파악에 주의해야 한다.

① 응, 그렇게 하고 싶어.

③ 와, 훌륭해!

④ 고마워! 그게 뭐야?

⑤ 천만에

어휘

come on in 들어오다 / housewarming party 집들이 / make oneself at home 편안히 하다 / take a look around 둘러보다

20　⑤

Script

M　<u>How can I help you</u>?

W　I'd like to get some information on a flight.

M　What flight number would that be for?

W　It's OZ 201. What time is <u>the expected departure</u>?

M　The departure time is 10:30 P.M.

해석

남　무엇을 도와 드릴까요?

여　항공편에 관한 정보를 좀 얻고 싶어요.

남　어떤 항공편이지요?

여　OZ 201입니다. 예상 이륙 시간이 몇 시인가요?

남　<u>이륙 시간은 오후 10시 30분입니다.</u>

해설

비행기의 이륙시간을 묻고 있으므로 가장 적절한 응답은 "이륙 시간은 오후 10시 30분입니다."이다.

① 제 좌석은 12C입니다.

② 아마 3시 30분에 도착할 것입니다.

③ 당신이 비행기를 타자마자예요.

④ 알려 주셔서 감사합니다.

어휘

flight[flait] 항공편 / expected[ikspéktid] 예정된 / departure[dipάːrtʃər] 출발

p.24~27

03 회 영어듣기모의고사

01 ⑤	02 ③	03 ③	04 ①	05 ③
06 ④	07 ④	08 ④	09 ②	10 ④
11 ①	12 ④	13 ①	14 ⑤	15 ③
16 ⑤	17 ②	18 ④	19 ⑤	20 ③

01　⑤

Script

M　How would you like to <u>have your hair done</u>?

W　I'd like a straight perm.

M　OK. You want to keep your beautiful long hair, am I right?

W　That's correct, but I'd like to cut it a little.

M　Then, how about keeping it 10 centimeters <u>below the shoulder</u>?

W　OK.

해석

남　머리를 어떻게 해 드릴까요?

여　스트레이트 파마를 해 주세요.

남　알았습니다. 당신은 이 아름다운 긴 머리를 유지하고 싶군요. 제 말이 맞죠?

여　맞아요. 하지만, 약간은 자르고 싶어요.

남　그러면, 어깨 아래로 약 10센티미터 정도 길이가 어때요?

여　좋아요.

해설

여자는 어깨에서 10센티미터 정도 내려온 길이의 생머리를 하기를 원한다.

어휘

straight[streit] 곧은 / perm[pə:rm] 파마 / correct[kərékt] 옳은, 정확한

02　③

Script

M　Sally, let's do homework together.

W　I already <u>did my homework</u>.

M　Really? Then, are you going to watch TV now?

W　No. I'd rather have supper first. I'm hungry.

M　Okay. I heard that you have a basketball game tomorrow.

W　Yes, I just practiced a lot <u>before I came home</u>.

M　You did?

W　Yes. I'm going to <u>take a shower</u> after supper and go to sleep early for tomorrow's game.

남	Sally, 같이 숙제하자.
여	나는 벌써 숙제를 다했어.
남	정말? 그러면 너 이제 텔레비전을 볼 거야?
여	아니. 저녁을 먼저 먹는 게 좋겠어. 배가 고프거든.
남	알았어. 너 내일 농구 시합이 있다고 그러던데.
여	응, 집에 오기 전에 연습을 많이 했어.
남	그랬어?
여	응. 저녁을 먹고 나서 샤워하고 내일의 시합을 위해서 일찍 잘 거야.

해설

여자는 배가 고파서 저녁을 먼저 먹겠다고 했다.

어휘

would rather+동사원형 ~하는 편이 낫다 / supper[sʌ́pər] 저녁 / practice[prǽktis] 연습하다 / take a shower 샤워하다

03 ③

Script

M	I'm here to return these three DVDs.
W	Can I see your membership card?
M	OK. Here you go.
W	Thank you. Let me see. Peter Kim. <u>Your due date</u> was yesterday, which means you have to pay a late charge.
M	Oh, I'm sorry. How much is that?
W	You pay a dollar <u>for each one late</u>.
M	OK. And I want to rent *Brave Heart*.
W	That one's 3 dollars.
M	I only have 5 dollars. What can I do?
W	Okay. I'll give you a discount since you're <u>a regular customer</u>.

해석

남	이 DVD 세 개를 반납하러 왔습니다.
여	회원증 좀 보여 주시겠어요?
남	알았습니다. 여기 있어요.
여	고맙습니다. 음. Peter Kim 씨. 반납일이 어제였네요. 연체료를 내셔야 합니다.
남	아, 죄송합니다. 얼마죠?
여	한 개에 1달러입니다.
남	알았습니다. 그리고 이 「브레이브 하트」를 빌릴게요.
여	그것은 3달러입니다.
남	저는 5달러밖에 없어요. 어떻게 하지요?
여	알았어요. 단골손님이시니 깎아 드릴게요.

해설

연체료 3달러에 「브레이브 하트」를 빌리는 값이 3달러이므로 총 6달러이지만, 남자가 5달러밖에 없어서 깎아 준다고 했으므로 남자가 지불할 금액은 5달러이다.

어휘

return[ritə́ːrn] ~을 반납하다, 돌려주다 / due date 만기일 / late charge 연체료 / rent[rent] ~을 빌리다 / regular customer 단골손님

04 ①

Script

M	Do you have a stapler?
W	Yes, <u>here it is</u>.
M	Thanks. There are no staples in it.
W	Don't worry. I'll get you some. <u>By the way</u>, do you have correction fluid?
M	I think I do. It's right here.
W	Thanks. I have <u>a few things to correct</u>.

해석

남	스테이플러(종이찍개)가 있나요?
여	네, 여기 있어요.
남	고맙습니다. 스테이플러(종이찍개) 심이 없네요.
여	걱정하지 마세요. 제가 좀 가져다 드릴게요. 그런데 수정액 있어요?
남	있는 것 같아요. 여기 있네요.
여	감사합니다. 고칠 것이 좀 있어서요.

해설

여자는 수정액을 필요로 하고 있다.

어휘

stapler[stéiplər] 스테이플러(종이찍개) / staple[stéipəl] 스테이플러(종이찍개) 심 / correction fluid 수정액 / correct[kərékt] ~을 고치다, 수정하다

05 ③

Script

W	<u>Suppose that</u> it takes 20 hours for Alan to read 4 books. <u>In other words</u>, it takes 5 hours for Alan to read one book <u>on average</u>. Then, how many books can Alan read in 30 hours?

해석

여	Alan이 네 권의 책을 읽는 데 스무 시간이 걸린다고 가정해보자. 다시 말해서, Alan이 한 권의 책을 읽는 데 평균적으로 다섯 시간이 걸린다는 말이다. 그러면, Alan은 서른 시간 동안 몇 권을 책을 읽을 수 있을까?

해설

한 권의 책을 읽는 데 다섯 시간이 걸리므로 서른 시간 동안에 여섯 권의 책을 읽을 수 있다.

어휘

suppose[səpóuz] 가정하다 / in other words 즉, 다시 말해서 / on average 평균하여, 대략

06 ④

Script

W	Hey, Chris. (slapping sound on his back)
M	Ouch! <u>Who is this</u>?
W	Chris, it's me. Joan.
M	Do I know you?
W	Of course. You and I went to Jackson Elementary School together.

M <u>Sorry to disappoint you</u>, but I went to St. Mary Elementary School, and my name is not Chris.

해석

여 야, Chris.

남 아야! 누구야?

여 Chris, 나야. Joan.

남 나 알아요?

여 물론이지. 너와 나는 잭슨 초등학교에 같이 다녔잖아.

남 실망시켜서 미안하지만, 나는 세인트 메리 초등학교에 다녔고, 내 이름은 Chris가 아니야.

해설

여자는 모르는 사람을 아는 사람으로 착각한 것을 깨닫고 당황했을 것이다.

어휘

elementary school 초등학교 / disappoint[dìsəpɔ́int] 실망시키다

07 ④

Script

① **W** I'm getting nervous.

　　M <u>Try to relax</u>. It'll be over soon.

② **W** How long does the movie run?

　　M It runs for one hundred and twenty minutes.

③ **W** Can you give me <u>something cold to drink</u>?

　　M How about some green tea with ice?

④ **W** What kind of movie is this?

　　M Yes, I like it. I'm sure you'll like it, too.

⑤ **W** How much do you think it's going to cost <u>to have my car fixed</u>?

　　M Well, I guess at least 200 dollars.

해석

① 여 저는 긴장돼요.

　 남 긴장을 풀도록 노력해 보세요. 곧 끝날 거예요.

② 여 이 영화는 상영 시간이 얼마나 되나요?

　 남 120분이요.

③ 여 찬 음료를 한 잔 주시겠어요?

　 남 얼음을 넣은 녹차는 어떠세요?

④ 여 이것은 어떤 종류의 영화인가요?

　 남 네. 저는 이 영화를 좋아해요. 당신도 분명히 마음에 드실 거예요.

⑤ 여 제 차를 고치는 데 비용이 얼마나 들 것 같아요?

　 남 글쎄요, 적어도 2백 달러는 들 거예요.

해설

④ 어떤 종류의 영화냐고 물었는데 그 영화를 좋아한다고 대답하고 있으므로 대화가 어색하다. 또한 의문사 의문문에는 yes, no로 대답하지 않는다.

어휘

nervous[nə́ːrvəs] 긴장한 / relax[riláeks] (긴장을) 풀게 하다 / be over ~이 끝나다 / run[rʌn] (영화, 연극 등을) 상영하다 / cost[kɔːst] (비용이) ~가 들다 / fix[fiks] 수리하다

08 ④

Script

W Julian, do you have my digital camera with you?

M No. But I can get it <u>if you want it</u>.

W Please go and get it then. I need it for my mother's birthday.

M OK. But before that, I have <u>something to tell you</u>.

W I'm listening.

M There are some scratches on it. The other day, I <u>bumped into</u> my brother and dropped it.

W Are you serious? Last time when you borrowed my MP3 player, you scratched it, too. Remember? You're always careless. I don't think I'll lend you my stuff anymore.

M I'm really sorry, but the camera still works fine.

해석

여 Julian. 너 내 디지털 카메라 가져왔어?

남 아니. 하지만 네가 원하면 가져올 수 있어.

여 그러면, 가서 가져와줘. 우리 어머니의 생신에 카메라가 필요해.

남 알았어, 하지만 그전에 너에게 할 말이 있어.

여 말해.

남 카메라가 약간 긁혔어. 요 전날 내가 동생하고 부딪쳐서 떨어뜨렸거든.

여 정말이야? 지난번에 내 MP3재생기를 빌렸을 때도 흠집을 냈었잖아. 기억나? 너는 항상 조심성이 없구나. 더는 내 물건을 너에게 빌려 줄 수 없을 것 같아.

남 정말 미안해. 하지만, 카메라는 여전히 잘 작동돼.

해설

여자는 남자가 여자에게 빌린 MP3재생기에 흠집을 낸 적이 있음에도, 빌려 간 카메라를 떨어뜨려 또 흠집을 내는 등 빌린 물건을 함부로 다루어서 화가 났다.

어휘

scratch[skrætʃ] 긁힌 상처 / bump into 부딪치다 / drop[drɑp] 떨어뜨리다 / serious[síəriəs] 진지한, 심각한 / careless[kɛ́ərlis] 부주의한, 조심성 없는 / stuff[stʌf] 물건 / work[wəːrk] 작동하다

09 ②

Script

W Did you finish the homework?

M Almost.

W <u>What do you mean</u>?

M My friend called me while I was doing it.

W Do you realize that you have been doing your homework for 3 hours? I've been watching you, but you haven't been concentrating at all.

M Sorry.

W This will be <u>the last time</u> I talk to you. Do it <u>within an hour</u>.

해석

여 너 숙제 다했니?

남 거의 요.

여 무슨 말이니?

남 제가 숙제를 하는데 친구가 전화했어요.

여 너는 네가 숙제를 세 시간 동안이나 하고 있다는 것을 아니? 내가 너를 지켜보았는데 숙제에 전혀 집중을 하질 않더구나.

남 죄송해요.

여 이번이 내가 너에게 마지막으로 말하는 거야. 한 시간 안에 끝내.

해설
여자는 남자에게 한 시간 안에 숙제를 끝내라고 마지막으로 경고하고 있다.

어휘
realize[ríːəlàiz] ~을 깨닫다, 인식하다 / concentrate[kánsəntrèit] 집중하다

10 ④

Script

① W What do you charge for a ticket?

M It's 5 dollars for an adult.

② W Where can I find the box office?

M It's right over there.

③ W Where would you like to go sightseeing?

M I'd like to go to N Seoul Tower.

④ W What's the purpose of your visit?

M I'm here on a business trip.

⑤ W Should I pay for it now?

M It's up to you.

해석

① 여 표 한 장에 얼마인가요?

남 성인은 5달러입니다.

② 여 매표소는 어디에 있죠?

남 바로 저기에 있습니다.

③ 여 어디를 관광하고 싶으세요?

남 저는 N 서울 타워에 가고 싶습니다.

④ 여 당신의 방문 목적은 무엇입니까?

남 저는 여기에 사업차 왔습니다.

⑤ 여 지금 돈을 내야 하나요?

남 당신 마음대로 하세요.

해설
출입국 관리소이므로 나라의 방문 목적을 묻는 대화가 상황에 가장 잘 어울린다.

어휘
charge[tʃɑːrdʒ] ~을 청구하다, 부과하다 / adult[ədʌ́lt] 성인, 어른 / box office 매표소 / sightseeing[sáitsiːiŋ] 관광 / purpose[pə́ːrpəs] 목적 / visit[vízit] 방문 / business trip 출장 / up to ~에게 달린

11 ①

Script

W Hey, James. What a surprise! I didn't expect to see you here.

M Hi, Sandra. My wife is in the delivery room. She's already been there for almost an hour. Are you visiting someone here?

W No, I'm pregnant. I'm on my 4th week now.

M Congratulations!

W Thanks. I have to go now. I'll call you later.

해석

여 안녕하세요. James. 뜻밖이네요! 당신을 여기서 보리라고는 예상하지 못했어요.

남 안녕하세요. Sandra. 부인이 분만실에 있어서요. 분만실에 있은 지 벌써 거의 한 시간이 다 되었어요. 누구를 방문하러 오셨나요?

여 아니요, 저 임신했어요. 지금 4주째예요.

남 축하해요!

여 고마워요. 저는 지금 가봐야 해요. 나중에 전화할게요.

해설
분만실이 있고, 임신한 여성이 가는 곳은 병원이다.

어휘
expect[ikspékt] ~을 예상하다 / delivery[dilívəri] 분만, 출산 / pregnant[prégnənt] 임신한

12 ④

Script

M Asia is made up of approximately 50 countries. These countries have different cultures and hardly have anything in common. Asia makes up nearly one third of the Earth's land and has more people than any other continent. In fact, two out of every three people on Earth are Asians. For the people of this continent, rice is a very common food.

해석

남 아시아는 대략 50개의 나라로 구성되어 있다. 이 나라들은 다른 문화를 가지고 있고, 공통점이 거의 없다. 아시아는 지구 땅의 거의 3분의 1을 차지하고 있고, 다른 어떤 대륙보다도 인구가 많다. 사실, 지구 상에서 세 명 중 두 명은 아시아 사람이다. 이 대륙 사람들에게는 쌀이 주식이다.

해설
각각의 나라는 다른 문화를 가지고 있고, 아시아 대륙은 지구 땅의 3분의 1을 차지하며, 지구 인구의 세 명 중 두 명은 아시아 사람이다. 주식이 쌀이라고 했으므로 언급되지 않은 것은 기후이다.

어휘
be made up of ~으로 구성되다, 이루어지다 / approximately[əpráksəmitli] 약, 대략 / in common 공통으로 / make up ~을 구성하다 / continent[kántənənt] 대륙 / in fact 사실상 / common[kámən] 흔한

13 ①

Script

[Telephone rings.]

W Best Airlines. How may I help you?

M I'd like to book a flight from New York to Seoul.

W That would be a one-way ticket, right?

M Yes, and I would like to leave this Sunday.

W I'm sorry, but Sunday is all booked. There are still seats available on Saturday or Monday.

M Um. Then, Saturday will be fine.

W Which class would you like?

M Business class, please.

해석

여   베스트 항공사입니다. 무엇을 도와드릴까요?

남   저는 뉴욕에서 서울로 가는 비행기를 예약하고 싶어요.

여   편도인가요, 맞지요?

남   맞아요. 그리고 이번 일요일에 떠나고 싶어요.

여   죄송하지만, 일요일은 예약이 다 찼어요. 토요일이나 월요일에는 아직 좌석이 남아 있어요.

남   음. 그러면, 토요일이 좋겠네요.

여   어떤 좌석을 원하시죠?

남   비즈니스석이요.

해설

도착지는 서울, 편도, 출발일은 토요일, 좌석 등급은 비즈니스석이다.

어휘

book[buk] ~을 예약하다 / one-way 편도의 / booked[búkt] 예약된 / available[əvéiləbəl] 이용 가능한

14 ⑤

Script

W This is something we usually do in winter. This is not only limited to our country. I have seen some people in other countries do this, and they have the same kind as we do. It is a light frame covered with colored paper or plastic, and it is easy to make. The windier it is, the higher you can make it fly. A long time ago, we used it during war as a signal.

해석

여   이것은 우리가 주로 겨울에 하는 것이다. 이것은 단지 우리나라에만 제한된 것은 아니다. 나는 다른 나라에서 사람들이 이것을 하는 것을 본 적이 있고, 그들도 우리가 가진 것과 같은 종류의 것을 가지고 있다. 그것은 색종이나 비닐로 덮여 있는 가벼운 틀이고, 만들기가 쉽다. 바람이 더 많이 불수록, 당신은 그것을 더 높이 날릴 수 있다. 오래전에, 우리는 전쟁을 하는 동안 신호를 보내는 데 그것을 사용했다.

해설

바람이 많이 불 때 더 잘 날며 전쟁 시에 신호를 보내는 데 사용할 수 있는 것은 연이므로 연날리기에 대한 설명이다.

어휘

limited[límitid] 제한된 / kind[kaind] 종류 / light[lait] 가벼운 / frame[freim] 틀 / covered with ~로 덮인 / windy[windi] 바람이 부는 / signal[sígnl] 신호

15 ③

Script

W Ralph, look at the floor.

M Oh, no. Where is this water coming from?

W I think the bathtub upstairs is leaking again.

M We need to call a plumber right now.

W I will, but before that, I need to wipe up this water first.

M Let me do that.

W Then, I'll call the manager and make some complaints.

M Hey, honey. I think you should let the upstairs tenants know what's happening here first.

W OK. I'll do that now.

해석

여   Ralph, 바닥을 좀 봐.

남   어, 이런. 이 물이 어디서 온 거지?

여   내 생각에는 위층 욕조가 또 새는 것 같아.

남   지금 당장 배관공을 불러야겠다.

여   내가 전화할게. 하지만 그 전에 물을 먼저 닦아야겠어.

남   내가 할게.

여   그러면 난 관리인에게 전화해서 항의를 할게.

남   여보, 내 생각엔 윗집 세입자들에게 여기에서 무슨 일이 일어나고 있는지 먼저 알려야 할 것 같아.

여   알았어. 지금 할게.

해설

여자는 윗집에 물이 새고 있다고 알리러 갈 것이다.

어휘

bathtub[bǽθtʌb] 욕조 / leak[liːk] 새다 / plumber[plʌ́mər] 배관공 / wipe up ~을 닦아내다 / complaint[kəmpléint] 항의, 불평 / tenant[ténənt] 세입자

16 ⑤

Script

M Have you been invited to Susie's birthday party?

W Sure. It's on July 4th, right?

M No, that's a national holiday, so it's being held three days later at her house.

W How come she didn't tell me?

M Maybe she hasn't had a chance to talk to you.

W It's still at 6 o'clock, right?

M Right. If you need a ride, call me the day before.

W Thank you.

해석

남   너 Susie의 생일 파티에 초대받았니?

여   물론이지. 7월 4일이지, 맞지?

남   아니, 그날이 국경일이잖아, 그래서 3일 후에 그녀의 집에서 하기로 했어.

여   왜 그녀가 나에게 말을 하지 않았지?

남   아마 너와 이야기를 할 기회가 없었겠지.

여   6시는 맞지, 그렇지?

남   맞아. 타고 갈 차편이 필요하면 하루 전에 전화해.

여   고마워.

해설

7월 4일의 3일 후이므로 7월 7일이다.

어휘
invite[inváit] ~을 초대하다 / national holiday 국경일 / hold[hould] 열다, 개최하다 / how come 왜 / ride[raid] 차편, 탈것 준비

17 ②

Script

W Are you here to <u>pick up your stuff</u>?

M No, I brought a dress shirt.

W Okay. Your name and phone number, please.

M John Hopkins. My phone number is 786-6131.

W Thank you.

M I have one thing to tell you. There is a stain on the left sleeve. Can you <u>get rid of</u> it?

W I guess I can do it easily <u>with no extra charge</u>. You can pick it up tomorrow.

해석

여 여기에 당신의 물건을 찾으러 오셨나요?

남 아니요, 셔츠 하나를 가져왔습니다.

여 알았습니다. 이름과 전화번호를 알려 주세요.

남 John Hopkins입니다. 제 전화번호는 786-6131입니다.

여 감사합니다.

남 한 가지 말할 게 있어요. 셔츠 왼쪽 소매에 얼룩이 있어요. 없앨 수 있나요?

여 제 생각에 추가 요금 없이 쉽게 제거할 수 있을 것 같습니다. 내일 가지러 오셔도 됩니다.

해설

남자는 옷을 맡기려고 세탁소에 갔다.

어휘
stuff[stʌf] 물건 / dress shirt 정장용 와이셔츠 / stain[stein] 얼룩 / sleeve[sliːv] 소매 / get rid of ~을 제거하다, 없애다 / pick up ~을 찾아가다

18 ④

Script

W I think I really studied hard, but my test result was terrible. I don't know <u>what's wrong with me</u>.

M How about talking to the school counselor? She will <u>give you some advice</u>.

W Where is her office?

M I'll show you, but you need to <u>make an appointment</u> first.

W Do you mean I have to call her?

M Yeah. Here's her phone number.

해석

여 나는 정말 열심히 공부했다고 생각하는데 결과가 좋지 않아. 무엇이 문제인지 모르겠어.

남 학교 상담 선생님과 이야기해 보는 게 어때? 선생님이 너에게 조언을 좀 해 주실 수 있을 거야.

여 선생님의 사무실이 어디야?

남 내가 알려 줄게. 하지만 예약을 먼저 해야 해.

여 선생님에게 전화해야 한다는 말이니?

남 응. 전화번호 여기 있어.

해설

여자는 상담교사를 찾아가기 전에 전화해서 약속을 잡을 것이다.

어휘
school counselor 상담교사 / advice[ədváis] 충고, 조언 / make an appointment 만날 약속을 정하다

19 ⑤

Script

M Hey, Judith. Let's <u>play a game</u>. I'll give you a quiz, and you give me an answer. OK?

W OK. I'll <u>play along</u>.

M The rule is very simple. Just repeat after me.

W OK.

M One yellow ball.

W One yellow ball.

M Two white balls.

W Two white balls.

M Three black balls.

W Three black balls.

M How many are there?

W How many are there?

M You're wrong. There are six balls.

W <u>You told me to repeat after you</u>.

해석

남 안녕, Judith. 우리 게임을 하자. 내가 너에게 문제를 낼게, 네가 대답을 하면 돼. 알았지?

여 알았어. 따라 할게.

남 규칙은 간단해. 그냥 나를 따라 하기만 하면 돼.

여 알았어.

남 노란 공 한 개

여 노란 공 한 개

남 하얀 공 두 개

여 하얀 공 두 개

남 검은 공 세 개

여 검은 공 세 개

남 (공이) 몇 개 있지?

여 (공이) 몇 개 있지?

남 틀렸어. 공은 여섯 개 있어.

여 <u>네가 너를 따라 하라고 했잖아.</u>

해설

남자의 틀렸다는 말에 "네가 너를 따라 하라고 했잖아."가 알맞은 응답이 된다.

① 농담이야.

② 여섯 개가 있어.

③ 너무 간단하고 쉽잖아.

④ 나는 답을 모르겠어.

어휘
play along ～와 협조하다 / rule[ru:l] 규칙 / repeat[ripíːt] ～을 반복하다

20 ③
Script

M How was your trip to Hawaii?

W It was raining every day, so we couldn't enjoy the beach.

M Sorry to hear that.

W It was nice for my father, though. He actually liked staying in the hotel.

M I see.

W The funny thing is that we spent rather a lot of money.

M How so?

W We went shopping almost every day.

해석

남 하와이 여행은 어땠어?

여 매일 비가 와서 해변에서 놀지 못했어.

남 안 됐다.

여 우리 아버지를 위해서는 좋았지만. 사실 아버지는 호텔에서 지내는 걸 좋아하셨어.

남 그렇구나.

여 재미있는 건 우리가 오히려 돈을 더 많이 썼다는 거야.

남 어떻게 그런 일이?

여 우리는 거의 매일 쇼핑을 했어.

해설

어떻게 해서 돈을 많이 썼느냐고 물었으므로 "우리는 거의 매일 쇼핑을 했어."라는 응답이 가장 적절하다.

① 우리는 텔레비전을 많이 봤어.

② 할 일이 아무것도 없었어.

④ 우리 어머니가 아버지에게 화가 나셨어.

⑤ 내가 말했듯이 우리는 호텔에 머물렀어.

어휘
though[ðou] 그래도 / actually[ǽktʃuəli] 사실 / rather[rǽðər] 오히려, 차라리

---

p.32~35

04회 영어듣기모의고사

01 ④	02 ③	03 ④	04 ②	05 ①
06 ⑤	07 ④	08 ②	09 ①	10 ①
11 ①	12 ②	13 ③	14 ③	15 ⑤
16 ②	17 ④	18 ③	19 ⑤	20 ①

---

01 ④
Script

W Is Mike going to visit us next Friday or this Friday?

M Next Friday. He told me if we buy him dinner, he'll take us to a baseball game.

W OK.

M So, which restaurant do you want to go?

W Let's go to a Korean restaurant.

M Sounds good. By the way, I'll mow the lawn this weekend. You are going to help me, right?

W Sure.

해석

여 Mike가 다음 금요일에 우리를 방문할 거예요, 아니면 이번 금요일에 우리를 방문할 거예요?

남 다음 금요일이요. 우리가 저녁을 사면 자기가 우리에게 야구 경기를 보여 주겠다고 했어요.

여 알았어요.

남 그럼, 어느 식당으로 가기를 원해요?

여 한식당에 가죠.

남 좋아요. 그런데 이번 주말에 잔디를 깎을 거예요. 당신이 나를 도와줄 거죠, 그렇죠?

여 물론이죠.

해설
두 사람은 이번 주말에 잔디를 깎을 것이다.

어휘
mow[mou] ～을 베다 / lawn[lɔːn] 잔디

02 ③
Script

M My name is Nick Campbell. I'm here to see Mr. Henderson.

W Do you have an appointment?

M Yes. At 10 o'clock.

W Okay. We have two Hendersons in our office.

M I mean James Henderson.

W It is hard to believe, but their first names are the same.

M He has a mustache, and he is bald.

W Okay. I'll contact him right away.

해석

남 저는 Nick Campbell입니다. Henderson 씨를 만나러 왔습니다.

여 약속을 하셨나요?

남 네. 10시예요.

여 알았습니다. 저희 사무실에는 Henderson 씨가 두 명입니다.

남 저는 James Henderson을 말하는 겁니다.

여 믿기 어려우시겠지만, 이름도 같습니다.

남 그는 콧수염이 있고 대머리입니다.

여 알았습니다. 바로 연락하겠습니다.

남자가 찾는 사람은 콧수염이 있고 대머리인 사람이다.

어휘
have an appointment 약속이 있다 / mustache[mʌ́stæʃ] 콧수염 /
bald[bɔːld] 대머리의 / contact[kɑ́ntækt] 연락을 취하다

03 ④

Script

W Two tickets, please.

M Which seat?

W Row A.

M That'll be 20 dollars each.

W That's too expensive. How about row B?

M That'll be 10 dollars each.

W Let me see. OK. I'll take those.

M All right. Is the boy your son? If he is over 5, he has to pay half price.

W I guess I have no choice. Tickets for two adults and one child in row B.

해석

여 표 두 장 주세요.

남 어느 좌석이요?

여 A열이요.

남 한 장에 20달러입니다.

여 너무 비싸네요. B열은 요?

남 한 장에 10달러입니다.

여 어디 볼까요. 알았어요. 그 자리로 할게요.

남 알았습니다. 저 남자아이가 아들인가요? 다섯 살이 넘었으면 반값을 내셔야 합니다.

여 선택의 여지가 없겠군요. B열로 어른 둘에 아이 한 명이요.

해설
어른 둘이 20달러, 아이는 5달러이므로 여자가 지불해야 할 금액은 25달러이다.

어휘
row[rou] 열 / pay[pei] 지급하다, 내다 / adult[ədʌ́lt] 성인, 어른

04 ②

Script

W Are you going to see off Mr. Kim?

M Yes. If you are too, we can go together.

W What time is his flight?

M His departure time is 6 P.M.

W I see. What time should we meet?

M I think we should be there at 5, and it takes one hour to get to the airport. So, I'll pick you up 30 minutes earlier. Is that OK?

W Yeah. I'll see you soon.

해석

여 너 김 선생님을 배웅하러 갈 거니?

남 응. 너도 갈 거면, 같이 가자.

여 몇 시 비행기야?

남 출발 시각이 6시야.

여 그렇구나. 몇 시에 만나야 하지?

남 거기에 다섯 시까지 도착해야 하고, 공항까지 가는 데는 한 시간 걸릴 거야. 그러니까 30분 일찍 데리러 갈게. 괜찮겠어?

여 응. 곧 보자.

해설
5시에 공항에 도착하려면 4시에 출발해야 하지만, 30분 일찍 데리러 온다고 했으므로 남자와 여자는 3시 30분에 만날 것이다.

어휘
see off 배웅하다 / flight[flait] 비행 / departure[dipɑ́ːrtʃər] 출발 /
get to ~에 도착하다 / pick up ~을 태워 주다

05 ①

Script

[Telephone rings.]

M Hey! Kelly. It's Jason. I got some tickets for a great concert.

W I'm sorry, but I'm kind of busy these days.

M That's not the reason I'm calling you. I want to get rid of them. I'll let them go for half the price.

W Okay. I'll check around, but I think it's going to be hard.

M Just ask around for me, okay?

해석

남 안녕! Kelly. 나야 Jason. 나 좋은 콘서트 표가 생겼어.

여 미안하지만, 나 요즈음 좀 바빠.

남 내가 전화를 한 이유는 그게 아니야. 표를 좀 팔고 싶어서. 반값에 팔 거야.

여 알았어. 내가 좀 알아볼게. 하지만, 내 생각엔 좀 어려울 것 같아.

남 그냥 나를 위해서 좀 알아봐 줘. 알았지?

해설
남자는 콘서트 표를 반값에 팔려고 전화를 했다.

어휘
get rid of ~을 없애다, 제거하다 / ask around 물어보며 다니다

06 ⑤

Script

M Where to?

W Seoul Plaza, please.

M OK.

W Excuse me, I'm a pretty forgetful person, so on the way I might forget where I'm going. So, please remind me if I ask, OK?

M Sure. Don't worry.

W Oh, no. Excuse me, where am I going?

M Hey! Where did you come from?

해석

남 어디로 모실까요?

여 서울 광장이요.

남 알았습니다.

여 실례합니다만, 제가 건망증이 매우 심해서 가는 동안 제가 어디로 가고 있는지 잊어버릴 수도 있거든요. 그래서 제가 물어보면 좀 상기시켜 주세요, 알았죠?

남 그러죠. 걱정하지 마세요.

여 오, 이런. 실례합니다만, 제가 어디를 가는 중이죠?

남 이봐요! 당신 어디에서 왔어요?

해설

여자가 건망증이 심해서 어디로 가고 있는지를 잘 잊어버리는데, 운전사는 건망증이 더 심해서 손님이 타는 것도 잊어버렸기 때문에 여자는 황당했을 것이다.

어휘

forgetful[fərgétfəl] 잘 잊어버리는 / on the way 도중에 / remind[rimáind] ~을 상기시키다

07 ④

Script

W May I help you?

M Yes. I'd like to open an account.

W Okay. Is this the first time with us?

M Yes, it is.

W Okay. Please fill out this form. Can I ask you how much you will deposit?

M 500 dollars. I'm done with the form.

W Thank you. I'll process an ATM card now.

M Thank you.

해석

여 도와드릴까요?

남 네. 저는 계좌를 개설하고 싶습니다.

여 알았습니다. 저희와는 처음이신가요?

남 네, 그렇습니다.

여 알았습니다. 이 양식을 작성해 주세요. 얼마를 입금하실 것인지 여쭤 봐도 될까요?

남 5백 달러요. 다 작성했습니다.

여 감사합니다. 이제 현금인출 카드를 처리하겠습니다.

남 감사합니다.

해설

은행에서 계좌를 개설해 주고, 입금을 도와주는 사람은 금전출납계원이다.

어휘

open an account 계좌를 개설하다 / fill out (양식을) 작성하다 / deposit[dipázit] (돈은) 맡기다, 예금하다 / ATM 현금자동입출금기(Automated Teller Machine)

08 ②

Script

W Do you know Alex Smith?

M Sure, I do. He lives next door. Why?

W He's my classmate. He got a perfect score on the final, and he is the top in our school.

M I didn't know that. He doesn't talk about himself much, and he is a good listener.

W And you know what? His ideas and ways of thinking are very creative. His science project got first prize last semester. We were all amazed.

M Wow! What an intelligent boy he is! He never brags about himself.

해석

여 너 Alex Smith를 아니?

남 물론, 알지. 그는 우리 옆집에 살아. 왜?

여 그 아이가 우리 반이거든. 기말고사에서 만점을 받아서 학교에서 일등을 했어.

남 몰랐어. 자신에 대해 별로 많이 이야기하지 않아서. 그리고 그 아이는 남의 말을 잘 들어주는 사람이야.

여 게다가, 내 이야기 좀 들어봐. 그 아이는 의견과 사고방식이 매우 창의적이야. 지난 학기에 그의 과학 과제물이 일등을 했어. 우리 모두 놀랐어.

남 왜! 그는 정말 똑똑하구나! 절대로 자신에 대해 자랑하지도 않고.

해설

말수가 적고, 조용한 사람이 생각이 깊거나 똑똑하다는 의미이므로 "잔잔한 물이 깊다."라는 속담이 정답이다.

① 사공이 많으면 배가 산으로 간다.

③ 무소식이 희소식이다.

④ 엎질러진 물이다.

⑤ 백지장도 맞들면 낫다.

어휘

next door 옆집(에) / listener[lísnər] 듣는 사람, 청취자 / creative[kriéitiv] 창의적인 / semester[siméstər] 학기 / amazed[əméizd] 놀란 / intelligent[intélədʒənt] 총명한, 지적인 / brag about ~에 대해 자랑하다

09 ①

Script

M I'm something bad. I'm not good for one's health. People in America even call me a cancer stick, but some people still like me. These days, a lot of women and teenagers try me, so I'd like to warn you that once you start me, it is almost impossible to stop. I have another warning for sellers of me. Please remember that it is illegal to sell me to teenagers.

해석

남 나는 나쁜 것입니다. 나는 건강에 좋지 않습니다. 미국에서는 많은 사람은 나를 암자라고 부르지만, 어떤 사람들은 그래도 나를 좋아합니다. 요즘에는 많은 여성과 십대들이 나를 피우고 있습니다. 그래서 일단 당신이 나를 시작하면 나를 끊는 것은 거의 불가능하다고 당신에게 경고하고 싶습니다. 나는 나를 판매하는 사람들에게 해 줄 또 다른 경고가 있습니다. 십대에게 나를 파는 것은 불법이라는 것을 기억하십시오.

암과자라고 불리며, 한 번 피우기 시작하면 끊기 어려운 것은 담배이다.

어휘
cancer[kǽnsər] 암 / stick[stik] 막대기 / warn[wɔːrn] ~에게 경고하다 /
once[wʌns] 일단 ~하면 / impossible[impásəbəl] 불가능한 /
illegal[ilíːgəl] 불법의

10 ①
Script

W Excuse me, Mr. Can you tell me <u>how</u> <u>to</u> <u>get</u> <u>to</u> the National Bank?

M Sure. It's a little far from here, but it's <u>within</u> <u>a</u> <u>walking</u> <u>distance</u>.

W Okay.

M Go straight for two blocks and make a left at the corner.

W Okay, and then?

M Then, go one more block and turn right at the corner. You'll see it on your left.

W That's pretty complicated. I think I should <u>write</u> <u>it</u> <u>down</u>.

해석
여 실례합니다만, 선생님. 국립은행에 가는 길을 알려 주실 수 있나요?
남 그러죠. 여기에서 약간 멀지만 걸어갈 수 있는 거리예요.
여 그렇군요.
남 두 블록을 곧장 가서 모퉁이에서 왼쪽으로 도세요.
여 알았어요, 그리고요?
남 그리고 나서 한 블록을 더 가서서 모퉁이에서 오른쪽으로 도세요. 당신의 왼쪽에 있을 거예요.
여 꽤 복잡하네요. 적어야겠어요.

해설
두 블록을 곧장 가서 왼쪽으로 돈 후, 한 블록을 더 가서 오른쪽으로 돌아서 왼쪽에 있는 것이다.

어휘
distance[dístəns] 거리 / pretty[príti] 꽤 /
complicated[kámpləkèitid] 복잡한

11 ①
Script

① **M** May I see your driver's license?
　 W What did I do wrong?
② **M** Your car is ready <u>to</u> <u>be</u> <u>picked</u> <u>up</u>.
　 W Thank you.
③ **M** I really like your car.
　 W Thanks. I bought it <u>for</u> <u>my</u> <u>children</u>.
④ **M** Excuse me, something is burning.
　 W Oh my God! I forgot to <u>turn</u> <u>off</u> <u>the</u> <u>stove</u>.
⑤ **M** What a terrific driver you are!
　 W Thank you! I learned <u>how</u> <u>to</u> <u>drive</u> from my father.

해석
① 남 운전 면허증을 좀 보여 주시겠습니까?
　 여 제가 무엇을 잘못했죠?
② 남 당신의 차는 가져갈 준비가 되어 있습니다.
　 여 감사합니다.
③ 남 나는 당신의 차가 정말 마음에 듭니다.
　 여 감사합니다. 아이들을 위해서 샀어요.
④ 남 실례합니다. 무엇인가 타고 있는데요.
　 여 맙소사! 가스불을 끄는 것을 깜빡했어요.
⑤ 남 너는 정말 훌륭한 운전자이구나!
　 여 감사합니다! 나는 아버지에게 운전하는 것을 배웠어요.

해설
경찰이 운전자에게 운전 면허증을 보여 달라고 하는 상황이다.

어휘
driver's license 운전 면허증 / pick up 줍다, 집어 올리다 /
burn[bəːrn] 타다 / turn off ~을 끄다 / stove[stouv] 스토브, 난로 /
terrific[tərífik] 훌륭한, 아주 멋진

12 ②
Script

M What can I do for you?

W How many books can I <u>check</u> <u>out</u>?

M You can check out <u>as</u> <u>many</u> <u>as</u> 10 items. But make sure you return them by the due date. Otherwise, you have to <u>pay</u> <u>a</u> <u>late</u> <u>charge</u>.

W I understand. Can I check out weekly magazines, too?

M I'm afraid you can't.

W I got it. Thank you.

해석
남 무엇을 도와드릴까요?
여 제가 책을 몇 권이나 대출할 수 있죠?
남 10권까지 대출할 수 있습니다. 하지만, 반납일까지는 책을 꼭 반납하셔야 해요. 그렇지 않으면 연체료를 내셔야 해요.
여 알았습니다. 주간 잡지도 대출할 수 있나요?
남 죄송하지만 안 됩니다.
여 알았어요. 감사합니다.

해설
책을 빌리려는 학생과 사서교사의 대화이다.

어휘
check out (책을) 대출하다 / due date 반납일 / otherwise[ʌ́ðərwàiz]
그렇지 않으면 / late charge 연체료 / weekly[wíːkli] 주간의, 매주의

13 ③
Script

W Hey, Eric. When do we fly?

M We still got 45 minutes.

W Then, let me go to the restroom. I need to <u>wash</u> <u>my</u> <u>hands</u>.

M Sure. But don't you think you go to the restroom too often? You've been to it five times already since we came to the airport.

W I know, but my stomach is upset. It is my first time to travel by air.

M Is it? It'll be okay. Try to take a deep breath and calm down.

해석

여 안녕, Eric. 우리 언제 비행기를 타니?

남 아직도 45분이나 남았어.

여 그러면, 나 화장실에 갔다 올게. 손을 좀 닦아야겠어.

남 그래. 근데, 너 화장실을 너무 자주 가는 것 같다고 생각하지 않니? 우리가 공항에 온 이후로 벌써 화장실에 다섯 번이나 갔다 왔잖아.

여 알지만, 속이 불편해서. 처음 비행기를 타는 거란 말이야.

남 그래? 괜찮을 거야. 심호흡을 하고, 진정하려고 노력해 봐.

해설

여자는 처음으로 비행기를 타게 되어 긴장하고 있다.

어휘

restroom[réstrùːm] 화장실 / stomach[stʌ́mək] 위, 배 / upset[ʌpsét] 불편한 / take a deep breath 심호흡을 하다 / calm down 진정하다

14 ③

Script

W Excuse me, do you have any vacancies?

M Yes, we do.

W That's great. I need one double bed for my parents and a single for me.

M OK.

W What's the rate for one night?

M 60 and 40 plus tax.

W That's pretty reasonable. I'd like to stay for 5 days.

M I see. How would you like to pay for it?

W Cash.

해석

여 실례합니다. 빈방이 있나요?

남 네, 있습니다.

여 잘 됐군요. 저의 부모님에게는 더블 침대가 있는 방 하나, 그리고 저에게는 싱글 침대가 있는 방 하나가 필요합니다.

남 알았습니다.

여 하룻밤에 얼마죠?

남 60달러와 40달러, 그리고 세금을 내셔야 합니다.

여 가격은 괜찮군요. 닷새 동안 머무르고 싶어요.

남 알았습니다. 지불은 어떻게 하시겠어요?

여 현금으로요.

해설

여자는 가격이 비싸다고 생각하는 것이 아니라 적당하다고 생각한다.

어휘

vacancy[véikənsi] 빈방 / rate[reit] 요금 /

reasonable[ríːzənəbəl] 비싸지 않은, 적당한

15 ⑤

Script

① **M** How would you like to get the money?

   W Please give it to me in twenty-dollar bills.

② **M** Excuse me, I'd like to check in.

   W Can I have your passport, please?

③ **M** Fill it up, please.

   W Absolutely.

④ **M** What are you majoring in?

   W Biology.

⑤ **M** Does Chris look like his grandfather?

   W Yes, he really likes his grandfather.

해석

① 남 돈을 어떻게 바꾸어 드릴까요?

   여 20달러짜리 지폐로 주세요.

② 남 실례합니다. 탑승 수속을 하고 싶습니다.

   여 여권을 좀 주시겠어요?

③ 남 가득 채워 주세요.

   여 물론이죠.

④ 남 전공이 무엇입니까?

   여 생물학이요.

⑤ 남 Chris는 자기 할아버지를 닮았나요?

   여 네, 그는 할아버지를 정말 좋아해요.

해설

⑤ 할아버지를 닮았느냐고 물어봤는데 할아버지를 좋아한다고 대답하는 것은 어색하다.

어휘

check in 탑승 수속을 하다, 숙박 수속을 하다 / fill up ~을 채우다 / absolutely[ǽbsəlùːtli] 정말로, 무조건으로 / major in ~을 전공하다 / biology[baiálədʒi] 생물학 / look like ~을 닮다

16 ②

Script

W My friend, Charles, who goes to the same school as I do, is too shy. He never says what he needs or wants. So, people around him think he is a little dumb, but it's not true. He's just too shy and cares too much about others' opinion. He's nice and friendly to everyone.

해석

여 내 친구 Charles는 나와 같은 학교에 다니는데 수줍음을 매우 많이 탄다. 그는 절대로 자신이 필요하거나 원하는 것을 말하지 않는다. 그래서 그의 주위 사람들은 그가 약간 멍청하다고 생각하지만, 그것은 사실이 아니다. 그는 단지 너무 수줍음을 많이 타고, 다른 사람의 의견에 신경을 지나치게 많이 쓰는 것이다. 그는 모든 사람에게 잘해 주고 친절하다.

해설

수줍음을 많이 타는 친구에게 "자신감 가져"라고 충고하는 것이 가장 적절하다.

23

① 진정해!

③ 행복하게 지내.

④ 너무 이기적으로 굴지 마!

⑤ 실망하지 마!

어휘

shy[ʃai] 수줍은, 부끄럼 타는 / dumb[dʌm] 바보 / care about ~에 대해 신경 쓰다, 걱정하다 / opinion[əpínjən] 의견 / friendly[fréndli] 친절한

17 ④

Script

W Excuse me.

M Hi, are you a member?

W No, I'm not.

M Then, take this card. One hour is 2,000 won.

W Okay. Where should I sit?

M You can sit anywhere you want.

W I see. Which section is non-smoking?

M On your left.

W Okay. I'm sorry, but I'm not familiar with this.

M Okay. Please type the card number on the screen, and then you are ready to go.

W Thank you.

해석

여 실례합니다.

남 안녕하세요. 회원이신가요?

여 아니요.

남 그러면 이 카드를 받으세요. 한 시간에 2천 원입니다.

여 알았습니다. 어디에 앉죠?

남 앉고 싶은 곳 어디든 앉으세요.

여 그렇군요. 어느 쪽이 금연 구역인가요?

남 손님의 왼쪽이요.

여 알았습니다. 미안하지만 제가 이곳이 익숙하지가 않아서요.

남 알았습니다. 이 카드 번호를 화면에 치세요. 그러면 사용할 준비가 된 것입니다.

여 감사합니다.

해설

시간 단위로 돈을 주고 컴퓨터를 사용할 수 있는 곳은 인터넷 카페이다.

어휘

anywhere[énihwὲər] 어디든지 / section[sékʃən] 부분, 잘라낸 부분 / non-smoking 금연 / type[taip] 자판을 치다, 타자기를 치다

18 ③

Script

M These days, lots of teenagers are becoming overweight. That might be because they eat too much fast food, or they get little exercise and watch TV too much. They also spend most of their free time playing computer games. Among them, the main problem is that they don't want to exercise. They even take a taxi or a bus when going a short distance.

해석

남 요즈음, 많은 십대들이 과체중이 되어 가고 있다. 그것은 그들이 패스트 푸드를 너무 많이 먹거나, 운동을 거의 하지 않고 텔레비전을 너무 많이 보기 때문일지도 모른다. 그들은 또한 한가한 시간의 대부분을 컴퓨터 게임을 하면서 보낸다. 그것 중에서 가장 큰 문제는 십대들이 운동을 하고 싶어하지 않는다는 것이다. 그들은 심지어 가까운 거리를 가는 데 버스나 택시를 탄다.

해설

과도한 패스트 푸드의 섭취, 부족한 운동, 지나친 텔레비전 시청, 지나친 컴퓨터 게임이 과체중의 원인으로 언급되었다.

어휘

overweight[óuvərwèit] 과체중의, 너무 살찐 / free time 여가, 한가한 시간 / distance[dístəns] 거리

19 ⑤

Script

W I heard that Mary is pretty mad at you.

M I know. I think I made her upset.

W What did you do to her?

M I asked her about her weight.

W That's terrible. You shouldn't have asked that kind of question.

M I know. I was just trying to help her find a way to lose weight.

W I understand your reasoning, but it was impolite.

해석

여 Mary가 너에게 화가 많이 나 있다고 들었어.

남 알아. 내가 그녀를 화나게 한 것 같아.

여 그녀에게 어떻게 했는데?

남 그녀에게 몸무게를 물어봤어.

여 저런. 그런 질문은 하지 말았어야지.

남 알아. 나는 단지 그녀가 살을 빼는 방법을 찾도록 도와주려고 한 거야.

여 왜 그랬는지 이해는 하지만, 그건 무례한 행동이었어.

해설

도와주려고 했던 것뿐이라고 말했으므로 "왜 그랬는지 이해는 하지만, 그건 무례한 행동이었어."라는 대답이 가장 적절하다.

① 감사합니다.

② 그녀는 너를 정말 보고 싶어해.

③ 네가 그렇게 느꼈다니 유감이야.

④ 걱정하지 마. 살은 빠질 거야.

어휘

be mad at ~에게 화가 나다 / upset[ʌpsét] 화난, 혼란한 / lose weight 살을 빼다, 몸무게가 줄다 / impolite[ìmpəláit] 무례한

20 ①

Script

M	Is everyone here?
W	Except Janet.
M	What happened to her?
W	Nobody knows.
M	Can you call her cell phone?
W	I already did, but her phone is turned off.
M	That's strange.
W	I think she's not interested in our club.
M	What makes you think that?
W	She's always late and often doesn't show up.

해석

남	모두 다 왔니?
여	Janet만 빼고
남	Janet에게 무슨 일이 있는 거야?
여	아무도 몰라.
남	그녀에게 휴대 전화로 전화를 좀 해 볼래?
여	벌써 해 봤는데 전화기가 꺼져 있어.
남	이상하다.
여	내 생각에 Janet은 우리 클럽에 흥미가 없는 것 같아.
남	왜 그렇게 생각하는데?
여	항상 늦고, 종종 오지 않잖아.

해설

Janet이 클럽에 흥미가 없다고 느끼는 것 같다고 생각한 이유를 물었으므로 "항상 늦고, 종종 오지 않잖아."라는 대답이 적절하다.
② 그녀는 클럽 회장이 되고 싶어해.
③ 내 생각에 그녀는 너무 자주 오는 것 같아.
④ 알았어. 내가 지금 당장 그녀에게 전화해 볼게.
⑤ 재미있기 때문이야.

어휘

except[iksépt] ~을 제외하고 / turn off ~을 끄다 / show up ~에 나타나다

---

p.40~43

05회 영어듣기모의고사

01 ③	02 ③	03 ⑤	04 ④	05 ①
06 ②	07 ①	08 ④	09 ③	10 ④
11 ②	12 ③	13 ④	14 ①	15 ⑤
16 ③	17 ⑤	18 ③	19 ①	20 ③

01 ③

Script

W Everybody, stand up. Put your feet apart and place your arms at your sides. Next lift your arms up straight. Okay, that's it. Now put your fingers together with your

palms up and push your arms up as far as possible. Hold this position for a second.

해석

여 모두, 일어서세요. 두 발을 벌리고 팔은 옆에 놓으세요. 다음에는 팔을 위로 곧게 올리세요. 됐어요. 그거예요. 이제 손바닥이 위로 가도록 해서 손가락을 모으고 가능한 한 멀리 밀어올리세요. 잠깐 그 자세를 유지하세요.

해설

발을 살짝 벌리고 팔을 양옆으로 내린 자세, 팔을 위로 곧게 들어 올린 자세, 깍지를 낀 손을 위로 향하게 하게 최대한 위로 뻗어 올린 자세의 순서이다.

어휘

apart[əpá:rt] 떨어져 / straight[streit] 똑바로 / palm[pɑ:m] 손바닥 / as ~ as possible 가능한 한 ~하게 / hold[hould] ~을 유지하다

02 ③

Script

W	I think Jason is much taller than last year.
M	I know. He was shorter than me last year, but he is far taller than me now.
W	But Kevin is taller than him, right?
M	I think so. I guess Kevin is a little over 180cm.
W	How about Mark, then?
M	In fact, I've never seen a boy taller than him.
W	Then, what about Henry?
M	He's as tall as me.

해석

여	Jason은 지난해보다 키가 훨씬 큰 것 같아.
남	그러게. 작년에는 나보다 작았는데 지금은 나보다 훨씬 커.
여	하지만 Kevin이 Jason보다 크지, 그렇지?
남	그런 것 같아. 내 생각에 Kevin은 180cm가 약간 넘을 걸.
여	그러면 Mark는 어때?
남	사실, 나는 그 아이보다 더 큰 아이는 본 적이 없어.
여	그러면 Henry는?
남	그는 나 정도야.

해설

Mark보다 큰 아이를 본 적이 없다고 했으므로 반에서 가장 큰 사람은 Mark이다.

어휘

much[mʌtʃ] (비교급을 수식하여) 훨씬 / far[fɑ:r] (비교급을 수식하여) 훨씬

03 ⑤

Script

M	What's your favorite sport, Susie?
W	Basketball. Do you like basketball, Andrew?
M	Yes, I do. But I like baseball better. I think baseball is more fun to play. What do you think?
W	Well, it is a little difficult for girls to play baseball,

and most girls really don't know how to play. It is so complicated.

M　That's true. Let me explain it to you, Susie.

W　Will you?

M　Sure, I've got plenty of time now.

W　Thanks a lot.

해석

남　Susie야, 너는 무슨 스포츠를 제일 좋아하니?

여　농구. Andrew, 너는 농구를 좋아하니?

남　응, 좋아해. 하지만 나는 야구가 더 좋아. 야구 경기를 하는 것이 더 재미있는 것 같아. 너는 어떻게 생각하니?

여　글쎄, 여자아이들이 야구를 하기는 좀 어려워. 그리고 여자아이들 대부분은 어떻게 해야 하는지도 잘 몰라. 너무 복잡해.

남　맞아. 내가 너에게 설명해 줄게, Susie야.

여　그럴래?

남　물론. 나 지금 시간 많아.

여　정말 고마워.

해설

남자는 여자에게 야구 경기 규칙을 설명해 줄 것이다.

어휘

favorite[féivərit] 가장 좋아하는 / complicated[kάmpləkèitid] 복잡한 / explain[ikspléin] 설명하다 / plenty of 많은

04 ④

Script

M　Have you met Shelly lately?

W　No, I haven't. Is she here?

M　Yes, she came here last night and is staying at her uncle's house.

W　That's surprising news.

M　I know no one would've expected her to come back here so early.

W　That's right. How is she, anyway?

M　She looks very healthy and even more beautiful.

W　I'm looking forward to seeing her soon.

해석

남　너 최근에 Shelly를 만난 적이 있니?

여　아니. 그녀가 여기 있니?

남　응, 그녀는 지난밤에 여기에 와서, 자신의 삼촌 집에 머물고 있어.

여　반가운 소식이네.

남　아무도 그녀가 그렇게 일찍 돌아오리라고는 생각하지 못했을 거야.

여　맞아. 그런데 그녀는 어때?

남　그녀는 매우 건강해 보이고 심지어 더 예뻐졌어.

여　빨리 그녀를 만나보고 싶다.

해설

"빨리 그녀를 만나보고 싶다"라는 말은 기대를 나타낸다.

어휘

lately[léitli] 최근에 / stay[stei] 머무르다. 지내다 / surprising[sərpráiziŋ] 놀라운 / expect[ikspékt] ~을 예상하다, 기대하다 / look forward to+명사 ~을 기대하다

05 ①

Script

W　Hey, Michael. Do you know there will be an election?

M　I know. It's going to be held on May 14th.

W　Can you tell me who you're voting for?

M　I can't tell you. You know that.

W　Come on! It's just between you and me.

M　Still, I can't tell you.

W　Oh, come on.

M　OK. I'll vote for you. Are you satisfied now?

W　I knew you would.

해석

여　이봐, Michael. 너 선거가 있는 거 알고 있니?

남　알아. 5월 14일에 하잖아.

여　누구를 뽑을 건지 말해 줄래?

남　말할 수 없어. 알잖아.

여　그러지 말고! 너와 나 사이잖아.

남　그래도 말할 수 없어.

여　아, 제발.

남　알았어. 나는 너를 뽑을 거야. 이제 만족하니?

여　나는 네가 그럴 줄 알았어.

해설

여자는 남자가 자신을 뽑아 준다고 했으므로 기쁠 것이다.

어휘

election[ilékʃən] 선거 / hold[hould] ~을 열다, 개최하다 / vote for ~에게 투표하다 / satisfy[sǽtisfài] 만족하게 하다

06 ②

Script

W　Mike, have you heard of James Powell?

M　No. Who's that?

W　He's a famous athlete from Jamaica.

M　What else do you know about him?

W　He has a world record in the 100 and 200 meters.

M　I see.

W　Don't you ever watch any sports games?

M　No, I don't. I'm not interested in any sports activities.

W　You are so different from your brother.

M　I know he is a real sports buff.

해석

여　Mike, James Powell에 대해서 들어 본 적 있니?

남　아니. 그게 누군데?

여　그는 자메이카 출신의 유명한 운동선수야.

남　그밖에 그에 대해 무엇을 알고 있어?

여　그는 100미터와 200미터에서 세계 신기록을 가지고 있어.

남　그렇구나.

여　너는 스포츠 경기는 전혀 보지 않니?

남　아니 안 봐. 나는 스포츠에는 전혀 관심이 없어.

여　너는 너의 형과 정말 다르구나.

남　알아. 그는 정말 운동광이야.

해설
육상 대회가 열릴 것이라는 말은 언급되지 않았다.

어휘
athlete[在θli:t] 운동 선수 / Jamaica[dʒəméikə] 자메이카 / world record 세계 신기록 / buff[bʌf] 광, 팬

07　①

Script

① W　Bless you. Did you catch a cold?

　　M　I'm not sure, but I feel a little bit cold.

② W　Did you bring any pills for a headache?

　　M　Yes, I did. Do you want some?

③ W　How long have you had it?

　　M　I've had it for a few days.

④ W　You must be healthy enough to do that.

　　M　How did you know?

⑤ W　What am I supposed to do?

　　M　You should stay away from her.

해석

① 여　(재채기를 한 사람에게) 몸조심하세요. 감기에 걸리셨어요?

　　남　잘 모르겠는데 약간 추워요.

② 여　두통약을 가져오셨습니까?

　　남　네, 좀 드릴까요?

③ 여　그것을 얼마 동안이나 가지고 있었어요?

　　남　며칠 되었습니다.

④ 여　그것을 하실 만큼 건강하신 것이 분명하군요.

　　남　어떻게 아셨죠?

⑤ 여　제가 어떻게 해야 합니까?

　　남　그녀를 멀리하세요.

해설
남자가 재채기를 해서 여자가 남자가 감기에 걸렸을까 봐 걱정을 하는 상황이다.

어휘
catch a cold 감기에 걸리다 / pill[pil] 알약 / be supposed to ~하기로 되어 있다 / stay away from ~에서 떨어져 있다, ~을 가까이 하지 않다

08　④

Script

W　Today is Christmas. Cindy bought some presents for her family. She had 50 dollars in total. She bought a ten-dollar necktie for her father and a ten-dollar scarf

for her mother. She also bought two five-dollar hairpins for her twin sisters. Lastly, she paid 5 dollars for her brother's pen. How much money does she have left?

해석

여　오늘은 크리스마스이다. Cindy는 가족을 위해 선물을 샀다. 그녀는 총 50달러를 가지고 있었다. 그녀는 아버지를 위해 10달러짜리 넥타이를, 어머니를 위해 10달러짜리 스카프를 샀다. 그녀는 또한 쌍둥이 여동생들을 위해 5달러짜리 머리핀 두 개를 샀다. 마지막으로 그녀는 오빠의 펜을 사는 데 5달러를 지불했다. 그녀에게 얼마의 돈이 남았습니까?

해설
Cindy는 총 50달러가 있었는데 아버지를 위해 10달러, 어머니를 위해 10달러, 쌍둥이 여동생들을 위해 10달러, 오빠를 위해 5달러를 썼으므로 총 35달러를 지출하였다. 남은 돈은 15달러이다.

어휘
in total 전체로, 통틀어 / lastly[læstli] 마지막으로

09　③

Script

[Telephone rings.]

W　Hello, New York Metro. May I help you?

M　Hi, my name is Mike Jackson. As you know, there will be a festival on Martin Street next week. I believe that the last train will be at 12:30 A.M., but there will still be a lot of people hanging around the festival. So, do you have any plans for them?

W　We sure do. There will be trains running until 1:30.

M　That's great. I really appreciate that.

W　You're welcome. Is there anything else I can help you with?

M　No, that's all.

해석

여　여보세요, 뉴욕 전철입니다. 도와드릴까요?

남　안녕하세요, 제 이름은 Mike Jackson입니다. 당신도 알다시피, 다음 주에 마틴 가에서 축제가 있을 겁니다. 제가 알기로 마지막 기차가 새벽 12시 30분인데 여전히 많은 사람이 축제를 즐기고 있을 거예요. 그래서 그들에 대한 대책이 있나요?

여　물론 있습니다. 1시 30분까지 기차를 운행할 것입니다.

남　잘됐군요. 정말로 감사합니다.

여　천만에요. 그밖에 다른 도와드릴 것이 있나요?

남　아닙니다.

해설
남자는 축제기간에 기차가 연장 운행을 하는지 묻기 위해 전화를 했다.

어휘
hang around 어슬렁거리며 돌아다니다 / run[rʌn] 운행하다 / appreciate[əprí:ʃièit] ~을 고마워하다

10　④

Script

W　Hey, John. Can you come over here? I got locked out

<u>of</u> the house.

M How did that happen?

W I heard someone <u>knocking on the door</u>, so I came out, but no one was there.

M I see. I need to get some tools to open the door.

W Go ahead. I'll stay here. Thanks. How much is it?

M I usually charge 5 dollars <u>for my service</u>. Isn't this the third time already?

W That's right. My carelessness is making you rich.

해석

여 안녕하세요, John. 이리로 좀 와 줄래요? 집의 문이 안에서 잠겼어요.

남 어쩌다 그랬어요?

여 누군가 문을 두드리는 소리가 들려서 나와 봤는데, 아무도 없었어요.

남 그렇군요. 당신을 들여보내 주려면 연장이 좀 필요해요.

여 그러세요. 저는 여기 있을게요. 고마워요. 얼마지요?

남 저는 대개 제 서비스에 대해 5달러를 받아요. 이것이 벌써 세 번째이지요?

여 맞아요. 제 부주의함이 당신을 부자로 만드는군요.

해설

남자는 문을 열어주는 열쇠 수리공이다.

어휘

come over 건너오다 / lock out 열쇠를 두고 나와 들어가지 못하게 되다 / knock[nɑk] 두드리다 / tool[tuːl] 연장, 도구 / charge[tʃɑːrdʒ] 부과하다 / carelessness[kɛ́ərlisnis] 부주의(함)

11 ②

Script

W Justin, I can't tell you <u>how sorry I am</u>.

M Why? What's wrong?

W Do you remember the textbook <u>I borrowed from you</u> last week? Well, I have to buy you another one.

M Really? What happened?

W My brother spilt milk <u>all over the book</u>. It wasn't my fault though.

M Oh, no. I wrote all my important notes from my class on it.

W I'm terribly sorry.

해석

여 Justin, 뭐라고 미안하다고 말을 해야 될지 모르겠어.

남 왜? 무슨 일이야?

여 내가 지난주에 내가 빌려 간 교과서를 기억하니? 음, 너에게 다른 것을 사주어야 해.

남 정말? 무슨 일인데?

여 내 남동생이 책에 우유를 엎질렀어. 하지만 내 잘못은 아니었어.

남 아, 저런. 수업시간에 중요한 것들을 적어 놓았는데.

여 정말 미안해.

해설

여자는 자신의 동생이 남자의 교과서에 우유를 쏟아 교과서를 못 쓰게 만들어서 미안해하고 있다.

어휘

borrow[bɔ́(ː)rou] 빌리다 / spill[spil] 엎지르다 / fault[fɔːlt] 잘못, 과실 / terribly[térəbli] 매우, 아주

12 ③

Script

M This is a very simple question, and I believe everyone can <u>give me a correct answer</u>. Listen carefully. There are 28 days in February. Kevin's mother works every tenth day in February. Her first day of work in February is on the first of February. <u>How many days will she work</u> in February?

해석

남 이것은 매우 간단한 문제이고, 저는 여러분 모두가 정확하게 대답할 수 있을 거라고 믿습니다. 주의 깊게 들어보세요. 2월에는 28일이 있습니다. Kevin의 어머니는 2월에는 열흘에 한 번씩 일을 하십니다. 2월에 그녀가 처음으로 일을 한 날은 2월 1일입니다. 그녀는 2월에 며칠 일을 하겠습니까?

해설

Kevin의 어머니는 2월 1일에 일을 시작했으므로 2월 1일, 2월 11일, 2월 21일 총 3일 일을 할 것이다.

어휘

correct[kərékt] 올바른 / carefully[kɛ́ərfəli] 주의 깊게, 신중하게

13 ④

Script

M Mom, what are we going to do <u>this holiday</u>?

W I'm not sure. Your father likes water sports, so he wanted to go to one of the islands in the Philippines.

M But you don't like water, and you don't even know <u>how to swim</u>.

W Right. I <u>prefer to</u> stay home and get some sleep. I'm exhausted these days.

M Mom, but don't you think we have to do something? I can't just stay home and spend my holiday here. What about going mountain climbing?

W That doesn't sound good. It's hard to <u>make a decision</u> when everyone has a different idea.

해석

남 엄마, 이번 휴가에 우리 무엇을 할 거예요?

여 글쎄다. 네 아버지는 수상 스포츠를 좋아하셔서 필리핀 섬 중의 한 곳에 가기를 원했어.

남 하지만 엄마는 물을 좋아하지 않잖아요. 그리고 수영도 못하시고요.

여 그래. 나는 집에 있으면서 잠을 좀 잤으면 좋겠구나. 요즘 좀 지쳤거든.

남 하지만 엄마 뭔가 해야 한다고 생각하지 않으세요? 그냥 집에 있으면서 휴일을 보낼 수는 없어요. 등산을 가는 건 어때요?

여 별로인 것 같구나. 모든 사람의 의견이 다르니 결정을 하기가 어렵구나.

해설

휴가 때 가족 모두 하고 싶은 일이 달라서 결정을 못하는 상황이므로 "사공이 많으면 배가 산으로 간다."라는 속담이 가장 적절하다.

① 식은 죽 먹기

② 쥐구멍에도 볕 들 날이 있다.

③ 시작이 반이다.

⑤ 겉을 보고 속을 판단하지 마라.

어휘

water sports 수상 스포츠 / the Philippines 필리핀 / prefer[prifɔ́ːr]
~을 선호하다 / exhausted[igzɔ́ːstid] 지친 / mountain climbing 등산 /
make a decision 결정하다

14 ①

Script

W Aden, what did you do on the weekend?

M I went to an art gallery with my sister, but the gallery was closed for renovation.

W Oh, really?

M Yes. So, we went to a movie instead. The movie was really boring. I almost fell asleep.

W That's too bad. I'm going hiking with my father this coming weekend. Do you want to join us?

M Sorry. I'm going to try the gallery again. They say they're going to reopen this weekend.

해석

여 Aden, 주말에 무엇을 했니?

남 여동생이랑 미술관에 갔었는데 수리를 한다고 문을 닫았더라.

여 어, 정말?

남 응. 그래서 대신에 영화를 보러 갔어. 영화는 정말 지루했어. 나는 거의 잠이 들었다니까.

여 그것참 안 됐다. 나 이번 주말에 우리 아버지랑 도보 여행을 갈 건데, 너도 같이 거야?

남 미안해. 나는 미술관에 다시 가 볼 거야. 이번 주말에 다시 문을 연다고 했거든.

해설

남자는 이번 주말에 미술관에 다시 가겠다고 했다.

어휘

art gallery 미술관 / renovation[rénəvéiʃən] 수리, 보수 /
instead[instéd] 대신에 / boring[bɔ́ːriŋ] 지루한 / fall asleep 잠들다 /
go hiking 도보여행하다 / reopen[riːóupən] 다시 열다

15 ⑤

Script

M Hoon is my best friend from Korea. He has been here for at least 2 years. He's very active and enthusiastic, but when he talks to other people, he has a problem. In America, when you have a conversation with a person, you should make eye contact, but he always avoids eye contact. The people he's talking to may get upset if they feel that he's not interested in what they say.

해석

남 훈이는 한국에서 온 나의 가장 친한 친구이다. 그는 적어도 2년은 여기

에 있었다. 그는 매우 활동적이고 열정적이지만, 다른 사람들과 이야기를 할 때 문제가 하나 있다. 미국에서는 누군가와 이야기를 할 때 눈을 마주쳐야 한다. 하지만, 그는 늘 눈이 마주치는 것을 피한다. 그와 이야기를 하는 사람들은 그가 그들이 하는 말에 관심이 없다고 느끼게 되면 화가 날 수 있다.

해설

남자는 말할 때 눈을 피하는 훈이에게 "말을 할 때는 눈을 쳐다봐."라고 충고해 줄 것이다.

① 친구들에게 '안녕'이라고 말해.

② 친구들과 악수를 해.

③ 도서관에서 떠들지 마.

④ 네 문제로부터 도망치지 마.

어휘

enthusiastic[enθúːziǽstik] 열정적인 /
make eye contact 시선을 마주치다 / avoid[əvɔ́id] 피하다 /
upset[ʌpsét] 화가 난

16 ③

Script

W Excuse me, is everything all right?

M Yes. This is the most excellent dish I've ever had.

W Thank you. Would you mind doing me a favor, sir?

M What's that?

W Is the boy running around your son?

M Yes, he is.

W Would you please keep him under control? Some customers are complaining about that.

M I'm terribly sorry. I'll make him stop.

해석

여 실례합니다. 모든 것이 괜찮나요?

남 네. 이것은 제가 먹어 본 것 중에서 가장 훌륭한 요리예요.

여 감사합니다. 저 손님, 부탁을 좀 들어주시겠습니까?

남 무엇이죠?

여 저기 뛰어다니는 아이가 손님의 아들인가요?

남 네, 그렇습니다.

여 뛰어다니지 못하게 해주시겠어요? 다른 손님들이 항의하고 있어요.

남 정말 죄송합니다. 제가 못하게 할게요.

해설

종업원과 손님의 대화로 식당에서 일어날 수 있는 대화이다.

어휘

excellent[éksələnt] 훌륭한 / under control 통제[제어]되는 /
complain about ~에 대해 불평하다

17 ⑤

Script

W Mike had one hotdog and two slices of pizza. John had spaghetti and a glass of water. Kevin had two hotdogs. Peter had a slice of pizza and spaghetti. David had one hamburger and one hotdog.

해석

여 Mike는 핫도그 한 개와 피자 두 조각을 먹었다. John은 스파게티와 물 한 잔을 먹었다. Kevin은 핫도그 두 개를 먹었다. Peter는 피자 한 조각과 스파게티를 먹었다. David는 햄버거 한 개와 핫도그 한 개를 먹었다.

해설

Mike는 핫도그 한 개(350)와 피자 두 조각(500)으로 총 850칼로리 섭취, John은 스파게티(630)를 먹었으므로 총 630칼로리 섭취, kevin은 핫도그 두 개(700)를 먹었으므로 총 700칼로리 섭취, Peter는 피자 한 조각(250)과 스파게티(630)를 먹었으므로 총 880칼로리 섭취, David는 햄버거 한 개(600)와 핫도그 한 개(350)를 먹었으므로 총 950칼로리를 섭취했다. 따라서 David가 가장 많은 칼로리를 섭취했다.

어휘

a slice of ~ 한 조각 / a glass of ~ 한 잔

18 ③

Script

W I have a close friend called David. He is very nice and generous to other people. One day, when he was getting on a train, one of his shoes fell to the ground. The train started to move, so he couldn't pick it up. But he didn't look sad. He quickly took off the other shoe and threw it out of the train. I asked him why he did that. David told me if a poor man finds the first shoe, he will now have a pair of shoes.

해석

여 나는 David라는 친한 친구가 있다. 그는 매우 착하고 다른 사람들에게 관대하다. 어느 날 그가 기차를 타는데 신발 한쪽이 땅으로 떨어졌다. 기차가 움직이기 시작해서 그는 신발을 주울 수가 없었다. 하지만 그는 슬퍼 보이지 않았다. 그는 재빨리 나머지 신발 한쪽을 벗어서 기차 밖으로 던졌다. 나는 그에게 왜 그랬는지 물어보았다. David는 나에게 첫 번째 신발을 발견한 불쌍한 사람이 이제 신발 두 쪽을 다 가지게 될 거라고 말했다.

해설

신발 한쪽을 실수로 떨어뜨리고 나서, 신발 한쪽을 주운 사람을 위해 나머지 한쪽 던져 준 행동은 배려심을 의미한다.

어휘

close[klous] 친한, 가까운 / generous[dʒénərəs] 관대한 / get on ~을 타다 / fall[fɔ:l] 떨어지다 / quickly[kwíkli] 빨리 / take off ~을 벗다 / throw[θrou] ~을 던지다

19 ①

Script

W Hey, Mark. Do you work out?

M Yes, I do. I do some weight training.

W I see. I work out, too. I play badminton sometimes.

M Sorry, but I think playing badminton sometimes is not a workout.

W What do you mean?

M That seems kind of like a hobby, not a workout. I think a workout is something you do regularly not just sometimes. Do you know what I mean?

W Yeah, I got it.

해석

여 안녕, Mark. 너는 운동을 하니?

남 응. 해. 나는 근육 운동을 좀 해.

여 그렇구나. 나도 운동을 해. 나는 가끔 배드민턴을 쳐?

남 미안하지만 내 생각에 가끔 배드민턴을 치는 것은 운동이 아닌 것 같아.

여 무슨 말이야?

남 그건 운동이 아니라 일종의 취미 같아. 나는 운동은 가끔씩만 하는 게 아니라 규칙적으로 하는 거라고 생각해. 무슨 말인지 알겠어?

여 응. 이해했어.

해설

남자가 자신이 생각하는 운동에 대해 이야기했으므로 "응. 이해했어."라는 응답이 가장 적절하다.

② 응. 나는 너무 바빴어.

③ 나도 알아. 근육을 만드는 것이 쉽지는 않지.

④ 응. 나는 배드민턴 치는 것을 정말 좋아해.

⑤ 언제 같이 배드민턴을 치는 것이 어때?

어휘

work out 운동하다 / weight training 근육 운동 / workout[wɔ́:rkàut] 운동 / regularly[régjələrli] 규칙적으로

20 ③

Script

M Where is John? He's supposed to be here today.

W I don't think he's going to make it.

M Why?

W I'm sure he's at home now.

M His mother won't let him go out, right?

W No, that's not it. He broke his leg yesterday, and it's in a cast.

M Do you know how it happened?

W He tripped over a rock.

해석

남 John은 어디에 있니? 그는 오늘 여기 오기로 했는데.

여 내 생각에 그는 올 것 같지 않아.

남 왜?

여 그는 지금 집에 있는 것이 분명해.

남 그의 어머니가 못 나가게 하는구나, 그렇지?

여 아니, 그게 아냐. 그는 어제 다리가 부러져서, 다리에 깁스하고 있어.

남 어떻게 그랬는지 알아?

여 그는 돌에 걸려 넘어졌어.

해설

어떻게 해서 다쳤느냐고 묻고 있으므로 다친 이유를 알려 주는 "그는 돌에 걸려 넘어졌어."라는 응답이 가장 적절하다.

① 정말 끔찍하구나.

② 그는 집에 있어야 해.

④ 무슨 일인지 살펴보자.

⑤ 아무도 그가 아픈지 몰라.

어휘
be supposed to ~할 예정이다 / make it 오다, 출석하다 / cast[kæst]
깁스, 붕대 / trip over ~에 걸려 넘어지다

06회 영어듣기모의고사

p.48~51

01 ⑤	02 ③	03 ②	04 ②	05 ④
06 ⑤	07 ③	08 ③	09 ④	10 ⑤
11 ④	12 ②	13 ⑤	14 ④	15 ⑤
16 ①	17 ④	18 ①	19 ⑤	20 ⑤

01 ⑤

Script

W How can I help you?

M Do you have these in size 5? It's for my daughter.

W I'm afraid we're out of size 5. How about these boots? They're very popular with young girls. Why didn't you bring your daughter with you?

M This is supposed to be a surprise gift for her birthday. She'll become 15 years old tomorrow.

W I understand. I'm sure she'll like those boots.

M OK. I'll take them.

해석

여 무엇을 도와드릴까요?

남 이것으로 치수가 5인 것이 있나요? 제 딸을 위한 것이에요.

여 치수가 5인 것은 다 떨어졌어요. 이 부츠는 어떠세요? 이 부츠는 여자 아이들에게 인기가 있어요. 딸을 데려오지 그러셨어요?

남 깜짝 생일 선물을 사주고 싶어서요. 제 딸은 내일 열다섯 살이 되거든요.

여 그렇군요. 따님은 분명히 이 부츠를 좋아할 거예요.

남 알겠어요. 그걸로 할게요.

해설

남자는 여자가 추천해 준 걸 사기로 했으므로 부츠를 살 것이다.

어휘
boot[buːt] 부츠 / be popular with ~에게 인기 있다

02 ③

Script

M What can I do for you?

W I'd like to send this package to Seoul.

M May I ask what is inside?

W It's a sweat suit for my son.

M I see. How would you like to send it?

W The faster, the better.

M OK. That'll be 5 dollars. It'll get there the day after tomorrow.

W Here you go. Thank you.

해석

남 무엇을 도와드릴까요?

여 저는 이 소포를 서울로 보내고 싶어요.

남 안에 무엇이 들어 있는지 물어봐도 될까요?

여 아들을 위한 운동복이에요.

남 그렇군요. 어떻게 보내 드릴까요?

여 빠를수록 좋아요.

남 알았습니다. 5달러입니다. 내일모레 도착할 겁니다.

여 여기 있습니다. 감사합니다.

해설

소포를 보내는 곳은 우체국이다.

어휘
package[pǽkidʒ] 소포, 꾸러미 / sweat suit 운동복 /
the day after tomorrow 내일모레

03 ②

Script

[Telephone rings.]

M Hello, can I speak to Andy?

W He's not in. Who's calling, please?

M This is Kelly's dad, Michael Barton.

W Hi, Mr. Barton. Andy went out to walk his dog. What is this about?

M The reason I'm calling is to thank him for what he did for my daughter.

W What did he do?

M There were a couple of boys who tried to rob her, and your son stopped them from doing so.

W He did?

M Yes. That's what I heard from my daughter.

해석

남 여보세요, Andy와 통화할 수 있을까요?

여 없는데요. 누구 시죠?

남 저는 Kelly의 아빠인, Michael Barton입니다.

여 안녕하세요, Barton 씨. Andy는 개를 산책시키러 나갔어요. 무슨 일이시죠?

남 제가 전화를 건 이유는 Andy가 제 딸을 위해 한 일에 대해 고맙다고 말하려고요.

여 그가 무슨 일을 했는데요?

남 제 딸의 돈을 빼앗으려고 하는 두 명의 소년이 있었는데 댁의 아드님이 그들을 막아줬어요.

여 그 애가 그랬어요?

남 네. 그게 제가 제 딸에게 들은 이야기예요.

해설

남자는 자신의 딸을 도와준 Andy에게 고맙다는 말을 하기 위해 전화했다.

어휘

go out 외출하다, 밖으로 나가다 / walk a dog 개를 산책시키다 /
thank[θæŋk] ~에게 고마워하다 / rob[rɑb] (물건을) 강탈하다, 빼앗다

04 ②

Script

M Congratulations! I heard you <u>won first prize</u> in the speech contest, Kate.

W Thanks.

M I envy you. I've never heard <u>such</u> a <u>good speech</u>.

W It's nice of you to say so. But anyone can be a good speaker if they practice enough.

M Really? I've found it's not easy. How come you are so good at speech?

W Well, I practice speaking in the Speech Club every Saturday. <u>Would you like to</u> join us?

M Sure. Why not?

해석

남 축하해! 말하기 대회에서 우승했다고 들었어, Kate.

여 고마워.

남 네가 부러워. 나는 그렇게 훌륭한 연설을 들어 본 적이 없어.

여 그렇게 말해 줘서 고마워. 하지만, 누구라도 충분히 연습하면 훌륭한 연설가가 될 수 있어.

남 정말? 나는 쉽지가 않은데. 너는 어떻게 그렇게 연설을 잘하니?

여 글쎄. 나는 매주 토요일에 말하기 클럽에서 연습해. 너도 함께할래?

남 물론. 왜 아니겠어?

해설

남자는 연설을 잘하기 위해 여자가 참여하는 연설 클럽에 가입할 것이다.

어휘

win first prize 일등을 하다 / speech[spiːtʃ] 연설, 말하기 /
practice[prǽktis] 연습하다 / how come 어째서, 왜 / join[dʒɔin] 참여하다

05 ④

Script

M Here we are. This is the place you requested?

W Yes. Thank you. <u>What's the fare</u>?

M It's 19 dollars.

W OK. Oh, no. Excuse me, but I'm afraid I don't have enough money. I only have 17 dollars on me. <u>What should I do</u>?

M Isn't there anybody inside that can lend you a few dollars?

W No one. Let me call my friend next door. She is not answering. I'm sorry.

M It's okay. I'll just take <u>what you have</u>.

W Thank you. You are very kind.

해석

남 다 왔습니다. 이곳이 당신이 말한 장소인가요?

여 네. 감사합니다. 요금은 얼마죠?

남 19달러입니다.

여 알았습니다. 아, 이런. 죄송합니다만 돈이 충분하지 않은 것 같아요. 겨우 17달러밖에 없네요. 어떻게 하죠?

남 집에 돈을 좀 빌려 줄 사람이 아무도 없나요?

여 아무도 없어요. 옆집에 사는 친구에게 전화해 볼게요. 친구가 전화를 안 받네요. 죄송해요.

남 괜찮습니다. 그거만 받죠.

여 감사합니다. 정말 친절한 분이시네요.

해설

여자는 택시 기사가 자신이 가지고 있는 17달러만 받겠다고 했으므로 안심했을 것이다.

어휘

request[rikwést] ~을 요청하다 / fare[fɛər] 요금

06 ⑤

Script

W Can you tell me why you chose this job? I know it's a very tough job.

M I saw my father saving many lives <u>in danger</u>.

W You mean your father works in this field, too?

M Yes. Well, he did. He retired last year.

W I see. Have you been injured <u>on the job</u> before?

M Of course. Once when I was trying to <u>put out fire</u>, my left leg got burned.

W Can you show me?

M Sure.

W Oh, that's terrible.

M It's OK now.

해석

여 이 직업을 왜 선택하셨는지 말해 주실래요? 이 일은 매우 힘든 직업이잖아요.

남 저는 아버지가 위험에 빠진 많은 생명을 구하는 것을 보았어요.

여 아버님도 이 분야에서 일을 하셨다는 말인가요?

남 네. 그러셨죠. 작년에 은퇴하셨어요.

여 그렇군요. 전에 일을 하시다가 부상을 당한 적이 있으세요?

남 물론이죠. 한번은 화재 진압을 하다가, 왼쪽 다리에 화상을 입었습니다.

여 보여 주실 수 있나요?

남 물론이죠.

여 저런, 끔찍하군요.

남 지금은 괜찮습니다.

해설

불은 끄는 사람은 소방관이다.

어휘

in danger 위험에 빠진 / field[fiːld] 분야 / retire[ritáiər] 은퇴하다 /
injured[índʒərd] 상처 입은 / put out (불을) 끄다 / get burned 화상을 입다

07 ③

Script

W How much you spend on traveling is really up to you. Here are some tips on saving your money. Number one: Go off-season. Popular destinations are very crowded, but after the peak-season they are less crowded. Usually, hotels offer special discounts during the off-season. Number two: Use coupons. From dozens of web pages you can find discount coupons for hotels and restaurants. Print them out, take them, and save money.

해석

여 여행을 할 때 얼마를 쓰느냐 하는 것은 정말 당신에게 달렸다. 여기에 당신의 돈을 절약할 수 있는 몇 가지 조언이 있다. 첫째, 비수기에 가라. 인기 있는 장소는 매우 복잡하지만, 성수기가 지나고 나서는 덜 붐빈다. 일반적으로 비수기 동안에 호텔은 특별 할인을 제공한다. 둘째, 쿠폰을 사용해라. 수많은 웹 사이트에서 호텔이나 식당의 할인 쿠폰을 찾을 수 있다. 할인 쿠폰을 출력해 가져가서 돈을 절약해라.

해설

비수기에 여행을 하는 것, 호텔이나 식당의 할인 쿠폰을 이용하는 것은 저렴하게 여행하는 방법이다.

어휘

up to ~에 달린 / off-season 비수기 / destination[dèstənéiʃən] 목적지, 행선지 / crowded[kráudid] 붐비는 / peak-season 성수기 / offer[ɔ́(:)fər] ~을 제공하다 / dozens of 많은, 수십의

08 ③

Script

① M The weather forecast said it would be raining hard.
　W Sometimes the weather forecast can be wrong.
② M Do you mind getting wet?
　W Yes. Let's run to the school.
③ M Would you like to share my umbrella?
　W Thanks. I didn't expect rain today.
④ M Is this your umbrella? Can I borrow it?
　W Sure, I have two. You can use this one.
⑤ M I left my umbrella on the bus.
　W Don't worry. It's in my bag.

해석

① 남 일기 예보에서 오늘 비가 많이 올 거라고 했는데.
　여 가끔은 일기 예보가 틀릴 수도 있지.
② 남 젖는 것이 싫으니?
　여 응. 학교까지 뛰어가자.
③ 남 우산을 같이 쓰실래요?
　여 감사합니다. 오늘 비가 올 거라고 생각하지 못했어요.
④ 남 이것이 네 우산이니? 내가 이것을 빌려도 될까?
　여 물론, 나는 우산이 두 개 있어. 이걸 사용하도록 해.
⑤ 남 버스에다 우산을 두고 내렸어.
　여 걱정하지 마. 그것은 나의 가방 안에 있어.

해설

남자가 여자에게 우산을 같이 쓰자고 제안하는 상황이다.

어휘

weather forecast 일기 예보 / share[ʃɛər] 함께 나누다, 같이 쓰다 / expect[ikspékt] 예상하다, 기대하다 / borrow[bɔ́(:)rou] ~을 빌리다

09 ④

Script

W In the United States and other western countries, students are allowed to use a calculator while they take a math test. Even though it sounds really strange to Korean students, it's pretty reasonable for students to use a calculator. Students can make mistakes when they calculate in their head, even though they know how to solve a problem. That's why teachers let students use a calculator. However, in Korea, calculating is also considered to be a part of a test.

해석

여 미국과 다른 서구 국가에서는 학생들이 수학 시험을 보는 동안 계산기를 사용하는 것이 허용된다. 한국 학생들에게 정말 이상하게 들리겠지만, 학생들이 계산기를 사용하는 것은 꽤 합리적인 일이다. 학생들은 그들이 문제를 어떻게 푸는지 알고 있더라도 머릿속으로 계산을 하다가 실수를 할 수도 있다. 그래서 선생님들은 학생들이 계산기를 사용하는 것을 허용한다. 하지만 한국에서는 계산하는 것 또한 시험의 일부분으로 여겨진다.

해설

미국이나 서구 국가에서는 수학 시험 시간에 계산기의 사용을 허용하고, 한국에서는 계산기의 사용을 허용하지 않는다는 이야기이다.

어휘

allow[əláu] ~을 허용하다 / calculator[kǽlkjəlèitər] 계산기 / reasonable[rí:zənəbəl] 합리적인 / calculate[kǽlkjəlèit] 계산하다 / consider[kənsídər] 고려하다, 간주하다

10 ⑤

Script

W Is this your first time in this country?
M Yes, it is. But I feel right at home.
W That's good. Where have you been so far?
M I don't know the exact names, but I have been to a few palaces. Those palaces were fantastic. I enjoyed seeing them a lot.
W I'm sure you had a lot of fun.

해석

여 이 나라에는 처음이세요?
남 네, 그렇습니다. 하지만 매우 편안하네요.
여 잘됐네요. 지금까지 어디에 가보셨어요?
남 정확한 이름은 잘 모르겠지만, 몇 곳의 궁에 가 보았어요. 정말 좋은 곳이더군요. 정말 즐거웠어요.
여 정말 즐겁게 지내셨군요.

해설

여자는 즐거웠다는 남자의 말에 분명히 그런 것 같다고 동의하고 있다.

어휘

so far 지금까지 / exact[igzǽkt] 정확한 / palace[pǽlis] 궁, 궁전 /

fantastic[fæntǽstik] 환상적인, 멋진

11 ④
Script

(Beep)

W You have reached the office of Happy Dental Clinic. Our office hours are <u>Monday</u> <u>through</u> <u>Friday</u> from 10 A.M. to 6 P.M. The office is located on Gulf Avenue. <u>Parking</u> <u>is</u> <u>available</u> at the rear of the building. If this is an emergency, press 1 <u>for</u> <u>immediate</u> <u>attention</u>. If you would like to make an appointment to have your teeth cleaned, press 2. If you want to talk to one of our nurses, press 0.

해석

여 당신은 행복 치과에 연결되셨습니다. 저희 치과는 월요일부터 금요일까지 오전 10시부터 오후 6시까지 문을 엽니다. 치과는 걸프 가에 자리 잡고 있습니다. 주차는 건물 뒤편으로 이용이 가능합니다. 응급 상황이시면, 즉각적인 처리를 위해 1번을 누르세요. 치아의 청결을 위해 예약을 원하시면, 2번을 누르세요. 간호사와 이야기를 하고 싶으시면, 0번을 누르세요.

해설

진료 시간은 오전 10시에서 오후 6시, 병원은 걸프 가에 위치, 주차는 건물 뒤편에. 진료과목은 치과이고, 담당의사는 알 수 없다.

어휘

reach[riːtʃ] ~에 도달하다, 도착하다 / dental clinic 치과 / office hours 근무 시간 / be located on ~에 위치하다 / avenue[ǽvənjùː] 가(街), 길 / available[əvéiləbəl] 이용 가능한 / rear[riər] 뒤의 / immediate[imíːdiət] 즉각적인 / attention[əténʃən] 처리, 대처

12 ②
Script

W Jake, can you <u>lend</u> <u>me</u> <u>some</u> <u>money</u>?

M How much do you want?

W I needed 200 dollars, but Jenny already gave me 80 dollars, and Mike gave me 50 dollars. Now I just need 70 dollars.

M Well, I have 100 dollars on me, so I can give you <u>what</u> <u>you</u> <u>need</u>.

W That's great. I'll <u>pay</u> <u>you</u> <u>back</u> next month. Thanks a lot.

M You're welcome.

해석

여 Jake, 너 나에게 돈을 좀 빌려 줄 수 있니?

남 얼마나 원하는데?

여 200달러가 필요했는데 Jenny가 이미 80달러를 주었고, Mike가 50달러를 주었어. 이제 70달러만 있으면 돼.

남 음, 나에게 100달러가 있으니까, 네가 필요한 돈을 줄 수 있어.

여 잘 됐다. 다음 달에 갚을게. 정말 고마워.

남 천만에.

해설

여자는 총 200달러가 필요했는데 Jenny가 80달러를, Mike가 50달러를

34

주었으므로 70달러가 더 필요하다.

어휘

lend[lend] ~을 빌려 주다 / pay back ~을 갚다, 상환하다

13 ⑤
Script

M What time do you want to leave?

W I'm not sure. What time is it now?

M It's <u>half</u> <u>past</u> <u>five</u>.

W Then let's make it a quarter to six.

M That early?

W Why? You've got something to do?

M Not really. I just need to check my email.

W How about <u>a</u> <u>quarter</u> <u>after</u> <u>six</u> then?

M OK.

해석

남 몇 시에 떠나기를 원해?

여 잘 모르겠어. 지금 몇 시야?

남 5시 30분이야.

여 그러면 6시 15분 전에 만나자.

남 그렇게 일찍?

여 왜? 뭐 할 일이 있니?

남 꼭 그런 건 아닌데. 그냥 이메일을 좀 확인하려고.

여 그러면 6시 15분은 어때?

남 좋아.

해설

두 사람은 6시 15분에 출발하기로 했다.

어휘

make it (서로) 만나기로 하다 / quarter[kwɔ́ːrtər] 15분, 4분의 1

14 ④
Script

W David was <u>having</u> <u>a</u> <u>birthday</u> <u>party</u>. He didn't want to invite all the boys from his class, but his mom told him he had to invite them all. David didn't listen to his mom. <u>There</u> <u>was</u> <u>no</u> <u>way</u> David was inviting Mark to his party. Mark gave him a black eye a few weeks ago. Besides he was mean to everyone. David didn't invite Jason, either. He was <u>a</u> <u>little</u> <u>jealous</u> <u>of</u> Jason being so smart.

해석

여 David는 생일 파티를 열었다. 그는 자기네 반 아이들 모두를 초대하고 싶지는 않았다. 하지만 David의 엄마는 반 아이들 모두를 초대해야 한다고 하셨다. David는 엄마의 말을 듣지 않았다. David는 자신의 파티에 결코 Mark를 초대할 수는 없었다. Mark는 몇 주 전에 David의 눈을 멍들게 했고, 게다가 그는 모든 아이들에게 심술궂게 굴었다. David는 Jason도 초대하지 않았다. David는 Jason이 너무 똑똑해서 약간 질투를 했다.

해설
Mark는 David에게뿐만 아니라 모든 아이에게 심술궂게 군다.

어휘
invite[inváit] 초대하다 / there is no way 결코 ~하지 않는다 /
give a person a black eye ~의 눈가에 멍이 들게 하다 /
besides[bisáidz] 더욱이, 게다가 / mean[mi:n] 심술궂은, 비열한 /
be jealous of ~을 시기하다, 질투하다

15 ⑤

Script

M Today is the last day of camp.

W Right. What do you want to do during our free time this afternoon?

M How about rock climbing? I want to get some fresh air.

W I'm afraid I can't. My legs are still hurting from rafting yesterday.

M Are they? Then, let's go bungee jumping.

W I'm sorry, but I'm afraid of heights. And it's 30 dollars a person. All I have is 20 dollars.

M I only have 20 bucks, too.

W In that case, there is only one thing left to do.

해석

남 오늘이 캠프의 마지막 날이야.

여 그러네. 오늘 오후 자유 시간에 무엇을 하고 싶어?

남 암벽 등반은 어때? 나는 신선한 공기를 마시고 싶어.

여 미안하지만 안 될 것 같아. 어제 급류타기를 해서 다리가 아직도 아파.

남 그래? 그러면 번지점프하자.

여 미안하지만 나는 높은 건 무서워. 그리고 한 사람에 30달러야. 내가 가진 거라곤 20달러가 전부야.

남 나도 20달러밖에 없어.

여 그러면, 할 것은 하나밖에 없네.

해설
남자와 여자는 각각 20달러씩밖에 없고, 암벽 등반은 여자의 다리가 아파서 할 수 없으므로 할 수 있는 것은 말 타기밖에 없다.

어휘
rock climbing 암벽 등반 / rafting[rǽftiŋ] 급류타기 /
bungee jumping 번지점프 / height[hait] 높이 / buck[bʌk] 달러 /
in that case 그 경우는, 그렇다면

16 ①

Script

W Hey, look at this article. It's about Japanese people's health. It says their rates of heart disease and cancer are much lower than those in other countries.

M Really? Are there any secrets behind that?

W Many scientists have tried to find the reasons, and they have come up with three most important factors: diet, exercise, and lifestyle.

M I think I can add one more thing.

W What is that?

M They never overeat.

W That's true.

해석

여 이봐, 이 기사를 좀 봐. 일본인의 건강에 관한 건데, 일본사람들의 심장병과 암 발생률이 다른 나라 사람들보다 훨씬 낮대.

남 정말? 그것에 대한 비법이라도 있니?

여 많은 과학자들이 이유를 찾아보고 식단, 운동, 생활 방식이라는 세 가지 중요한 요소를 알아냈어.

남 내가 한 가지 더 추가할 수 있을 것 같아.

여 그게 뭔데?

남 그들은 절대 과식하지 않아.

여 맞아.

해설
일본인이 건강한 이유로 식단, 운동, 생활 방식, 소식의 네 가지가 언급되었다.

어휘
article[á:rtikl] 기사 / rate[reit] 비율 / heart disease 심장병 /
cancer[kǽnsər] 암 / secret[sí:krit] 비밀 / reason[rí:zən] 이유 /
come up with ~을 발견하다 / factor[fǽktər] 요소 / diet[dáiət] 식단 /
lifestyle[laifstail] 생활 방식 / add[æd] ~을 추가하다, 더하다 /
overeat[òuvərí:t] 과식하다

17 ④

Script

W Did you do the dishes?

M Sure, they're done. I'm going to watch TV.

W Wait a second. Can you get some hangers for me?

M Where are they?

W In the closet.

M OK. Don't ask me anything else though. I'm really tired.

W Give me a break! All you did was do the dishes. How about me? I cleaned the living room, did the laundry, and fed the dog.

M All right.

해석

여 설거지는 다 했어요?

남 물론 했어요. 텔레비전을 볼 거예요.

여 잠깐만요. 나에게 옷걸이를 좀 갖다줄래요?

남 어디에 있죠?

여 옷장에요.

남 알았어요. 그밖에 다른 것은 시키지 마세요. 난 정말로 피곤해요.

여 잠깐만요! 당신이 한 건 설거지가 전부 잖아요. 나는 어때요? 나는 거실 청소에 빨래, 그리고 개에게 먹이도 줬어요.

남 알았어요.

해설
여자는 남자에게 옷걸이를 갖다달라고 부탁하고 있다.

어휘
do the dishes 설거지하다 / hanger[hǽŋər] 옷걸이 / closet[klázit]
옷장 / Give me a break! 잠깬 그만! / living room 거실 / do the laundry

빨래하다 / feed[fiːd] 먹이를 주다

18 ①
Script
① **M** She caught a thief, and she was awarded <u>a medal for bravery</u>.
   W That's terrible.
② **M** I think we should help the poor.
   W <u>I can't agree with you more</u>.
③ **M** Why do you want to get a red one?
   W Hey, people have different tastes.
④ **M** Can I talk to Mr. Kim?
   W Sure, I'll <u>connect you to him</u> right away.
⑤ **M** Would you do me a favor?
   W What is it?

해석
① 남 그녀는 도둑을 잡아서 용감한 시민상을 받았어.
   여 저런 끔찍하군.
② 남 나는 우리가 가난한 사람들을 도와야 한다고 생각해.
   여 네 말에 전적으로 동의해.
③ 남 너는 왜 빨간색으로 하려고 하니?
   여 야, 사람마다 취향이 다르잖아.
④ 남 Mr. Kim 좀 바꿔 주세요.
   여 네, 바로 연결해 드리겠습니다.
⑤ 남 부탁을 좀 들어주시겠어요?
   여 무엇이죠?

해설
① 좋은 일에 대한 반응으로 끔찍하다는 말은 어울리지 않는다.

어휘
catch[kætʃ] 잡다 / thief[θiːf] 도둑 / award[əwɔ́ːrd] ~을 수여하다 / bravery[bréivəri] 용기, 용감성 / terrible[térəbəl] 끔찍한 / agree with ~에게 동의하다, ~와 의견이 일치하다 / taste[teist] 취향, 기호; 맛 / connect[kənékt] 연결하다 / do a person a favor ~의 부탁을 들어주다

19 ⑤
Script
[Telephone rings.]

M Hello, may I speak to John?
W I think you've <u>got the wrong number</u>.
M Isn't this 245-2451?
W Yes, the phone number is right.
M That's strange. John gave me this number last night.
W <u>There is no one here by that name</u>.

해석
남 여보세요, John 좀 바꿔주세요.
여 전화를 잘못 거신 것 같군요.
남 245-2451 아닌가요?
여 네, 전화번호는 맞아요.

남 이상하네요. John이 지난밤에 이 전화번호를 저에게 주었거든요.
여 <u>여기 그런 사람은 없어요</u>.

해설
잘못 걸었다고 했으므로 "여기 그런 사람은 없어요."라고 대답하는 것이 가장 적절하다.
① 그는 방금 나갔어요.
② John은 금방 돌아올 거예요.
③ 그래요? 그거 잘 됐군요.
④ 미안해요. 지금 당장은 그를 찾을 수가 없네요.

20 ⑤
Script
W Today is the last day of the semester. Enjoy your vacation. You have some homework to do <u>during the summer vacation</u>. It's not a lot, so don't worry.
M What do we have to do, Mrs. Smith?
W You have to <u>write an essay</u> that is at least three A4-sized pages long.
M What do we have to write about?
W <u>You can write about whatever you want</u>.

해석
여 오늘은 이번 학기의 마지막 날이에요. 방학 즐겁게 보내세요. 여름 방학 숙제가 있어요. 많지 않으니까 걱정하지 마세요.
남 무엇인가요, Smith 선생님?
여 A4 크기 종이에 최소한 세 쪽 이상의 작문을 해 와야 해요.
남 무엇에 대해 써야 하나요?
여 <u>원하는 것은 무엇이든지 쓸 수 있어요</u>.

해설
무엇에 대해 글을 쓰느냐고 물었으므로 "원하는 것은 무엇이든지 쓸 수 있어요."라는 응답이 가장 적절하다.
① 너는 일기를 써야 해.
② 미안하지만, 나는 몰라.
③ 물론, 너는 그것에 대해 써도 돼.
④ 나는 여름 방학에 대해서 썼어.

어휘
semester[siméstər] 학기 / write an essay 수필을 쓰다 / at least 최소한

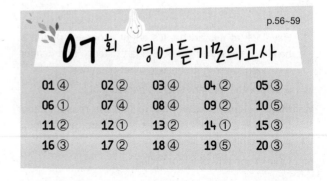

p.56~59

07회 영어듣기모의고사

01 ④	02 ②	03 ④	04 ②	05 ③
06 ①	07 ④	08 ④	09 ②	10 ⑤
11 ②	12 ①	13 ②	14 ①	15 ③
16 ③	17 ②	18 ④	19 ⑤	20 ③

01 ④

Script

W Hi. I'd like to adopt a puppy. Could you recommend a smart one?

M The white one beside the black puppy is pretty smart.

W Oh, you mean the one on the left side of the black one?

M No, the one on the right side.

W The one holding a bone in his mouth?

M Yes, that's him.

W Oh, he looks very cute. I'll take him.

해석

여 안녕하세요. 저는 애완견을 입양하고 싶습니다. 똑똑한 것으로 하나 추천해 주시겠어요?

남 검은 강아지 옆에 하얀 강아지가 매우 똑똑합니다.

여 아, 검은 강아지의 왼쪽에 있는 것 말인가요?

남 아니요, 오른쪽에 있는 거요.

여 잎에 뼈다귀를 문 것 말인가요?

남 네, 바로 그것입니다.

여 아, 매우 귀엽게 생겼네요. 그 강아지로 할게요.

해설

검은 강아지 오른쪽에 있고, 입에 뼈다귀를 문 것이다.

어휘

adopt[ədápt] ~을 입양하다 / recommend[rèkəménd] ~을 추천하다 / beside[bisáid] ~ 옆에 / hold[hould] ~을 붙들다, 쥐다

02 ②

Script

W Everyone of us has this at home, and it is the most useful piece of equipment for housewives. Recently, some companies have invented a robot version, and it can do its job on its own. Once you plug it in, it automatically moves around, sucking up all the dust from the floor of your house.

해석

여 우리 모두는 이것을 집에 가지고 있고, 이것은 주부에게 가장 유용한 장비이다. 최근에 어떤 회사가 로봇 형태로 이것을 개발했고, 이것은 스스로 일을 할 수 있다. 일단 그것을 플러그에 꽂으면 집 바닥의 먼지를 모두 빨아들이면서 자동으로 돌아다닌다.

해설

집의 먼지를 빨아들이는 것은 청소기이다.

어휘

useful[júːsfəl] 유용한 / equipment[ikwípmənt] 장비 / housewife[háuswàif] 주부 / recently[ríːsəntli] 최근에 / invent[invént] ~을 발명하다 / on one's own 혼자서, 자력으로 / once[wʌns] 일단 ~하면 / plug in (전기) 플러그에 꽂다, 콘센트에 연결하다 / automatically[ɔ̀ːtəmǽtikəli] 자동으로 / suck[sʌk] ~을 흡수하다 / dust[dʌst] 먼지

03 ④

Script

[Telephone rings.]

M Hello, Christine. I need your help. Can you help me?

W Sure, go ahead.

M I'm making potato stew, and I don't know what to do next.

W Tell me what you have done so far.

M I have boiled a couple of potatoes and have rinsed them with cold water.

W And?

M And have cut the potatoes into edible sizes and have put them into a pot. This is pretty much what I've done so far.

W Okay. Add two spoonfuls of soy sauce and sugar, and stir the potatoes. That's it.

M Thank you so much.

해석

남 안녕, Christine. 네 도움이 필요한데. 나를 좀 도와줄래?

여 물론이지, 말해 봐.

남 내가 감자조림을 만들고 있는데, 다음에 뭘 해야 할지 모르겠어.

여 지금까지 네가 한 일을 말해 봐.

남 감자 두 개를 삶아서 찬물에 헹궜어.

여 그리고?

남 그리고 먹기 좋은 크기로 썰어서 냄비에 넣었어. 이게 내가 지금까지 한 거야.

여 알았어. 간장과 설탕을 두 숟가락 넣고, 감자를 저어 줘. 그게 다야.

남 정말 고마워.

해설

남자가 전화를 끊고 가장 먼저 할 일은 간장을 넣는 것이다.

어휘

stew[stjuː] 스튜(요리) / boil[bɔil] ~을 끓이다 / rinse[rins] 헹구다 / edible[édəbəl] 먹을 수 있는 / pot[pat] 냄비 / spoonful[spúːnfùl] 한 숟가락(의 분량) / soy sauce 간장 / stir[stəːr] ~을 휘젓다, 뒤섞다

04 ②

Script

W Excuse me, could you come over here?

M Yes, ma'am. Is there something wrong?

W Yes. I have an allergy to peanuts. Did you make this sauce with peanuts?

M I'm not sure. I have to check with the kitchen. Could you wait for a second?

W Okay. Please check.

M Ma'am. There are a few peanuts in this sauce. I'll replace this salad with one without any sauce.

W Thank you. Could you put some olive oil on top

instead?

M Okay.

해석

여　실례지만, 이리로 좀 와 주시겠어요?

남　네, 손님. 뭐가 잘못되었나요?

여　네. 제가 땅콩 알레르기가 있어요. 이 소스를 땅콩으로 만드셨나요?

남　잘 모르겠네요. 주방에 확인해 봐야 합니다. 잠시만 기다려 주시겠어요?

여　알았어요. 확인해 주세요.

남　손님. 이 소스에 약간의 땅콩이 들어가 있답니다. 제가 이 샐러드를 소스가 없는 걸로 바꿔 드릴게요.

여　감사합니다. 대신 위에 올리브 기름을 좀 뿌려 주시겠어요?

남　알았습니다.

해설

음식점 종업원과 손님과의 대화이므로 남자는 종업원이다.

어휘

come over (말하는 사람 쪽으로) 오다 /
have an allergy to ~에 알레르기가 있다 / peanut[píːnʌt] 땅콩 /
replace[ripléis] ~을 바꾸다, 교환하다

05 ③

Script

W What's the result?

M It is not as good as I expected. It's kind of disappointing actually.

W That's too bad, but don't you have another chance?

M Yes, I do.

W Then, you don't need to be disappointed.

M Thanks, but I really worked hard this time.

W I know, but don't take it so hard.

해석

여　결과는 어때?

남　내가 기대한 것만큼 좋지는 않아. 사실 약간 실망스러워.

여　안 됐다. 하지만 또 한 번의 기회가 있지 않아?

남　응.

여　그러면, 실망할 필요 없어.

남　고마워. 하지만 이번에 정말 열심히 했거든.

여　알아, 하지만 너무 심각하게 받아들이지 마.

해설

여자는 너무 심각하게 받아들이지 말라고 위로하고 있다.

어휘

expect[ikspékt] 기대하다, 예상하다 / disappointing[dìsəpɔ́intiŋ]
실망시키는 / disappointed[dìsəpɔ́intid] 실망한 /
take something hard ~을 걱정하다, 신경 쓰다

06 ①

Script

W Hi, Henry. What's up?

M Don't ask. I have pimples on my face. I really don't know what to do.

W Don't worry. Many people get them.

M I know, but mine are a lot worse than others'.

W Wash your face without using any soap in the morning and evening.

M Will that work?

W Just give it a try.

M Okay. I'll try it from now on.

해석

여　안녕, Henry. 무슨 일이야?

남　묻지 마. 얼굴에 여드름이 났어. 정말로 어떻게 해야 할지 모르겠어.

여　걱정하지 마. 많은 사람이 여드름이 나잖아.

남　알아, 하지만 내 것은 다른 사람들의 것보다 훨씬 심해.

여　비누는 사용하지 말고 아침, 저녁으로 얼굴을 씻어 봐.

남　효과가 있을까?

여　그냥 한번 해 봐.

남　알았어. 지금부터 해 볼게.

해설

남자는 여드름이 나서 외모에 대해 고민을 하고 있다.

어휘

pimple[pímpl] 여드름 / soap[soup] 비누 /
give it a try 시도하다, 한 번 해보다 / from now on 지금부터

07 ④

Script

W How much are the oranges?

M They're 2 dollars each, but the more you buy, the cheaper each one is.

W How is that possible?

M If you buy 5, they're 1 dollar 50 cents each, but if you buy more than 10, they're a dollar each.

W That's a good bargain. But since I live alone, I don't need that many oranges. I'll just take 5.

M OK. Let me put them in a plastic bag for you.

W Thank you.

해석

여　이 오렌지 얼마죠?

남　하나에 2달러예요. 하지만, 더 사면 더 싸게 살 수 있어요.

여　그것이 어떻게 가능하죠?

남　다섯 개를 사면, 하나에 1달러 50센트이지만, 열 개 이상을 사면 하나에 1달러예요.

여　정말 싸군요. 하지만 저는 혼자 사니까, 오렌지가 그렇게 많이 필요하지 않아요. 다섯 개만 주세요.

남　알았습니다. 제가 비닐봉지에 담아 드리죠.

여　감사합니다.

해설

다섯 개를 사면 한 개에 1달러 50센트에 준다고 했으므로 지불해야 할 금액은

7달러 50센트이다.

어휘
cheap[tʃi:p] 값이 싼 / bargain[bά:rgən] 거래, 싼 물건 /
plastic bag 비닐봉지

08 ④
Script

W What time is your flight?

M It is scheduled to leave at 3:30, but it's going to be delayed 30 minutes.

W What's the reason?

M They say the incoming flight is delayed.

W This seems to happen a lot. Mine is delayed, too.

M Then, what time is your flight going to depart?

W 30 minutes later than yours.

M Then, let's get something to eat. I feel a little hungry.

해석

여 너의 비행기는 몇 시에 출발하니?

남 3시 30분이 예정인데 30분 연착할 거야.

여 이유가 뭔데?

남 들어오는 비행기가 연착했대.

여 이런 일이 많이 있는 것 같아. 내 비행편도 지연됐어.

남 그러면 네 비행기는 몇 시에 출발하는데?

여 네 비행기보다 30분 후에.

남 그러면 뭘 좀 먹자. 나 배가 좀 고파.

해설
남자의 비행기가 연착으로 4시 출발이므로 여자의 비행기는 그보다 30분 후인 4시 30분에 출발할 것이다.

어휘
flight[flait] 비행, 항공편 / delay[diléi] 연기하다, 지체시키다 /
incoming[ínkÀmiŋ] 들어오는 / depart[dipά:rt] 출발하다, 떠나다

09 ②
Script

W Thanks for calling Big Boy. May I help you?

M Yes, my name is Peter Brown, and I just had dinner there. I think I left my book on the table. Could you please go and check if it's still there?

W Sir, a waitress found a book and put it beside the cashier a few minutes ago.

M I see. The name of the book is *The Old Man and The Sea*.

W OK. It must be yours, then.

M I'll drop by within 30 minutes and pick it up. Thank you.

해석

여 Big Boy에 전화 주셔서 감사합니다. 도와드릴까요?

남 네, 제 이름은 Peter Brown이고, 방금 거기서 저녁을 먹었습니다. 제

책을 테이블에 놓고 온 것 같아서요. 아직도 그곳에 있는지 가서 확인 좀 해 주시겠어요?

여 손님, 종업원 한 명이 몇 분전에 책 한 권을 계산대에 갖다 놓았습니다.

남 그렇군요. 책의 제목은 「노인과 바다」입니다.

여 알았습니다. 그럼 손님 것이 확실하군요.

남 30분 안에 들러서 가져갈게요. 감사합니다.

해설
남자는 식당에 책을 두고 와서 책을 찾으려고 전화를 걸었다.

어휘
check[tʃek] ~을 확인하다 / cashier[kæʃíər] 계산대 / drop by 들르다

10 ⑤
Script

① **W** Tom, take a look at this.
   M Wow, it's wonderful.

② **W** Someone stole my notebook.
   M That's too bad.

③ **W** Hey, you stepped on me.
   M I'm terribly sorry.

④ **W** Is this your paper?
   M Where did you find it?

⑤ **W** Hey, stop cheating and bring your paper to me.
   M Please forgive me this time.

해석

① 여 Tom, 이것 좀 봐.
   남 와, 멋있다.

② 여 누군가가 나의 공책을 훔쳐 갔어.
   남 그것참 안됐구나.

③ 여 이봐요, 제 발을 밟았잖아요.
   남 정말 죄송합니다.

④ 여 이것이 너의 시험지니?
   남 어디서 찾았어?

⑤ 여 얘, 커닝하지 마. 그리고 네 시험지 이리 가져와.
   남 이번만 봐주세요.

해설
학생이 커닝을 하다가 선생님에게 들킨 상황이다.

어휘
take a look at ~을 훑어보다 / steal[sti:l] ~을 훔치다 / step on ~을 밟다 /
cheat[tʃi:t] 커닝하다, 부정 행위를 하다 / paper[péipər] 시험 문제, 답안;
종이; 논문 / forgive[fərgív] 용서하다

11 ②
Script

M You don't seem to eat breakfast.

W I don't have an appetite in the morning, so I skip breakfast every day.

M That's because you get up too late, and you're always in a rush.

W I know, but whether it is good or not, it is a habit I've had for a long time.

M I understand. The reason why I'm telling you this is that once you skip your breakfast, you are likely to eat a lot at lunch. So, it's hard for you to get in shape.

W That's why I'm exercising these days.

해석

남 아침을 안 먹은 것 같아 보이는데.

여 나는 아침에 입맛이 없어서 매일 건너뛰어.

남 그건 네가 너무 늦게 일어나서 항상 서두르기 때문이잖아.

여 알아, 하지만 그것이 좋든 나쁘든 간에, 내 오랜 습관이야.

남 이해해. 내가 이것을 너에게 말하는 이유는 일단 네가 아침을 건너뛰면 점심때 많이 먹게 되잖아. 그래서 건강 유지가 힘들어져.

여 그래서 나 요즘에 운동하잖아.

해설

남자는 여자에게 아침을 거르지 말라고 하고 있다.

어휘

appetite[ǽpitàit] 식욕 / skip[skip] (식사 등을) 거르다 / in a rush 서두르는 / whether[hwéðər] ~이든지 아니든지 / once[wʌns] 일단 ~하면 / be likely to+동사원형 ~할 것 같다 / in shape (건강이) 호조로, 본래의 상태로

12 ①

Script

M How much do I owe you?

W You owe me 40 dollars.

M Here you go. Let me see if you did a good job.

W Don't worry.

M Hey, take a close look at these trousers.

W What is it?

M There are a lot of wrinkles on the back.

W That can't be. Can I see that? Oh, I'm terribly sorry. Could you wait a minute?

M OK.

해석

남 얼마입니까?

여 40달러입니다.

남 여기 있어요. 잘 되었는지 좀 볼게요.

여 걱정하지 마세요.

남 이것 보세요, 이 바지를 좀 자세히 보세요.

여 무엇이죠?

남 뒤쪽에 주름이 많잖아요.

여 그럴 리가요. 제가 좀 볼까요? 아, 정말 죄송합니다. 잠시만 기다려 주시겠어요?

남 알았습니다.

해설

바지의 주름을 펴 주는 곳은 세탁소이다.

어휘

owe[ou] 빚지고 있다, 지불할 의무가 있다 / take a look at ~을 훑어보다 /

close[klous] 자세한, 세심한 / trouser[tráuzər] 바지 / wrinkle[ríŋkəl] 주름 / terribly[térəbli] 매우, 아주

13 ②

Script

W Did you get the job you applied for?

M No. I wasn't even given the chance to interview for the position.

W That doesn't make sense.

M I guess I'm not the person they are looking for.

W Don't worry. I think you have a lot of skills and experience, so you'll get a better one.

M That was what my parents told me, but now I'm starting to doubt myself.

해석

여 네가 지원했던 일자리를 얻었니?

남 아니. 나는 면접을 볼 기회조차도 얻지 못했어.

여 말도 안 돼.

남 내 생각에 나는 그들이 찾는 사람이 아닌가 봐.

여 걱정하지 마. 너는 기술과 경력이 많으니까 더 좋은 직업을 구할 수 있을 거야.

남 우리 부모님도 그렇게 말씀하셨어. 하지만 내 자신이 의심스럽게 시작했어.

해설

남자는 지원한 일자리에 면접을 볼 기회조차 얻지 못해 실망했다.

어휘

apply for ~에 지원하다 / make sense 말이 되다, 이치에 맞다 / skill[skíl] 솜씨, 기술 / experience[ikspíəriəns] 경험 / doubt[daut] ~을 의심하다

14 ①

Script

M Unlike other senses located on your head, this sense is all over your body. Throughout your life, you receive an endless flow of information about the world and yourself from this sense. It tells you if something is hot or cold, hard or soft. It sends messages of pain, such as a headache or a sore throat.

해석

남 당신의 머리에 위치한 다른 감각과는 달리, 이 감각은 당신의 몸 전체에 있다. 사는 동안 당신은 이것을 통해서 세계와 당신 자신에 대해 끊임없는 정보를 받아들인다. 그것은 어떤 것이 뜨거운지 차가운지, 혹은 단단한지 부드러운지 알려 준다. 그것은 두통이나 목이 부은 것과 같은 통증을 전달해 준다.

해설

뜨거운지 차가운지, 단단한지, 부드러운지를 알려 주는 것은 촉각이다.

어휘

unlike[ʌnláik] ~와 달리 / sense[sens] 감각 / locate on ~에 위치하다 / all over 도처에, 전부에 / throughout[θruːáut] ~의 도처에, ~의 구석까지 / receive[risíːv] ~을 받다, 얻다 / endless[éndlis] 끝이 없는 / flow[flou] 흐름, 유입 / such as ~와 같은 / headache[hédèik] 두통 /

sore throat 인후염, 목의 통증

15 ③

Script

W Look! There are <u>so many road signs</u> over there.

M Do you know what they mean?

W No, I don't. Can you <u>explain them to me</u>?

M Sure.

W What does this sign say?

M It says it's only <u>for the disabled</u>.

W I get it.

해석

여 봐! 저기에 정말 많은 표지판이 있어.

남 너는 저것들이 무엇을 의미하는지 아니?

여 아니, 몰라. 네가 그것들에 대해 좀 설명해 줄래?

남 물론이지.

여 이 표지판은 무슨 뜻이야?

남 이것은 장애인들만 이용할 수 있다는 거야.

여 이해했어.

해설

여자가 물어본 표지판은 장애인 전용 표지판이다.

어휘

road sign 도로 표지 / mean[miːn] 의미하다 /
explain[ikspléin] ~을 설명하다 / the disabled 신체장애인

16 ③

Script

W Have you been to a flea market before?

M No, I haven't.

W I'm going to one now. Do you want to <u>come along</u>? You'll see many interesting things at the market.

M Like what?

W Various used products from <u>all over the world</u>.

M I see. What else?

W Antique furniture, <u>cheap clothes</u>, and second-hand accessories. You can even see some magic shows.

해석

여 너는 전에 벼룩시장에 가 본 적이 있니?

남 아니.

여 나 지금 갈 건데, 같이 갈래? 시장에서 흥미로운 것을 많이 볼 수 있을 거야.

남 예를 들면?

여 전 세계에서 모인 다양한 중고품들.

남 그렇구나. 그밖에는?

여 고가구, 싼 옷들, 중고 액세서리도 있어. 심지어 마술쇼도 볼 수 있을 거야.

해설

중고품, 고가구, 저렴한 의류, 마술쇼가 볼 수 있는 것으로 언급되었다.

어휘

flea market 벼룩시장 / come along 함께 가다 / various[véəriəs] 다양한 /
used[juzd] 중고의, 써서 낡은 / product[prάdəkt] 생산품 /
all over the world 전 세계에서 / antique[æntíːk] 골동의, 고미술의 /
furniture[fə́ːrnitʃər] 가구 / cheap[tʃiːp] 값이 싼, 저렴한 /
clothes[klouðz] 옷, 의복 / second-hand 중고의, 고물의 /
accessory[æksésəri] 액세서리

17 ②

Script

① W How do you like these cookies?
    M They're so delicious.

② W Would you like some pizza?
    M <u>Help yourself</u>.

③ W What does this sign say?
    M There's <u>no swimming allowed</u>.

④ W Are you interested in popular music?
    M Sure. I listen to it often.

⑤ W May I help you?
    M No, thanks. <u>I'm just browsing</u>.

해석

① 여 이 쿠키들이 어떤가요?
    남 정말로 맛있어요.

② 여 피자 좀 드실래요?
    남 마음껏 드세요.

③ 여 어 표지판은 무슨 뜻인가요?
    남 수영이 허락되지 않습니다.

④ 여 대중음악에 관심이 있습니까?
    남 네, 저는 자주 듣습니다.

⑤ 여 도와 드릴까요?
    남 아니요, 괜찮아요. 저는 그냥 구경하는 중이에요.

해설

② 음식을 권한 사람에게 반대로 마음껏 드시라는 대답은 어울리지 않는다.

어휘

delicious[dilíʃəs] 맛있는 / Help yourself. 마음껏 드세요. / allow[əláu]
~을 허락하다 / browse[brauz] (상품을) 훑어보다

18 ④

Script

W When Eric was on his way home, he found someone illegally parked <u>in front of</u> his house. There was a parking lot near the park, but the driver wanted <u>to save on</u> parking fees. The car is blocking his driveway, so he might have a hard time getting his car <u>out of the garage</u>. In this situation, what would Eric say to the driver?

해석

여 Eric은 집에 오는 길에 자신의 집 앞에 불법으로 주차한 사람을 발견했다. 공원 근처에 주차장이 있지만, 그 운전자는 돈을 절약하고 싶었다. Eric은 그 차가 자신의 차고 진입로를 막고 있어서 차고에서 차를 꺼내는 데 어려움을 겪을 수도 있다. 이 상황에서 Eric 그에게 뭐라고 말을 할까?

when it's ready, okay?

W Thanks. I appreciate it.

여 안녕하세요, Simpson 씨. 이 시계를 수리하고 싶어요.

남 아, 뭐가 문제인 것 같죠?

여 약간 빠른 것 같아요.

남 그렇구나. 시계는 나에게 두고 가고, 준비가 되면 전화해 줄게, 알았지?

여 감사해요. 감사합니다.

해설

시계를 고치면 연락 주겠다는 말에 "감사해요. 감사합니다."라는 응답이 적절하다.

① 시간을 내 주셔서 감사합니다.

② 무엇이 잘못되었나요?

④ 제가 언제 오면 되나요?

⑤ 네 시계가 문제가 아니라 네 태도가 문제야.

어휘

repair[ripέər] ~을 수리하다 / run[rʌn] (기계가) 돌아가다, 작동하다 / appreciate[əpríːʃièit] ~에 감사하다

---

19 ⑤

Script

M Hey, Diana. Watch your step!

W Ouch!

M Does it hurt?

W Yeah. I think I sprained my ankle. I can't get up.

M You'd better go to see a doctor.

W I don't think I can walk.

M Don't worry. I can carry you on my back.

W Thank you. I should have been more careful.

해석

남 이봐, Diana. 발 조심해!

여 아야!

남 아프니?

여 응. 발목을 삔 것 같아. 일어서지 못하겠어.

남 병원에 가 보는 게 좋겠다.

여 걸을 수 없을 것 같아.

남 걱정하지 마. 내가 너를 업을 수 있어.

여 고마워. 좀 더 조심했어야 했는데.

해설

업어 주겠다는 말에 "고마워. 좀 더 조심했어야 했는데."라는 응답이 가장 적절하다.

① 하지만 정말 무거워 보인다.

② 미안하지만, 나는 빨리 걸을 수가 없어.

③ 나는 대개 그 가방을 들고 다니지 않아.

④ 나는 너를 업고 갈 만큼 튼튼해.

어휘

watch one's step 발밑을 조심하다 / sprain[sprein] 삐다 / ankle[ǽŋkl] 발목 / carry someone on one's back 등에 업다

---

20 ③

Script

W Hello, Mr. Simpson. I'd like to have this watch repaired.

M Oh, what seems to be the problem with it?

W It's running a bit fast.

M I see. You can leave the watch with me, and I'll call you

---

p.64~67

08회 영어듣기모의고사

01 ①	02 ③	03 ⑤	04 ③	05 ④
06 ②	07 ④	08 ⑤	09 ④	10 ⑤
11 ③	12 ①	13 ⑤	14 ②	15 ③
16 ③	17 ②	18 ④	19 ③	20 ④

---

01 ①

Script

W When you're sitting down, you need to do some exercises to relax your muscles. First, bend your upper body forward and lift your heels as high as possible. At the same time put your hands on your knees. If you hold this position for 5 seconds, your muscles will feel more relaxed.

해석

여 앉아 있을 때 근육의 긴장을 풀어 주기 위해 운동이 필요합니다. 우선 상체를 앞으로 구부리고 발뒤꿈치는 가능한 한 높이 드십시오. 동시에 손은 무릎에 올려놓으십시오. 이 자세를 5초 동안 유지하면, 근육의 긴장이 풀릴 것입니다.

해설

의자에 앉은 자세에서 상체는 구부리고, 발뒤꿈치는 최대한 들고, 손은 무릎에 놓은 자세이다.

어휘

relax[rilǽks] (긴장을) 완화하다, 풀게 하다 / bend[bend] ~을 구부리다 / upper[ʌ́pər] 위에 있는 / forward[fɔ́ːrwərd] 앞으로 / lift[lift] ~을 들어

올리다 / heel[hi:l] 발뒤꿈치 / at the same time 동시에 / knee[ni:] 무릎 /
hold[hould] (어떤 상태를) 유지하다

02 ③

Script

M Mom, you promised to buy me a suit, right?

W Well, I was going to buy you a suit, but your uncle told
me that he has one that he used to wear, but looks
good as new.

M I don't want to wear a used suit.

W Listen! It looks brand-new.

M It's like a new one, but it's not a new one.

W Mark, if the suit looked old and out of fashion, I would
buy you a new one. But just like I told you, it looks
fantastic. I'm sure you'll like it once you see it.

해석

남 엄마, 저에게 정장을 사 주기로 약속했잖아요, 그렇죠?

여 있잖아, 네게 정장을 사 주려고 했는데, 네 삼촌이 자기가 입던 것이지
만 새것처럼 좋아 보이는 것이 하나 있다고 말을 하잖니.

남 나는 누가 입던 것을 입고 싶지 않아요.

여 들어 봐! 새것 같단다.

남 새것 같지만, 새것은 아니잖아요.

여 Mark, 그 정장이 낡고, 구식이라면 새것을 사주겠지만, 내가 말한 것처
럼 아주 좋아 보여. 네가 그것을 보면 분명히 좋아할 거야.

해설

남자는 엄마가 정장을 사 주지 않고, 삼촌이 입던 양복을 주겠다고 해서 기분
이 언짢을 것이다.

어휘

suit[su:t] 정장 / used to+동사원형 ~하곤 했다 / used[juzd] 중고의,
사용된 / brand-new 신품의 / out of fashion 구식의, 유행이 지난

03 ⑤

Script

W What a mess!

M I'm sorry. I'm always like this.

W Look at those things on your desk. What would you do
if you needed something?

M I know. That's why every time I look for something, it
takes me all day.

W You should get yourself more organized.

M I know, but it's not easy. I'll try.

해석

여 정말 지저분하네!

남 미안해. 나는 항상 이래.

여 책상 위에 있는 것들을 좀 봐. 뭔가 필요하면 어떻게 찾니?

남 알아. 그래서 내가 무엇인가를 찾을 때마다 온종일 걸리는 거야.

여 너의 물건들을 좀 더 정리 정돈해야겠다.

남 알아, 하지만 쉽지가 않네. 노력할게.

해설

남자는 정리 정돈을 못한다.

어휘

mess[mes] 엉망진창, 뒤죽박죽 / all day 온종일 / organized[ɔ́:rɡənàizd]
정돈된, 정리된

04 ③

Script

M I'm having a surprise party for my sister. Can you come
and lend me a hand with the party preparations?

W Absolutely. What time?

M At 5 in the evening.

W Well, I'm afraid I may be about a half an hour late.
Since I haven't bought a present for her, I have to stop
by the department store.

M That's all right. She'll probably come home around 7.

W Okay. See you then.

해석

남 내 여동생을 위해 깜짝 파티를 할 거야. 와서 내가 파티 준비하는 것을
도와줄래?

여 물론이지. 몇 시에?

남 저녁 5시에.

여 음, 미안하지만 한 30분 정도 늦을 것 같다. 선물을 아직 안 사서 백화
점에 들러야 하거든.

남 괜찮아. 내 동생은 아마 7시쯤에 집에 올 거야.

여 알았어. 그때 봐.

해설

여자는 5시보다 30분 늦는다고 했으니까 5시 30분에 도착할 것이다.

어휘

lend A a hand A를 도와주다 / preparation[prèpəréiʃən] 준비 /
absolutely[ǽbsəlù:tli] (대답으로) 물론, 그렇고말고 / stop by ~에 들르다
/ department store 백화점

05 ④

Script

M I just can't find my gym bag anywhere.

W When was the last time you had your bag with you?

M I had it with me when I came out of the gym.

W Then?

M I put the bag on the front seat.

W And?

M I picked up my shirts at the cleaners. Until then, I
was holding the bag in my hand. I think I left it on the
counter.

W You'd better call them before they close.

해석

남 나의 운동용 가방이 어디 있는지 찾을 수가 없어.

여 언제 마지막으로 가지고 있었는데?

남 체육관에서 나올 때 가방을 가지고 있었어.

여 그러고 나서는?

남 앞좌석에 가방을 놓았어.

여 그리고?

남 세탁소에 가서 셔츠를 찾았어. 그때까지는 손에 가방을 들고 있었어. 내 생각에 계산대에 둔 것 같아.

여 세탁소가 문을 닫기 전에 전화해 보는 게 좋겠다.

해설

남자가 마지막에 가방을 놓았다고 생각하는 곳은 세탁소 계산대이다.

어휘

gym[dʒim] 체육관 / front[frʌnt] 앞의 / the cleaners 세탁소 / hold[hould] ~을 잡다 / had better ~하는 것이 좋겠다

06 ②

Script

W Jimmy, I'm ready. It took almost 5 hours to do that, but I'm satisfied. How about you?

M I am not ready yet, but let's go.

W What do you mean?

M I didn't even start, and I don't think I can do it. I'm just going to give up.

W Hey. Starting is difficult, but once you start doing it, you can finish it.

M Do you think so?

W Yes, just do it.

해석

여 Jimmy, 나는 준비됐어. 그것을 하는 데 거의 다섯 시간이 걸렸지만 만족해. 너는?

남 나는 아직 준비가 안 됐지만 가자.

여 무슨 말이야?

남 나는 시작도 하지 못했어. 그리고 할 수 있을 것 같지가 않아. 그냥 포기하려고.

여 야. 시작은 어렵지만, 일단 시작하고 나면 끝마칠 수 있어.

남 그렇게 생각해?

여 응. 그냥 해.

해설

남자는 시작도 해 보지 않고 포기하려 하고 있다. 시작을 하는 것이 중요하다는 의미를 담고 있는 대화이므로 "시작이 반이다."라는 속담이 적절하다.

① 고통이 없으면 얻는 것도 없다.

③ 이미 엎질러진 물이다.

④ 돌멩이 하나로 새 두 마리를 잡는다. (일석이조)

⑤ 사공이 많으면 배가 산으로 간다.

어휘

almost[ɔ́:lmoust] 거의, 대략 / satisfied[sǽtisfàid] 만족한 / give up 포기하다

07 ④

Script

M What time does the movie start?

W In 5 minutes. The previews they show us before the movie are pretty interesting.

M I know, but there's a trick. They only show us interesting scenes, but when we actually watch the movie, it is sometimes not interesting at all.

W That's true. Peter, the movie is starting now. Why don't you set your cell phone to vibration? I already did mine.

M No problem.

해석

남 영화가 몇 시에 시작하니?

여 오 분 후에. 영화 전에 보여 주는 예고편이 정말 재미있네.

남 그래. 하지만 함정이 있어. 그들은 재미있는 장면만 보여 주는데, 우리가 실제 영화를 보면 때때로 전혀 재미있지가 않잖아.

여 맞아. Peter, 이제 영화 시작한다. 전화기를 진동으로 바꾸지 그러니? 나는 벌써 했어.

남 그래.

해설

여자는 남자에게 전화기를 진동으로 바꾸라고 부탁하고 있다.

어휘

preview[prí:vjù:] 예고편 / trick[trik] 계교, 함정, 속임수 / scene[si:n] 장면 / set[set] (상태로) 되게 하다, 상태로 하다 / vibration[vaibréiʃən] 진동

08 ⑤

Script

W Welcome. What can I do for you?

M Yes. May I have a map of the town?

W Sure. Here you are.

M Can you recommend some interesting places around here?

W This map helps you search for famous sights such as palaces, skyscrapers, and national museums. They are within a walking distance.

M Thank you. It's very kind of you.

W Not at all. That's my job, and I hope you have a good time.

해석

여 어서 오세요. 무엇을 도와드릴까요?

남 네. 도시의 지도를 얻을 수 있을까요?

여 네. 여기 있습니다.

남 이 주변에 흥미로운 장소를 좀 추천해 주실래요?

여 이 지도가 궁이나, 고층빌딩, 국립 박물관과 같은 유명한 관광지를 찾는 데 도움이 될 거예요. 그것들은 걸을 수 있는 거리에 있습니다.

남 감사합니다. 매우 친절하시군요.

여 아닙니다. 그것이 저의 일인걸요. 그리고 좋은 시간을 보내기를 바라요.

해설

남자는 여행 안내소에서 관광 정보를 얻고 있다.

09 ④
Script

M It was the first class at a new school. I was very nervous because I didn't know anyone and didn't speak fluent English. When the class ended, all of the students left the room. No one came over to talk to me. I felt very sad. Then, suddenly, I heard someone call my name. I turned around and saw a girl from my class. She gave me a big, friendly smile. I felt better right away.

해석

남 새로운 학교에서의 첫 수업이었다. 나는 매우 긴장을 했다. 왜냐하면, 나는 아는 사람이 아무도 없었고, 영어도 유창하게 하지 못했기 때문이다. 수업이 끝나고, 모든 학생이 교실을 떠났다. 나에게 말을 하러 다가오는 사람이 아무도 없었다. 나는 매우 슬펐다. 그때 갑자기 누군가 나의 이름을 부르는 것을 들었다. 나는 뒤를 돌았고, 우리 반 소녀 한 명을 보았다. 그녀는 나에게 크고, 친근한 미소를 보냈다. 나는 바로 기분이 나아졌다.

해설

전학 간 학교에는 친구가 한 명도 없었고, 첫 수업에 매우 긴장을 했으며, 영어를 잘하지 못했다.

어휘

nervous[nə́:rvəs] 긴장한 / fluent[flú:ənt] 유창한 / suddenly[sʌ́dnli] 갑자기 / turn around 뒤돌아보다 / friendly[fréndli] 친근한 / right away 곧바로, 즉시

10 ⑤
Script

W Hello, sorry I'm late. The streets are so crowded.

M That's all right. I just got here, too.

W I'd like to tell you how sorry I am about the mix-up yesterday.

M What happened to you? I thought we were going to have lunch together.

W I really apologize. I completely forgot about our appointment.

M Don't worry about it.

해석

여 안녕, 늦어서 미안해. 길이 너무 붐벼서.

남 괜찮아. 나도 방금 왔어.

여 어제의 혼란에 대해서 정말 미안하다고 말하고 싶어.

남 무슨 일이었어? 같이 점심을 먹기로 했다고 생각했는데.

여 정말로 사과할게. 우리 약속을 완전히 잊어버렸어.

남 신경 쓰지 마.

해설

여자는 남자와 같이 점심을 먹기로 한 약속을 잊어버렸다.

11 ③
Script

W Excuse me, could you tell me the way to the nearest bank?

M Let me see. Go straight along Maple Street and turn right at the second corner. Then go one more block and turn left at the corner. It's on your right.

W That's not simple. Turn right at the second corner. Go one more block and turn left, and it is on my right.

M That's right.

W Thank you very much.

해석

여 실례합니다. 가장 가까운 은행에 가는 길을 좀 알려 주시겠어요?

남 어디 볼까요. 메이플가를 따라 곧장 가다가 두 번째 모퉁이에서 오른쪽으로 도세요. 그리고 나서 한 블록을 더 가시다가 모퉁이에서 왼쪽으로 도세요. 은행은 당신의 오른쪽에 있을 거예요.

여 간단하지 않네요. 두 번째 모퉁이에서 우회전, 한 블록 더 가서 좌회전하면 제 오른쪽에 있군요.

남 맞아요.

여 정말 감사합니다.

해설

두 번째 모퉁이에서 우회전, 한 블록 더 가서 좌회전한 후 오른쪽에 있는 건물이다.

어휘

nearest[niərist] 가장 가까운 / straight[streit] 곧장 / along[əlɔ́:ŋ] ~을 따라서 / turn right 오른쪽으로 돌다 / turn left 왼쪽으로 돌다

12 ①
Script

W Excuse me, but you are not supposed to drink here.

M Why not?

W Look at the floor. It's all carpeted. If you spill your drink, it will cost a lot to have it cleaned.

M OK. Where is a trash can?

W There is one right next to the restroom.

M Thank you. By the way, I saw the sign saying you will be closed for a week.

W That's right. We'll be remodeling inside the building.

M OK, thank you.

해석

여 실례합니다만, 여기서 음료수를 마시면 안 됩니다.

남 왜 안 돼요?

여 바닥을 좀 보세요. 카펫이 전부 깔려 있잖아요. 당신이 음료수를 흘리면, 그것을 청소하는데 비용이 많이 들 거예요.

남 알겠어요. 쓰레기통은 어디에 있나요?

여　화장실 바로 옆에 하나 있습니다.

남　감사합니다. 그런데 일주일 동안 이곳이 문을 닫을 거라는 게시물을 보았어요.

여　맞습니다. 우리는 건물 내부수리를 할 거예요.

남　알았습니다. 감사합니다.

해설

여자는 건물을 지키고, 관리하는 관리인이다.

어휘

cost[kɔːst] 비용이 ~가 들다 / trash can 쓰레기통 / restroom[réstrùːm] 화장실 / remodel[riːmάdl] ~을 개조하다

13 ⑤

Script

M　Are you ready to order?

W　Yes. I'd like to have a tuna sandwich and a chicken salad.

M　Anything to drink?

W　Sprite, please. And I'd like some take-out for my brother. A cheese burger and a Coke.

M　OK. It'll be ready by the time you finish your meal.

W　Thank you. Wait a minute! Can you cancel the soda? I think I have some at home.

M　Sure.

해설

남　주문할 준비가 되셨습니까?

여　네. 참치 샌드위치하고 닭고기 샐러드로 할게요.

남　마실 것은요?

여　스프라이트 주세요. 그리고 제 남동생을 위해 테이크 아웃을 하고 싶어요. 치즈 버거하고 콜라로요.

남　네. 손님께서 식사를 마치실 때쯤에 준비될 것입니다.

여　감사합니다. 잠깐만요! 음료수는 취소해 주실래요? 집에 있는 것 같아요.

남　물론이죠.

해설

여자가 마지막에 음료수를 취소했으므로 주문하지 않은 음식은 Coke이다.

어휘

tuna[tjúːnə] 참치 / take-out 사가지고 가는 요리 / meal[miːl] 식사 / cancel[kǽnsəl] ~을 취소하다

14 ②

Script

M　Who wrote all those?

W　I'm not sure, Mr. Brown.

M　Who was in this classroom?

W　Jacob and Harry. When I got here, they were leaving.

M　I see. Do you know where they went?

W　I wish I knew, Mr. Brown.

M　Could you erase the board for me, Sally?

W　Yes, sir.

해설

남　저것들을 누가 다 쓴 거니?

여　잘 모르겠어요, Brown 선생님.

남　누가 이 교실에 있었지?

여　Jacob하고 Harry요. 제가 여기 왔을 때, 그들이 떠나고 있었어요.

남　알았다. 그 애들이 어디로 갔는지 아니?

여　몰라요, Brown 선생님.

남　나를 위해 칠판을 지워 주겠니, Sally?

여　네, 선생님.

해설

여자는 선생님을 위해 칠판을 지울 것이다.

어휘

erase[iréis] ~을 지우다 / board[bɔːrd] 칠판; 널빤지

15 ③

Script

W　Attention, please. As you all know, we run two different libraries. One is for students, and the other is for adults. Since last week, there have been some complaints from the adults that some students are using their building and are making a lot of noise. That library is limited to adults only. Any student caught entering the library will be banned from the student library. Thank you.

해설

여　주목해 주십시오, 여러분. 모두 알다시피, 우리는 두 개의 다른 도서관을 운영하고 있습니다. 하나는 학생을 위한 것이고, 다른 하나는 성인을 위한 것입니다. 지난주 이후로 성인들에게서 학생들 몇 명이 성인 도서관을 사용하면서 시끄럽게 한다는 항의가 들어오고 있습니다. 그 도서관은 성인들만 사용하도록 제한되어 있습니다. 그 도서관에 들어가다가 발각된 학생은 학생 도서관의 출입이 금지될 것입니다. 감사합니다.

해설

일반 성인들을 위한 도서관에 학생들의 출입을 통제한다는 안내 방송이다.

어휘

Attention, please! 여러분께 알립니다! 주목해 주십시오! / run[rʌn] ~을 운영하다 / adult[ədʌ́lt] 성인 / complaint[kəmpléint] 불평 / make noise 떠들다, 소란을 피우다 / limited[límitid] 제한된, 한정된 / ban[bæn] ~을 금지하다

16 ③

Script

W　Do you like jazz? If you do, you're going to like the jazz music of Stevie Wonder. You can see him this weekend at 7 P.M. Stevie Wonder is playing two concerts this Friday and Saturday at the "All That Jazz Club." The cover charge is 25 dollars which includes a glass of wine served with your dinner. Thank you.

해설

여　재즈를 좋아하십니까? 좋아한다면, Stevie Wonder의 재즈 음악을

좋아할 것입니다. 여러분은 이번 주말 밤 7시에 그를 볼 수 있습니다. Stevie Wonder는 이번 금요일과 토요일에 All That Jazz Club에서 두 번의 연주를 할 것입니다. 입장료는 25달러이며, 저녁과 포도주가 함께 제공됩니다. 감사합니다.

해설
공연은 매주 주말이 아니라, 이번 금요일과 토요일에 있다.

어휘
cover charge 입장료, 봉사료(전체적인 서비스 요금) / include[inklúːd] ~을 포함하다 / serve[səːrv] 제공하다

17 ②
Script

M I'm very closely related to students. Sometimes they feel very happy, and sometimes they feel very sad because of me. At the same time, some students are longing to receive me, while others are not. When students receive me, they show me to their parents. It's my duty to show the students' grades.

해석
남 나는 학생들과 매우 밀접한 관련이 있습니다. 때때로 그들은 나 때문에 매우 행복하고, 나 때문에 매우 슬픕니다. 동시에 어떤 학생들은 나를 받기를 애타게 바라고, 또 다른 학생들은 그렇지 않습니다. 학생들이 나를 받으면, 그들은 나를 부모님께 보여 줍니다. 학생들의 성적을 알려 주는 것이 나의 의무입니다.

해설
학생들의 성적을 보여 주는 나는 성적표이다.

어휘
closely[klóusli] 밀접하게 / be related to ~와 관련이 있다 / long[lɔːŋ] ~을 열망하다, 애타게 바라다 / duty[djúːti] 의무 / grade[greid] 성적

18 ④
Script

① **M** How often does the bus run?
   W As far as I know, you can catch it every 15 minutes.
② **M** We have some guide books for tourists. What would you like to know?
   W We're interested in the historical sites.
③ **M** What's the best way to explore Seoul?
   W The city tour bus is a good option.
④ **M** I'm planning to fly to New York. Have you ever been there?
   W Maybe 13 hours or so.
⑤ **M** I bought this CD player yesterday, but it doesn't work.
   W Let me see. I'm sorry for the inconvenience.

해석
① 남 이 버스는 얼마나 자주 운행을 합니까?
   여 제가 알기로 15분마다 이 버스를 탈 수 있습니다.
② 남 우리는 관광객을 위한 안내 책자가 좀 있습니다. 무엇을 알고 싶으세요?

   여 우리는 역사 유적지에 관심이 많습니다.
③ 남 서울을 살펴보는 가장 좋은 방법은 무엇입니까?
   여 시내 관광버스가 좋은 선택이죠.
④ 남 나는 비행기를 타고 뉴욕에 가려고 계획 중이야. 뉴욕에 가 본 적이 있니?
   여 아마 열세 시간 정도.
⑤ 남 제가 어제 이 CD 플레이어를 샀는데, 작동이 안 되네요.
   여 좀 보겠습니다. 불편을 끼쳐드려 죄송합니다.

해설
④ 뉴욕에 가 본 적이 있느냐고 물었는데 13시간 정도라고 대답하는 것은 어색하다.

어휘
run[rʌn] ~을 운행하다 / historical[histɔ́(ː)rikəl] 역사의, 역사적인 / explore[iksplɔ́ːr] ~을 탐험하다, 답사하다 / option[ápʃən] 선택, 선택하는 것 / inconvenience[ìnkənvíːnjəns] 불편

19 ③
Script

W Julian, what are you doing now?
M I'm playing computer games.
W Could you stop playing computer games and help me, please?
M OK. What do you want me to do?
W The house needs to be clean before Mom and Dad get home. They will be arriving shortly. Can you take out the garbage?
M Yes, I'd be glad to help you.

해석
여 Julian, 너 지금 뭐 하고 있니?
남 컴퓨터 게임을 하고 있어.
여 컴퓨터 게임 그만하고 나를 좀 도와줄래?
남 알았어. 내가 무엇을 하기를 바라는데?
여 부모님이 집에 오시기 전에 집을 청소해야 해. 엄마, 아빠가 곧 도착하실 거야. 쓰레기를 내다 버려 줄래?
남 응. 기꺼이 해 줄게.

해설
쓰레기를 버려 달라는 부탁에 "응. 기꺼이 해 줄게."라는 응답이 가장 적절하다.
① 저녁을 준비하자.
② 무엇을 도와드릴까요?
④ 응. 다음번에는 내가 그것을 쓰레기통에 넣을게.
⑤ 나와 같이 컴퓨터 게임 하기를 원하니?

어휘
shortly[ʃɔ́ːrtli] 곧 / take out ~을 가지고 나가다 / garbage[gáːrbidʒ] 쓰레기

20 ④
Script

W John, what happened? Your clothes are all dirty.

M We <u>got</u> <u>a</u> <u>flat</u> <u>tire</u> on the way here. While I was helping my father change the tire, I got <u>covered</u> <u>in</u> <u>dirt</u>.

W I'm glad you didn't have an accident.

M Yeah, me too. But look at me. What am I supposed to do?

W Oh, don't worry. You can wear my brother's suit. He is <u>about</u> <u>your</u> <u>size</u>.

M OK, I will. Thanks.

해석

여 John, 무슨 일이야? 옷이 전부 더럽네.

남 여기로 오는 길에 우리 차의 타이어가 바람이 빠졌어. 아버지가 타이어 갈아 끼우는 것을 돕다가 먼지를 뒤집어썼어.

여 사고가 나지 않아서 다행이다.

남 응, 나도 그래. 하지만 날 좀 봐. 내가 어떻게 해야 하지?

여 어, 걱정하지 마. 우리 오빠의 정장을 입어도 돼. 그는 대략 너의 사이즈야.

남 알았어, 그렇게. 고마워.

해설

오빠의 옷을 입으라는 호의에 "알았어. 그렇게. 고마워."라는 응답이 가장 적절하다.

① 너는 정말 운이 좋구나.

② 제발 조심해.

③ 너는 곤경에 처했어.

⑤ 지금 주문해도 되나요?

어휘

flat[flæt] 바람이 빠진, 터진 / dirt[dəːrt] 먼지 / be supposed to+동사원형 ~하기로 되어 있다 / wear[wɛər] ~을 입다 / suit[suːt] 신사복 한 벌

---

p.72-75

09회 영어듣기모의고사

01 ①	02 ⑤	03 ③	04 ②	05 ③
06 ⑤	07 ④	08 ③	09 ②	10 ⑤
11 ④	12 ③	13 ⑤	14 ②	15 ②
16 ①	17 ④	18 ④	19 ①	20 ①

01 ①

Script

W Listen carefully. I'd like you to <u>draw</u> <u>something</u> I'm going to describe now. If you do well, I'll <u>let</u> <u>you</u> <u>go</u> <u>home</u> right away. Now draw a circle inside a triangle and draw a square <u>inside</u> <u>the</u> <u>circle</u>. It's a very simple drawing. Please show me what you have drawn now.

해석

여 잘 들으세요. 저는 여러분이 제가 지금 묘사하는 것을 그리기를 원합니다. 여러분이 잘하면, 집에 바로 보내 줄게요. 자, 삼각형 안에 원을 그리시고, 그리고 그 원 안에 사각형을 그리세요. 매우 간단한 그림입니다.

당신이 지금 그린 것을 저에게 보여 주세요.

해설

삼각형 안에 원, 원 안에 사각형이 있는 그림이다.

어휘

carefully[kɛ́ərfəli] 주의하여, 조심스럽게 / draw[drɔː] ~을 그리다 / describe[diskráib] ~을 묘사하다, 말로 설명하다 / triangle[tráiæŋɡəl] 삼각형 / square[skwɛər] 사각형 / drawing[drɔ́ːiŋ] 그림

02 ⑤

Script

M Excuse me, are you Ms. Baker? I'm a huge fan of yours. It's a great pleasure meeting you here.

W Thank you. It's my pleasure, too.

M I've read every play you have written. Are you <u>working</u> <u>on</u> <u>another</u> <u>piece</u>?

W Yes. I'm writing a new play about my life.

M That sounds interesting.

W <u>It's</u> <u>coming</u> <u>out</u> <u>soon</u>.

M I hope your writing <u>goes</u> <u>well</u>.

W Thank you.

해석

남 실례합니다. 당신 Baker 씨이지요? 저는 당신의 열성팬입니다. 여기서 당신을 만나다니 정말 기쁘네요.

여 감사합니다. 저도 기쁘네요.

남 저는 당신이 쓴 모든 작품을 다 읽어 보았습니다. 또 다른 작품을 쓰고 계시나요?

여 네. 제 인생에 관한 새 작품을 쓰고 있습니다.

남 재미있겠네요.

여 곧 출간될 거예요.

남 집필 활동이 잘되기를 바랍니다.

여 감사합니다.

해설

여자는 연극을 쓰는 극작가이다.

어휘

huge[hjuːdʒ] 엄청난, 거대한 / pleasure[pléʒər] 기쁨 / play[plei] 연극, 희곡 / work on ~에 착수하다 / piece[piːs] 작품; 조각 / come out (책이) 출간되다, (상품이) 출시되다

03 ③

Script

W Hello, Mr. Johnson.

M Hi, Kelly. What can I do for you today?

W I'd like to <u>have</u> <u>my</u> <u>picture</u> <u>taken</u>.

M What's it for?

W It's for my passport.

M You must be going somewhere.

W Yes, <u>I'm</u> <u>planning</u> <u>to</u> <u>join</u> a language program in the States.

M I see.

해석

여 안녕하세요, Johnson 씨.

남 안녕, Kelly. 오늘은 무엇을 해 줄까?

여 사진을 찍으려고요.

남 무엇에 쓸 건데?

여 여권 사진이요.

남 어디 가는구나.

여 네, 미국에 어학연수 받으러 갈 계획이에요.

남 그렇구나.

해설

여자는 여권 사진을 찍으러 사진관에 왔다.

어휘

passport[pǽspɔ̀ːrt] 여권 / somewhere[sʌ́mʰwɛ̀ər] 어딘가, 어떤 장소 /
the States 미국

04 ②

Script

W Are you OK?

M Yes. Mrs. Kim told me if it happens again, she'll call my
   mother.

W Aren't you going to tell your mom about what
   happened?

M Are you crazy? If I do, she would kill me.

W Then, I am not supposed to tell her, right?

M That's exactly what I had in mind.

해석

여 너 괜찮니?

남 응. 김 선생님이 다시 그런 일이 있으면, 우리 어머니에게 전화할 거라
   고 했어.

여 무슨 일이 있었는지 엄마에게 말하지 않을 거니?

남 미쳤니? 내가 얘기하면, 엄마는 나를 가만두지 않을 거야.

여 그러면 나도 말하지 않아야겠네, 그렇지?

남 그게 바로 내 생각이야.

해설

"그게 바로 내 생각이야."라는 말은 동의를 의미한다.

어휘

happen[hǽpən] 발생하다, 일어나다 / be supposed to ～할 예정이다,
～하기로 되어 있다 / have something in mind ～을 뜻하다, ～에 관해 생각
하고 있다

05 ③

Script

W My father's birthday is coming, so I'm making a card
   for my dad.

M That's a good idea. What are you going to write on it?

W I'm going to write, "Thank you, Dad. Be happy. I'll try

my best to be a good daughter."

M Good. By the way, when is his birthday?

W It's the third Sunday in May. It's the day after tomorrow.

M I see. Your dad will be glad to know you love him so
   much.

해석

여 우리 아버지의 생신이 다가와서 아빠를 위해 카드를 만들고 있어.

남 좋은 생각이다. 뭐라고 쓸 거야?

여 "감사합니다, 아빠, 행복하세요. 좋은 딸이 되도록 최선을 다 할게요."라
   고 쓸 거야.

남 좋은데. 그런데, 아빠 생신이 언제야?

여 5월 셋째 일요일이야. 내일모레지.

남 그렇구나. 네가 아빠를 그렇게 많이 사랑한다는 걸 아시면 아빠가 기뻐
   하실 거야.

해설

아버지의 생신은 5월 셋째 일요일인 18일이고, 18일이 내일모레이므로 오늘
은 16일이다.

어휘

write on ～에 글씨를 쓰다 / daughter[dɔ́ːtər] 딸 /
the day after tomorrow 내일모레

06 ⑤

Script

W John, can you come over and help me?

M Sure. What is it?

W I need you to replace this light bulb for me.

M Where?

W It's the one in the kitchen.

M Then, I need a chair. I don't think I'm tall enough to
   reach it.

W You can bring the chair from your room.

M OK, Mom.

해석

여 John, 이리 와서 좀 도와줄래?

남 네. 무엇이에요?

여 네가 이 전등을 좀 갈아 끼워 줬으면 좋겠다.

남 어디요?

여 부엌에 있는 거.

남 그러면 의자가 필요해요. 제가 그것에 닿을 정도로 크지 않은 것 같거
   든요.

여 네 방에서 의자를 가져오면 되겠다.

남 네, 엄마.

해설

엄마가 아들에게 부엌의 전구를 갈아 끼워 달라고 부탁하고 있다.

어휘

replace[ripléis] ～을 바꾸다, 갈다 / light bulb 전구 / reach[riːtʃ] ～에 닿다

07 ④

Script

W Wow! You have really a lot of <u>laundry to do</u>.

M This is my first time to wash my clothes in this Laundromat. I'm going to wash these and dry them afterward.

W It'll take <u>quite a long time</u> to wash and dry them all.

M How long will it take?

W It'll take one and a half hours to wash them.

M That doesn't seem so long.

W But the drying takes 30 minutes <u>longer than the washing</u>.

M Yeah. That's quite a long time.

해석

여 와! 너는 정말 빨래가 많구나.

남 이번이 이 빨래방에서 처음으로 빨래하는 거야. 이 옷들을 빨아서 말릴 거야.

여 그걸 모두 세탁하고, 건조까지 하려면 시간이 꽤 걸릴 거야.

남 얼마나 걸리는데?

여 옷을 세탁하는데 한 시간 반 정도 걸릴 거야.

남 그 정도는 별로 오래 걸리는 것 같지 않은데.

여 하지만 옷을 말리는 데는 세탁하는 것보다 30분이 더 걸려.

남 응. 그건 정말 긴 시간이구나.

해설

세탁하는 데 한 시간 반, 건조하는 데 두 시간이 걸리므로 총 세 시간 반이 걸린다.

어휘

laundry[lɔ́:ndri] 세탁물 / Laundromat[lɔ́:ndrəmæt] 빨래방 / afterward[ǽftərwərd] 그 후에

08 ③

Script

W Hi, Mr. Johnson. I'd like to change my class schedule.

M OK. What do you want to change?

W I want to switch my biology class to English.

M I'm sorry, but you can't do that. The English class <u>is already full</u>.

W Ah, no way!

M Is there <u>any other class</u> you want to take?

W What about history?

M Let me check. Good, <u>that's available</u>.

해석

여 안녕하세요, Johnson 선생님. 제 수업 일정을 바꾸고 싶어요.

남 알았다. 무엇을 바꾸고 싶니?

여 생물학을 영어로 바꾸고 싶어요.

남 미안하지만, 그것은 안 될 것 같구나. 영어수업은 벌써 다 찼단다.

여 아, 안 돼요!

남 다른 듣고 싶은 과목이 있니?

여 역사는 어때요?

남 어디 보자. 좋아, 그건 가능하구나.

해설

여자는 생물학 수업을 다른 과목으로 바꾸고 싶어한다.

어휘

switch A to B A를 B로 바꾸다 / available[əvéiləbəl] 이용 가능한

09 ②

Script

W David, what are you interested in the most?

M My main interest is writing poems. I've written two poems <u>for our school newspaper</u>.

W That's great!

M How about you, Kathy?

W <u>I'm interested in</u> teaching ice-skating to young children. I've taught skating for 3 years. I only get 20 dollars <u>for a month</u> for bus fare. I'm not making any money from that.

M Then, you can say it's voluntary work.

해석

여 David, 가장 관심이 있는 것이 무엇이니?

남 나의 주요 관심사는 시를 쓰는 거야. 나는 우리 학교 신문에 두 편의 시를 게재했어.

여 대단하다!

남 너는 어때, Kathy?

여 나는 어린아이들에게 아이스 스케이트를 가르치는 것에 관심이 있어. 나는 스케이트를 3년 동안 가르쳤어. 나는 한 달에 버스비로 20달러를 받아. 나는 그 일로는 돈을 버는 것이 전혀 아니야.

남 그러면 자원 봉사라고 말할 수 있겠다.

해설

남자는 학교 신문에 자신의 시를 게재하고 싶어하는 것이 아니라 두 편의 시를 게재한 적이 있다.

어휘

interest[íntərist] 관심사 / fare[fɛər] 요금 / voluntary work 자원 봉사

10 ⑤

Script

W What are you going to do this weekend?

M I'm not sure. I guess I'll just stay home. Maybe I'll help my father <u>fix up the house</u>. What about you? Do you have any plans?

W My parents have <u>made a reservation</u> at a beach resort. I plan on getting a little sun.

M Sounds fantastic!

W Why don't you join us? We have enough room.

M Great! <u>I'd love to</u>.

해석

여 너는 이번 주말에 무엇을 할 거니?

남 확실하지는 않아. 그냥 집에 있으려고. 아마도 아버지가 집을 수리하는 것을 도울 거야. 너는? 무슨 계획이 있니?

여 우리 부모님이 비치 리조트에 예약을 하셨어. 나는 선탠을 좀 할 거야.

남 좋겠다!

여 같이 가지 그러니? 자리는 충분해.

남 좋은데! 나도 가고 싶어.

해설

여자는 주말에 해변에서 선탠을 할 것이다.

어휘

fix up 수리하다, 손질하다 / make a reservation 예약하다 / get some sun 선탠하다, 햇볕에 그을리다

11 ④
Script

M It took 2 years for me to invent my Super Bike. I'll show you what's special about it. First, there's a big headlight in the middle of the handlebar. Next, there are two robot arms from the main frame on each side. The tires are also very special. There are little pins on the tires. They make your bike-riding safe when it snows. There is also a button near the seat. If you push it, an umbrella will pop up to protect you from rain and sun.

해석

남 나는 Super Bike를 발명하는 데 2년이 걸렸습니다. 슈퍼 자전거가 무엇이 특별한지 알려 드리겠습니다. 우선, 핸들의 가운데 커다란 전조등이 있습니다. 다음으로, 양옆에 자전거의 본체에 붙어 있는 두 개의 로봇 팔이 있습니다. 타이어도 매우 특별합니다. 타이어에 작은 핀이 달려 있습니다. 그것들은 눈이 올 때 자전거 타는 것을 안전하게 해 줍니다. 의자 근처에 버튼도 있습니다. 당신이 그것을 누르면, 햇빛이나 비로부터 당신을 보호하기 위해 우산이 펼쳐집니다.

해설

Super Bike에는 도난 방지용 알람은 설치되어 있지 않다.

어휘

invent[invént] ~을 발명하다 / headlight[hédlàit] 전조등, 헤드라이트 / handlebar[hǽndlbɑ̀ːr] (자전거 등의) 핸들 / pop up 갑자기 나타나다 / protect A from B B로부터 A를 보호하다

12 ③
Script

W Excuse me, how much do you charge for renting a bike?

M 4 dollars an hour.

W That's too expensive. My brother and I don't have enough money.

M How much do you have?

W We had 10 dollars, but we each ate a hotdog. The hotdogs were 2 dollars each. So, this is all I got.

M Okay. Then, I'll just take that.

W Thank you very much.

해석

여 실례합니다. 자전거를 한 대 빌리는 데 얼마지요?

남 시간당 4달러란다.

여 너무 비싸네요. 저와 제 동생은 돈이 충분하지 않아요.

남 얼마가 있니?

여 10달러 있었지만, 우리는 핫도그를 하나씩 먹었어요. 핫도그가 하나에 2달러였어요. 그래서 이게 저희가 가진 전부예요.

남 알았다. 그러면 그것만 받으마.

여 정말 감사합니다.

해설

여자는 동생과 자신의 핫도그를 4달러에 사 먹었고, 자전거를 빌리는 데 10달러에서 남은 돈 6달러를 지불할 것이다.

어휘

charge[tʃɑːrdʒ] 지불을 요구하다, 청구하다 / rent[rent] ~을 빌리다 / expensive[ikspénsiv] 값비싼

13 ⑤
Script

W I'm very cold.

M Let me see. You've got a fever.

W How bad is it?

M I think you should go and see a doctor now.

W I can't even walk. Could you bring me a blanket first?

M Sure. I'll turn on the heater for you, OK?

W Would you give me the blanket first? My body is shaking now.

M OK. I'll be right back.

해석

여 나 너무 추워.

남 어디 보자. 열이 있구나.

여 얼마나 심해?

남 내 생각에 지금 병원에 가야겠다.

여 걷지도 못하겠어. 우선 담요를 좀 가져다줄래?

남 그래. 내가 난방기를 켜 줄게, 알았지?

여 담요를 먼저 가져다줄래? 이제는 몸이 떨려.

남 알았어. 곧 돌아올게.

해설

남자는 가장 먼저 담요를 가져다줄 것이다.

어휘

fever[fíːvər] 열 / turn on ~을 켜다 / heater[hìːtər] 난방기 / shake[ʃeik] (몸, 목소리가) 떨리다

14 ②

Script

W What time does your flight depart?

M 3:30. My boarding time is 3:10, so I have to get to the gate before 3:10.

W I see. Then, you only have one hour left before the flight. When is Tom going to be here?

M He should be here soon. He'll probably be here 10 minutes before boarding time. He's always like that.

W I see.

해석

여 비행기가 몇 시에 출발하니?

남 3시 30분. 탑승 시각이 3시 10분이니까 3시 10분 전에는 탑승 게이트에 도착해야 해.

여 알았어. 그러면 비행기 시간까지 한 시간밖에 안 남았네. Tom은 언제 여기에 오는 거야?

남 곧 올 거야. 그는 아마 탑승 시간 10분 전에 여기에 도착할 거야. 그는 항상 그러거든.

여 그렇구나.

해설

탑승 시간은 3시 10분이고 Tom은 탑승 시간 10분 전에 도착할 것이므로 3시에 도착할 것이다.

어휘

flight[flait] 항공편, 비행 / depart[dipáːrt] 출발하다, 떠나다 / boarding[bɔ́ːrdiŋ] 탑승, 승선

15 ②

Script

① **W** Sorry, but I have to leave now.
  M Then, when can I see you again?

② **W** Hey, you are not supposed to cut in line.
  M I'm sorry. I thought you were not in line.

③ **W** Watch out!
  M Thanks, I couldn't see the bike coming.

④ **W** Would you help me carry these boxes?
  M Sorry. My hands are full right now.

⑤ **W** I can't contact him right now.
  M That's OK. I'll call him later.

해석

① 여 미안하지만 나는 지금 가야 해.
  남 그러면 언제 다시 볼 수 있을까?

② 여 이것 봐요, 새치기를 하면 안 되지요.
  남 미안합니다. 당신이 줄을 안 서 있는 줄 알았어요.

③ 여 조심해요!
  남 고마워요, 자전거가 오는 것을 보지 못했어요.

④ 여 이 상자들을 옮기는 것을 좀 도와줄래요?
  남 미안해. 지금 당장은 빈손이 없어.

⑤ 여 지금 당장은 그와 연락이 안 돼요.

남 괜찮아요. 제가 나중에 전화할게요.

해설

줄을 서 있는데 다른 사람이 새치기하려는 상황이다.

어휘

be supposed to+동사원형 ~하기로 되어 있다 / cut in line 새치기하다 / carry[kǽri] ~을 운반하다 / full[ful] 가득 찬 / contact[kántækt] ~와 연락하다, 접촉하다

16 ①

Script

W Is anyone out there?

M Yes. Who is it?

W It's Cindy. It's very dark here, and I can't see anything. Please help me.

M What are you doing there?

W The power has gone out, and the elevator has stopped.

M Why don't you push the yellow button there?

W I tried, but no one answered.

M Did you call 911 to help you?

W My cell phone doesn't work in here. Can you call them for me?

해석

여 밖에 누구 있어요?

남 네, 누구 시죠?

여 Cindy에요. 여기는 너무 어두워서 아무것도 볼 수가 없어요. 저를 좀 도와주세요.

남 너 거기서 뭐해?

여 전기가 나가서 엘리베이터가 멈췄어.

남 거기에 있는 노란 버튼을 누르지그래?

여 눌렀는데 응답이 없어.

남 911에 전화해서 도움을 청했니?

여 내 휴대 전화가 여기서 작동을 안 해. 네가 나를 위해서 전화를 좀 해줄래?

해설

여자는 엘리베이터에 갇혀서 무서워하고 있다.

어휘

power[páuər] 전력, 전기 / go out 꺼지다, 나가다 / elevator[éləvèitər] 엘리베이터 / push[puʃ] ~을 누르다, 밀다 / answer[ǽnsər] 응답하다

17 ④

Script

W What if there was a natural disaster here in your town?

M You mean like an earthquake, typhoon, or flood?

W Yes. Something like that.

M I don't know. I might get frightened. How about you?

W I would find somewhere safe to go like a basement.

M   What if you are not inside a building?

W   I haven't really thought about that.

해석

여   만약에 자연재해가 여기 너의 마을에서 발생하면 어떨 거 같아?

남   지진이나, 태풍, 홍수 같은 것을 말하는 거야?

여   응. 그런 것들.

남   몰라. 무섭겠지. 너는?

여   지하실 같은 안전한 곳을 찾아야겠지.

남   만약에 네가 건물 안에 있지 않으면?

여   그것은 생각을 안 해 봤는데.

해설

지진, 태풍, 홍수, 대피 장소(지하실)가 언급되었고, 언급되지 않은 것은 산사태이다.

어휘

What if ~?(= What will[would] happen if의 줄임말) ~라면 어떻게 될까? / natural disaster 자연재해 / earthquake[ɔ́ːrθkwèik] 지진 / typhoon[taifúːn] 태풍 / flood[flʌd] 홍수 / frightened[fráitnd] 무서운, 두려운 / basement[béismənt] 지하

18 ④
Script

W   Hey, John. Wake up! I'm kind of sleepy. Please start talking to me.

M   Okay. Are we almost there?

W   No, not yet.

M   How much farther do we still have to go?

W   We have to go for 2 hours more.

M   It takes longer than we expected.

W   Yeah, we still have a long way to go. And what's more, I'm afraid we've run out of gas.

해석

여   얘, John. 일어나! 나 좀 졸려. 나에게 말을 좀 걸어 봐.

남   알았어. 우리 거의 다 왔니?

여   아니, 아직.

남   아직 얼마나 더 가야 하니?

여   두 시간은 더 가야 해.

남   우리가 예상했던 것보다 오래 걸리네.

여   응, 우리는 아직도 갈 길이 멀었어. 게다가 연료가 다 떨어져가서 걱정이야.

해설

여자는 기름이 떨어져가서 걱정을 하고 있다.

어휘

kind of 어느 정도, 약간 / sleepy[slíːpi] 졸리는 / farther[fáːrðər] 더 멀리 / expect[ikspékt] 예상하다 / what's more 게다가 / run out of gas (차가) 기름이 떨어지다

19 ①
Script

M   Wow! Summer vacation is almost here.

W   Right. Only one more week to go.

M   Do you have any plans for the vacation?

W   Not really. My mom told me if I don't prepare for the next semester, I'll be in trouble. My grades are getting lower and lower. By the way, I heard you're going to Paris this summer vacation.

M   Right. I can't wait.

해석

남   와! 여름 방학이 눈앞이다.

여   그래. 겨우 한 주 남았지.

남   방학에 무슨 계획이 있니?

여   아니 별로. 우리 엄마가 그러시는데 내가 다음 학기를 대비하지 않으면 힘들 거래. 성적이 계속 떨어지고 있거든. 그건 그렇고, 나는 네가 이번 여름 방학에 파리에 간다고 들었어.

남   맞아. 기다릴 수가 없어. (정말 가고 싶어.)

해설

파리에 간다고 들었다는 말에 "맞아, 기다릴 수가 없어. (정말 가고 싶어.)"라는 응답이 가장 적절하다.

② 늦어서 미안해.

③ 응, 나는 에펠 탑을 봤어.

④ 여름 방학이 거의 끝났어.

⑤ 고마워. 굉장한 경험이었어.

어휘

prepare for ~을 준비하다 / semester[siméstər] 학기 / be in trouble 곤경에 처하다 / grade[greid] 성적

20 ①
Script

W   Have you lost some weight since you went on a diet?

M   Just a little.

W   You told me you don't eat anything after 7, right?

M   That's true, but it doesn't work much.

W   Why don't you try working out?

M   I don't like exercising.

해석

여   너 다이어트 시작한 이후로 살이 좀 빠졌니?

남   그저 약간.

여   저녁 7시 이후에 아무것도 먹지 않는다고 했었지, 그렇지?

남   맞아, 하지만 효과가 크지 않아.

여   운동을 하지 그러니?

남   난 운동을 좋아하지 않아.

해설

운동을 하라고 권하는 말에 "난 운동을 좋아하지 않아."라는 응답이 가장 적절하다.

② 그러고 싶지만, 나는 일을 할 수 없어.

③ 일자리를 구하고 싶지 않아.

④ 요즘에는 일자리를 구하기가 어려워.

⑤ 그렇게 말하지 마. 나는 돈이 하나도 없어.

어휘

go on a diet 다이어트를 시작하다 / work out 운동하다

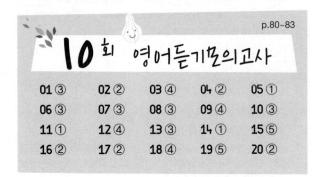

p.80~83

10회 영어듣기모의고사

01 ③	02 ②	03 ④	04 ②	05 ①
06 ③	07 ③	08 ③	09 ④	10 ③
11 ①	12 ④	13 ③	14 ①	15 ⑤
16 ②	17 ②	18 ④	19 ⑤	20 ②

01 ③

Script

M ① The TV set is between the two windows.

② There is a bed on the right side of the room.

③ A picture frame is on the left wall above the dresser.

④ There is a dresser on the other side of the bed.

⑤ The lamp stand is right next to the dresser.

해석

남 ① 텔레비전세트가 두 개의 창문 사이에 있다.

② 방의 오른쪽에 침대가 하나 있다.

③ 액자가 옷장 위 왼쪽 벽에 걸려 있다.

④ 옷장이 침대 반대쪽에 있다.

⑤ 전등이 옷장 바로 옆에 있다.

해설

액자는 벽에 걸려 있는 것이 아니라 옷장 위에 놓여 있다.

어휘

frame[freim] 액자, 틀 / dresser[drésər] 옷장 / lamp stand 전등 / next to ~ 옆에

02 ②

Script

M Good morning, how can I help you?

W I'm looking for a house for my family.

M Okay. Tell me what type you're looking for.

W I'm looking for a three-bedroom apartment near the subway.

M We surely have a place close to the subway.

W What's the monthly rent?

M 1,800 dollars a month including water and electricity.

Would you like to go and have a look around the apartment?

W Sure.

해석

남 안녕하세요, 어떻게 도와드릴까요?

여 저는 제 가족과 살 집을 찾고 있습니다.

남 알았습니다. 어떤 형태를 원하는지 말씀해 보세요.

여 저는 전철역 근처로 방이 세 개 있는 아파트를 찾고 있어요.

남 물론 전철 가까이에 있는 집이 있습니다.

여 한 달 월세가 얼마인가요?

남 수도와 전기를 포함해서 한 달에 1,800달러입니다. 가서 한 번 둘러보시겠어요?

여 그러죠.

해설

부동산 중개인과 고객 사이에서 일어날 수 있는 대화이다.

어휘

surely[ʃúərli] 물론, 확실히 / monthly[mʌ́nθli] 한 달에 한 번의, 매달의 / rent[rent] 집세 / including[inklú:diŋ] ~을 포함하여 / electricity[ilèktrísəti] 전기 / have a look around ~을 둘러보다

03 ④

Script

W I'd like to send this package by airmail to San Francisco.

M Sure. It weighs 20 pounds. That'll be 60 dollars.

W OK. I'd like to have it insured.

M Then, I need to know the exact price of the contents.

W It's 200 dollars.

M Then, it's 5 dollars extra for insurance.

W Thank you. Here you are.

해석

여 이 소포를 항공 우편으로 샌프란시스코에 보내고 싶습니다.

남 네. 무게가 20파운드 나가네요. 60달러입니다.

여 알았습니다. 보험을 들고 싶어요.

남 그러면 내용물의 정확한 가격을 알아야 합니다.

여 200달러입니다.

남 그러면 보험료가 5달러입니다.

여 감사합니다. 여기 있어요.

해설

항공 우편 요금이 60달러, 보험료가 5달러이므로 여자가 지불해야 할 금액은 65달러이다.

어휘

package[pǽkidʒ] 소포 / airmail[ɛ́ərmèil] 항공 우편 / weight[weit] (무게가) ~가 나가다 / insure[inʃúər] 보험에 들다 / exact[igzǽkt] 정확한 / content[kəntént] 내용물 / insurance[inʃúərəns] 보험

04 ②

Script

W Thank God it's Friday.

M It sure was a long week. The day before yesterday was terrible.

W What happened?

M While walking to work, I bumped into a bike and ended up being late.

W Are you all right?

M Not really. I still have a backache.

W I hope you get better.

M Thank you.

해석

여 오늘이 금요일이라 다행이다.

남 정말 긴 한 주였지. 그제는 끔찍했어.

여 무슨 일이 있었는데?

남 회사에 가는 길에 자전거하고 부딪쳐서 회사에 늦었어.

여 괜찮아?

남 괜찮지 않아. 아직 허리가 아파.

여 나아지길 바라.

남 고마워.

해설

오늘은 금요일이고, 그저께 사고를 당했으므로 사고를 당한 요일은 수요일이다.

어휘

the day before yesterday 그저께 / bump into ~와 부딪치다 / end up 결국 ~이 되다 / backache[bǽkèik] 허리 통증, 등의 아픔

05 ①

Script

① M What was the problem?

  W The way he did it was excellent.

② M Can I have this?

  W You can have whatever you want except that.

③ M Do you have time to talk to me?

  W Sure. Will it take long?

④ M Why did she refuse your offer?

  W Because she can't move to another city.

⑤ M What do you think of this computer game?

  W To me, it's the best I've seen.

해석

① 남 무엇이 문제였어?

  여 그가 했던 방식은 정말 훌륭했어.

② 남 제가 이것을 가져도 될까요?

  여 그것만 제외하고 무엇이든 가져도 돼.

③ 남 나와 이야기할 시간이 좀 있니?

  여 물론. 오래 걸릴 것 같니?

④ 남 그녀는 왜 너의 제안을 거절했니?

여 왜냐하면 다른 도시로 이사할 수 없기 때문이야.

⑤ 남 이 컴퓨터 게임에 대해 어떻게 생각하니?

  여 내가 본 최고의 게임이야.

해설

① 문제가 무엇이었냐고 묻는 말에 그가 했던 방식은 훌륭했다는 대답은 적절하지 않다.

어휘

whatever[hwɑtévər] ~하는 것은 무엇이든지 / except[iksépt] ~을 제외하고 / refuse[rifjúːz] ~을 거절하다 / offer[ɔ́(ː)fər] 제안

06 ③

Script

M There have been serious problems due to what our children eat at the school cafeteria. Every year many students become hospitalized due to food poisoning. The government keeps telling us they will take action against this, but nothing has been done so far. Therefore, we parents should do something to protect our kids from food poisoning. I'd be happy to get any suggestions from parents as to how to move forward with this issue.

해석

남 우리의 아이들이 학교 구내식당에서 식사하는 것 때문에 심각한 문제들이 있어 왔습니다. 매년 많은 학생들이 식중독 때문에 병원에 입원하게 됩니다. 정부는 우리에게 계속 그것에 대한 대책을 세울 것이라고 말을 하지만, 지금까지 달라진 것은 전혀 없습니다. 따라서 우리 부모들이 우리의 아이들을 식중독으로부터 보호하기 위해 무엇인가를 해야만 합니다. 저는 이 사안을 진전시킬 방안에 대한 부모님들의 어떤 제안이라도 환영합니다.

해설

아이들의 식중독 문제를 해결하기 위해 부모들의 참여를 촉구하는 글이다.

어휘

due to ~ 때문에; ~에 기인하는 / hospitalize[hɑ́spitəlàiz] 입원시키다 / food poisoning 식중독 / government[gʌ́vər(n)mənt] 정부 / take action ~에 대해 조치를 취하다 / protect A from B B로부터 A를 보호하다 / suggestion[səgdʒéstʃən] 제안 / move forward 진전시키다 / issue[íʃuː] 쟁점, 사안

07 ③

Script

M Are you excited about the trip?

W Of course, it's my first overseas trip.

M Right. You'll have a wonderful experience in the USA.

W I think so. I'm going to travel to 15 different states.

M That's a pretty busy schedule. By the way, do you have a suitcase?

W Yes. I just bought one.

해석

남 여행을 하게 되어 신이 나니?

여 물론이죠, 제 첫 번째 외국여행이잖아요.

남	맞아. 너는 미국에서 훌륭한 경험을 하게 될 거야.
여	그럴 것 같아요. 저는 열다섯 개의 다른 주를 여행할 거예요.
남	꽤 바쁜 일정이구나. 그런데 여행 가방은 있니?
여	네. 방금 샀어요.

해설

누구와 함께 여행을 갈 것인지는 언급되지 않았다.

어휘

overseas[ouvərsíːz] 외국의, 외국으로 가는 / state[steit] 주; 상태 /
pretty[príti] 꽤 / suitcase[súːtkèis] 여행 가방

08 ③
Script

W They are the most beautiful and <u>useful of all creatures</u>. They serve us well by destroying harmful insects, and they also give us pleasure. Their various colors, their beautiful flight, and their musical songs always delight us. And we <u>are fascinated by</u> their mysterious migration practices. How do they find their way <u>over thousands of miles</u>?

해석

여 그들은 모든 창조물 중에서 가장 아름답고 유용하다. 그들은 해로운 곤충들을 없앰으로써 우리에게 좋은 역할을 한다. 그리고 그들은 또한 우리에게 즐거움을 주기도 한다. 그들의 다양한 색채와 아름다운 비행, 가락이 좋은 노래는 항상 우리를 즐겁게 한다. 그리고 우리는 그들의 신비로운 이주에 매료된다. 어떻게 그들이 수천 마일에 걸친 긴 길을 찾아낼 수 있을까?

해설

곤충을 잡아 먹고, 날아다니며 이주를 하는 것은 새이다.

어휘

useful[júːsfəl] 유용한, 쓸모있는 / creature[kríːtʃər] 창조물 /
serve[səːrv] 섬기다, 봉사하다 / destroy[distrɔ́i] ~을 파괴하다 /
harmful[háːrmfəl] 해로운 / insect[ínsekt] 곤충, 벌레 /
pleasure[pléʒər] 기쁨 / various[vέəriəs] 다양한 / flight[flait] 비행 /
delight[diláit] ~을 기쁘게 하다 / be fascinated by ~에 매료되다 /
mysterious[mistíəriəs] 신비로운 / migration[maigréiʃən] 이주, 이민 /
practice[prǽktis] 습관, 관습, 실행

09 ④
Script

M Look at these cushions, Jessica. How about this one?

W The heart-shaped one? Oh, 30 dollars is too much.

M What about that square one?

W 20 dollars isn't bad, but the shape is <u>too common</u>.

M Then, how about the round one?

W I want something more practical. I might use it <u>as a pillow</u>.

M Then, what do you think about this long and narrow one?

W It <u>looks like</u> a pillow. And the price is reasonable, only 15 dollars. Okay. I'll take that one.

해석

남	이 쿠션들 좀 봐, Jessica. 이것은 어때?
여	하트모양? 아, 30달러는 너무 비싼데.
남	그러면 저 사각형은 어때?
여	20달러는 나쁘지 않지만, 모양이 너무 평범해.
남	그러면 둥근 것은 어때?
여	나는 더 실용적인 것을 원해. 베개로 사용할 수도 있잖아.
남	그럼, 이 길고 좁은 건 어때?
여	베개처럼 생겼네. 그리고 가격도 적당하고, 겨우 15달러야. 알았어. 그것으로 할게.

해설

여자는 길고 좁은 모양의 베개처럼 생긴 쿠션을 살 것이다.

어휘

shaped[ʃeipt] ~형의 / square[skwɛər] 사각형 / shape[ʃeip] 형태, 모양 /
common[kámən] 평범한, 흔한 / practical[prǽktikəl] 실용적인 /
pillow[pílou] 베개 / narrow[nǽrou] 좁은 / look like ~처럼 생기다 /
reasonable[ríːzənəbəl] 적당한, 합리적인

10 ③
Script

W Nick, did you buy the milk and bread I asked you to?

M Yes, they are <u>on the table</u>.

W Thank you. Now go to the cleaners and pick up the laundry. And when you get back, could you <u>empty the trash cans</u>?

M OK. I'll get everything done, Mom.

W Thank you. <u>One last thing</u>, clean all the windows, okay?

M Sure, I think Dad will be happy to see the house cleaned.

해석

여	Nick, 너 내가 부탁한 우유랑 빵 사왔니?
남	네, 테이블 위에 있어요.
여	고맙구나. 이제 세탁소에 가서 세탁물을 좀 찾아오렴. 그리고 돌아오면 쓰레기통을 비워 주겠니?
남	알았어요. 다 할게요, 엄마.
여	고맙구나. 마지막으로 유리창을 좀 모두 닦으렴. 알았지?
남	네, 아빠가 집이 깨끗해진 것을 보면 좋아하시겠어요.

해설

여자는 남자에게 우유와 빵 사오기, 세탁물 찾아오기, 쓰레기통 비우기, 유리창 청소를 부탁했다.

어휘

cleaners[klíːnərs] 세탁소 / laundry[lɔ́ːndri] 세탁물 / empty[émpti]
~을 비우다 / trash can 쓰레기통

11 ①
Script

M Can I see what you have in your bag?

W Sure. Do you want me to open it?

M Please, do. What is this?

W It's for my brother. It's worth only 50 dollars.

M OK. How about this?

W It's a digital camera for my sister. It's only 200 dollars.

M Do you have any other items to declare in that small bag?

W No, just clothes.

M OK. Thank you. You may go.

해석

남 당신의 가방에 무엇이 있는지 좀 볼까요?

여 네. 열어 드릴까요?

남 그렇게 해 주세요. 이것은 뭐죠?

여 그것은 제 동생을 위한 거예요. 겨우 50달러예요.

남 알겠어요. 이것은요?

여 그것은 제 여동생을 위한 디지털 카메라예요. 그것도 200달러밖에 안 해요.

남 그 작은 가방에 다른 신고해야 할 품목이 있나요?

여 아니요, 그냥 옷이에요.

남 알았습니다. 감사합니다. 가셔도 됩니다.

해설

세관 검사를 하는 곳은 공항이다.

어휘

worth[wəːrθ] ~의 가치가 있는 / item[áitəm] 항목, 품목 / declare[diklέər] 신고하다 / clothes[klouðz] 의류

12 ④

Script

W How long will it take to get to our destination?

M We're almost there. What's the problem? You look pale.

W I feel like I have motion sickness.

M Why don't you open the window and get some fresh air?

W Okay. I feel better now.

M Come on. We'll have a great time in Waikiki. It's a perfect place for surfing.

해석

여 목적지까지 얼마나 걸려?

남 거의 다 왔어. 무슨 일이야? 너 창백해 보여.

여 나 멀미를 하는 것 같아.

남 창문을 열고 신선한 공기를 좀 마시는 게 어때?

여 알았어. 이제 좀 나아졌어.

남 자. 우리는 와이키키에서 좋은 시간을 보낼 거야. 그곳은 서핑하기에 완벽한 장소야.

해설

여자는 지금 멀미가 나서 불편해하고 있다.

어휘

destination[dèstənéiʃən] 행선지, 목적지 / pale[peil] 창백한 /

feel like ~할 것 같다 / motion sickness 멀미, 메스꺼움 / surf[səːrf] 서핑을 하다

13 ③

Script

M Young kids' bodies are growing and changing at a rapid rate, which requires a lot of energy. In addition, the world is filled with so many interesting things to discover and so many new skills to learn, and all that stimulation can make a child pretty tired. Whether big or little, people don't perform at their best when they are too tired. Therefore, young kids need not only a good night's sleep but also a little nap. This extra sleep keeps them healthy.

해석

남 어린아이들의 몸은 빠른 속도로 성장하고 변하는데, 그것은 많은 에너지가 필요하다. 게다가 세상은 알아야 할 많은 흥미로운 것들과 배워야 할 많은 새로운 기술로 가득 차 있다. 그리고 그 모든 자극이 아이들을 매우 피곤하게 만든다. 어른이든 아이든 간에, 사람들은 너무 피곤하면 최상의 상태로 일을 수행할 수 없다. 따라서 어린이들은 충분한 밤잠뿐만 아니라 약간의 낮잠도 필요로 한다. 이 여분의 잠이 그들을 건강하게 유지해 준다.

해설

어린아이들은 빠른 속도로 성장하고 변하기 때문에 낮잠이 필요하다는 내용이다.

어휘

at a rapid rate 빠른 속도로 / require[rikwáiər] ~을 필요로 하다 / in addition 게다가, 더욱이 / be filled with ~로 가득 차 있다 / discover[diskʌ́vər] 알다, 깨닫다, 발견하다 / stimulation[stìmjəléiʃən] 자극 / perform[pərfɔ́ːrm] ~을 수행하다 / at one's best 가장 좋은 상태에 / nap[næp] 낮잠

14 ①

Script

W May I help you, sir?

M Yes. I bought this golf club 2 weeks ago. I have a complaint about it.

W What did you find wrong with it?

M I found a scratch on the club. Will you be able to give me a new one?

W I'm not sure if I can. We can only replace goods within 10 days of purchase.

M I noticed it yesterday, and I've never used it.

W I don't think we can exchange it for you. The period has to be within 10 days of purchase as mentioned.

해석

여 도와드릴까요, 손님?

남 네. 저는 2주 전에 이 골프채를 샀습니다. 이 골프채에 대해 항의할 것이 있습니다.

여 뭔가 잘못되었나요?

남 채에 긁힘이 있습니다. 새것으로 주실 수 있습니까?

여　제가 그럴 수 있는지 확신은 못하겠습니다. 저희는 구매 후 10일 이내에만 교환해 드릴 수 있거든요.

남　저는 어제 그것을 발견했어요. 그리고 그것을 한 번도 사용하지 않았어요.

여　교환해 드릴 수 없을 것 같아요. 말씀드렸듯이 구매 후 10일 이내가 기한이거든요.

해설

남자는 새 골프채에 긁힘이 있고, 가게에서 교환을 안 해주려고 해서 기분이 언짢을 것이다.

어휘

golf club 골프채 / complaint[kəmpléint] 불평 / scratch[skrætʃ] 긁힘, 긁힌 자국 / replace[ripléis] ~을 교환하다 / goods[gudz] 상품 / purchase[pə́ːrtʃəs] 구입 / notice[nóutis] ~을 알아채다, 인지하다 / exchange[ikstʃéindʒ] ~을 교환하다 / period[píəriəd] 기간 / mention[ménʃən] 언급하다

15 ⑤

Script

① M What is your father doing now?
　 W He is fixing the roof.

② M Wow, you're wearing nice shoes!
　 W Thanks. I just bought them.

③ M Do you need any help washing the dishes?
　 W No, thank you. I can do it myself.

④ M Excuse me, do you know where a shoe-repair shop is?
　 W Yes. There's one in the shopping mall over there.

⑤ M We've got a flat tire. I don't know how to change the tire.
　 W Then, what can we do?

해석

① 남　너의 아버지는 지금 무엇을 하고 계시니?
　 여　지붕을 고치고 계세요.

② 남　와, 정말 좋은 신발을 신었네!
　 여　고마워. 방금 샀어.

③ 남　설거지를 하는 데 도움이 필요하니?
　 여　아니, 괜찮아. 혼자서 할 수 있어.

④ 남　실례합니다. 구두 수선하는 곳이 어디 있는지 아세요?
　 여　네. 저기 있는 쇼핑몰 안에 하나 있어요.

⑤ 남　타이어의 바람이 빠졌어. 나 타이어 갈 줄 모르는데.
　 여　그럼 우린 어떻게 하지?

해설

자동차 타이어의 바람이 빠져서 곤란해하고 있는 상황이다.

어휘

fix[fiks] ~을 수리하다 / roof[ruːf] 지붕 / wear[wɛər] (신을) 신다 / wash the dishes 설거지하다 / repair[ripɛ́ər] 수리, 수선 / flat[flæt] 바람이 빠진, 터진

16 ②

Script

W Let's do something exciting for this weekend. Do you

have any suggestions?

M How about water skiing?

W I'm not in the mood for that. Any other suggestions?

M How about going to an amusement park?

W The closest one is too far. Let's ride a bike along the river.

M Sounds great.

해석

여　이번 주말에 뭔가 신나는 것을 하자. 제안할 것이 있니?

남　수상 스키는 어때?

여　그런 걸 할 기분은 아니야. 다른 의견은?

남　놀이공원에 가는 건 어때?

여　가장 가까운 곳도 너무 멀어. 강을 따라 자전거를 타는 것은 어때?

남　그거 괜찮겠다.

해설

두 사람은 주말에 강을 따라 자전거를 타기로 했다.

어휘

suggestion[səgdʒéstʃən] 제안; 암시 / in the mood for+명사 ~할 기분이 나서 / amusement park 놀이공원 / closest[klousist] 가장 가까운 / far[faːr] 먼 / ride a bike 자전거를 타다 / along[əlɔ́ːŋ] ~을 따라서

17 ②

Script

[Telephone rings.]

M Hey, Betty. It's Johnny.

W What's up?

M I need to find a nice restaurant. My relatives from Japan will be here tomorrow.

W I see. Do they like Korean food? I know a good restaurant in downtown. It's really great.

M Where is it?

W It's behind the Charles Hotel. And it's open from 11 A.M. to 11 P.M.

M Do you think I need to make a reservation?

W Yes. I think so.

해석

남　안녕, Betty. 나 Johnny야.

여　웬일이야?

남　괜찮은 식당을 좀 알아봐야 해서. 나의 친척이 일본에서 내일 여기에 오거든.

여　그렇구나. 그 사람들은 한국 음식을 좋아하니? 내가 시내에 있는 좋은 식당을 알아. 정말 좋아.

남　어딘데?

여　Charles 호텔 뒤에 있어. 오전 11시에서 밤 11시까지 문을 열어.

남　내가 예약을 해야 할까?

여　응. 그럴걸.

해설

남자는 일본에서 오는 친척과 함께 갈 식당을 알아보려고 여자에게 전화를

걸었다.

어휘
relative[rélətiv] 친척 / downtown[dáuntaun] 도심지에 / behind[biháind] ~의 뒤에 / make a reservation 예약하다

18 ④
Script

M Where were you born, Jenny?

W I was born and brought up in Germany.

M Oh! So, you weren't born in the USA.

W No, I came here in 2003.

M Did you go to college right away?

W No. My English wasn't very good, so I took language courses for one year and then went to college.

M I think you speak English fluently now.

W Thanks. I majored in English Literature at a university in New York.

해석

남 Jenny야, 너는 어디서 태어났니?

여 나는 독일에서 태어나고 자랐어.

남 아! 그러면 너는 미국에서 태어나지 않았구나.

여 아니. 나는 여기에 2003년도에 왔어.

남 바로 대학에 입학했니?

여 아니. 나는 영어를 잘하지 못해서, 일 년 동안은 어학연수를 하고 나서 대학에 갔어.

남 지금은 영어를 유창하게 하는 것 같은데.

여 고마워. 나는 여기 뉴욕에 있는 대학에서 영문학을 전공했어.

해설
출생지는 독일이고, 현재 거주지는 미국의 뉴욕이며, 대학 입학 연도는 2004년이고, 대학에서 영문학을 전공했다. 직업은 알 수 없다.

어휘
be born in ~에서 태어나다 / bring up 양육하다, 기르다 / Germany[dʒə́:rməni] 독일 / college[kálidʒ] 대학 / fluently[flú:əntli] 유창하게 / major in ~을 전공하다 / literature[lítərətʃər] 문학

19 ⑤
Script

M What are you looking at?

W I'm thinking of buying a new computer. Mine is too old and too slow. The worst thing is that it breaks down too often.

M That's why you are looking at the computers.

W But my mother told me if I wait for another 6 months, there will be a newer model with more powerful chips at a cheaper price.

M You know it's always like that.

W I know, so I'm trying to decide whether to buy now or wait for another 6 months.

M I think you'd better buy a used one. They're cheaper.

해석

남 너는 무엇을 보고 있니?

여 나는 새 컴퓨터를 사려고 생각 중이야. 내 것은 너무 낡고 느려. 가장 나쁜 건 너무 자주 고장이 난다는 거야.

남 그래서 컴퓨터를 보고 있었구나.

여 하지만 우리 어머니는 6개월을 더 기다리래. 그러면 더 저렴한 가격에 더 강력한 칩을 가진 더 최신 기종이 나올 거라고.

남 항상 그렇다는 걸 너도 알잖아.

여 나도 알아. 그래서 지금 살지 아니면 6개월을 더 기다릴지 결정하려고 하는 중이야.

남 내 생각에 중고를 사는 게 나을 것 같은데. 그게 더 싸잖아.

해설
지금 살지 말지를 결정하려 한다는 말에 "내 생각에 중고를 사는 게 나을 것 같은데. 그게 더 싸잖아."라는 응답이 가장 적절하다.

① 왜 더 일찍 그것을 사지 않았니?

② 맞아. 나중에 사는 게 나아.

③ 내 생각에 너는 돈을 좀 더 모아야겠다.

④ 지금은 둘 중에 어느 것도 선택할 수 없어.

어휘
look at ~을 쳐다보다 / break down 고장 나다 / powerful[páuərfəl] 강력한 / chip[tʃip] 전자칩, 반도체 조각 / decide[disáid] ~을 결정하다 / used[juzd] 중고의

20 ②
Script

M Can I look around your room?

W No. Please don't.

M Why not?

W It's my private space.

M Come on! We've been friends for a long time.

W Okay, come on in.

M Wow, you have so many things in your room.

W I spent a few hours arranging things last night.

M That's why it's so neat.

해석

남 네 방을 둘러봐도 될까?

여 안 돼. 그러지 마.

남 왜 안 돼?

여 이곳은 나의 개인 공간이야.

남 그러지 마! 우리는 오랫동안 친구였잖아.

여 알았어. 들어와.

남 와, 네 방에는 정말 많은 것이 있구나.

여 지난밤에 물건들을 정리하느라 몇 시간을 보냈어.

남 그래서 이렇게 정돈이 잘 되어 있구나.

해설
지난밤에 정리를 하느라 많은 시간을 썼다는 말에 "그래서 이렇게 정돈이 잘 되어 있구나."라는 응답이 가장 적절하다.

① 엉망진창이구나!
③ 왜 그렇게 했니?
④ 네 어머니가 너에게 벌을 주셨니?
⑤ 내가 네 방을 청소하는 걸 도와줄게.

어휘
look around ~을 둘러보다 / private[práivit] 사적인 / space[speis] 공간 / come on in 들어오다 / arrange[əréindʒ] ~을 정돈하다 / neat[ni:t] 깨끗한, 산뜻한

p.88~91
11회 영어듣기모의고사

01 ②	02 ④	03 ④	04 ③	05 ③
06 ④	07 ②	08 ②	09 ①	10 ⑤
11 ④	12 ②	13 ①	14 ⑤	15 ⑤
16 ⑤	17 ③	18 ②	19 ②	20 ③

01 ②
Script
W Please help me. Some man snatched my bag and ran that way.
M Tell me what he looks like.
W He doesn't look like one of those common criminals. He has short hair, and... I don't know.
M Take your time.
W He just looks ordinary. He has big eyes.
M Does he have a mustache or a beard?
W No, nothing.

해석
여 저를 좀 도와주세요. 어떤 사람이 제 가방을 낚아채서 저쪽으로 달려갔어요.
남 그 사람이 어떻게 생겼는지 말해 보세요.
여 그는 보통 범죄자들 중 한 명처럼 생기지는 않았어요. 그는 머리가 짧고 그리고…… 잘 모르겠어요.
남 천천히 얘기하세요.
여 그냥 평범하게 생겼어요. 눈이 컸어요.
남 콧수염이나 턱수염이 있었나요?
여 아니요, 없었어요.

해설
범인은 머리가 짧고, 눈이 크며, 수염이 나지 않은 평범한 사람이다.

어휘
snatch[snætʃ] ~을 잡아채다 / look like ~처럼 생기다 / criminal[krímənəl] 범죄자 / take one's time 시간을 들이다, 서두르지 않다 / ordinary[ɔ́:rdənèri] 평범한, 보통의 / mustache[mʌ́stæʃ] 콧수염 / beard[biərd] 턱수염

02 ④
Script
W Hey! The train is late! I've been waiting here so long.
M Which train are you waiting for?
W The three thirty to San Jose.
M To San Jose? I'm afraid you've made a mistake, ma'am.
W A mistake? But I took this train last week.
M We've changed the schedule recently.
W Changed it? Why didn't you put up a notice?
M Oh, that...
W I don't believe this! You've changed the train schedule, but commuters were not notified at all. How could you do that?

해석
여 여보세요! 기차가 늦는군요! 여기서 매우 오래 기다렸어요.
남 어떤 기차를 기다리시는데요?
여 산호세로 가는 3시 30분 기차요.
남 산호세요? 유감스럽지만 실수를 하신 것 같은데요, 부인.
여 실수요? 하지만 지난주에도 이 기차를 탔는데요.
남 최근에 기차 시간이 바뀌었습니다.
여 시간을 바꿨다고요? 왜 고지를 하지 않았지요?
남 아, 그거요…….
여 믿을 수가 없군요! 기차 시간을 변경하고, 통근자들에게 전혀 알리지 않다니요. 어떻게 그럴 수가 있죠?

해설
여자는 기차 시간을 바꿨음에도 통근자들에게 어떤 고지도 하지 않은 기차회사에 화가 났을 것이다.

어휘
make a mistake 실수하다 / recently[rí:sntli] 최근에 / notice[nóutis] 게시, 벽보, 고시 / commuter[kəmjú:tər] 통근자 / notify[nóutəfai] 통지하다, 발표하다

03 ④
Script
W I'm looking for some souvenirs for my daughters.
M How about these key rings?
W They are too common.
M Oh, I see. What about those necklaces? Most girls like them.
W I'm afraid my daughters don't wear necklaces.
M How about the earrings?
W No, they don't fit their style. What about these bracelets?
M Bracelets? You made a good choice. They're 18 dollars each.
W OK. I'll take them.

해석

여　제 딸들에게 줄 기념품을 찾고 있습니다.

남　이 열쇠고리는 어떠세요?

여　그것들은 너무 흔해요.

남　아, 그렇군요. 이 목걸이는 어때요? 여자아이들 대부분이 좋아합니다.

여　유감스럽게도 제 딸들은 목걸이를 안 해요.

남　그러면 귀걸이는요?

여　아니요, 그것들은 제 딸들의 스타일이 아니에요. 이 팔찌는 어떨까요?

남　팔찌요? 선택 잘하셨어요. 그것들은 각각 18달러입니다.

여　네. 그것으로 할게요.

해설

여자는 팔찌를 사기로 했다.

어휘

souvenir[sùːvəníər] 기념품 / key ring 열쇠고리 /
common[kámən] 흔한, 평범한 / necklace[néklis] 목걸이 /
earring[íərìŋ] 귀걸이 / bracelet[bréislit] 팔찌

04 ③

Script

M　Excuse me, I'm looking for a book about the Joseon Dynasty.

W　Let me find one for you. Here you go.

M　Thank you. What's the price of the book?

W　It's 50 dollars. But if you have a membership card, you can get 20 percent off.

M　Yes, I do. Here you are.

해석

남　실례합니다. 조선 왕조에 관한 책을 찾고 있어요.

여　제가 하나 찾아 드리죠. 여기 있어요.

남　감사합니다. 책값은 얼마인가요?

여　50달러입니다. 하지만 회원카드가 있으면, 20% 할인을 받을 수 있어요.

남　네, 있어요. 여기요.

해설

책값이 50달러인데 20% 할인을 받으면 40달러가 된다.

어휘

dynasty[dáinəsti] 왕조 / off[ɔːf] 감하여, 공제하여

05 ③

Script

W　I enjoy climbing mountains. I climb mountains every weekend. It helps me build my leg muscles. When I first started climbing mountains, I couldn't climb all the way up to the peak. A few months later, I made it to the top of the mountain. These days, I climb many different mountains with my friends and family. The higher I reach, the happier I am, and the higher I reach, the fresher the air I can breathe. I'm used to climbing up mountains now.

해석

여　나는 등산을 즐긴다. 나는 주말마다 산에 오른다. 그것은 나의 다리 근육을 단련하는 데 도움이 된다. 나는 처음 등산을 하기 시작했을 때 정상까지 올라갈 수 없었다. 몇 달 후, 나는 산의 정상까지 오를 수 있었다. 요즘에 나는 친구들과 가족과 함께 많은 다른 산으로 등산을 간다. 더 높이 오를수록, 더 행복하고, 더 높이 오를수록 더 신선한 공기를 마실 수 있다. 나는 산에 오르는 데 익숙해졌다.

해설

정상에 오르면 좋은 경치를 볼 수 있다는 말은 없다.

어휘

climb[klaim] ~을 오르다, 등반하다 / muscle[mʌ́səl] 근육 /
up to ~에 이르기까지 / peak[piːk] 산꼭대기, 정상 /
make it ~에 도달하다, 이르다 / reach[riːtʃ] ~에 도착하다 /
breathe[briːð] 숨 쉬다, 호흡하다 / be used to + -ing ~하는 데 익숙하다

06 ④

Script

[Telephone rings.]

W　Hello?

M　Hello, Ms. Benson. This is Mr. Brown in apartment 771.

W　Oh, yes. What can I do for you? Is it the leaking problem again?

M　No, it's not that. It's the heating system this time. I think something's wrong with the temperature control. It's too cold in here.

W　Really? OK. I'll get someone to look at it right away.

해석

여　여보세요?

남　여보세요. Benson 부인. 저는 771호에 사는 Brown입니다.

여　아, 네. 무엇을 도와드릴까요? 또 무언가가 새나요?

남　아니요, 그게 아니라요. 이번에는 난방기예요. 온도 조절 장치에 문제가 있는 것 같아요. 여기는 너무 추워요.

여　정말요? 알겠어요. 제가 사람을 시켜 당장 살펴보라고 할게요.

해설

남자는 난방기가 고장이 나서 고쳐달라고 전화를 했다.

어휘

leak[liːk] 새는 물, 누수; 새다 / heating system 난방 장치 /
temperature[témpərətʃər] 온도 / control[kəntróul] 조절 장치; 지배, 통제

07 ②

Script

[Telephone rings]

W　Green Tour, may I help you?

M　Hi, this is Mike Cowen. I just called to make sure that my trip is all set.

W　Yes. It's all set. You paid for everything, and you are ready to go.

M　Thanks. Can I check the information again?

W　Yes. The package deal includes hotels, meals, local transportation, and the plane fare.

M Okay. Thanks. Then, I'll see you at the airport.

W Sure thing.

해석

여 그린 여행사입니다. 도와드릴까요?

남 안녕하세요, 저는 Mike Cowen입니다. 제 여행준비가 다 되었는지 확인차 전화했습니다.

여 네. 준비가 다 되었습니다. 모두 지불하셨고 갈 준비가 되셨습니다.

남 감사합니다. 다시 한번 정보를 확인할 수 있을까요?

여 네. 여행 상품은 호텔, 식사, 현지 교통, 비행기 요금을 포함합니다.

남 알았습니다. 감사합니다. 그러면 공항에서 뵙죠.

여 그래요.

해설

여행 경비로 호텔, 식사, 현지 교통비, 비행기 요금이 포함된다고 했으므로 가이드 팁은 언급되지 않았다.

어휘

make sure ~을 확실히 하다 / all set 만반의 준비가 되어 / package deal 세트 판매. 일괄 거래 / include[inklú:d] ~을 포함하다 / meal[mi:l] 식사 / local[lóukəl] 지역의 / transportation[trænspərtéiʃən] 교통 / fare[fɛər] 요금

08 ②

Script

M Good morning, ma'am. May I help you?

W Yes, please. Would you fill it up?

M Regular or premium?

W Regular, please.

M Do you want me to check under the hood?

W Yes, please.

M Your oil is still OK. Now, just let me clean your windshield.

W Thank you.

해석

남 안녕하세요, 부인. 도와드릴까요?

여 네, 가득 채워 주시겠어요?

남 일반이요 아니면 프리미엄이요?

여 일반으로 해 주세요.

남 후드 아래도 좀 점검해 드릴까요?

여 네, 그래 주세요.

남 오일은 아직 괜찮네요. 자, 앞 유리창을 닦아 드릴게요.

여 감사합니다.

해설

기름을 넣는 곳은 주유소이다.

어휘

fill up ~을 채우다 / regular[régjələr] 보통의, 일반의 / check[tʃek] 점검하다, 조사하다 / hood[hud] (자동차 엔진의) 덮개, 보닛 / windshield[wíndʃì:ld] (자동차의) 앞유리

09 ①

Script

M Hi, ma'am. What can I do for you?

W I want to print these rolls of film.

M Sure.

W When can I pick them up?

M They'll be ready by tomorrow afternoon.

W Can you make it a little bit sooner than that?

M We can develop them in about 40 minutes, but it'll cost more.

W All right. I'll pick them up in 40 minutes.

해석

남 안녕하세요, 부인. 무엇을 도와 드릴까요?

여 저는 이 필름을 현상하고 싶어요.

남 네.

여 언제 가져갈 수 있지요?

남 내일 오후면 준비가 될 거예요.

여 그것보다 좀 더 빨리할 수 있나요?

남 약 40분 정도면 현상을 할 수 있지만 비용이 좀 더 듭니다.

여 알겠어요. 40분 후에 가져갈게요.

해설

사진을 현상해 주는 사람은 사진관 직원이다.

어휘

roll[roul] 한 통, 롤 / pick up ~을 가져가다 / develop[divéləp] (사진을) 인화하다; 개발하다 / cost[kɔːst] (비용이) ~가 들다

10 ⑤

Script

① **M** Which would you rather do, watch or play?

W I can't make up my mind.

② **M** Excuse me, could you take our picture?

W Sure. Do I just push this button?

③ **M** Ma'am, you dropped your handkerchief.

W Thank you. You are so kind.

④ **M** I bought a round-trip ticket to Hawaii.

W Is that right?

⑤ **M** Hello. I'd like to have this shirt pressed.

W Sure. It will be ready tomorrow.

해석

① 남 보는 거하고, 하는 것 중에 어떤 걸 더 좋아해?

여 결정을 못하겠어.

② 남 실례합니다. 저희 사진을 좀 찍어 주시겠어요?

여 물론이죠. 이 버튼만 누르면 되나요?

③ 남 부인, 손수건을 떨어뜨리셨습니다.

여 감사합니다. 정말 친절하시군요.

④ 남 하와이행 왕복표를 샀어.

여 그래?

⑤ 남 안녕하세요. 이 셔츠를 좀 다리고 싶은데요.

여 네. 내일이면 될 거예요.

해설

세탁소에 옷을 다림질해 달라고 맡기는 상황이다.

어휘

make up one's mind 결정하다 / take a picture 사진 찍다 /
drop[drap] ∼을 떨어뜨리다 / handkerchief[hǽŋkərtʃif] 손수건 /
round-trip 왕복여행의 / press[pres] 다리미질하다

11 ④

Script

W Hurry up. We're late already.

M Okay, okay. What time is it now?

W It's 6 P.M.

M Then, we <u>don't need to hurry</u>.

W What do you mean? It starts at 7 sharp.

M I thought it starts at 8. All right, I'm coming. What theater is it?

W How many times have I told you? It's at the Modern Theater. The traffic will be terrible, so we'd better <u>take the subway</u>.

M That's a good idea.

해설

여 서둘러, 우리는 이미 늦었어.

남 알았어, 알았다고. 지금 몇 신데?

여 6시

남 그러면 서두를 필요 없잖아.

여 무슨 말이야? 7시 정각에 시작하는데.

남 나는 8시에 시작하는 줄 알았어. 알았어. 갈게. 무슨 극장이지?

여 내가 몇 번이나 말을 했니? Modern Theater야. 교통체증이 심할 테니 전철을 타고 가는 게 낫겠다.

남 좋은 생각이야.

해설

7시에 시작하며, Modern Theater에서 하는 것은 Ballet "Swan Lake"이다.

어휘

hurry[hə́:ri] 서두르다 / sharp[ʃɑːrp] 정각에 / had better ∼하는 게 낫다

12 ②

Script

W Let's go.

M David hasn't come yet.

W I know, but we don't need to wait for him. He has a ticket, and he knows <u>where to go</u>, right?

M I know, but I want to go there with him as well.

W We don't have much time.

M Christine, <u>listen to me</u>. He's usually not late.

W So, do you think he'll be here in a minute?

M Yes. There's <u>no doubt about that</u>.

해설

여 가자

남 David가 아직 안 왔어.

여 알아. 하지만, 그를 기다릴 필요는 없잖아. 그는 표도 가지고 있고 어디로 가야 하는지도 알잖아, 그렇지?

남 알아. 하지만, 그와 함께 가고 싶어.

여 우리는 시간이 별로 없어.

남 Christine, 내 말을 들어 봐. 그는 늦을 사람이 아니야.

여 그래서 너는 그가 곧 올 거라고 생각을 하니?

남 응. 의심의 여지가 없어.

해설

남자는 David가 늦지 않고 올 것이라고 확신하고 있다.

어휘

wait for ∼을 기다리다 / as well 또한, 같이 / doubt[daut] 의심, 의문

13 ①

Script

W Please <u>draw a table</u>, 3 blocks by 3. In the center, draw a smiley face. From there, go one block to the right, and then <u>go up one block</u>. Draw a triangle there. And now, put a star right next to it. Finally, put another star below the smiley face. <u>Are you following me</u>?

해석

여 위와 옆으로 각각 세 블록인 표를 그려 보세요. 한가운데 웃는 얼굴을 그려 주세요. 거기에서 오른쪽으로 한 블록 가서, 위로 한 블록 가세요. 거기에 삼각형을 그리세요. 그리고 이제, 바로 옆에 별을 그리세요. 마지막으로 웃는 얼굴 아래에 별 하나를 더 그려 주세요. 이해가 되죠?

해설

가운데 칸에 웃는 얼굴, 오른쪽 맨 위에 칸에 삼각형, 웃는 얼굴 위아래로 별이 있는 것이 정답이다.

어휘

draw[drɔː] ∼을 그리다 / smiley[smáili] 미소 띤 /
triangle[tráiæŋɡl] 삼각형 / right[rait] 바로 / next to ∼의 옆에 /
below[bilóu] ∼의 아래 / follow[fálou] ∼을 따라가다, 이해하다

14 ⑤

Script

① W Hello, can I talk to Mr. Brown?

M This is he.

② W Is Mike there?

M He just <u>stepped out</u>. He'll be back in 30 minutes.

③ W Do you think it is possible?

M No, <u>no one can do it</u>.

④ W Isn't this 786-6131? I'm sure that this is the right number.

M It can't be.

⑤ **W** How did he get the money?

M He got the money yesterday.

해석

① 여 여보세요, Brown 씨와 이야기할 수 있을까요?
남 접니다.

② 여 Mike 있나요?
남 방금 나갔어요. 30분 후에 돌아올 거예요.

③ 여 너는 그것이 가능할 것 같니?
남 아니. 아무도 할 수 없을 거야.

④ 여 786-6131번 아닌가요? 분명히 이 번호가 맞는 것 같은데요.
남 그럴 리가요.

⑤ 여 그가 돈을 어떻게 구했어?
남 그는 어제 그 돈을 구했어.

해설

⑤ 돈을 어떻게 구했느냐는 질문에 어제 구했다는 대답은 어울리지 않는다.

어휘

step out 밖으로 나가다 / be back 돌아오다 / possible[pάsəbəl] 가능한

15 ⑤

Script

M I heard you are taking a trip to Europe.

W That's right. I'm leaving the day after tomorrow.

M Who are you going with, anyway?

W I'm going alone.

M Alone? Isn't that a little dangerous?

W I guess so, but I prefer to go alone because I can do whatever I want. If I go with my friends, we may argue a lot, especially about where to go, when to go, what to eat, and things like that.

M That's true.

해석

남 나는 네가 유럽으로 여행을 간다고 들었어.
여 맞아. 내일모레 떠나.
남 그런데, 누구와 같이 가니?
여 혼자서 가.
남 혼자? 약간 위험하지 않겠니?
여 그렇게 생각하지만, 난 혼자 가는 게 좋아. 내가 하고 싶은 건 뭐든지 할 수 있잖아. 친구들과 같이 가면, 특히 어디로 갈지, 언제 갈지, 뭘 먹을지, 뭐 그런 것들로 말다툼을 많이 하게 될지도 몰라.
남 맞아.

해설

여자는 원하는 것을 다 할 수 있고, 친구와 싸울 염려도 없이 자유롭게 여행을 하고 싶어서 혼자 여행을 가려고 하고 있다.

어휘

take a trip 여행하다 / alone[əlóun] 혼자서 /
prefer[prifə́ːr] ~을 선호하다 /
argue about ~에 관해 언쟁하다. 말다툼하다 / especially[ispéʃəli] 특히

16 ⑤

Script

M Jennifer, let's play tennis this afternoon.

W Sorry, but I don't feel like it.

M Come on. You are looking pale because you haven't been outside for a few days.

W I know, but I really don't want to.

M Then, let's go to the movies.

W I'm really sorry, John. I don't feel like going out. Today, I'd rather read a book at home than play outside.

해석

남 Jennifer, 오늘 오후에 테니스 치자.
여 미안하지만, 치고 싶지 않아.
남 그러지 마. 너 며칠 동안 밖에 나가지 않아서 창백해 보여.
여 알아. 하지만 정말로 하기 싫어.
남 그러면 영화를 보러 가자.
여 정말 미안해, John. 나는 밖에 나가고 싶지 않아. 오늘은 밖에 나가서 노는 것보다 집에서 책을 읽는 것이 낫겠어.

해설

여자는 오늘 집에서 책을 읽겠다고 했다.

어휘

feel like ~하고 싶다 / pale[peil] 창백한 / go out 외출하다 /
would better ~하는 편이 낫겠다

17 ③

Script

M What time is it now?

W It's 8:30.

M I can't find the way to the village.

W Do you have a flashlight?

M If I had one, I would already be using it.

W What are we supposed to do then?

M I don't know. We should have listened to the guide.

해석

남 지금 몇 시야?
여 8시 30분.
남 마을로 가는 길을 못 찾겠어.
여 너 손전등 있니?
남 있다면, 벌써 사용하고 있겠지.
여 그러면 우리는 어떻게 해야 하지?
남 몰라. 우리는 가이드 말을 들었어야 했는데.

해설

남자가 가이드의 말을 들을 걸 그랬다고 후회하고 있으므로 "엎질러진 물이다."라는 속담이 가장 적절하다.

① 고통이 없으면 얻는 것도 없다.

② 안 하는 것보다 늦게라도 하는 게 낫다.

④ 사공이 많으면 배가 산으로 간다.

⑤ 시작이 가장 어렵다.

어휘
village[vílidʒ] 마을 / flashlight[flǽʃlàit] 손전등 /
guide[gaid] 가이드, 안내원

18 ②
Script

W I need to get a new pair of glasses.

M What's wrong?

W I left them at the bookstore, and when I went back there to get them, they had gone.

M That's too bad. Do you want to get a new pair from the place I know?

W I don't have any money.

M That's okay. My uncle owns it, and you can pay little by little every month.

W That's a great idea. Thank you. Let's go.

해석

여 나 안경을 새로 사야 해.

남 뭐가 잘못됐어?

여 서점에 안경을 두고 왔는데, 내가 그것을 가지러 다시 갔을 때는 없어졌더라고.

남 저런 안 됐다. 너 내가 아는 곳에서 하나 살래?

여 나는 돈이 없어.

남 괜찮아. 우리 삼촌이 그것을 하고 계시는데 매달 조금씩 돈을 내면 돼.

여 그거 좋은 생각인데. 고마워. 가자.

해설
안경을 잃어버려서 새 안경을 하러 안경점에 갈 것이다.

어휘
pair[pɛər] 쌍 / glasses[glǽsis] 안경 / own[oun] 소유하다 /
little by little 조금씩

19 ②
Script

W Mike, tell me how you get perfect scores in your English tests all the time.

M Well, it's not as hard as you think.

W It's easy for you to say, but not me.

M You should review what you learn every day. I've never missed even one day.

W That's tough.

M I know, but it will work for everyone.

W Thanks for your advice.

해석

여 Mike, 어떻게 영어 시험에서 항상 만점을 맞는지 말 좀 해봐.

남 그게, 네가 생각하는 것만큼 어렵지 않아.

여 네가 그렇게 말하기는 쉽지만, 난 아냐.

남 매일 복습을 해야 해. 난 단 하루도 빼 먹은 적이 없어.

여 정말 힘들겠는데.

남 알아. 하지만 그것은 모든 사람에게 효과가 있어.

여 충고 고마워.

해설
시험을 잘 볼 수 있도록 조언을 해 주었으므로 "충고 고마워."라는 응답이 가장 적절하다.

① 나는 그것을 위해서 열심히 일했어.
③ 내가 내일 영어 시험을 내줄게.
④ 알았어. 내가 답을 찾도록 도와줄게.
⑤ 내가 한 말을 명심해

어휘
keep in mind 명심하다 / review[rivjúː] ~을 복습하다; 검토 /
miss[mis] ~을 빠뜨리다, 거르다

20 ③
Script

W John didn't come to class today.

M Really? What's his reason?

W He said he was sick.

M That's pretty strange.

W What do you mean?

M I saw him across the street with his girlfriend 10 minutes ago. He didn't look sick.

W That can't be. He must have lied to me.

해석

여 John이 오늘 수업에 오지 않았어.

남 정말? 이유가 뭐래?

여 아프다고 말을 했어.

남 정말 이상하군.

여 무슨 말이야?

남 10분 전에 길 건너편에 John이 여자 친구하고 있는 것을 보았는데 아파 보이지는 않았어.

여 그럴 리가. 그가 나에게 거짓말을 한 것이 틀림없어.

해설
아프다고 한 John이 여자 친구와 함께 있는 것을 보았다는 말에 "그럴 리가. 그가 나에게 거짓말을 한 것이 틀림없어."라는 응답이 가장 적절하다.

① 그는 영화를 보러 갈지도 몰라.
② 그의 여자 친구는 분명히 예쁠 거야.
④ 그가 수업에 가는 것이 불가능해.
⑤ 너는 밤에 그가 길을 건너는 것을 볼 수 있어.

어휘
reason[ríːzən] 이유 / pretty[príti] 꽤, 아주; 예쁜 /
across[əkrɔ́ːs] 맞은 편에

12회 영어듣기모의고사

p.96~99

01 ⑤	02 ③	03 ④	04 ③	05 ⑤
06 ⑤	07 ①	08 ④	09 ②	10 ⑤
11 ④	12 ①	13 ③	14 ④	15 ②
16 ⑤	17 ③	18 ③	19 ②	20 ②

01 ⑤

Script

W Dad, are you going to buy me a shirt?

M Sure. Go ahead and pick out anything you want.

W Okay. I like the one with the stripes.

M I don't think it suits you.

W How about the checkered one, then?

M That one, either.

W Okay. Then, I'll just pick the black round neck T-shirt.

M Okay.

해석

여 아빠, 제게 셔츠를 사 주실 거예요?

남 물론이지. 가서 네가 원하는 것을 고르렴.

여 알았어요. 저는 줄무늬 셔츠가 좋아요.

남 내 생각에 너에게 어울릴 것 같지 않구나.

여 그러면 체크무늬는 어때요?

남 그것도 아닌 것 같다.

여 알았어요. 그러면 그냥 검은색 라운드 티셔츠로 할게요.

남 알았다.

해설

여자는 아버지의 의견에 따라 검은색 라운드 티셔츠를 살 것이다.

어휘

stripe[straip] 줄무늬 / suit[su:t] ~에게 어울리다 / checkered[tʃékərd] 체크무늬의

02 ③

Script

M Excuse me, do you know how to use this machine?

W Sure. First, put the money into the slot. Then, choose the size and press the button.

M All right. And then, what do I do?

W Look at the front. Can you see the red laser point? You need to look at it and wait for a few seconds.

M Thank you.

W If you wait for two or three minutes, your pictures will be ready, but try to dry them first.

해석

남 실례합니다. 이 기계를 어떻게 사용하는지 아세요?

여 물론이죠. 우선 구멍에 돈을 넣으세요. 그러고 나서 크기를 고른 다음 버튼을 누르세요.

남 알았습니다. 그런 다음에는 무엇을 하죠?

여 앞을 보세요. 저 빨간 레이저 불빛이 보이죠? 거기를 보고 몇 초간 기다리세요.

남 감사합니다.

여 2, 3분 정도 기다리면, 사진이 나올 거예요. 하지만 먼저 말리세요.

해설

남자는 즉석 증명 사진기를 이용해서 사진을 찍으려 하고 있다.

어휘

slot[slɑt] 동전 넣는 구멍 / press[pres] ~을 누르다 / look at ~을 보다 / wait for ~을 기다리다 / dry[drai] ~을 말리다

03 ④

Script

W Good morning, Mr. Smith.

M Good morning, Ms. Anderson. Thanks for coming here.

W Thank you for inviting me here. I'm so excited to be here.

M We'd like to know more about you. We have lots of interesting questions. Are you ready to answer them?

W Sure. Go ahead.

M Your new movie just came out. Could you tell us about the new release?

W Yes, I was a marathoner and had an accident.

M Really? How interesting! We'll be right back after this commercial break.

해석

여 안녕하세요, Smith 씨.

남 안녕하세요, Anderson 씨. 와 주셔서 감사합니다.

여 저를 여기에 초대해 주셔서 감사합니다. 여기에 오게 되어 매우 기쁩니다.

남 우리는 당신에 대해 좀 더 알고 싶어요. 재미있는 질문이 많이 있습니다. 그 질문들에 답변하실 준비가 되셨나요?

여 물론이죠. 어서 질문하세요.

남 당신의 새 영화가 막 개봉이 되었지요. 당신의 새 영화에 대해 좀 이야기해 주시겠어요?

여 네, 저는 마라톤 선수였는데 사고를 당하게 돼요.

남 정말요? 흥미있군요! 광고 방송 후에 바로 돌아오겠습니다.

해설

두 사람의 관계는 방송 진행자와 배우이다.

어휘

invite[inváit] ~을 초대하다 / come out ~가 나오다, 출시되다 / marathoner[mǽrəθɑnər] 마라톤 선수 / commercial[kəmə́:rʃəl] 광고 방송의, 상업의

04 ③

66

Script

M I'd like to book a ticket to Sweden.

W Is that a round trip?

M Yes, it is.

W When would you like to fly?

M September, 25th.

W And return date?

M I'm not sure. Can I decide later?

W If you return within a month, it'll be nine hundred and fifty dollars, but after a month it would be 100 dollars more.

M I see. I don't think I can return within a month.

W OK.

해석

남 스웨덴으로 가는 표를 예약하고 싶은데요.

여 왕복인가요?

남 네.

여 언제 떠나시길 원하시죠?

남 9월 25일이요.

여 돌아오는 날짜요?

남 확실하지는 않아요. 나중에 결정해도 되나요?

여 한 달 이내에 돌아오시면, 가격은 950달러이지만 한 달 후에 오시면 100달러가 추가될 거예요.

남 그렇군요, 한 달 이내에 돌아올 수는 없을 것 같아요.

여 알았습니다.

해설

남자는 한 달 이내에 돌아오지 않을 것이므로 항공료로 1050달러를 내야 할 것이다.

어휘

book[buk] ~을 예약하다 / round trip 왕복여행 / return[ritə́:rn] 돌아옴; 돌아오다 / decide[disáid] ~을 결정하다

05 ⑤

Script

M Hi, do you have anything to declare?

W No, nothing to declare.

M Do you have any food, agricultural products, drugs, or weapons?

W No. All I have are clothes and some souvenirs for my family and relatives.

M Okay. Can you open your bag, please? What are these?

W They are vitamin pills. I take them every day.

M All right. I think you can go now. Thanks for your cooperation.

해석

남 안녕하세요, 신고하실 물품이 있으신가요?

여 아니요, 신고할 것은 없어요.

남 음식이나, 농산물, 약물, 무기를 가지고 있나요?

여 아니요. 제가 가지고 있는 건 옷하고, 가족과 친척들을 위한 약간의 기념품이에요.

남 알았습니다. 가방을 좀 열어 주시겠어요? 이것들은 무엇인가요?

여 그것들은 비타민정제입니다. 저는 매일 그것들을 복용해요.

남 알았습니다. 당신은 이제 가셔도 될 것 같습니다. 협조해 주셔서 감사합니다.

해설

공항에서 입국할 때 일어날 수 있는 대화로 남자는 세관원이다.

어휘

declare[diklέər] (세관에서) 신고하다 / agricultural products 농산물 / drug[drʌɡ] 약물 / weapon[wépən] 무기 / souvenir[sù:vəníər] 기념품 / relative[rélətiv] 친척 / pill[pil] 알약 / take[teik] ~을 복용하다 / cooperation[kouɑ̀pəréiʃən] 협조

06 ⑤

Script

M Kelly, do you have time tomorrow?

W I'm supposed to pick up a relative from Canada at 3 P.M. Why, Mark?

M I want to see the ballet *Swan Lake* with you. It starts at 7. Do you think you can go with me?

W Sure.

M Don't be late since the ballet starts at 7 sharp. We have to be there at least 30 minutes early.

W Let's meet one hour before the ballet at the bus stop.

M Okay. See you then.

해석

남 Kelly, 너 내일 시간 있니?

여 오후 3시에 캐나다에서 오는 친척을 마중하러 갈 건데. 왜, Mark?

남 너와 함께 「백조의 호수」 발레 공연을 보고 싶어서. 7시에 시작하거든. 네 생각에 나랑 같이 갈 수 있을 것 같니?

여 물론이야.

남 발레는 7시 정각에 시작하니까 늦지 마. 우리는 늦어도 30분 전에는 도착해야 해.

여 버스 정류장에서 발레 시작 한 시간 전에 만나자.

남 알았어. 그때 봐.

해설

Kelly와 Mark는 6시 30분이 아니라 6시에 만나기로 약속했다.

어휘

ballet[bǽlei] 발레 / sharp[ʃɑːrp] 정각에 / at least 적어도 / bus stop 버스 정류장

07 ①

Script

M Sarah, can I ask you what you want to be in the future?

W Sure. I want to be a flight attendant because I'd like to travel all over the world.

M That sounds wonderful.

W How about you?

M Me? I'm interested in architecture. I'd like to <u>build a</u> <u>building</u> that many people will remember.

해석

남 Sarah, 나중에 뭐가 되고 싶은지 물어봐도 될까?

여 응. 나는 승무원이 되고 싶어. 전 세계를 여행하고 싶거든.

남 그거 좋은데.

여 너는?

남 나? 나는 건축에 관심이 있어. 나는 사람들이 기억할 만한 건물을 짓고 싶어.

해설

남자는 사람들의 기억에 남을 만한 건물을 짓는 건축가가 되기를 원한다.

어휘

flight attendant 승무원 / all over the world 전 세계에 / be interested in ~에 관심이 있다 / architecture[ɑ́ːrkətèktʃər] 건축

08 ④

Script

① **W** What do you think of this movie?

　M I think it's very interesting.

② **W** <u>How far</u> do you think it is to the airport?

　M I guess it's almost 5 miles.

③ **W** <u>Have you ever been to</u> Rome before?

　M No, but I want to go there someday.

④ **W** Where do you think you will stay in Paris?

　M I'll stay for 3 days in Paris.

⑤ **W** <u>How would you like</u> your coffee?

　M With sugar, please.

해석

① 여 이 영화에 대해서 어떻게 생각하십니까?

　남 매우 재미있다고 생각합니다.

② 여 공항까지 얼마나 멀 것 같나요?

　남 제 생각에 약 5마일 정도 될 것 같습니다.

③ 여 너는 전에 로마에 가 본 적 있니?

　남 아니, 언젠가 가 보고 싶어.

④ 여 파리에서 어디에 머물 거예요?

　남 저는 파리에서 사흘 동안 머물 거예요.

⑤ 여 커피를 어떻게 해 드릴까요?

　남 설탕을 넣어 주세요.

해설

④ 어디에 머물 거냐는 질문에 사흘 동안 머물 거라는 대답은 어울리지 않는다.

09 ②

Script

W I had a chance to talk with an American, and he taught me a few interesting gestures.

M <u>Like what</u>?

W I'll teach you <u>one of them</u>. Make a fist and lift up your thumb, index finger, and the little finger.

M Like this?

W Yes. It's a combination of the letters, I, L, and Y, and it's <u>an expression of love</u>.

M I see.

해석

여 나는 어떤 미국 사람하고 이야기할 기회가 있었는데, 그가 나에게 몇 가지 재미있는 동작을 가르쳐줬어.

남 뭔데?

여 내가 그것들 중 하나를 알려 줄게. 주먹을 쥔 다음, 엄지와 검지 그리고 새끼손가락을 들어 올리는 거야.

남 이렇게?

여 응. 이것은 아이, 엘, 와이의 세 글자가 합쳐진 거야. 사랑이라는 표현이야.

남 그렇구나.

해설

주먹을 쥔 손에서 엄지, 검지, 새끼손가락을 편 동작으로 사랑을 뜻하는 손동작이다.

어휘

gesture[dʒéstʃər] 동작 / fist[fist] 주먹 / lift up 들어 올리다 / thumb[θʌm] 엄지 / index finger 검지 / the little finger 새끼손가락 / combination[kàmbənéiʃən] 결합 / expression[ikspréʃən] 표현, 표시

10 ⑤

Script

M How was your trip to Australia? Did you see anything particular?

W Australia <u>is very similar to</u> the States, but there are several animals you can't see there.

M Like what?

W Like koalas, kangaroos, and alligators.

M I see. Did you see <u>all those animals</u>?

W Yeah, and the alligators were scary. I've also been to the opera house.

M Did you see any glaciers?

W No, but I saw them in New Zealand.

해석

남 호주로의 여행은 어땠어? 뭐 특별한 것을 보았어?

여 호주는 미국하고 매우 비슷한데 미국에서는 볼 수 없는 몇몇 동물들이 있더라.

남 어떤 건데?

여 코알라, 캥거루, 악어 같은 것들.

남 그렇구나. 그 동물들을 다 보았니?

여 응, 그리고 악어는 무서웠어. 오페라 하우스에도 갔다 왔어.

남 빙하도 봤어?

여 아니, 하지만 빙하는 뉴질랜드에서 봤어.

+해설
빙하는 뉴질랜드에서 본 것이다.

어휘
particular[pərtíkjulər] 특별한 / be similar to ~와 유사하다 /
the States 미국 / several[sévərəl] 몇몇의 / koala[kouá:lə] 코알라 /
kangaroo[kæ̀ŋgərúː] 캥거루 / alligator[ǽligèitər] 악어 / scary[skɛ́əri]
무서운 / glacier[gléiʃər] 빙하

11 ④
Script

W How are you going to get to the museum?

M I'm going to ride a bike.

W Don't do that. It's too far and very dangerous. It'll take at least 2 hours.

M OK. Then, I'll take the subway. It's very convenient.

W I know, but it'll be a long journey.

M Then, what should I take?

W You should take bus 3431 since the route is shorter.

M OK. Thanks for your help.

해석

여 너는 박물관에 무엇을 타고 갈 거니?

남 나는 자전거를 타고 갈 거야.

여 그러지 마. 너무 멀고 정말 위험해. 최소한 두 시간은 걸릴 거야.

남 알았어. 그러면 전철을 탈게. 매우 편리하잖아.

여 나도 알지만, 오래 걸릴 거야.

남 그러면 무엇을 타야 하지?

여 버스 노선이 더 짧으니까 3431 버스를 타.

남 알았어. 도와줘서 고마워.

해설
여자는 남자에게 버스 노선이 짧으니까 버스를 타고 가라고 권하고 있다.

어휘
museum[mjuːzíːəm] 박물관 / ride a bike 자전거를 타다 / far[faːr] 먼 /
convenient[kənvíːnjənt] 편리한 / route[ruːt] 노선

12 ①
Script

W Robert, I need someone to help me with my school project.

M Haven't you finished it yet?

W No, I started it last night.

M I think you will need to do it all day today.

W That's why I need some help.

M But as far as I know, everyone has done it by themselves. Your success depends on your effort not others' help.

해석

여 Robert, 학교 숙제를 도와줄 사람이 좀 필요해.

남 아직 못 끝냈어?

여 응, 어젯밤에 시작했어.

남 내 생각에 너 그 숙제를 오늘 온종일 해야 될 것 같아.

여 그래서 바로 도움이 필요한 거야.

남 하지만, 내가 알기로 다른 사람들은 모두 자기들 스스로 했어. 네 성공 여부는 다른 사람의 도움이 아니라 너의 노력에 달린 거야.

해설
남자는 여자에게 혼자 힘으로 숙제하라고 충고하고 있다.

어휘
success[səksés] 성공 / depend on ~에 달려있다. 의존하다 /
effort[éfərt] 노력

13 ③
Script

① **W** What can I do for you, sir?
　M I'm just looking around.

② **W** Look! A fire in the trash can!
　M Let me take care of that.

③ **W** May I help you?
　M I'd like to have this prescription filled, please.

④ **W** You have a lot of packages to send! Just put them on the counter here.
　M Thanks. Most of my family live far away.

⑤ **W** Would you mind closing the door?
　M Of course not.

해석

① 여 무엇을 도와드릴까요, 손님?
　남 그냥 좀 둘러보는 중입니다.

② 여 저길 좀 봐! 쓰레기통에 불이 났어!
　남 내가 처리할게.

③ 여 도와드릴까요?
　남 이 처방전대로 조제를 해 주세요.

④ 여 당신은 보내야 할 소포가 많군요! 그냥 여기 계산대에 올려놓으세요.
　남 감사합니다. 제 가족 대부분이 멀리 살아서요.

⑤ 여 창문 좀 닫아 주실래요?
　남 그러죠.

해설
남자가 약국에 와서 처방전대로 약을 지어달라고 하는 상황이다.

어휘
trash can 쓰레기통 / take care of ~을 처리하다; ~을 돌보다 /
prescription[priskrípʃən] 처방전 / fill[fil] (처방약을) 조제하다 /
package[pǽkidʒ] 소포 / far away 멀리

14 ④
Script

M I've been putting on a lot of weight recently.

W Is that right?

M Yes. I need to do something to lose weight.

W How about going to a fitness center?

M There's no fitness center near my house.

W Then, do some simple exercises at home.

M I don't feel like exercising at home.

W Then, make it a rule to go to work on foot.

M That's a great idea. I'll start doing that.

해석

남 나는 최근에 살이 많이 쪘어.

여 그래?

남 응. 살을 좀 빼려면 뭔가를 해야겠어.

여 헬스장에 가는 건 어때?

남 우리 집 근처에 헬스장이 없어.

여 그러면 집에서 간단한 운동을 해.

남 나는 집에서는 운동하고 싶지 않아.

여 그러면 회사에 걸어가도록 해봐.

남 그거 좋은 생각이다. 그렇게 하도록 할게.

해설

남자는 회사에 걸어갈 것이다.

어휘

put on weight 살이 찌다 / lose weight 살을 빼다, 체중이 줄다 / fitness center 헬스장 / make it a rule to+**동사원형** 늘 ~하기로 하다

15 ②
Script

W Have you finished writing the essay?

M No, I haven't. How about you?

W I've finished. As you know, I like writing.

M I know, and I think you are a talented writer. I envy you. By the way, when is it due?

W It's due Tuesday, the 17th.

M Right. We still have plenty of time.

W I don't think two days is enough time to write an essay, but you think that way...

M Maybe that's the reason I'm not a good writer.

해석

여 에세이 다 썼니?

남 아니. 너는?

여 나는 다 썼어. 너도 알다시피 나는 글 쓰는 것을 좋아하잖아.

남 알아, 그리고 넌 글을 쓰는 데 재능이 있는 것 같아. 네가 부러워. 그런데, 마감이 언제지?

여 17일 화요일이야.

남 맞다. 아직 시간은 많네.

여 작문을 하는 데 이틀이 많은 시간인 것 같지는 않지만, 네가 그렇게 생각한다면 뭐……

남 아마 그래서 나는 글을 잘 못 쓰나 봐.

해설

수필이 마감이 17일 화요일인데 이틀이 남았다고 했으므로 오늘은 15일 일요일이다.

어휘

talented[tǽləntid] 재능이 있는, 유능한 / envy[énvi] ~을 부러워하다 / due[djuː] ~할 예정인, ~하기로 되어 있는 / plenty of 많은

16 ⑤
Script

M Most parents in Korea want their children to do well in school, so they make their children stay home and study. However, when we watch kittens and puppies playing, we realize that they're learning how to live through play. They learn not only physical skills but also social interaction. The same is true for our children. Some experts say that it's important for children to play outdoors with others for two to three hours a day.

해석

남 한국 부모들 대부분은 자녀가 학교에서 잘하기를 원한다. 그래서 그들은 자녀를 집에 붙들어 놓고 공부를 시킨다. 하지만 고양이와 강아지가 노는 것을 보면, 우리는 그들이 놀이를 통해서 사는 법을 배운다는 것을 알 수 있다. 그들은 신체적인 활동기술뿐만 아니라 사회적인 상호작용도 배운다. 우리의 아이들도 마찬가지이다. 어떤 전문가들은 아이들이 하루에 두세 시간 정도 다른 아이들과 함께 야외에서 노는 것이 중요하다고 말한다.

해설

동물이 놀이를 통해 사회 활동을 배우는 것처럼 아이들도 타인과의 놀이를 통해 학습한다는 내용으로 타인과의 놀이의 중요성을 설명한 글이다.

어휘

kitten[kítn] 새끼 고양이 / puppy[pʎpi] 강아지 / realize[ríːəlàiz] 알다, 깨닫다 / physical[fízikəl] 신체적인 / social[sóuʃəl] 사회의 / interaction[ìntərǽkʃən] 상호작용 / expert[ékspəːrt] 전문가 / outdoors[autdɔ́ːrz] 야외에서

17 ③
Script

W What are you going to do this afternoon?

M I'm thinking of playing computer games.

W Oh, not again. I think you are a computer addict.

M No, I'm not.

W Yes, you are. You spend most of your free time doing it.

M That's not true. I'll do something else today.

W Will you? Then, clean the garage for your dad.

M Okay, but you take back what you just said to me.

해석

여 너 오늘 오후에 뭐 할 거니?

남 나는 컴퓨터 게임을 하려고 생각 중인데.

여 이런, 또 그러지 마. 내 생각에 너는 컴퓨터 중독 같아.

남 아냐.

여 맞아, 너는 네 한가한 시간 대부분을 컴퓨터 게임을 하면서 보내잖아.

남 그건 사실이 아니야. 오늘은 다른 것을 하도록 할게.

여　그럴래? 그러면 아빠를 위해서 차고를 청소하도록 해.

남　알았어. 하지만 네가 방금 나에게 한 말은 취소해.

해설

남자는 오늘 오후에 아버지를 위해 차고 청소를 할 것이다.

어휘

addict[ədíkt] 중독자 / free time 여가, 한가한 시간 /
garage[ɡərɑ́:ʒ] 차고 / take back ~을 취소하다

18　③

Script

M　A long time ago, many scientists in Europe found <u>why</u> <u>this happened</u>, but people in Asia thought of this as a kind of disaster. This occurs when the Moon passes between the Sun and the Earth. This occurs at least twice and <u>up</u> <u>to</u> <u>five</u> <u>times</u> each year.

해석

남　오래전에, 유럽의 많은 과학자들이 이것이 일어나는 이유를 알아냈지만, 아시아에 사는 사람들은 이것을 일종의 재앙으로 생각했다. 이것은 달이 태양과 지구 사이를 지날 때 일어난다. 이것은 일 년에 최소한 두 번에서 최대 다섯 번까지 일어난다.

해설

달이 지구와 태양 사이와 와서 태양을 가리는 현상은 일식이다.

어휘

disaster[dizǽstər] 재앙 / occur[əkə́:r] 발생하다

19　②

Script

M　You don't like our English teacher, do you?

W　<u>Honestly</u>, <u>I</u> <u>don't</u>.

M　Why not?

W　I think our English teacher likes you <u>more</u> <u>than</u> <u>me</u>.

M　Why are you saying that?

W　When I don't do my homework, <u>he</u> <u>punishes</u> <u>me</u>, but I've never seen him punish you.

M　I'm afraid you're wrong.

해석

남　너 영어 선생님 싫어하지, 그렇지?

여　솔직히, 싫어.

남　왜 싫어?

여　나는 우리 영어 선생님이 나보다 너를 더 좋아하는 것 같아.

남　왜 그렇게 말을 해?

여　내가 숙제를 안 하면, 선생님은 나에게 벌을 주지만, 나는 선생님이 너에게 벌을 주는 것을 본 적이 없어.

남　<u>유감이지만 네가 잘못 알고 있는 거야.</u>

해설

선생님이 자신에게만 벌을 준다는 말에 "유감이지만 네가 잘못 알고 있는 거야."라는 응답이 가장 적절하다.

① 너 정말 피곤하구나.

③ 왜 그가 나에게 벌을 주니?

④ 나는 매일 숙제를 할 거야.

⑤ 맞아. 그는 여자아이들을 가르치는 것을 더 좋아해.

어휘

honestly[ɑ́nistli] 솔직히 / punish[pʌ́niʃ] ~을 벌하다, 처벌하다

20　②

Script

W　John, I heard that you <u>argued</u> <u>with</u> Jenny.

M　That's right. She <u>was</u> <u>mad</u> <u>at</u> me because I didn't give her the free ticket to the concert.

W　Why didn't you?

M　I just don't like her.

W　Hey, listen. You should <u>treat</u> <u>your</u> <u>friends</u> <u>equally</u>, and if there is something you don't like about her, you should tell her.

M　Okay.

W　<u>How</u> <u>would</u> <u>you</u> <u>feel</u> if someone treated you that way?

M　<u>I would feel terrible.</u>

해석

여　John, Jenny와 말다툼을 했다고 들었어.

남　맞아. 내가 공짜 콘서트 표를 주지 않아서 나에게 화가 났어.

여　왜 안 줬는데?

남　나는 그냥 그녀가 싫어.

여　자, 들어 봐. 너는 친구들을 공평하게 대해야 해. 그리고 네가 그녀에 대해 싫은 점이 있다면 그녀에게 말을 해야지.

남　알았어.

여　누군가 너를 그런 식으로 대한다면 너는 기분이 어떻겠니?

남　<u>불쾌할 거야.</u>

해설

친구에게 함부로 대하는 친구에게 반대의 입장을 생각해 보라고 한 말에 "불쾌할 거야."라는 응답이 가장 적절하다.

① 그것은 좋을 것 같아.

③ 그녀는 나에게 화가 났어.

④ 표 고마워.

⑤ 알았어, 내가 너에게 저녁을 살게.

어휘

argue with ~와 말다툼하다 / be mad at ~에게 화를 내다 / free[fri:] 무료의 / treat[tri:t] ~을 대하다, 다루다 / equally[í:kwəli] 동등하게, 공평하게 / terrible[térəbəl] 불쾌한, 무시무시한

13회 영어듣기모의고사

01 ①	02 ④	03 ①	04 ②	05 ③
06 ③	07 ②	08 ④	09 ⑤	10 ⑤
11 ④	12 ④	13 ⑤	14 ①	15 ④
16 ③	17 ④	18 ①	19 ⑤	20 ③

01 ①

Script

W Andrew, who's your mother among them?

M My mother is wearing a pair of glasses.

W There are three ladies wearing glasses, but let me guess. I'll say the one with long hair in the white shirt.

M No, that's Susie's mom. My mother has short curly hair. She's right next to Susie's mom.

W Now, I got it.

해석

여 Andrew, 저분들 중에서 누가 너의 어머니이시니?

남 우리 어머니는 안경을 끼고 계셔.

여 안경을 쓰고 계신 분이 세 명이나 되지만, 내가 맞혀 볼게. 긴 머리에 흰 셔츠를 입은 분일 것 같아.

남 아니. 그분은 Susie의 엄마야. 우리 어머니는 짧은 곱슬머리야. Susie의 엄마 바로 옆에 계셔.

여 이제 알았다.

해설

Susie의 엄마가 안경을 쓰고, 긴 머리에 흰 셔츠를 입고 있으므로, 그 바로 옆에 있는 짧은 곱슬머리의 여자가 남자의 엄마이다.

어휘

among[əmʌ́ŋ] ~ 사이에 / wear[wɛər] ~을 쓰다; 입다 / glasses[glǽsiːz] 안경 / curly[kə́ːrli] 곱슬곱슬한 / right[rait] 바로; 바른; 오른쪽의

02 ④

Script

W How is everything, Mike?

M I'm doing fine. How about you?

W It couldn't be better. Do you still teach kids?

M No, I used to but not anymore.

W Then, what do you do?

M I'm shooting motion pictures these days. It's mainly about life in a country.

W Is it kind of an independent film?

M That's right.

해석

여 어떻게 지내, Mike?

남 나는 좋아. 너는?

여 최고로 좋아. 너는 여전히 아이들을 가르치니?

남 아니. 그랬지만 지금은 아냐.

여 그러면 무엇을 하는데?

남 나는 요즘 영화를 찍고 있어. 전원생활에 관한 거야.

여 독립 영화 같은 거야?

남 맞아.

해설

남자는 예전에는 아이들을 가르쳤지만, 지금은 영화를 찍고 있으므로 현재의 직업은 영화감독이다.

어휘

used to+동사원형 ~하곤 했다 / shoot[ʃuːt] ~을 촬영하다; ~을 쏘다 / motion picture 영화 / mainly[méinli] 주로 / kind of 일종의 / independent film 독립영화

03 ①

Script

W Today is the most important day of my life. I have to be fully prepared.

M I know. Just tell me what you need.

W First of all, I need some hairspray and a comb.

M OK. Let me write it down.

W And I need a small mirror and a hairdryer.

M OK. What else do you need?

W Well, I think that's all.

해석

여 오늘은 내 생애에서 가장 중요한 날이야. 준비를 완벽하게 해야 해.

남 알아. 무엇이 필요한지 나에게 말만 해.

여 우선, 헤어스프레이와 빗이 필요해.

남 알았어. 좀 적을게.

여 그리고 작은 거울과 헤어드라이어기가 필요해.

남 알았어. 그밖에 무엇이 필요하니?

여 음, 그게 다인 것 같아.

해설

여자가 헤어스프레이, 빗, 작은 거울, 헤어드라이어가 필요하다고 했다.

어휘

fully[fúli] 충분히, 완전히 / prepared[pripέərd] 준비가 되어 있는 / first of all 우선 / hairspray[hέərsprei] 헤어스프레이 / comb[koum] 빗 / hairdryer[hέərdráiər] 헤어드라이어

04 ②

Script

W Mark, do you know who John picked?

M I'm not sure, but it wasn't you.

W How do you know?

M He told me he wouldn't pick you.

W Do you know why?

M He said he needed someone good at Japanese, but your specialty is English.

W That's not fair.

해석

여 Mark, John이 누구를 뽑았는지 아니?

남 잘 모르지만 너는 아니었어.

여 어떻게 알아?

남 그가 나에게 너를 뽑지 않을 것이라고 말을 했어.

여 왜 그런지 알아?

남 일본어를 잘하는 사람이 필요하다고 했는데 너의 전공은 영어잖아.

여 그것은 공평하지 않아.

해설

여자는 자신이 뽑히지 않을 것이라는 것을 알아서 실망했을 것이다.

어휘

specialty[spéʃəlti] 전공, 특기 / fair[fɛər] 공평한

05 ③

Script

W Did you plant all these flowers?

M I did some but not all of them.

W Where did you get them?

M I bought them at the garden shop. I also bought some grass, too.

W I see. What are these flowers?

M They are not flowers. They're weeds.

W Are they? What are you going to do with them?

M I'm about to pull them up.

해석

여 네가 이 꽃들을 모두 심었니?

남 일부는 내가 심었지만 전부는 아니야.

여 그것들은 어디서 났어?

남 꽃가게에서 샀어. 잔디도 좀 샀고.

여 그렇구나. 이 꽃들은 뭐야?

남 그것들은 꽃이 아니고 잡초야.

여 그래? 그것을 어떻게 할 건데?

남 막 뽑으려던 참이야.

해설

남자는 잡초를 뽑으려 하고 있다.

어휘

plant[plænt] (식물을) 심다 / grass[græs] 잔디 / weed[wi:d] 잡초 / pull up ~을 뽑다, 근절하다

06 ③

Script

M I heard that you're going to Florence.

W Yes, my aunt invited me there.

M What is that place famous for?

W It's known for its art and architecture. People there are very polite and kind.

M I see. I'm sure there are many famous buildings.

W Of course, but most of all, I like its beautiful scenery.

M I really want to go there, too.

해석

남 네가 플로렌스에 간다고 들었어.

여 응, 우리 이모가 나를 그곳에 초대하셨어.

남 플로렌스는 무엇으로 유명하니?

여 그곳은 예술과 건축물로 유명해. 그곳 사람들은 아주 예의 바르고 친절해.

남 그렇구나. 분명히 유명한 건물이 많이 있겠지.

여 물론, 하지만 나는 그중에서도 플로렌스의 아름다운 경치가 제일 좋아.

남 나도 정말 그곳에 가고 싶다.

해설

여자가 가장 좋아하는 것은 플로렌스의 아름다운 경치이다.

어휘

be famous for ~으로 유명하다 / architecture[á:rkətèktʃər] 건축물, 건축 / polite[pəláit] 예의 바른 / most of all 무엇보다도, 그 중에서도 / scenery[sí:nəri] 경치, 풍경

07 ②

Script

M I believe that this is one of the most important acts in our society. This is something you can learn when you work with others to reach a goal. School is a good place to practice it. We are often given projects so that we can learn how to work together. When we work in a group, we can't bring a good result without this.

해석

남 나는 이것이 우리의 사회에서 가장 중요한 행동 중 하나라고 믿는다. 이것은 목표를 이루기 위해 다른 사람들과 함께 일을 하면서 배울 수 있다. 학교는 이것을 연습할 수 있는 좋은 장소이다. 우리에게 종종 프로젝트가 주어져서 함께 일하는 법을 배울 수 있다. 우리가 단체로 일할 때, 이것이 없으면 좋은 결과를 가져올 수 없다.

해설

함께 일하면서 배울 수 있는 것, 함께 일할 때 가장 필요한 것은 협력하는 것이다.

어휘

society[səsáiəti] 사회 / reach[ri:tʃ] ~에 도달하다

08 ④

Script

M It looks really wonderful.

W Thank you, but please don't touch it. It took me 5 hours to build this sandcastle.

M You spent so much time, but one big wave will sweep

it away completely.

W I know, but I wanted to do it.

M Can I take a picture of it?

W Sure, go ahead. It'll be destroyed soon.

M Thank you. Why don't you stand right next to it? I'll take a picture of you and your wonderful work.

W Thanks.

해석

남 정말로 훌륭하네요.

여 감사합니다. 하지만 만지지는 말아 주세요. 이 모래성을 쌓는 데 다섯 시간이 걸렸어요.

남 정말 많은 시간을 들였는데 한 번의 큰 파도가 그것을 완전히 휩쓸어 가겠군요.

여 알아요. 하지만 모래성을 쌓고 싶었어요.

남 사진을 찍어도 될까요?

여 네, 그러세요. 곧 무너질 거예요.

남 감사합니다. 바로 옆에 서 보실래요? 제가 당신하고 당신의 훌륭한 작품을 찍어 드릴게요.

여 고마워요.

해설

모래성을 쌓고, 파도가 모래성을 휩쓸어 갈 수 있는 곳은 바닷가이다.

어휘

sandcastle[sǽn∂kæsl] 모래성 / sweep[swiːp] 휩쓸어 가다, 휩쓸다 / completely[kəmplíːtli] 완전히 / destroy[distrɔ́i] ~을 파괴하다 / stand[stænd] 서다

09 ⑤

Script

M Hi, I'd like to buy a card for my parents.

W Here is a heart-shaped one. It looks really lovely.

M Yeah, but that's a card for girlfriends. I need a thank-you card.

W Okay, then. I think that one would be good. It says "Special Thanks."

M You mean the one with no pictures or the one with flowers?

W Neither. I mean the one with the ribbon above the letters.

M That looks great! I'll take it.

해석

남 안녕하세요. 부모님에게 드릴 카드를 사고 싶어요.

여 여기 하트모양 카드가 있어요. 정말 예쁘지요.

남 네. 하지만 그건 여자 친구를 위한 것이지요. 저는 감사 카드가 필요해요.

여 알겠어요. 그러면, 제 생각엔 저것이 좋을 것 같네요. "Special Thanks"라고 쓰여 있어요.

남 그림이 없는 걸 말하는 건가요, 아니면 꽃 그림이 있는 걸 말하는 건가요?

여 둘 다 아니에요. 글자 위에 리본이 있는 걸 말하는 거예요.

남 좋아 보이네요! 그걸로 할게요.

해설

남자 'Special Thanks'라는 글 위에 리본이 달린 카드를 선택했다.

어휘

heart-shaped 하트 모양의 / lovely[lʌ́vli] 귀여운, 사랑스러운 / ribbon[ríbən] 리본

10 ⑤

Script

M Hi. I'm David. I'm going to tell you what happened to me yesterday. I went to Big Mountain Amusement Park with my friends. We really had a good time riding all kinds of roller coasters. When it was time to leave, we realized that none of us had any money to return home. My friends and I had to ask passersby for money. When we finally got home, it was 9 o'clock at night. I was exhausted.

해석

남 안녕. 나는 David야. 내가 너에게 어제 있었던 일을 말해 줄게. 나는 친구들과 함께 빅마운틴 놀이공원에 갔어. 우리는 온갖 종류의 롤러코스터를 타면서 정말 즐거운 시간을 보냈어. 떠날 때쯤 되어서 우리는 우리 중 누구도 집에 돌아갈 돈을 가지고 있지 않다는 것을 알았어. 내 친구들과 나는 지나가는 사람들에게 돈을 좀 달라고 부탁해야 했어. 결국 우리가 집에 도착했을 때는 밤 9시였어. 나는 완전히 지쳤어.

해설

부모님이 많이 걱정을 하셨다는 언급은 없다.

어휘

amusement park 놀이공원 / ride[raid] ~을 타다 / roller coaster 롤러코스터 / realize[ríːəlàiz] ~을 알다, 깨닫다 / passerby[pǽsərbài] 행인 / exhausted[igzɔ́ːstid] 지친

11 ④

Script

W Eric, do you know Monica is having a recital next Monday?

M I know she's having a recital, but as far as I know, it's not next Monday.

W Is that right?

M She said it's been rescheduled to Thursday.

W I see. It starts at 6, right?

M That also has been changed to 7.

W Okay. Then, we can meet at 6 to help her get ready.

M OK. See you then.

해석

여 Eric, Monica가 다음 월요일에 연주회 하는 것을 아니?

남 Monica가 연주회를 한다는 것은 아는데 내가 알기로 다음 월요일은 아니야.

여 그래?

남 Monica가 목요일로 일정이 변경되었다고 했어.

여 그렇구나. 6시에 시작하지, 맞지?

남 그것도 7시로 변경되었어.

여　알았어. 그러면, 우리가 그녀의 준비를 도와주려면 6시에 만나자.

남　알았어. 그러면 그때 봐.

해설
두 사람은 목요일 6시에 만나기로 했다.

어휘
recital[risáitl] 연주회, 독주회 / reschedule[ri:skédʒu(:)l] 일정을 변경하다

12 ④

Script

M　This was certainly a delicious meal.

W　I enjoyed it, too. I think it was the most delicious food I've recently had. How much is it, anyway?

M　Don't worry about it. I'll pay this time.

W　Then, I'll take care of the tip. How much should we tip?

M　Let's see. The bill is 50 dollars. I think in a restaurant like this, 10 percent is usual.

W　The food was good, and the waitress was kind. So, I'll tip an extra 2 dollars more than the usual.

M　Okay. Sounds great.

해석

남　정말 맛있는 음식이었어.

여　저도 맛있게 먹었어요. 제가 최근에 먹은 음식 중에 가장 맛있는 음식인 것 같아. 어쨌든, 얼마지?

여　걱정하지 마. 이번에는 내가 낼게.

남　그러면, 팁은 내가 낼게. 팁은 얼마나 줘야 하지?

여　어디 볼까. 50달러가 나왔네. 이런 식당에서는 보통 10퍼센트를 주는 것 같아.

남　음식도 맛있었고, 종업원도 친절했으니까, 일반적인 것보다 2달러를 더 줄게.

여　그래. 좋아.

해설
음식값이 50달러, 팁이 5달러이고, 2달러를 더 주기로 했으므로 57달러가 된다.

어휘
certainly[sə́:rtənli] 분명히, 확실히 / delicious[dilíʃəs] 맛있는 / recently[rí:səntli] 최근에 / tip[tip] 팁; ~에게 팁을 주다 / usual[jú:ʒuəl] 통상의, 일상의

13 ⑤

Script

W　Mike said he would not join the club.

M　Why not?

W　He said he found a better one.

M　He will regret it. Our club is the best.

W　I understand you are proud of your club, but not everyone has to join your club. And you should respect another person's opinion, too.

M　Okay. I see what you mean.

해석

여　Mike는 클럽에 가입하지 않겠대.

남　왜 안 해?

여　더 좋은 클럽을 찾았대.

남　그는 후회하게 될 거야. 우리 클럽이 최고야.

여　네가 너의 클럽을 자랑스러워 하는 것은 이해하지만, 모두가 너의 클럽에 가입해야 하는 건 아니잖아. 그리고 다른 사람의 의견도 존중해 줘야지.

남　알겠어. 네가 무슨 말을 하는 건지 알았어.

해설
여자는 남자에게 남의 의견을 존중해야 한다고 충고하고 있다.

어휘
join[dʒɔin] ~에 가입하다 / regret[rigrét] ~을 후회하다 / be proud of ~을 자랑스러워하다 / respect[rispékt] ~을 존중하다 / opinion[əpínjən] 의견

14 ①

Script

M　Jenny, what's wrong?

W　I'm so depressed, and I lost my appetite, too.

M　Why did you lose your appetite? Did the test result come back already?

W　No, not yet. But I'm sure I didn't do very well.

M　Why do you think that?

W　The test was very difficult for me. How about you?

M　Me? I'm not sure. I even don't remember the questions anyway. Don't worry too much.

해석

남　Jenny, 무슨 안 좋은 일이라도 있니?

여　나 너무 우울해. 식욕도 없고.

남　왜 식욕을 잃은 거야? 시험 결과가 벌써 나왔어?

여　아니, 아직. 하지만 좋은 성적을 받지 못할 것은 분명해.

남　왜 그렇게 생각하는데?

여　시험이 나에게 너무 어려웠거든. 너는?

남　나? 잘 모르겠어. 나는 시험문제조차도 생각나지 않는 걸 뭐. 너무 걱정하지 마.

해설
시험에 대해 걱정하는 학생과 위로해 주는 학생의 대화이다.

어휘
depressed[diprést] 우울한 / lose one's appetite 식욕을 잃다

15 ④

Script

①　**M**　Would you like to take a picture with me?

　　W　Sure. I want to take a picture of us with my camera, too.

②　**M**　Can I borrow your digital camera?

　　W　No problem.

75

③ M Excuse me, how much is this paint?

W The pink paint is 10 dollars.

④ M These are real masterpieces.

W That's right. I like paintings by Pablo Picasso.

⑤ M Wow! Have you ever seen this many people here before?

W Never. This is going to be a very exciting game.

해석

① 남 나랑 같이 사진 찍을래?

여 물론. 내 카메라로도 우리 사진을 찍고 싶어.

② 남 당신의 디지털 카메라를 좀 빌릴 수 있을까요?

여 네.

③ 남 실례합니다, 이 페인트는 얼마인가요?

여 분홍색 페인트는 10달러예요.

④ 남 이것들은 정말 명작들이지.

여 맞아. 나는 파블로 피카소가 그린 그림을 좋아해.

⑤ 남 와! 너는 전에 여기에 이렇게 많은 사람들이 있는 걸 본 적이 있니?

여 한 번도 없어. 정말로 흥미진진한 경기가 될 거야.

해설

두 사람이 피카소의 그림을 감상하고 있는 장면이다.

어휘

take a picture 사진 찍다 / borrow[bɔ́(:)rou] ~을 빌리다 / masterpiece[mǽstərpìːs] 명작, 걸작

16 ③

Script

M A huge car accident happened on the Autobahn in Germany. It involved 256 cars. Miraculously, no one died, although 66 people were injured. It is believed that the accident was caused by slippery road conditions as it was raining heavily at that time. Some motorists who were driving at high speed on the Autobahn might also be to blame.

해석

남 독일에 있는 아우토반에서 대형 자동차 사고가 일어났습니다. 그것은 256대의 자동차가 연관되어 있었습니다. 비록 66명의 부상자가 있었지만, 기적적으로 아무도 죽지 않았습니다. 그 사고는 그 당시 심한 폭우로 미끄러워진 도로 때문에 일어났다고 합니다. 아우토반에서 고속으로 운전했던 일부 운전자들의 책임도 있을 것입니다.

해설

많은 사람이 다쳤지만 죽은 사람은 없었다.

어휘

Germany[dʒə́ːrməni] 독일 / involve[inválv] 관련시키다 / miraculously[mirǽkjələsli] 기적적으로 / injured[índʒərd] 상처 입은, 부상한 / cause[kɔːz] ~의 원인이 되다, 일으키다 / slippery[slípəri] 미끄러운 / heavily[hévili] 심하게, 몹시 / motorist[móutərist] 운전자 / high speed 고속 / blame[bleim] ~의 탓으로 돌리다, ~에게 책임지우다

17 ④

Script

M This is a piece of cloth with a special colored pattern or picture on it that is the symbol of a particular country or organization, or has a particular meaning. It's also used in some sports as a signal or as a sign showing the position of something. This can be attached to a pole or held in one's hand.

해석

남 이것은 특정한 나라나 조직의 상징이 되거나, 특별한 의미를 가지는 독특한 색깔의 패턴이나 그림이 그려진 천 조각이다. 그것은 또한 일부 운동경기에서 신호로 사용되거나 사물의 위치를 알려 주는 표시로 사용된다. 이것은 막대에 붙이거나 손에 들 수 있다.

해설

특정한 나라나 조직의 상징이 되거나 어떤 신호를 보내는 용도로 쓰일 수 있는 천 조각은 깃발이다.

어휘

cloth[klɔ(ː)θ] 천 / pattern[pǽtərn] 패턴, 형태 / particular[pərtíkjulər] 특정한, 특별한 / organization[ɔ̀ːrgənəzéiʃən] 조직 / signal[sígnl] 신호 / attach[ətǽtʃ] 붙이다 / pole[poul] 막대기 / hold A in one's hand A를 ~의 손에 들고 있다

18 ①

Script

W Kevin meets Rebecca on the way to school. Kevin tells her he had a very hard time last night. All the other students in his English class went to a party at their teacher's house, but Kevin couldn't get there. From their school, he took the subway, but he took the one on the opposite side and got completely lost. He really wanted to go to the party last night, but he missed it because of his mistake. In this situation, what would Rebecca most probably say to him?

① I'm sorry to hear that.

② We're going to miss you.

③ Why didn't you come to the party?

④ It's a pity that you weren't invited.

⑤ That's okay. You can do better next time.

해석

여 Kevin은 학교 가는 길에 Rebecca를 만난다. Kevin은 그녀에게 자신이 지난밤에 매우 어려움을 겪었다고 말한다. 영어 수업을 같이 듣는 반 학생들 모두 선생님 집에서 하는 파티에 갔지만, Kevin은 갈 수 없었다. 그는 학교에서 지하철을 탔는데 반대 방향에서 타서 완전히 길을 잃어버렸다. 그는 지난밤에 정말로 파티에 가고 싶었지만 자신의 실수 때문에 갈 수 없었다. 이러한 상황에서 Rebecca는 그에게 무엇이라고 말을 할까?

① 그런 이야기를 들어서 유감이야.

② 우리는 네가 그리울 거야.

③ 파티가 가 그러니?

④ 네가 초대받지 않았다니 안 됐어.

⑤ 괜찮아. 다음번에는 더 잘할 수 있을 거야.

해설

Rebecca는 안 좋은 일을 겪은 Kevin에게 "그런 이야기를 들어서 유감이야."라는 위로의 말을 해줄 수 있다.

어휘

opposite[ɑ́pəzit] 반대쪽의 / get lost 길을 잃다 /
completely[kəmplíːtli] 완전히 / mistake[mistéik] 실수 / pity[píti]
동정, 불쌍히 여김 / invite[inváit] ~을 초대하다

19 ⑤

Script

M Can you tell me <u>how to use</u> this machine?

W Don't you have instructions for this?

M Yes, I do. But I don't quite understand them.

W Well. Can you see that red button? It's the start button.

M I know.

W Push that button first and <u>grab</u> that <u>yellow handle</u> and pull it when it moves. <u>Is that clear</u>?

M Sure, thanks. You're really helpful.

해석

남 이 기계를 어떻게 사용하는지 알려 주실래요?

여 이 기계의 사용설명서를 가지고 있지 않나요?

남 가지고 있어요. 하지만 잘 이해가 안 돼요.

여 음. 저 빨간 버튼이 보이나요? 그것이 시작 버튼이에요.

남 알아요.

여 먼저 그 버튼을 누르고 노란 손잡이를 잡으세요. 그리고 손잡이가 움직이면 잡아당기세요. 이제 아시겠어요?

남 네, 고마워요. 정말 도움이 되었어요.

해설

기계의 사용법을 설명해 준 사람에게 "네, 고마워요. 정말 도움이 되었어요."라는 응답이 가장 적절하다.

① 네. 그것은 깨끗해요. 고마워요.

② 나는 당신이 혼자 할 수 있을 거라고 확신해요.

③ 미안해요. 제가 지금 바로 치울게요.

④ 이제 버튼을 누르셔도 돼요.

어휘

instructions[instrʌ́kʃəns] 사용설명서 / grab[græb] 부여잡다, 움켜잡다 /
pull[pul] ~을 당기다 / clear[kliər] 명백한, 분명한

20 ③

Script

W Jake, my computer won't work again.

M What happened?

W I don't know. I just turned it on, and <u>nothing came up</u>.

M Let me see it. I think there is some problem with the hardware.

W Do you think you can <u>repair this computer</u> right now?

M <u>Well, I don't think it's possible.</u>

해석

여 Jake, 내 컴퓨터가 또 작동이 안 돼.

남 무슨 일이 있었는데?

여 몰라. 그냥 컴퓨터를 켰는데 아무것도 뜨지 않아.

남 좀 보자. 내 생각엔 하드웨어에 문제가 있는 것 같아.

여 네 생각에 지금 당장 이것을 고칠 수 있을 거 같니?

남 글쎄, 불가능할 것 같은데.

해설

지금 당장 컴퓨터를 수리해 줄 수 있느냐는 질문에 "글쎄, 불가능할 것 같은데."라는 응답이 가장 적절하다.

① 그것을 수리해 줘서 고마워.

② 물론, 얼마나 빠른지 보자.

④ 아니. 내 생각에는 지금 당장 켜야 할 것 같아.

⑤ 응. 그것은 오래되고 느려서 너는 새것이 하나 필요해.

어휘

turn on ~을 켜다 / come up 나타나다 / hardware[hɑ́ːrdwɛ̀ər] (컴퓨터)
하드웨어 / repair[ripɛ́ər] ~을 수리하다 / right now 지금 당장

p.112~115

14회 영어듣기모의고사

01 ①	02 ⑤	03 ②	04 ⑤	05 ①
06 ③	07 ③	08 ①	09 ④	10 ④
11 ②	12 ③	13 ②	14 ①	15 ②
16 ③	17 ④	18 ③	19 ①	20 ④

01 ①

Script

W This is an animal that mainly lives in water and has a soft body <u>covered by</u> a hard shell. It cannot breathe underwater, but it can <u>hold its breath</u> for various lengths of time. In fact, it breathes air. Although many of them live in or around water, they don't <u>lay eggs</u> underwater. They can also spend much of their lives on dry land. Surprisingly, they are commonly kept <u>as pets</u>.

해석

여 이것은 주로 물에서 사는 동물이며 단단한 껍질에 의해 덮인 부드러운 몸을 가지고 있다. 그것은 물속에서는 숨을 쉴 수 없지만, 숨을 참을 수 있는 기간이 다양하다. 물 주위나 물속에 많이 살지만, 그들은 물속에 알을 낳지는 않는다. 그들은 또한 그들의 삶에서 많은 시간을 육지에서 보낼 수도 있다. 놀랍게도, 그들은 흔히 애완동물로 길러진다.

해설

등껍질이 딱딱하며 속살은 부드럽고, 물속에서도, 육지에서도 살 수 있는 동물은 거북이이다.

어휘

covered by ~으로 덮인 / shell[ʃel] 등딱지, 껍데기 / breathe[briːð]
숨을 쉬다 / underwater[ʌ̀ndərwɔ́ːtər] 수면 아래에, 수중 /
hold one's breath 숨을 멈추다, 숨을 돌리다 / various[vɛ́əriəs] 다양한 /
lay[lei] ~을 낳다 / dry land 육지 / pet[pet] 애완동물

02 ⑤

Script

W What do you want to be in the future, Henry?

M I'm thinking of studying law, but my parents want me to be a doctor.

W I see.

M What do you think about that?

W I think your opinion is more important.

M Thanks. How about you, Sarah?

W I'm thinking of becoming a social worker.

M I knew you would because you always like to help others.

해석

여 너는 장차 무엇이 되길 원하니, Henry?

남 나는 법을 공부하려고 생각 중인데, 우리 부모님은 내가 의사가 되길 원하셔.

여 그렇구나.

남 너는 어떻게 생각해?

여 나는 너의 의견이 더 중요하다고 생각해.

남 고마워. Sarah 너는?

여 나는 사회복지사가 되고 싶어.

남 네가 항상 다른 사람들을 돕는 것을 좋아하니까 사회복지사가 되고 싶어 할 거라고 생각했어.

해설

여자는 사회복지사가 되고 싶어한다.

어휘

law[lɔː] 법률 / opinion[əpínjən] 의견, 생각 / social worker 사회복지사

03 ②

Script

M Do you have any plans for tomorrow?

W I'm going to study English. I really hate to memorize English vocabulary, but I have no other choice. How about you?

M My mom has bought some furniture, and I have to get rid of the old stuff with my father.

W I see. If you need any help, just let me know. I can carry the small pieces.

M Thanks.

해석

남 너는 내일 무슨 계획이라도 있니?

여 나는 영어 공부를 할 거야. 나는 정말 영어 단어 외우는 것을 싫어하지만, 선택의 여지가 없어. 너는?

남 우리 엄마가 가구를 좀 사셔서 나는 우리 아버지하고 낡은 가구를 버려야 해.

여 그렇구나. 도움이 필요하면, 나에게 알려 줘. 나는 작은 것들은 운반할 수 있어.

남 고마워.

해설

남자는 아버지와 함께 낡은 가구를 버릴 것이다.

어휘

memorize[méməràiz] ~을 암기하다 / vocabulary[voukǽbjəlèri] 어휘 / furniture[fə́ːrnitʃər] 가구 / get rid of ~을 제거하다, 없애다 / stuff[stʌf] 물건 / carry[kǽri] ~을 운반하다

04 ⑤

Script

W Hi, Tom. You don't look happy. Is there something wrong?

M I have a final exam tomorrow.

W Don't worry too much. You will do fine.

M I don't think I'm ready yet.

W I don't think you need to feel so anxious because I've seen you work very hard.

해석

여 안녕, Tom. 너 안 좋아 보이는데. 무슨 일이 있니?

남 내일 기말 시험이 있어.

여 너무 걱정하지 마. 너는 잘할 거야.

남 나는 아직 준비가 된 것 같지 않아.

여 나는 네가 열심히 공부를 해왔기 때문에 걱정할 필요가 없다고 생각해.

해설

여자는 남자에게 걱정할 필요가 없다고 격려해 주고 있다.

05 ①

Script

W Hi, Mr. Adams. I dropped by to say goodbye.

M Going back to your country? When are you leaving?

W This coming Friday. My flight is at 7 P.M.

M I really enjoyed having you here.

W I just want to thank you and all the other teachers.

M We're going to miss you. Did you say goodbye to your classmates?

W Sure, I did. And some of them are going to see me off at the airport.

M Then, have a good trip. Goodbye.

해석

여 안녕하세요, Adams 선생님. 작별 인사를 하려고 들렀어요.

남 너의 나라로 돌아가니? 언제 떠나니?

여 이번 금요일이요. 오후 7시 비행기예요.

남 네가 여기에서 함께 지내서 정말 즐거웠단다.

여 선생님과 다른 선생님들에게 감사하다는 말을 전하고 싶어요.

남 네가 그리울 거야. 반 친구들에게 작별 인사는 했니?

여 물론, 했어요. 그리고 몇 명은 공항으로 배웅 나올 거예요.

남 그럼, 잘 가거라. 안녕.

해설

자신의 나라로 돌아가는 유학생과 선생님의 대화이다.

어휘
drop by 들르다 / say goodbye 작별 인사하다 / go back 돌아가다 /
coming[kʌ́miŋ] 다가오는 / flight[flait] 항공편, 비행 / see off 배웅하다

06 ③

Script

M May I take your order?

W Yes, I'd like two slices of pizza and a large Coke.

M Here or to go?

W Here, please.

M That comes to 5 dollars and 25 cents.

W Here's 10 dollars.

M Thanks.

W Just a moment. I have a quarter.

M Okay. Here's your change.

해석

남 주문을 하시겠어요?

여 네, 피자 두 조각하고, 콜라 큰 것으로 하나 주세요.

남 가져갈 것인가요, 아니면 먹고 갈 것인가요?

여 먹고 갈 거예요.

남 전부 5달러 25센트입니다.

여 여기 10달러 있어요.

남 감사합니다.

여 잠깐만요. 저에게 25센트가 있어요.

남 알았습니다. 잔돈 여기 있습니다.

해설

10달러 25센트를 냈고, 내야 할 돈이 5달러 25센트이므로 거스름돈으로 5
달러를 받을 것이다.

어휘
order[ɔ́:rdər] 주문; 명령 / slice[slais] 얇게 썬 조각 /
to go (식당 등의 음식을) 싸 가지고 갈 / come to 금액이 ~가 되다 /
quarter[kwɔ́:rtər] 25센트; 4분의 1 / change[tʃeindʒ] 잔돈

07 ③

Script

W Can you check the fuel tank, please?

M I'm sure there is enough.

W I want to know the exact amount.

M OK. There was 25 liters when I first checked the fuel
tank this morning. After that, John took 5 liters, and
then Kevin took 10 liters. That's all I know.

W OK. Mike also used 3 liters.

M Is that right?

W Yes. Since then no one has used it.

해석

여 연료 탱크 좀 확인해 줄래?

남 충분히 있어. 확실해.

여 정확한 양을 알고 싶어.

남 알았어. 내가 오늘 아침에 처음 확인했을 때는 25리터가 있었고, 그러
고 나서 John이 5리터, Kevin이 10리터를 가져갔어. 그것이 내가 아
는 전부야.

여 알았어. Mike도 3리터를 썼어.

남 그래?

여 응. 그 이후로 사용한 사람은 없어.

해설

연료 탱크에 25리터 있었는데 John이 5리터, Kevin이 10리터, 마이크가
3리터를 사용했으므로 7리터가 남았다.

어휘
fuel tank 연료 탱크 / enough[inʌ́f] 충분한 / exact[igzǽkt] 정확한

08 ①

Script

W Ken, I'll be there around 6. Do you want me to bring
anything?

M Nothing. My mother has already prepared everything,
but I have a favor to ask you.

W What is it?

M I invited Harry to the party, but he doesn't want to
come.

W Why not?

M Since he argued with Kate, he doesn't want to see her
anymore.

W I see. So, you want me to bring Harry to the party?

M That's right.

해석

여 Ken, 여섯 시쯤에 갈게. 내가 뭘 가져다주길 바라니?

남 아무것도 필요 없어. 우리 어머니가 벌써 모든 것을 다 준비하셨어.
하지만 부탁이 하나 있어.

여 뭔데?

남 내가 파티에 Harry를 초대했는데 Harry가 오려고 하지 않아.

여 왜 안 와?

남 Kate와 말다툼을 해서, 더는 그녀를 보고 싶어하지 않아.

여 그렇구나. 그래서 너는 내가 Harry를 파티에 데려오기를 원하는구나.

남 바로 그거야.

해설

남자는 여자에게 파티에 친구인 Harry를 데려오라고 부탁하고 있다.

어휘
bring[briŋ] ~을 가져오다 / prepare[pripέər] ~을 준비하다 /
ask a favor ~을 부탁하다 / argue with ~와 말다툼하다

09 ④

Script

W Excuse me, can you help me?

M Sure. What do you need?

W I've lost my friends, and I can't find them. What should I do?

M Where did you last see them?

W I think it was at the roller coaster. I was with them when we bought the tickets.

M If I were you, I would ask the main office to page them.

W I think I will. Thank you for your advice.

해석

여 실례합니다. 좀 도와주시겠어요?

남 물론이죠. 무엇이 필요하시죠?

여 제가 친구를 잃어버렸는데 찾을 수가 없어요. 제가 어떻게 해야 하죠?

남 어디서 그들을 마지막으로 보았나요?

여 제 생각에는 롤러코스터에서요. 표를 살 때 그들과 같이 있었어요.

남 제가 당신이라면, 사무실에 그들의 이름을 불러서 찾아 달라고 부탁하겠어요.

여 그래야겠군요. 조언 감사합니다.

해설

롤러코스터를 탈 수 있는 곳은 놀이공원이다.

어휘

roller coaster 롤러코스터 / page[peidʒ] ~의 이름을 불러 찾게 하다 / advice[ədváis] 조언, 충고

10 ④

Script

M Can I help you?

W Yes. I need to get something for my brother.

M Pen sets are always a good gift. We have a set with 3 pencils and an eraser, and another with 3 ballpoint pens and correction fluid. If you can afford colored pencils, there are 12 different colored pencils in a set.

W But I don't think he needs colored pencils. He is a middle school student.

M I see. Then choose this set. It has a pencil, a ballpoint pen, and an eraser.

W I'll take that. Can you gift-wrap it, please?

M No problem. Wait a second, please.

해석

남 도와드릴까요?

여 네. 제 남동생을 위해 뭘 좀 사고 싶어서요.

남 펜 세트는 항상 좋은 선물이죠. 연필 세 자루와 지우개 하나가 들어 있는 세트가 있고, 또 볼펜 세 자루와 수정액이 들어 있는 세트가 있어요. 색연필을 사 주실 여유가 되신다면 열두 가지 색깔의 색연필 세트가 있고요.

여 하지만 색연필이 필요할 것 같진 않아요. 그는 중학생이거든요.

남 알겠어요. 그럼 이 세트로 하시죠. 연필 한 자루와 볼펜 한 자루, 지우개 한 개가 들어 있어요.

여 그걸로 할게요. 선물 포장을 좀 해 주시겠어요?

남 네. 잠시만 기다리세요.

해설

여자는 남동생을 위해서 연필 한 자루, 볼펜 한 자루, 지우개 한 개가 들어 있는 세트를 사려고 한다.

어휘

eraser[iréisər] 지우개 / ballpoint pencil 볼펜 / correction fluid 수정액 / afford[əfɔ́ːrd] ~할 여유가 있다. ~할 수 있다 / colored pencil 색연필 / gift-wrap 선물 포장을 하다

11 ②

Script

W Hi, Daniel. I'm sorry I hung up on you last night.

M Oh, that! Actually I was wondering why.

W I'm really sorry. My mother scolded me for staying on the phone too long.

M I see. I thought you were mad at me.

W No, not at all.

M OK. Then, are we still doing our homework together tonight?

W Sure. I'll see you at 6.

해석

여 안녕, Daniel. 어젯밤에는 전화하다가 끊어서 미안해.

남 아, 그게! 사실 왜 그랬는지 궁금해하고 있었어.

여 정말 미안해. 전화를 너무 오래 한다고 어머니한테 혼이 났거든.

남 그랬구나. 나는 네가 나에게 화가 난 줄 알았어.

여 아니, 전혀 아니야.

남 알았어. 그럼 오늘 밤에 숙제 같이하기로 한 거는 유효한 거지?

여 물론. 6시에 보자.

해설

여자는 전화를 오래 한다고 어머니에게 혼이 나서 전화를 끊었다.

어휘

hang up on 전화를 끊다 / scold[skould] ~을 꾸짖다, 잔소리하다 / mad[mæd] 화난 / not at all 전혀 ~이 아니다

12 ③

Script

① **W** Where do you want me to place this vase?

　M Please put it on the table.

② **W** She seems to have been punished.

　M Yeah. She looks depressed.

③ **W** Don't forget to pay your rent.

　M Don't worry. I already returned the books.

④ **W** What's tomorrow's schedule?

　M It depends on the weather.

⑤ **W** Did you attend the English class?

　M Sure. I never miss any English classes.

해석

① 여 이 꽃병을 어디에 놓을까요?

　남 테이블 위에 놓아 주세요.

② 여 그녀는 벌을 받은 것처럼 보여.

남 응. 우울해 보인다.
③ 여 월세 내는 것을 잊지 마세요.
    남 걱정하지 마세요. 저는 책을 이미 반납했어요.
④ 여 내일의 일정은 무엇입니까?
    남 날씨에 달렸어요.
⑤ 여 너는 영어 수업은 들었니?
    남 물론이지. 나는 영어 수업은 절대로 빼먹지 않아.

③ 월세를 내는 것을 잊지 말라는 말에 책을 이미 반납했다는 대답은 어울리지 않는다.

어휘
place[pleis] ∼을 놓다 / vase[veis] 꽃병 / punish[pʌ́niʃ] 벌하다, 처벌하다 / depressed[diprést] 우울한 / pay[pei] ∼을 지불하다 / rent[rent] 집세, 임대료 / return[ritə́:rn] ∼을 반납하다 / depend on ∼에 달려있다 / attend[əténd] ∼에 참석하다, 출석하다

13 ②
Script

W Hi, Eden! How was your trip to Bangkok?

M Great! I enjoyed sailing on a yacht.

W Did you visit the famous fish market?

M No, I didn't have enough time. I just went to a buffet restaurant. It was so huge that the waiters and waitresses use roller skates to serve customers.

W That's great. Did you also go to the International Movie Festival?

M Sure. The movies were fantastic! A sightseeing tour of the city was fun, too.

해설
여 안녕, Eden! 방콕 여행은 어땠니?
남 좋았어! 요트 타는 것이 즐거웠어.
여 그 유명한 수산시장에 갔었니?
남 아니, 시간이 충분하지 않았어. 그냥 뷔페식당에 갔었어. 정말 커서 종업원들이 손님을 접대할 때 롤러스케이트를 타고 다녀.
여 대단하다. 국제 영화제에도 갔었니?
남 물론. 영화들이 정말 훌륭했어! 시내 관광도 재미있었고.

해설
남자는 시간이 부족해서 수산 시장에는 가지 못했다.

어휘
buffet[bʌféi] 뷔페 / roller skate 롤러스케이트 / serve[sə:rv] 접대하다, 주문받다, 봉사하다 / customer[kʌ́stəmər] 고객 / sightseeing[sáitsì:iŋ] 관광

14 ①
Script

① W You are not supposed to litter.
    M I'm sorry. I'll pick it up.
② W Stop bothering your sister.
    M She started it first.

③ W Do not play with the ball on the street.
    M I'm sorry. I won't do it again.
④ W I hope that it stops pouring.
    M Me, too. I want to go out and play.
⑤ W It looks really dirty.
    M No, it's not. I cleaned it this morning.

해설
① 여 쓰레기를 버리면 안 돼요.
    남 죄송합니다. 제가 주울게요.
② 여 너의 여동생을 그만 괴롭혀.
    남 쟤가 먼저 그랬어요.
③ 여 길거리에서 공을 가지고 놀지 마라.
    남 죄송합니다. 다시 안 그럴게요.
④ 여 억수같이 퍼붓는 비가 그만 그쳤으면 좋겠어.
    남 나도. 밖에 나가서 놀고 싶어.
⑤ 여 그것은 정말 더러워 보인다.
    남 아니야. 내가 오늘 아침에 청소했어.

해설
소년이 바닥에 쓰레기를 버려서 어른이 꾸짖는 상황이다.

어휘
litter[lítər] (물건을) 흐트리다, 어질러 놓다 / bother[bάðər] ∼을 괴롭히다 / pour[pɔːr] 억수같이 퍼붓다

15 ②
Script

M Hi, Cindy. Would you do me a favor?

W What is it?

M I need to call Mrs. Adams, so can you give me her phone number? And can I use your cell phone, too?

W My cell phone is here, and Mrs. Adams's phone number is... I need to check my phonebook.

M Could you hurry it up? It's urgent.

W Oh my God! I've just erased all of the phone numbers in my phonebook. I think I pushed the wrong button by accident. This is terrible.

M I've lost my cell phone. You've erased all of your phone numbers. Now, what can we do?

해설
남 안녕, Cindy. 내 부탁 좀 들어줄래?
여 뭔데?
남 Adams 선생님한테 전화해야 하는데 전화번호 좀 알려 줄래? 그리고 네 휴대 전화를 좀 쓸 수 있을까?
여 내 휴대 전화는 여기 있고, Adams 선생님의 전화번호는…… 전화번호부를 확인해 봐야 해.
남 좀 서둘러 줄래? 급하거든.
여 이런! 전화번호부에 있던 전화번호를 다 지워버렸네. 실수로 버튼을 잘못 누른 것 같아. 끔찍하군.
남 나는 휴대 전화를 잃어버렸고, 너는 전화번호를 모두 지워버렸으니. 이제 우리가 뭘 할 수 있지?

남자는 휴대 전화를 잃어버렸고, 여자는 전화번호를 모두 지워버려서 전화를 걸 수 없으므로 남자는 좌절감을 느낄 것이다.

어휘

do someone a favor ~의 부탁을 들어주다 / phonebook[founbuk] 전화번호부 / hurry[hə́ːri] 서두르다 / urgent[ə́ːrdʒənt] 긴급한 / erase[iréis] ~을 지우다 / by accident 우연히

16 ③

Script

W We're talking today with Mike, a famous soccer player. Good evening, Mike.

M Good evening. Thank you for inviting me.

W Is this your first visit to New Haven?

M No. I've been here before many times for games.

W Oh, really? Where's your hometown?

M San Francisco. I moved to New York when I was 12. Since then, I've lived in here.

W And you went to university in New York?

M That's right.

W Thanks. Let's have a break. We'll be right back. Stay tuned!

해석

여 오늘은 유명한 축구선수인 Mike 씨와 이야기를 나눠 보겠습니다. 안녕하세요, Mike 씨.

남 안녕하세요. 초대해 주셔서 감사합니다.

여 이번이 뉴 헤이븐에 첫 방문이신가요?

남 아니요. 경기 때문에 여러 번 왔었습니다.

여 아, 그래요? 고향은 어디시죠?

남 샌프란시스코입니다. 제가 열두 살 때 뉴욕으로 이사를 왔어요. 그때부터 여기에 살고 있어요.

여 그리고 뉴욕에서 대학을 다녔나요?

남 맞습니다.

여 감사합니다. 잠시 휴식을 취하고 곧 돌아오겠습니다. 채널을 고정해 주세요!

해설

남자는 현재 샌프란시스코에 사는 것이 아니라 뉴욕에 산다.

어휘

famous[féiməs] 유명한 / visit[vízit] 방문; 방문하다 / hometown[hóumtàun] 고향 / have a break 휴식을 취하다 / stay tuned (채널, 주파수를) 고정하다

17 ④

Script

M This is the system or type of money that a country uses. Each country has its own unit for this and its famous people or symbol on this. This has many kinds of different values and types. Mainly there are coins and bills. The most common one is the US dollar, which can be used in most countries worldwide.

해석

남 이것은 한 나라가 사용하는 돈의 형태이거나 체계이다. 각 나라는 이것에 대해서 그 나라 만의 단위를 가지고 있고, 이것에는 유명한 사람이나 상징이 그려져 있다. 이것은 많은 다른 종류의 가치를 지니고 있고, 형태도 다양하다. 주로 동전과 지폐가 있다. 가장 흔한 것은 미국 달러인데 전 세계적으로 대부분의 나라에서 사용되어 질 수 있다.

해설

각 나라에서 사용되는 돈의 형태나 체계는 화폐이다.

어휘

own[oun] 자신의 / unit[júːnit] 단위 / symbol[símbəl] 상징 / value[vǽljuː] (통화의) 가치 / coin[kɔin] 동전 / bill[bil] 지폐 / common[kámən] 흔한 / worldwide[wə́ːrldwàid] 전 세계적으로

18 ③

Script

W Secret Garden, may I help you?

M Hi, I'd like to make a reservation for 4 people. My name is John Cooper.

W Okay. When will that be for?

M On the fifth of July

W Okay, for what time?

M 7 P.M.

W Okay. Can I have your phone number, please?

M It's 212-223-5186.

W I see. If there is any change, please let us know in advance.

M Okay. Thank you.

해석

여 시크릿 가든입니다. 도와드릴까요?

남 안녕하세요, 네 명 예약을 하고 싶습니다. 제 이름은 John Cooper입니다.

여 알았습니다. 며칠이지요?

남 7월 5일이요.

여 알았습니다. 몇 시지요?

남 저녁 7시요.

여 알았습니다. 전화번호를 주시겠어요?

남 212-223-5186입니다.

여 알았습니다. 만약 변경사항이 있으시면 미리 알려 주세요.

남 네. 감사합니다.

해설

예약한 날은 7월 15일이 아니라 7월 5일이다.

어휘

make a reservation 예약하다 / in advance 미리

19 ①

Script

M What are you doing?

W I'm trying to memorize this passage.

M What for?

W I'm supposed to make a five-minute speech in class.

M It must be very difficult.

W No, not at all. But the problem is that I get so nervous when I speak in front of other people.

M Isn't that normal for everyone?

해석
남 뭐 하고 있어?
여 이 글을 외우려고 노력 중이야.
남 왜?
여 수업 시간에 5분 연설을 해야 하거든.
남 정말 어렵겠다.
여 아니, 전혀. 하지만 문제는 다른 사람들 앞에서 말을 할 때 너무 긴장을 한다는 거야.
남 모든 사람들이 그러는 거 아니야?

해설
사람들 앞에서 말을 할 때면 긴장을 한다는 말에 "모든 사람들이 그러는 거 아니야?"라는 응답이 가장 적절하다.
② 네가 원한다면 내가 해 줄 수 있어.
③ 너는 그것에 천부적인 재능이 있어.
④ 책을 구해서 계속 연습을 해 봐.
⑤ 이해해. 마이크를 사용하도록 해 봐.

어휘
memorize[méməràiz] ~을 암기하다 / passage[pǽsidʒ] (글의) 한 구절 / make a speech 연설하다 / nervous[nə́:rvəs] 긴장한 / in front of ~의 앞에 / normal[nɔ́:rməl] 정상인

20 ④

Script

M Kelly, is that you?

W Mike! Long time no see. I haven't seen you for a long time.

M Yeah, but look at you! You haven't changed at all.

W Thank you for saying so. I think we should stay in touch with each other more often.

M That's what I was thinking.

해석
남 Kelly, 너니?
여 Mike! 정말 오랜만이다. 오랫동안 못 만났지.
남 응. 하지만 너 좀 봐! 하나도 안 변했네.
여 그렇게 말해 줘서 고마워. 내 생각에 우리는 좀 더 자주 서로 연락을 하고 지내야 할 것 같아.
남 그게 바로 내가 생각하는 거야.

해설
더 자주 연락하고 지내자는 말에 "그게 바로 내가 생각하는 거야."라는 응답이 가장 적절하다.
① 나는 우리가 결론에 도달할 수 있을 거라고 생각해.

② 내 생각에 너는 우리 집에서 지낼 수 있을 것 같아.
③ 우리는 더는 그것을 만질 수 없어.
⑤ 너는 어떻게 그것을 얻었어?

어휘
Long time no see. 오랜만이야. / stay in touch with ~와 연락을 유지하다

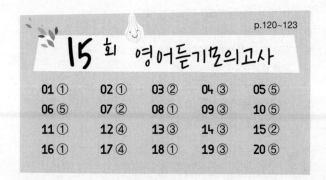

p.120~123

15 회 영어듣기모의고사

01 ①	02 ①	03 ②	04 ③	05 ⑤
06 ⑤	07 ②	08 ①	09 ③	10 ⑤
11 ①	12 ④	13 ③	14 ③	15 ②
16 ①	17 ④	18 ①	19 ③	20 ⑤

01 ①

Script

W Hello, I'd like to make some stickers for myself.

M Okay. Can you write down what you want on the sticker?

W Sure. "A Lovely Girl"

M That's it?

W Please make each word begin with a capital and put a rose at each side.

M Okay.

해석
여 안녕하세요, 저를 위한 스티커를 만들고 싶어요.
남 알았습니다. 스티커에 쓸 말을 적어 주시겠어요?
여 네. "A Lovely Girl"
남 그게 전부 인가요?
여 각각의 글자를 대문자로 시작해 주시고, 양쪽에 장미를 하나씩 넣어 주세요.
남 알았습니다.

해설
'A Lovely Girl'이라는 글씨가 쓰여 있고 양쪽에 장미가 한 개씩 있는 스티커이다.

어휘
write down ~을 적다 / capital[kǽpitl] 대문자

02 ①

Script

W You look like you've put on some weight.

M Yes, I know. I haven't exercised at all lately.

W If I were you, I would start dieting or jogging.

M I'm already on a diet, but I don't like jogging.

W Why don't you <u>play</u> basketball <u>after</u> <u>school</u>?

M I don't like to sweat, and my left elbow isn't good.

W <u>How</u> <u>about</u> <u>swimming</u> then?

M Swimming? Well, I can't swim.

해석

여 너 살이 좀 찐 것 같아 보여.

남 응, 알아. 최근에 운동을 전혀 안 했거든.

여 내가 너라면 다이어트를 하거나 조깅을 시작하겠어.

남 나는 벌써 다이어트 중이야. 하지만 조깅은 싫어.

여 방과 후에 농구를 하지 그러니?

남 나는 땀나는 것이 싫어. 그리고 나의 왼쪽 팔꿈치도 좋지 않고.

여 그러면 수영은 어때?

남 수영? 글쎄, 나는 수영을 못 해.

해설

남자는 체중을 줄이기 위해 다이어트, 즉 식이요법을 하고 있는 중이다.

어휘

put on weight 살이 찌다 / lately[léitli] 최근에 / diet[dáiət] 식이요법하다, 다이어트하다 / jog[dʒɑg] 조깅하다 / be on a diet 다이어트[식이요법]하다 / sweat[swet] 땀을 흘리다; 땀 / elbow[élbou] 팔꿈치

03 ②

Script

M This is an instrument used for <u>measuring</u> <u>weights</u>. To use it properly, you have to put it <u>on</u> <u>an</u> <u>even</u> <u>floor</u>. Older versions have a pointer on the scale that indicates how much a certain item weighs. But these days <u>most</u> <u>of</u> <u>them</u> are digitalized. However, you can still see the old ones in a market or you might even have one at home.

해석

남 이것은 무게를 측정하는 데 사용되는 도구이다. 이것을 올바르게 사용하기 위해서, 당신은 이것을 평평한 바닥에 놓아야 한다. 옛날에 이것은 특정 물건이 얼마나 나가는지를 보여 주는 바늘이 눈금 위에 있었다. 그러나 요즈음에는 이것들 대부분이 디지털화되었다. 하지만 여러분은 아직도 시장에서 구식 저울을 볼 수 있고, 혹은 당신 집에 하나 가지고 있을 수도 있다.

해설

사물의 무게를 재는 것은 저울이다.

어휘

instrument[ínstrəmənt] 도구 / measure[méʒər] ~을 재다, 측정하다 / weight[weit] 무게 / properly[prápərli] 올바르게, 적당히 / even[íːvən] 평평한 / scale[skeil] 저울, 저울눈 / indicate[índikèit] ~을 나타내다, 표시하다 / certain[sə́ːrtən] 특정한 / weigh[wei] 무게가 ~나가다 / digitalize[dídʒitəlàiz] 디지털화되다

04 ③

Script

M Can I talk to you for a second?

W Sure, come on in and <u>have</u> <u>a</u> <u>seat</u>. What can I do for you, Edward?

M I was wondering who you're going to select for the contest.

W Why do you want to know about that?

M Because I would like to <u>participate</u> <u>in</u> the contest.

W I'm sorry, but I don't think you will be chosen.

M I think I have pretty good skills. I should <u>be</u> <u>given</u> <u>an</u> <u>opportunity</u>.

W I understand, but I'll choose the most competitive applicant.

해석

남 잠시 얘기 좀 나눌 수 있을까요?

여 물론이지, 들어와서 앉아라. 무엇을 도와줄까, Edward?

남 저는 이번 대회를 위해 누구를 고를 것인지 알고 싶습니다.

여 왜 그것에 대해 알고 싶은데?

남 저도 대회에 참가하기를 원해서요.

여 미안하지만 너는 뽑힐 것 같지 않아.

남 저는 그것을 꽤 잘하는 것 같아요. 저에게 기회를 줘야 해요.

여 이해는 하지만 나는 가장 경쟁력이 있는 지원자를 선택할 거야.

해설

남자는 대회에 참여할 기회를 달라고 부탁하고 있다.

어휘

wonder[wʌ́ndər] 궁금해하다, 의아해하다 / select[silékt] 선택하다 / participate in ~에 참여하다 / opportunity[ὰpərtjúːnəti] 기회 / competitive[kəmpétətiv] 경쟁력이 있는 / applicant[ǽplikənt] 지원자

05 ⑤

Script

W What are you doing tomorrow afternoon?

M I have to take care of my brother since my parents are <u>going</u> <u>shopping</u>. Why? Do you have any plans?

W I was thinking of asking you to the movies, but you <u>have</u> <u>things</u> <u>to</u> <u>do</u>...

M Yeah, <u>maybe</u> <u>next</u> <u>time</u>.

W OK. But you'll still go rollerblading with me tomorrow morning, right?

M Yes.

해석

여 너 내일 오후에 뭘 할 거야?

남 부모님이 쇼핑을 가셔서 동생을 돌봐야 해. 왜? 무슨 계획이라도 있어?

여 너에게 영화 보러 가자고 하려고 했었는데 너는 할 일이 있으니까……

남 응. 아마도 다음에.

여 알았어. 그래도 내일 아침에 나랑 롤러블레이드 타러 갈 거지, 맞지?

남 응.

해설

여자는 내일 아침에 롤러블레이드를 타러 갈 것이다.

어휘

take care of ~을 돌보다 / rollerblade[róulərbèid] 롤러블레이드를 타다

06 ⑤

Script

① **W** How was the exhibition?
  M There weren't <u>many</u> <u>things</u> <u>to</u> <u>see</u>.
② **W** <u>What</u> <u>time</u> <u>shall</u> <u>we</u> <u>make</u> <u>it</u>?
  M How about 7:30?
③ **W** What is Seoul like?
  M It's so crowded, and traffic is terrible.
④ **W** Where did you get that bike?
  M It's my birthday present from my dad.
⑤ **W** <u>Can</u> <u>you</u> <u>show</u> <u>me</u> your ID, please?
  M I'm sorry, but I sold it yesterday.

해석

① 여 전시회는 어땠습니까?
  남 볼만한 것이 별로 없었어요.
② 여 몇 시로 정할까요?
  남 7시 반은 어때요?
③ 여 서울은 어떤 곳인가요?
  남 사람도 많고, 교통은 끔찍합니다.
④ 여 너 그 자전거 어디서 났어?
  남 우리 아빠가 준 생일 선물이야.
⑤ 여 신분증 좀 보여 주시겠어요?
  남 미안하지만, 어제 팔았습니다.

해설

⑤ 신분증을 보여 달라는 말에 어제 팔았다는 대답은 적절하지 않다.

어휘

exhibition[èksəbíʃən] 전시회 / make it 만나기로 하다 /
crowded[kráudid] 붐비는

07 ②

Script

W ① Playing computer games is the students' <u>least</u>
    <u>favorite</u> <u>activity</u>.
② Students like watching TV more than reading <u>in</u>
    <u>their</u> <u>free</u> time.
③ Few students like spending time with their friends.
④ Students like exercising more than reading.
⑤ <u>More</u> <u>than</u> <u>half</u> <u>of</u> the students like exercising.

해석

여 ① 컴퓨터 게임을 하는 것이 학생들이 가장 덜 좋아하는 활동이다.
  ② 학생들은 여가에 독서를 하는 것보다 텔레비전 보는 것을 더 좋
    아한다.
  ③ 친구들과 시간을 보내는 것을 좋아하는 학생들이 거의 없다.
  ④ 학생들은 독서보다 운동을 더 좋아한다.
  ⑤ 학생들 반 이상이 운동하는 것을 좋아한다.

해설

학생들은 독서보다 텔레비전 보는 것을 좋아한다.

어휘

least[liːst] 가장 적은, 최소한의 / favorite[féivərit] 아주 좋아하는 /
free time 여가, 한가한 시간

08 ①

Script

M I know you want to go <u>by</u> <u>car</u> when you go to your
  hometown this New Year's Day. However, I think taking
  a train is faster, especially on days like New Year's, and
  more convenient than taking a car. It's <u>far</u> <u>safer</u> <u>as</u> <u>well</u>.
  If you go by train, you won't have to worry about traffic
  jams. And you won't have to worry about parking when
  you arrive there. Nowadays, it's really difficult to find a
  parking space even <u>in</u> <u>a</u> <u>small</u> <u>city</u>. Moreover, you can
  save money since you don't have to spend money on
  fuel and toll fees.

해석

남 나는 당신이 이번 새해 첫날 고향에 갈 때 자동차로 가고 싶어한다는
  것을 알고 있습니다. 하지만, 나는 특히 새해 같은 날에는 기차를 타고
  가는 것이 차를 타고 가는 것보다 더 빠르고 편리하다고 생각합니다.
  훨씬 안전하기도 합니다. 당신이 기차를 타고 간다면 교통체증을 걱정
  할 필요가 없습니다. 그리고 그곳에 도착했을 때 주차를 걱정할 필요가
  없습니다. 요즈음은 작은 도시에서조차도 주차공간을 찾기가 정말 어
  렵습니다. 더욱이 당신은 연료비나 통행료를 쓸 필요가 없어서 돈을 절
  약할 수 있습니다.

해설

자동차 이용의 단점과 기차 이용의 장점을 제시하여 기차 이용을 권유하고
있다.

어휘

hometown[hóumtàun] 고향 / convenient[kənvíːnjənt] 편리한 /
as well 또한, 역시 / traffic jam 교통체증 / parking space 주차 공간 /
moreover[mɔːróuvər] 더욱이, 게다가 / fuel[fjúːəl] 연료, 가스 /
toll fee 통행료

09 ③

Script

W Excuse me, <u>can</u> <u>you</u> <u>tell</u> <u>me</u> how to get to Hyde Park?
M Sure. You should take the subway.
W I see. Which line should I take?
M Take the yellow line and <u>transfer</u> <u>to</u> the green line at
  City Hall.
W I got it. How long does it take?
M It takes a little <u>less</u> <u>than</u> <u>half</u> <u>an</u> <u>hour</u> to City Hall, and
  about 15 minutes to the park.
W Do you happen to know the fare?
M Yes. It's 1 dollar 50 cents. You'll just need a dollar if
  you are a student.
W No, I'm not. Thanks.

해석

여 실례합니다. 하이드 공원에 어떻게 가는지 알려 주시겠어요?
남 네. 전철을 타야 합니다.

여	그렇군요. 어떤 선을 타야 하나요?
남	노란색 선을 타시고 시청에서 녹색 선으로 갈아타세요.
여	알았습니다. 얼마나 걸리죠?
남	시청까지는 30분 약간 덜 거리고, 시청에서 공원까지 15분 정도 걸려요.
여	혹시 요금을 아시나요?
남	네. 1달러 50센트입니다. 학생이면 1달러만 있으면 됩니다.
여	아니에요. 감사합니다.

해설
시청까지 약 30분, 시청에서 공원까지 약 15분이 걸리므로 총 약 45분 정도 걸리고 남자는 학생이 아니므로 요금은 1달러 50센트이다.

어휘
transfer[trænsfə́ːr] 갈아타다 / happen[hǽpən] 우연히 발생하다 / fare[fɛər] 요금

10 ⑤
Script
M	Erica invited us over for dinner tomorrow.
W	We were planning to go to the movies at 7:30, right?
M	You're right. I forgot.
W	Why don't we have lunch with her?
M	Well, she said she has an important meeting at 1. What should we do?
W	How about going to the next movie after dinner?
M	What time does the next movie begin?
W	It begins two hours later.
M	Okay.

해석
남	Erica가 우리를 내일 저녁 식사에 초대했어.
여	우리 내일 7시 30분에 영화 보기로 했지, 그렇지?
남	맞다. 깜빡했어.
여	점심을 같이하는 건 어때?
남	글쎄, 그녀가 1시에 중요한 회의가 있어. 어떻게 하지?
여	저녁식사 후에 그다음 영화를 보는 게 어때?
남	다음 영화가 몇 시에 시작하는데?
여	두 시간 후에.
남	알았어.

해설
원래 영화를 보기로 한 시간은 7시 30분이었는데 두 시간 후에 시작하는 다음 영화를 보기로 계획을 변경했으므로 영화를 볼 시간은 9시 30분이다.

11 ①
Script
[Telephone rings.]
M	Hello?
W	Hi, Jake! Are you having fun with Linda? What are you doing now?
M	We're playing a board game.

W	Sounds fun. What time are you going to visit grandma?
M	As soon as I finish playing.
W	She misses you a lot, so make sure you drop by today.
M	Don't worry. I miss her, too.
W	Tell Grandma I'll be there on Sunday.
M	Okay.

해석
남	여보세요?
여	안녕, Jake! Linda와 좋은 시간 보내고 있니? 지금 뭐 하고 있니?
남	보드게임하고 있어요.
여	재미있겠구나. 몇 시에 할머니를 뵈러 갈 거니?
남	게임이 끝나자마자요.
여	할머니가 너를 많이 보고 싶어하시니 오늘 꼭 가라.
남	걱정하지 마세요. 저도 할머니가 보고 싶어요.
여	할머니에게 내가 일요일에 간다고 말씀드려라.
남	알겠어요.

해설
어머니와 아들 사이에서 할 수 있는 대화이다.

어휘
as soon as ~하자마자 / make sure 확실히 ~하다 / drop by ~에 들르다

12 ④
Script
W	Could I have a word with you?
M	Yes, sure.
W	Well, it's about the idea you suggested.
M	Yes, what about it?
W	Thank you for your ideas, but they are a little out of date. I saw the same thing on other internet sites.
M	Oh, right. Okay.
W	I know you did your best, but next time you should be more creative, OK?
M	Okay. Thank you.

해석
여	잠시 이야기를 좀 할 수 있을까?
남	네, 물론이죠.
여	음, 네가 제안한 아이디어에 관한 것인데.
남	네, 그게 뭐 어때서요?
여	의견은 고마운데, 약간 구식이야. 똑같은 것을 다른 인터넷 사이트에서 봤어.
남	아, 그렇구나. 알았어요.
여	나는 네가 최선을 다 한 줄 알지만, 다음에는 좀 더 창의적이었으면 해, 알았지?
남	알았어요. 고마워요.

해설
여자는 남자에게 좀 더 창의적이었으면 좋겠다고 조언하고 있다.

어휘

have a word ~와 잠깐 이야기를 하다 / suggest[səgdʒést] 제안하다 /
out of date 구식인 / do one's best 최선을 다하다 / creative[kriːéitiv]
창의적인

13 ③
Script

M David had a tour in Germany after leaving Italy. He wanted to see historic sites in Germany. It's not good to drive around or ride a bike in Germany. He took the bus to explore the sites, and he joined a tour group. He met many tourists from other countries. When he visited the Berlin Wall, he bought some souvenirs.

해석
남 David는 이탈리아를 떠나고 나서 독일을 여행했다. 그는 독일에서 유적지를 보기를 원했다. 독일에서 운전하거나 자전거를 타는 것은 좋지 않다. 그는 유적지들을 돌아보려고 버스를 탔다. 그리고 단체 관광에 합류했다. 그는 다른 나라에서 온 많은 관광객을 만났다. 그는 베를린 장벽을 방문했을 때 기념품을 샀다.

해설
David는 베를린 장벽을 방문했으므로 베를린 장벽을 보았을 것이다.

어휘
historic site 유적지 / explore[iksplɔ́ːr] 탐험하다 / souvenir[sùːvəníər] 기념품

14 ③
Script

① **W** John, wake up. It's time to go to school.
  M 5 more minutes, please.
② **W** Open your eyes to the new world.
  M Thank you for your advice.
③ **W** William, this is not a place for a nap.
  M Sorry. I stayed up last night.
④ **W** Get up and go to your class.
  M Okay. I will go right now.
⑤ **W** Is this your classmate?
  M Yes, he is very kind and smart.

해석
① 여 John, 일어나. 학교에 갈 시간이야.
  남 5분만 더요.
② 여 새로운 세계를 좀 봐.
  남 조언 고마워.
③ 여 William, 여기는 낮잠을 자는 장소가 아니야.
  남 죄송해요. 지난밤에 늦게 자서요.
④ 여 일어나서 너의 반으로 가라.
  남 알았어요. 지금 바로 갈게요.
⑤ 여 이 애가 너의 반 친구이니?
  남 응, 그는 아주 친절하고 똑똑해.

해설
수업시간에 졸고 있는 학생을 선생님이 깨우는 상황이다.

15 ②
Script

M Good morning, ma'am. May I help you?
W Good morning, I want to buy some US dollars.
M How much do you need?
W 200 dollars.
M Sure. Please fill out this form, and I need your passport.
W OK. Here it is.
M Thank you. How would you like them?
W Ten twenties.
M OK. Here you go.
W Thank you.

해석
남 안녕하세요, 부인. 도와드릴까요?
여 안녕하세요, 미국 달러를 좀 사고 싶어요.
남 얼마가 필요하시죠?
여 200달러요.
남 네. 이 서류를 작성해 주세요. 그리고 여권을 주세요.
여 알았습니다. 여기 있습니다.
남 감사합니다. 어떻게 드릴까요?
여 20달러짜리 열 개요.
남 알았습니다. 여기 있어요.
여 감사합니다.

해설
은행에서 환전할 때 할 수 있는 대화이다.

어휘
fill out ~을 기재하다 / passport[pǽspɔ̀ːrt] 여권

16 ①
Script

M I finally got the tickets for Beyonce's concert!
W No way! They are so expensive!
M Well, it's my birthday tomorrow, so my dad gave me some money for the tickets!
W That's fantastic!
M Let's go downtown early in the afternoon and have dinner before the concert.
W That's terrific.

해석
남 나 드디어 Beyonce 콘서트 표를 샀어.
여 말도 안돼! 그 표는 정말 비싸잖아.
남 있잖아, 내일이 내 생일이라서 우리 아빠가 표를 사라고 돈을 좀 주셨어!
여 훌륭한데!

남 오후에 일찍 시내로 가서 콘서트 전에 저녁을 먹자.

여 좋았어.

해설

두 사람은 콘서트에 가게 되어 신이 났을 것이다.

어휘

downtown[dàuntáun] 시내 / terrific[tərífik] 훌륭한

17 ④

Script

M Did you bring your report card?

W Yes, I did. I've got my mother's signature.

M Okay. What did she say?

W She said I should study harder.

M I see. Do you know what your problem is?

W Yes, I do. Lack of concentration.

M Now that you know that, you need to fix it. Okay? Go back to your seat.

W Thank you.

해석

남 성적표를 가져왔니?

여 네. 어머니의 서명을 받아 왔어요.

남 알았어. 뭐라고 하셨니?

여 더 열심히 공부하라고 말씀하셨어요.

남 그렇구나. 너의 문제가 무엇인지 아니?

여 알아요. 집중력 부족이죠.

남 너도 이제 알았으니 고치도록 하렴. 알았지? 자리로 돌아가라.

여 감사합니다.

해설

여자의 문제점은 집중력 부족이다.

어휘

bring[briŋ] ~을 가져오다 / report card 성적표 / signature[sígnətʃər] 서명 / lack[læk] 부족, 결핍 / concentration[kànsəntréiʃən] 집중 / fix[fiks] ~을 고치다

18 ①

Script

W What is the hardest part of studying English?

M It's memorizing words. There are too many words to memorize.

W I see. Let me give you a piece of advice. If there is little snow, it melts quickly, but if there is a lot of snow, it doesn't melt easily. Likewise, if you keep memorizing words, they will pile up in your brain.

M I see.

W Just do it little by little every day, and you'll end up with thousands of words memorized in your head.

M OK. I'll do that from now on.

해석

여 영어를 공부하는 데 가장 어려운 점이 무엇이니?

남 단어를 외우는 것이에요. 외울 단어가 너무 많아요.

여 그렇구나. 내가 조언을 하나 해 줄게. 눈이 약간 있다면, 빠르게 녹겠지. 하지만 눈이 많이 있다면 쉽게 녹지 않겠지. 그것처럼 네가 단어를 계속 외운다면, 단어가 네 머릿속에 쌓이게 될 거야.

남 그렇군요.

여 매일 조금씩 해. 그러면 머릿속에 수천 개의 단어를 암기할 수 있게 될 거야.

남 알겠어요. 지금부터 그렇게 할게요.

해설

단어를 조금씩 계속 외우면 나중에는 머릿속에 단어가 많이 쌓일 거라는 내용이므로 작은 것이 모여 큰 것이 된다는 의미의 티끌 모아 태산이 가장 적절하다.

어휘

memorize[méməràiz] ~을 암기하다 / melt[melt] 녹다 / likewise[láikwàiz] 같이, 마찬가지로 / pile up ~을 쌓다 / little by little 조금씩 / end up 결국 ~이 되다 / thousands of 수천의 / from now on 지금부터

19 ③

Script

M Hey, Mary. Have you seen Kate?

W Yes. I saw her at the library.

M Was she with Mark?

W No. I didn't see Mark there. Why are you looking for them?

M We're doing a school project together, and we were supposed to meet this morning, but I forgot. I just called them, but none of them answered my phone.

W Maybe they didn't notice their phone ringing.

M Yeah, maybe you are right.

W You'd better go and look for them.

해석

남 안녕, Mary. 너 Kate를 봤니?

여 응. 도서관에서 봤어.

남 그녀가 Mark하고 같이 있었니?

여 아니. 거기서 Mark는 못 봤어. 그 애들은 왜 찾고 있는데?

남 우리는 학교 프로젝트를 같이하고 있거든. 오늘 아침에 만나기로 했었는데 내가 깜빡했어. 막 전화를 했는데 아무도 내 전화를 받지 않아.

여 아마 전화가 울리는지 모르고 있었겠지.

남 응. 네 말이 맞는 거 같아.

여 네가 가서 그들은 찾아보는 게 좋겠다.

해설

전화를 진동으로 해 놓아서 못 들었을 것 같다는 말에 동의했으므로 "네가 가서 그들을 찾아보는 게 좋겠다."라는 응답이 가장 적절하다.

① 그들은 너에게 화가 났어.

② 그들은 새 전화를 사야 해.

④ 도서관은 공부하기 좋은 장소야.

⑤ 도서관에서는 전화기를 사용하지 마.

be supposed to ~하기로 되어 있다, ~할 예정이다 / notice[nóutis]
~을 알아채다 / had better ~하는 게 좋겠다

20 ⑤

Script

W Mike, I'm so tired. I couldn't sleep at all last night.

M Why?

W I saw a ghost. It was terrible.

M Really? I can't believe it.

W It's true. I left my room to use the bathroom. There was a woman outside the window in the living room.

M What did she do? Did she follow you?

W No. As soon as I saw her, I shouted and rushed into my parents' room.

M Well, forget it. It'll never happen again.

W I won't be able to sleep alone tonight.

해석

여 Mike, 나 너무 피곤해. 지난밤에 잠을 하나도 못 잤어.

남 왜?

여 유령을 봤거든. 너무 끔찍했어.

남 정말? 믿을 수가 없는 걸.

여 사실이야. 화장실에 가려고 내 방을 나갔는데, 거실에 있는 유리창 밖에 어떤 여자가 있었어.

남 그녀가 뭘 했는데? 그녀가 널 따라왔어?

여 아니. 나는 그녀를 보자마자, 비명을 지르면서 부모님 방으로 뛰어갔어.

남 음, 잊어버려. 다시는 그런 일 없을 거야.

여 오늘 밤에는 혼자서 잠을 잘 수 없을 거야.

해설

다시는 귀신을 보는 일이 없을 거라는 위로에 "오늘 밤에는 혼자서 잠을 잘 수 없을 거야."라는 응답이 가장 적절하다.

① 그녀를 찾는 걸 도와줄래?

② 귀신 같은 건 없어.

③ 그녀가 분명히 너 때문에 놀랐겠구나.

④ 괜찮아. 그녀는 우리 어머니야.

어휘

ghost[goust] 귀신, 유령 / bathroom[bǽθrù(:)m] 욕실 / follow[fálou] 따라오다 / as soon as ~하자마자 / rush into 빠르게[급하게] 가다

---

p.128~131

16회 영어듣기모의고사

01 ③	02 ①	03 ③	04 ①	05 ③
06 ④	07 ④	08 ②	09 ④	10 ②
11 ④	12 ③	13 ④	14 ①	15 ⑤
16 ②	17 ⑤	18 ③	19 ④	20 ⑤

---

01 ③

Script

① M I came to pick up my wallet.
    W What does it look like, and what's inside?

② M Who is the lady in this picture?
    W She is my grandmother when she was young.

③ M Could you take a picture for us?
    W Sure. Where would you like to stand?

④ M I'd like to change my reservation.
    W May I have your name?

⑤ M Where are the books on driving?
    W They're on the third aisle on your right.

해석

① 남 제 지갑을 가지러 왔습니다.
    여 어떻게 생겼고, 안에는 무엇이 들었나요?

② 남 사진에 있는 이 여자 분은 누구시죠?
    여 그녀는 젊었을 때의 우리 할머니예요.

③ 남 저희를 위해서 사진을 좀 찍어 주시겠어요?
    여 물론이죠. 어디에 서고 싶으세요?

④ 남 저는 예약을 변경하고 싶습니다.
    여 성함이 어떻게 되시죠?

⑤ 남 운전에 관한 책은 어디에 있습니까?
    여 당신의 오른쪽 세 번째 칸에 있습니다.

해설

남자가 여자에게 사진을 찍어 달라고 부탁하는 상황이다.

어휘

pick up 되찾다, 집다 / wallet[wálit] 지갑 / look like ~처럼 생기다 / stand[stænd] 서다 / reservation[rèzərvéiʃən] 예약 / aisle[ail] 복도, 통로

---

02 ①

Script

W Here is our five-day forecast. Tomorrow should be sunny and slightly warmer with temperatures around twenty. On Thursday and Friday, things will cool down again, with temperatures in the low teens. Unfortunately the weekend will be rainy, but hopefully a little warmer with temperatures back up to twenty. Now you will be watching our headline news in a second. Thank you.

해석

여 5일 일기 예보입니다. 내일은 화창하고 약 20도로 조금 따뜻하겠습니다. 목요일과 금요일은 10도 초반으로 기온이 다시 차가워질 것입니다. 안타깝게도 주말에 비가 내리겠지만, 다행스럽게도 기온이 20도까지 오르면서 약간 따뜻해질 것으로 예상됩니다. 이제 곧 저희 주요 뉴스를 시청하시겠습니다. 감사합니다.

해설

내일모레가 목요일이므로 오늘은 화요일이다.

어휘

forecast[fɔ́ːrkæst] 일기 예보 / slightly[sláitli] 약간 /

temperature[témpərətʃər] 기온, 온도 / cool down 서늘해지다 / teen[tiːn] 10을 뜻함(thirteen ~ nineteen에서) / unfortunately[ʌnfɔ́ːrtʃənitli] 불행하게도 / rainy[réini] 비가 오는 / hopefully[hóupfəli] 잘하면, 희망을 갖고 / back[bæk] 본래 자리로, 되돌아가서 / up to ~까지 / headline news 주요 뉴스

03 ③

Script

W You don't look good, George. What's wrong?

M I dropped my cell phone into the toilet, and I picked it up very quickly, but…

W Oh, dear. So, what did you do?

M I took the battery out and dried it.

W Is it okay?

M No. I tried to turn my phone on several times. It's not working. The worst thing is that I bought it yesterday.

해석

여 너 안 좋아 보인다. George. 무슨 일이야?

남 휴대 전화를 변기에 빠뜨렸어. 재빨리 줍기는 했지만……

여 저런. 그래서 어떻게 했어?

남 배터리를 빼서 말렸어.

여 괜찮아?

남 아니. 여러 번 전원을 켜봤는데, 작동하지 않아. 가장 나쁜 건 전화기를 어제 샀다는 거야.

해설

남자는 어제 산 전화기를 변기에 빠뜨려서 말렸지만, 전화기가 작동하지 않아서 좌절감을 느낄 것이다.

어휘

drop[drɑp] ~을 떨어뜨리다 / toilet[tɔ́ilit] 화장실, 변기 / turn on ~을 켜다 / several[sévərəl] 몇 번의, 서너 번의

04 ①

Script

M Can you bring me a blanket?

W Sure, anything else?

M Yes, can you bring me something to read?

W Sure, I'll bring you a weekly magazine. Is that all right?

M Thanks. It's such a long flight that I have already read a couple of books of my own.

W I'm sure you like reading. I'll be right back.

해석

남 저에게 담요를 좀 가져다주시겠어요?

여 물론이죠, 그 밖에는 다른 것은요?

남 네, 읽을 것을 좀 가져다주시겠어요?

여 물론입니다. 주간 잡지를 가져다드리죠. 괜찮으시겠어요?

남 감사합니다. 너무 긴 비행이라 제가 가져온 두 권의 책을 벌써 다 읽었거든요.

여 분명히 독서하는 것을 좋아하시는군요. 곧 돌아오겠습니다.

해설

긴 비행에 가져온 책을 다 읽어서 다른 읽을 만한 것을 가져다달라고 부탁하는 상황이므로 장소는 비행기임을 알 수 있다.

어휘

bring[briŋ] ~을 가져오다 / blanket[blǽŋkit] 담요 / weekly[wíːkli] 주간의 / magazine[mǽgəzíːn] 잡지 / right back 곧

05 ③

Script

M Have you heard about the University of Yale?

W Sure, it's one of the best universities in the world.

M It was founded in 1701 and has almost 2,000 professors now.

W That's an incredible number. What is the student population?

M There are 6,000 undergraduate students at the university, and another 6,000 in graduate courses.

W I guess there aren't many students compared to the number of professors.

해석

남 예일 대학에 대해 들어 본 적이 있니?

여 물론이지. 세계에서 가장 좋은 대학 중 하나잖아.

남 예일 대학은 1701년에 설립되었고, 지금은 교수가 거의 2천 명이야.

여 놀라운 수치구나. 학생 수는 어때?

남 대학생이 6천 명이고, 대학원생도 6천 명이야.

여 교수의 수에 비하면 학생들의 수가 많은 편은 아닌 것 같아.

해설

대학생이 6천 명, 대학원생이 6천 명으로 총 1만 2천 명이고 교수가 2천 명이므로 교수 한 명당 학생의 수는 6명이다.

어휘

found[faund] 설립하다 / incredible[inkrédəbəl] 놀라운, 믿기 어려운 / undergraduate[ʌndərgrǽdʒuit] 대학생의 / graduate course 대학원 과정 / compared to ~과 비교하여

06 ④

Script

M How did you know about the job openings in the sales department at Wise Department Store?

W I read an advertisement in the paper.

M How many employees are they hiring?

W It says that they are hiring about 20 people.

M Does one have to speak any foreign languages?

W Yes, it says applicants need to speak either Japanese or English.

M How about job experience? Do we need any?

W It says a minimum of two years.

해석

남	Wise 백화점에서 판매직에 일자리가 생겼다는 건 어떻게 알았니?
여	신문에서 광고를 봤어.
남	직원은 몇 명이나 뽑아?
여	약 스무 명을 뽑는대.
남	외국어를 해야만 하니?
여	응, 지원자들은 일어나 영어 중 하나를 해야 한대.
남	경력은 어때? 필요해?
여	최소한 2년이라고 쓰여 있더라.

해설
지원자는 영어와 일어를 둘 다 해야 하는 것이 아니라 영어나 일어 중 하나를 할 줄 알아야 한다.

어휘
job opening 취직자리 / sales department 판매부, 영업부 / advertisement[æ̀dvərtáizmənt] 광고 / employee[emplɔ́iiː] 고용인 / hire[háiər] ~을 고용하다 / foreign language 외국어 / applicant[ǽplikənt] 지원자 / either A or B A, B 중 둘 중 하나 / job experience 경력

07 ④

Script

M What did you think about the boy you met last night?

W He was very friendly, but talked too much.

M Oh, I thought the same way.

W He kept talking and talking. I felt like he was a lecturer.

M I know. He was the only one that asked many questions about the environment.

W Anyway, the lecture was good.

M That's right. I learned a lot about our environment.

해설

남	지난밤에 만난 소년에 대해서 어떻게 생각하니?
여	그는 매우 친절했지만, 말이 너무 많았어.
남	아, 나도 그렇게 생각했어.
여	그는 계속해서 말을 했지. 나는 그가 강사인 것처럼 느껴졌어.
남	맞아. 그가 환경에 대해 많은 질문을 한 유일한 사람이었지.
여	어쨌든, 강의는 좋았어.
남	맞아. 나도 우리의 환경에 대해서 많이 배웠어.

해설
두 사람은 어제저녁에 환경 관련 강의에 참석했다.

어휘
friendly[fréndli] 친절한, 정다운 / lecturer[léktʃərər] 강사 / environment[inváiərənmənt] 환경

08 ②

Script

M I'd like to buy a bottle of whisky.

W Do you have any ID?

M I have my passport. Is that good enough?

W Sure, can I see it?

M Here it is.

W Thank you. I see you're old enough to buy alcohol. How would you like to pay?

M By credit card.

해설

남	위스키 한 병을 사고 싶어요.
여	신분증 있으세요?
남	여권이 있어요. 그거면 충분한가요?
여	네, 보여 주시겠어요?
남	여기 있어요.
여	감사합니다. 당신은 술을 살 수 있을 만한 나이이군요. 어떻게 지불하시겠어요?
남	카드로요.

해설
가게에서 술을 파는 사람은 점원이다.

어휘
whisky[hwíski] 위스키 / ID=identification[aidèntəfikéiʃən] 신분증 / alcohol[ǽlkəhɔ̀ːl] 알코올

09 ④

Script

[Telephone rings.]

M Hello.

W Hello. May I speak to Peter?

M Sorry, but he's not here. He went to the library.

W Oh, did he? Then, when will he be back?

M I'm not sure. Would you like to leave a message?

W Yes. This is Cathy. I'm his classmate. I'm calling to tell him that our history homework is due on the 13th, Tuesday, not the 14th, Wednesday. And the pages are from 128 to 140.

M OK. I'll pass it on to him.

W Thank you.

해설

남	여보세요.
여	여보세요. Peter랑 통화할 수 있을까요?
남	미안하지만, 지금 여기 없구나. 도서관에 갔단다.
여	아, 그래요? 그러면 언제 돌아오나요?
남	잘 모르겠는데. 메시지를 남기겠니?
여	네. 저는 Cathy이고요, 같은 반 친구예요. 역사 숙제가 마감일이 14일 수요일이 아니고 13일 화요일이라고 말해주려고 전화했어요. 페이지는 128에서 140쪽까지예요.
남	알았다. 그렇게 전해 주마.
여	감사합니다.

해설
역사 숙제의 마감일은 14일 수요일이 아니라 13일 화요일이다.

어휘
leave a message 메시지를 남기다 / classmate[klǽsmèit] 급우 /

due[dʲuː] ~하기로 되어 있는 / pass A on to B B에게 A를 전하다

10 ②
Script

W World Airlines. How may I help you?

M I'd like to make a reservation. Are there any flights to New York on October 25th?

W There is a flight at 10 in the morning. Is that all right?

M Yes. I'd like to reserve that flight.

W May I have your name and phone number, please?

M My name is Jake Smith, and my phone number is 786-6131.

W OK. You're booked on Flight 201 leaving San Francisco International Airport on the 25th. And you should arrive at the airport one and a half hours prior to the departure time.

M I see. Thank you.

해석

여 월드 항공사입니다. 무엇을 도와드릴까요?

남 예약을 하고 싶습니다. 10월 25일에 뉴욕으로 가는 비행편이 있습니까?

여 아침 10시에 있습니다. 괜찮으시겠어요?

남 네. 그 비행편을 예약하고 싶습니다.

여 성함과 전화번호를 주시겠어요?

남 제 이름은 Jake Smith이고, 전화번호는 786–6131입니다.

여 알았습니다. 25일 샌프란시스코 국제공항에서 출발하는 201호 편에 예약이 되었습니다. 그리고 비행기 출발 한 시간 반 전에 공항에 도착하셔야 합니다.

남 알았습니다. 감사합니다.

해설

남자는 비행기 출발 한 시간 반 전에 도착해야 하므로 8시 30분까지 도착해야 한다.

어휘

make a reservation 예약하다 / flight[flait] 비행편, 비행 / reserve[rizə́ːrv] ~을 예약하다 / booked[bukt] 예약된 / prior to ~전에 / departure[dipáːrtʃər] 출발

11 ④
Script

W What are you reading?

M An article on elementary school.

W What is it about?

M It says boys make up 70 percent of all elementary school students.

W I see. I also heard that there are too many boys, so some boys don't have an opportunity to sit next to a girl.

M You got that right.

W But I think it can't be helped.

M I know.

해석

여 너 무엇을 읽고 있니?

남 초등학교에 관련된 기사.

여 무슨 내용인데?

남 초등학생의 70퍼센트가 남자아이래.

여 무슨 말인지 알겠다. 나도 남자아이들이 너무 많아서, 어떤 남자아이들은 여자 짝꿍 옆에 앉을 기회를 얻지 못한다고 들었어.

남 맞아.

여 하지만 어쩔 수 없잖아.

남 알아.

해설

문제점은 초등학교에 남학생이 여학생보다 훨씬 많다는 것이다.

어휘

article[áːrtikl] 기사 / make up ~로 구성되다, 이루어지다 / opportunity[àpərtʲúːnəti] 기회

12 ③
Script

W How much is this TV?

M It's 2,000 dollars, but it's on sale for 10 percent off.

W Can you give me a bigger discount?

M How much are you asking for?

W How about a 20 percent discount?

M That much? Sorry, but I can't. All I can give you is 10 percent.

해석

여 이 텔레비전은 얼마입니까?

남 2천 달러인데, 10% 할인 중입니다.

여 좀 더 할인해 주시면 안 되요?

남 얼마를 원하시는데요?

여 20% 할인해 주세요.

남 그렇게나 많이요? 미안하지만 그럴 수 없습니다. 제가 해 드릴 수 있는 건 10%예요.

해설

텔레비전의 원래 가격은 2천 달러이고 10%를 할인해 준다고 했으므로 여자가 지불할 금액은 1,800달러이다.

어휘

on sale 할인 판매 중인 / ask for ~을 달라고 요구하다, 청하다

13 ④
Script

[Telephone rings.]

W Hello, this is Cathy from Top Travel. May I speak to Mr. Smith, please?

M Speaking.

W I have a new schedule for your trip to Rome. You leave Seoul this coming Friday instead of Thursday at 10 A.M. and you arrive in Rome the next day at noon.

M I see. I'll stop by your office to pick up my flight ticket this afternoon.

W That's fine with me.

해석

여 여보세요, 저는 탑 여행사의 Cathy입니다. Smith 씨와 이야기할 수 있을까요?

남 접니다.

여 로마행 여행의 새 일정이 나왔어요. 목요일 대신에 이번 금요일 오전 10시에 서울을 떠나 로마에 그 다음 날 정오에 도착하실 거예요.

남 그렇군요. 오늘 오후에 비행기 표를 가지러 사무실에 들르겠습니다.

여 그렇게 하세요.

해설

여행은 변경된 여행 일정을 알려 주려고 전화했다.

어휘

instead of ∼ 대신에 / stop by ∼에 들르다

14 ①

Script

M Richard moved out last weekend. I was there with Robert to help him.

W Were you?

M Yes, he's now living in a very nice quiet neighborhood with a great view.

W Do you know why he moved to the new apartment?

M He couldn't sleep at night because of the noises coming from upstairs.

W Really? I didn't know about that.

해석

남 Richard가 지난 주말에 이사했어. 나는 그를 도우려고 Robert와 함께 거기에 있었어.

여 그랬어?

남 응, 그는 이제 전망 좋은 방에, 매우 조용하고 좋은 동네에서 살고 있어.

여 그가 왜 새 아파트로 이사했는지 아니?

남 그는 위층 소음 때문에 밤에 잠을 못 잤어.

여 정말? 몰랐어.

해설

Richard는 위층의 소음 때문에 시끄러워서 이사했다.

어휘

move out 이사하다 / quiet[kwáiət] 조용한 / neighborhood[néibərhùd] 이웃, 주민 / view[vju:] 전망 / upstairs[ʌ̀pstέərz] 위층에

15 ⑤

Script

M Now wonderful Neverland finally opens on the first of March. We have everything for the whole family. This exciting tourist spot provides an Animal Park where children can touch and feed farm animals. We also have world-class shopping malls, white sand beaches,

and restaurants serving exotic international dishes. We will make your time worthwhile.

해석

남 이제 환상의 네버랜드가 3월 1일 마침내 개장을 합니다. 우리는 온 가족을 위한 모든 것을 가지고 있습니다. 이 흥미진진한 관광 명소는 아이들이 가축을 만져 보고 먹이를 줄 수 있는 동물원을 제공합니다. 우리는 또한 세계적인 수준의 쇼핑몰과 백사장, 이국적인 요리를 맛볼 수 있는 식당도 갖추고 있습니다. 우리는 당신의 시간을 가치있게 만들어 드릴 것입니다.

해설

Neverland에는 동물원, 쇼핑몰, 이국적인 풍의 식당, 해변이 있다.

어휘

tourist spot 관광명소 / provide[prəváid] ∼을 공급하다 / feed[fi:d] ∼에게 먹이를 주다 / world-class 세계적인 수준의 / exotic[igzátik] 이국적인 / international[ìntərnǽʃənəl] 국제적인 / dish[diʃ] 요리; 접시 / worthwhile[wə́:rθhwàil] ∼할 보람이 있는, 훌륭한

16 ②

Script

W I'm too cold. Please tell the driver to turn off the air conditioner.

M I don't think he will listen to me.

W Why not?

M See, there are more than 30 passengers on this bus, but you are probably the only one that feels cold.

W How do you know that?

M As you can see, no one has complained yet.

W Then what should I do?

M How about putting on my jacket?

해석

여 너무 춥다. 운전사에게 에어컨을 좀 꺼 달라고 말해 줘.

남 내 말을 들을 것 같지 않은데.

여 왜 안 들어?

남 있잖아. 이 버스에는 30명 이상의 승객이 있는데, 너만 춥다고 느끼는 것 같아.

여 네가 어떻게 아니?

남 너도 보다시피, 아직 아무도 불평하는 사람이 없잖아.

여 그러면 어떻게 해야 하지?

남 내 재킷을 입는 게 어때?

해설

남자는 춥다는 여자에게 자신의 재킷을 입으라고 제안하고 있다.

어휘

turn off ∼을 끄다 / air conditioner 에어컨, 냉방기 / passenger[pǽsəndʒər] 승객 / complain[kəmpléin] 불평하다 / put on ∼을 입다

17 ⑤

Script

① **W** Do you know what she does for a living?

M   I think she is a firefighter.

② **W**   Do you think you can finish it today?

    M   To be honest, I don't think so.

③ **W**   What brought you here?

    M   I'm here to meet Mr. Kim.

④ **W**   Can you buy me a snack?

    M   Sorry, I left my wallet in the car.

⑤ **W**   What makes you really happy?

    M   I was scolded for failing the test.

해석

① 여   너는 그녀의 직업이 무엇인지 아니?

   남   그녀는 소방관인 것 같아.

② 여   네 생각에 오늘 그것을 끝낼 수 있을 것 같아?

   남   솔직히 말해서, 그럴 수 없을 것 같아.

③ 여   여기에 무슨 일로 왔니?

   남   Kim 선생님을 만나러 왔어.

④ 여   나에게 간식을 좀 사 줄래?

   남   미안해, 지갑을 차에 두고 왔어.

⑤ 여   너를 정말 행복하게 해 주는 것이 무엇이니?

   남   나는 시험에 떨어져서 꾸지람을 들었어.

해설

⑤ 행복하게 해주는 것이 무엇이냐고 물었는데 시험에서 떨어져서 혼났다는 대화는 어울리지 않는다.

어휘

for a living 생계를 위해 / firefighter[fáiərfàitər] 소방관 / to be honest 솔직하게 / wallet[wάlit] 지갑 /scold[skould] 꾸짖다 / fail the test 시험에 떨어지다

18   ③

Script

M   When I was young, my father always woke me up around 6 o'clock in the morning. He never skipped a day until he passed away. He died of cancer when I was 16 years old. After that, I thought I could sleep longer, but I got used to getting up early in the morning. It was really helpful when I joined the army.

해석

남   내가 어렸을 때 우리 아버지는 매일 아침 여섯 시쯤에 나를 깨웠다. 아버지는 돌아가실 때까지 단 하루도 건너뛰지 않았다. 우리 아버지는 내가 열여섯 살 때 암으로 돌아가셨다. 그 후에, 나는 더 오래 잘 수 있을 거라고 생각했지만, 아침에 일찍 일어나는 것에 익숙해져 있었다. 그것은 내가 육군에 입대했을 때 정말로 도움이 되었다.

해설

16년 동안 아침 일찍 일어난 것이 아니라 화자가 열여섯 살에 아버지가 돌아가셨다.

어휘

wake up ~을 깨우다 / skip[skip] ~을 건너뛰다 / pass away 죽다, 돌아가시다 / die of ~로 죽다 / cancer[kǽnsər] 암 / get used to+-ing ~하는 데 익숙해지다 / join the army 육군에 입대하다

19   ④

Script

M   Hi, Susie! What a surprise! It's great to see you.

W   Hi, Mark! How are you?

M   Pretty good. I thought you went to Paris with Jenny and Susan.

W   Well, Jenny and Susan did go to Paris on a trip, but not me.

M   Why didn't you go with them?

W   My father didn't allow me.

해석

남   안녕, Susie! 뜻밖이다! 만나서 반가워.

여   안녕, Mark! 어떻게 지내?

남   꽤 잘 지내. 나는 네가 Jenny하고 Susan과 파리에 간 줄 알았어.

여   음, Jenny하고 Susan은 진짜 파리로 여행을 갔지만, 난 아니야.

남   왜 그들과 같이 가지 않았어?

여   우리 아버지가 허락하지 않으셨어.

해설

너는 왜 함께 여행을 가지 않았느냐는 말에 "우리 아버지가 허락하지 않으셨어."라는 응답이 가장 적절하다.

① 그거 정말 좋을 것 같은데!

② 나는 지금 그들과 함께 있어.

③ 저는 괜찮아요.

⑤ 그들이 파리로 날 초대할 거야.

20   ⑤

Script

W   Do you know the guy who played table tennis with us?

M   Yes, he is my classmate.

W   Is he a new student?

M   Yes, he came from New York. I think his father is a lawyer, and his mother is a doctor.

W   I see.

M   Do you want me to introduce him to you?

W   Yes. I would like to make friends with him.

해석

여   너 우리와 탁구 쳤던 아이를 아니?

남   응, 우리반 친구야.

여   새로 온 학생이야?

남   응, 뉴욕에서 왔어. 아버지가 변호사고, 엄마가 의사라는 것 같아.

여   그렇구나.

남   내가 그를 너에게 소개해 줄까?

여   응. 그와 친구가 되고 싶어.

해설

그를 소개시켜 주느냐고 물었으므로 "응. 그와 친구가 되고 싶어."라는 응답이 가장 적절하다.

① 그는 공부를 스스로 열심히 해.

② 그는 정말 다정하고 활발해.

③ 아니. 나는 그를 잘 몰라.

④ 응. 그는 탁구를 잘 쳐.

어휘

table tennis 탁구 / lawyer[lɔ́ːjər] 변호사 / introduce[ìntrədjúːs] ~을 소개하다 / make friends with A A와 친구가 되다

1회 실전모의고사

p.136~139

01 ①	02 ⑤	03 ⑤	04 ②	05 ⑤
06 ③	07 ⑤	08 ②	09 ③	10 ④
11 ③	12 ④	13 ④	14 ②	15 ②
16 ③	17 ①	18 ②	19 ①	20 ⑤

01 ①

Script

W Isn't that Jane March at the bus stop?

M I think so. She looks so different today. Did she change her hairstyle? Last time when we met her, she was blond.

W Right! I think she's dyed her hair black. And she used to wear jeans, didn't she?

M Yes, but now she is wearing a skirt.

W I'm sure she has a boyfriend.

M I guess so.

해석

여 저기 버스 정류장에 있는 사람이 Jane March 아니니?

남 그런 것 같아. 오늘은 굉장히 달라 보이는데. 머리 스타일을 바꿨니? 지난번에 우리가 그녀를 만났을 때는 금발이었잖아.

여 맞아! 내 생각에 검은색으로 염색을 한 것 같아. 그리고 청바지를 주로 입었잖아, 그렇지 않니?

남 응. 하지만 지금은 치마를 입고 있네.

여 남자 친구가 생긴 것이 확실해.

남 그런 것 같다.

해설

두 사람이 가리키는 사람은 검은 머리에 치마를 입은 사람이다.

어휘

bus stop 버스 정류장 / blond[blɑnd] 금발의 / dye[dai] 염색하다

02 ⑤

Script

W Excuse me, if you don't mind, can I ask you what you do for a living?

M What made you ask that?

W Your clothes are interesting. I mean you are wearing Korean traditional clothes on a normal day, so...

M I see. I read people's palms. I tell people what's going to happen to them in the future by looking at the lines on their hands.

W I see. You are like a fortune teller.

M That's right.

해석

여 실례합니다. 괜찮으시다면, 직업이 무엇인지 물어봐도 될까요?

남 무엇 때문에 그걸 물어보시는 건가요?

여 의상이 흥미로워서요. 제 말은 평일에 한복을 입고 있어서요.

남 그렇군요. 저는 사람들의 손금을 봅니다. 저는 사람들의 손금을 보고 미래에 그들에게 무슨 일이 일어날지 말해 주죠.

여 알겠어요. 점술가와 같은 것이군요.

남 맞아요.

해설

남자는 손금을 봐주는 점술가이다.

어휘

if you don't mind 괜찮다면 / for a living 생계로 / traditional[trədíʃənəl] 전통의 / normal[nɔ́rməl] 보통의, 평범한 / read someone's palm 손금을 보다 / fortune teller 점쟁이

03 ⑤

Script

W Hey, Jacob. You look completely different today.

M Thank you. My mother bought me a new jacket.

W Really? I envy you.

M Some girls kept looking at me on my way this morning.

W Is that right? I know why they did.

M Why? Do I look good in this jacket?

W Sorry to tell you, but the label is still hanging off your jacket.

M Oh, no. I forgot to take that off.

해석

여 안녕, Jacob. 너 오늘 완전히 달라 보인다.

남 고마워. 우리 어머니가 새 재킷을 사 주셨어.

여 정말? 부럽다.

남 오늘 아침에 오는 길에 어떤 여자애들이 계속 나를 바라봤어.

여 그래? 왜 그랬는지 알겠다.

남 왜? 이 재킷을 입으니 멋있어 보이니?

여 이런 말을 해서 미안하지만, 상표가 아직도 달려 있잖아.

남 이런, 안돼. 가격표 떼는 것을 깜빡했어.

해설

남자는 옷이 예쁘다고 해서 자랑스러웠다가 가격표를 떼지 않을 것을 깨닫고는 창피했을 것이다.

어휘
completely[kəmplíːtli] 완전히 / envy[énvi] ~을 부러워하다 /
hang off 매달리다, 늘어지다 / take off 떼다

04 ②

Script

W Good evening, sir. Did I do something wrong?

M Could you pull your car over, first?

W Okay.

M We just saw that you were holding your cell phone and talking. Can I see your driver's license?

W I'm sorry. I wasn't talking too long. Could you give me a break?

M We can't do that. You should know how dangerous talking on the phone is while you're driving.

W Okay. I won't do that again.

해석

여 안녕하세요, 경찰관님. 제가 뭘 잘못했나요?

남 우선 차를 먼저 갓길에 대 주시겠어요?

여 알았습니다.

남 방금 전화기를 드시고 통화를 하는 것을 보았습니다. 운전면허증 좀 보여 주시겠어요?

여 죄송합니다. 그렇게 오래 이야기하지 않았어요. 한 번만 봐주세요.

남 그럴 수는 없습니다. 운전을 하면서 전화를 하는 것이 얼마나 위험한 일인지 아셔야 해요.

여 알았습니다. 다시는 안 그러겠습니다.

해설

운전을 하면서 전화 통화를 하다가 경찰에게 걸린 상황이다.

어휘

pull over (차를) 갓길에 대다 / hold[hould] ~을 들다 /
driver's license 운전면허 / give someone a break ~을 한 번 봐주다

05 ⑤

Script

W How did you do on the test?

M I didn't answer any questions. Nothing at all.

W Oh, no. I thought you really studied hard.

M I did. I stayed up all night to study for the test, but I think I studied the wrong part.

W What do you mean?

M I studied from page 24 to 74, but there was nothing I knew on the test.

W Oh my God! Those pages were for history, not biology.

해석

여 시험 잘 봤니?

남 나 한 문제도 답을 하지 못했어. 하나도.

여 저런. 나는 네가 정말 열심히 공부했다고 생각했는데.

남 그랬어. 시험공부를 하느라고 밤을 새웠는데 다른 부분을 공부한 것 같아.

여 무슨 말이야?

남 나는 24쪽에서 74쪽까지 공부를 했는데, 시험에 내가 아는 것이 하나도 없더라고.

여 저런! 그것은 생물이 아니라 역사 시험범위잖아.

해설

남자는 역사 시험을 본 것이 아니라, 생물 시험을 보았다.

어휘

stay up 늦게까지 자지 않고 깨어 있다 / all night 밤새도록 /
biology[baiálədʒi] 생물학

06 ③

Script

W Finally we are here in New York.

M I think we need to exchange some money into dollars.

W Sure, but I have some dollar bills from our last trip. I think this is enough money for the museum and lunch. Since we are in front of the museum, let's check the special exhibition and then see the rest of the museum.

M That's a good idea, but I'm a little bit hungry. So, why don't we eat lunch first?

W Okay. That sounds great.

해석

여 마침내 우리가 뉴욕에 왔어.

남 내 생각에 돈을 좀 달러로 교환해야 할 것 같아.

여 그래. 하지만 나 지난번 여행에서 남은 달러가 약간 있어. 내 생각에 이 돈이면 충분히 박물관을 관람하고, 점심을 먹을 수 있을 것 같아. 우리 박물관 앞이니까 특별 전시회도 확인하고, 박물관을 돌아보자.

남 좋은 생각이긴 한데, 난 약간 배가 고파. 그러니까 점심을 먼저 먹는 게 어때?

여 알았어. 좋아.

해설

배가 고파서 박물관에 가기 전에 점심을 먼저 먹기로 했다.

어휘

exchange[ikstʃéindʒ] ~을 교환하다 / last[læst] 지난번의 /
exhibition[èksəbíʃən] 전시

07 ⑤

Script

W Hi, Lucy. This is Rebecca. I'm calling to invite you to my 15th birthday party. We're going to have a big party at 6 o'clock this Friday evening. I invited Susie, Richard, and Ray. My parents promised to make a great birthday cake and a variety of food. I hope you can come and enjoy the party. When you get this message, please call me back. Goodbye.

해석

여 안녕, Lucy. 나 Rebecca야. 나의 열다섯 번째 생일에 너를 초대하려고 전화를 하는 거야. 우리는 이번 금요일 저녁 6시에 파티를 열 거야.

나는 Susie와 Richard, Ray를 초대했어. 우리 부모님이 나에게 커다란 생일 케이크와 다양한 음식을 만들어 주시겠다고 약속했어. 나는 네가 와서 파티를 즐길 수 있으면 좋겠어. 네가 이 메시지를 받으면 나에게 전화해 줘. 안녕.

해설

메시지를 받으면 전화를 해 달라고 했으므로 응답전화가 필요 없다는 내용은 알맞지 않다.

08 ②

Script

M What can I do for you?

W I bought this book yesterday, but a couple of pages are missing.

M Really? Let me take a look at it. I don't know how that happened. I'm really sorry. I'll exchange it for you. Do you have the receipt?

W Sure. Here you go.

M OK. I'll go and get another copy for you.

W Okay. Thank you. Can I have it wrapped? It's a gift for my friend.

M Of course. I hope she will enjoy it. Come again, please.

해석

남 무엇을 도와드릴까요?

여 제가 어제 이 책을 샀는데요. 몇 쪽이 없네요.

남 정말요? 한 번 보죠. 어떻게 이런 일이 생겼는지 모르겠네요. 정말로 죄송합니다. 다른 것으로 교환해 드릴게요. 영수증은 가지고 있으세요?

여 물론이죠. 여기 있어요.

남 알았습니다. 제가 가서 다른 것으로 하나 가지고 오겠습니다.

여 알았습니다. 감사합니다. 포장을 좀 해 주실래요? 친구에게 줄 선물이 거든요.

남 물론이죠. 친구가 그 책을 재미있어 하기를 바랍니다. 또 오세요.

해설

여자는 책이 파본 이라서 책을 교환하려고 한다.

어휘

a couple of 몇 개의, 둘의 / missing[mísiŋ] 없어진 /
take a look at ~을 보다 / exchange[ikstʃéindʒ] ~을 교환하다 /
receipt[risíːt] 영수증 / wrap[ræp] ~을 포장하다

09 ③

Script

W May he rest in peace.

M He was a really nice man.

W I know everyone respected him.

M He left everything he had to the orphanage he often used to help. He even left nothing for his family.

W What a great man!

M I can feel how great he was by the number of people at his funeral. I'll miss him a lot.

해석

여 고이 잠드소서.

남 그는 정말로 좋은 사람이었어.

여 모든 사람이 그들 존경했다는 것을 알아.

남 그는 자신이 가진 모든 것을 그가 종종 도와줬던 보육원에 남겼어. 그는 심지어 가족에게 아무것도 남기지 않았지.

여 정말 훌륭한 사람이구나!

남 그의 장례식에 모인 사람들의 수를 보면 그가 얼마나 훌륭한 사람이었는지 느낄 수 있어. 그가 많이 그리울 거야.

해설

돌아가신 분을 추모하는 장례식장이다.

어휘

May someone rest in peace. 편히 잠드소서. /
respect[rispékt] ~을 존경하다 / orphanage[ɔ́ːrfənidʒ] 보육원 /
funeral[fjúːnərəl] 장례식

10 ④

Script

M In the USA, when you meet other people for the first time, it's OK to ask questions like "Where do you live?," "Do you have any brothers or sisters?," or "What kind of sports do you like?" However, it's very impolite to ask personal or private questions about age, marriage, religion, salary, and especially their physical appearance. We may think we can easily ask each other about such things, but people are very sensitive about those matters.

해석

남 미국에서 처음으로 다른 사람들을 만났을 때, "어디에 사세요?", "형제나 자매가 있으세요?", 무슨 운동을 좋아하세요?"와 같은 질문을 하는 것은 괜찮다. 하지만, 나이나 결혼, 종교, 봉급, 특히 그들의 신체적 외모에 대한 사적이고 개인적인 질문을 하는 것은 매우 예의 없는 행동이다. 우리는 서로에게 그런 것에 대해 쉽게 물어볼 수 있다고 생각할 수도 있지만, 사람들은 그러한 문제에 대해 매우 민감하다.

해설

형제나 자매가 있느냐고 물어볼 수 있다고 했으므로 "형제, 자매가 있으세요?"라는 질문은 피하지 않아도 된다.

① 몇 살이세요?

② 결혼하셨나요?

③ 신을 믿으세요?

⑤ 수입이 얼마나 되세요?

어휘

impolite[ìmpəláit] 무례한, 예의 없는 / personal[pə́ːrsənəl] 개인의 /
private[práivit] 사적인 / marriage[mǽridʒ] 결혼, 혼인 /
religion[rilídʒən] 종교 / physical[fízikəl] 육체적인 /
appearance[əpíərəns] 겉모습 / sensitive[sénsətiv] 민감한 /
matter[mǽtər] 일, 사건

11 ③

Script

M Mom, will you be able to go shopping with me this

evening? On the way home, I got this leaflet. It says jeans are on sale now, and we can get a pair of free jeans.

W I don't think we can get a pair of jeans for nothing. Why don't you read it carefully again?

M Ah, I missed something. We have to buy three pairs of jeans to get one free.

W Ads are always like that. You cannot see the important information because it's written in very fine print.

M I got it, Mom. I must read ads more carefully from now on.

해석

남 엄마, 오늘 저녁에 저와 함께 쇼핑 가실 수 있어요? 집에 오다가 이 전단을 받았어요. 청바지가 지금 할인판매를 한대요. 그리고 공짜 청바지를 얻을 수 있어요.

여 청바지를 그냥 얻을 수 있을 것 같지는 않다. 다시 한 번 주의 깊게 읽어 보지 그러니.

남 이런, 제가 뭔가를 놓쳤네요. 청바지를 공짜로 하나 얻으려면 청바지를 세 개 사야 해요.

여 광고는 항상 그렇단다. 중요한 정보는 너무 작은 글씨로 쓰여 있어서 볼 수가 없단다.

남 알았어요, 엄마. 이제부터는 광고를 좀 더 주의 깊게 읽어야겠어요.

해설

어머니가 아들에게 광고에서 중요한 정보는 작은 글씨로 쓰여 있어서 놓치기 쉬우니 광고에 현혹되지 말라고 조언하고 있다.

어휘

leaflet[líːflit] 전단, 광고지 / free[friː] 무료의 / for nothing 이유없이, 무료로 / ad[æd] 광고 / fine print 매우 작은 활자(체) / from now on 이제부터, 지금부터

12 ④

Script

M Hello. It's John. Is Mr. Brown in?

W I'm sorry, but Mr. Brown is out now.

M When do you expect him back?

W Well, he said it would take almost 3 hours to have his car repaired.

M When did he leave?

W He left right before noon, and it would probably take him one hour to go and come back.

M I see. Then, I'll call him back later.

W Okay.

해석

남 여보세요. 저는 John인데, Brown 씨 계신가요?

여 죄송하지만, Brown 씨는 지금 외출하셨습니다.

남 언제 돌아오시나요?

여 글쎄요, 차를 고치는 데 세 시간 정도 걸릴 거라고 하셨어요.

남 언제 나가셨는데요?

여 정오가 되기 바로 전에 나갔어요. 그리고 오고 가는 데 아마 한 시간 정도 걸릴 거예요.

남 알았습니다. 그러면 나중에 전화하죠.

여 알았습니다.

해설

남자는 정오에 나갔고, 자동차 수리에 세 시간, 오고 가는 데 한 시간이 소요되므로 4시쯤 돌아올 것이다.

어휘

expect[ikspékt] ~을 기대하다 / repair[ripέər] ~을 수리하다

13 ④

Script

W The first international modern Olympics were held in Greece in 1896 and at that time, only men took part in the games, and winners were only given a silver and a bronze medal. In addition, the Olympics were only held in developed countries such as France, Germany, and England. Nowadays, however, the Olympics are held on different continents every four years, and more and more women participate in the games.

해석

여 첫 번째 근대 국제올림픽이 1896년에 그리스에서 열렸다. 그 당시에는 오직 남자들만 게임에 참가했고, 승자들에게는 은메달과 동메달만이 수여되었다. 게다가 올림픽은 프랑스, 독일, 영국과 같은 선진국에서만 열렸다. 하지만 요즈음은 4년마다 다른 대륙에서 개최되고, 점점 더 많은 여성들이 참여한다.

해설

초창기 올림픽은 대륙별로 열린 것이 아니라 선진국에서만 열렸다.

어휘

hold[hould] 개최하다 / at that time 그 당시에 / take part in ~에 참가하다 / bronze[brɑnz] 청동 / in addition 더구나, 게다가 / developed country 선진국 / continent[kántənənt] 대륙 / more and more 점점 더 / participate in ~에 참가하다

14 ②

Script

M This sign tells people not to honk their horns. The symbol is usually shown in a quiet area such as a school zone or a residential area. As traffic becomes heavy, some drivers tend to honk their horns. So the government prohibits drivers from honking their horns in a neighborhood by posting this sign.

해석

남 이 표지판은 사람들에게 경적을 울리지 말라고 말한다. 이 표시는 일반적으로 어린이보호구역(스쿨존)이나 주거지역과 같은 조용한 곳에서 보인다. 교통이 막히면, 어떤 운전자들은 경적을 울리고 싶어한다. 그래서 정부는 이런 표지판이 게시된 지역에서는 운전자들이 경적을 울리는 것을 금지한다.

해설

경적을 울리지 말라는 의미의 표지판이 답이다.

어휘

honk[hɔːŋk] 경적을 울리다 / horn[hɔːrn] 경적 / quiet[kwáiət] 조용한 / residential[rèzidénʃəl] 주거의 / tend to ~하는 경향이 있다 /

prohibit[prouhíbit] 금지하다 / neighborhood[néibərhùd] 이웃 /
post[poust] ~을 게시하다

15 ②
Script

M Look at him. He is crossing the street at the red light.

W A lot of people do that these days.

M They should be fined.

W I don't think that's going to work. I think people should learn what to do and what not to during their early childhood.

M That's what I am saying.

해석

남 저 사람을 좀 봐. 빨간 신호에 길을 건너고 있어.

여 요새 저런 사람들 많아.

남 저런 사람들은 벌금을 물려야 해.

여 그런 것은 효과가 없을 것 같아. 나는 사람들이 무엇을 해야 되고 무엇을 하지 말아야 할지 어린 시절에 배워야 한다고 생각해.

남 그것이 내 말이야.

해설

"그것이 내 말이야."라는 남자의 말은 동의를 의미한다.

어휘

cross[krɔːs] ~을 건너다 / fine[fain] ~에게 벌금을 과하다 /
childhood[tʃáildhùd] 어린 시절

16 ③
Script

① M Can we see the Great Wall of China from space?
   W I don't think we can.

② M What is the longest river in the world?
   W It is the Nile.

③ M Where did she bury her treasure?
   W I think she will buy a house on the hill.

④ M Why is she mad?
   W Her mother made her wash the car.

⑤ M Don't you agree with me?
   W Sorry, but I'm against your plan.

해석

① 남 우주에서 만리장성을 볼 수 있니?
   여 못 볼 것 같은데.

② 남 세계에서 가장 긴 강은 무엇이니?
   여 나일 강이야.

③ 남 그녀가 어디에 보물을 묻었어?
   여 내 생각에 그녀는 언덕 위에 있는 집을 살 것 같아.

④ 남 그녀는 왜 화가 났니?
   여 그녀의 어머니가 자동차 세차를 시켰거든.

⑤ 남 너는 나에게 동의하지 않니?
   여 미안하지만 나는 너의 계획에 반대해.

해설

③ 어디에 보물을 묻었느냐는 질문에 언덕 위에 있는 집을 살 것 같다는 대답은 어울리지 않는다.

어휘

the Great Wall of China 만리장성 / space[speis] 우주; 공간 /
bury[béri] ~을 묻다 / treasure[tréʒər] 보물 / hill[hil] 언덕 /
mad[mæd] 화난 / agree with ~에게 동의하다

17 ①
Script

M Can I help you?

W I'm looking for a scarf. It's for my friend's birthday.

M How about this one?

W That's nice. I think my friend will like it. How much is it?

M 40 dollars. That's after 10 percent off.

W All right. I'll buy two, one for me and the other for my friend.

M These two scarves? Anything else?

W No, that's all. Here's 100 dollars.

M Thank you. Here's your change. Have a good day.

해석

남 도와드릴까요?

여 저는 스카프를 찾고 있어요. 제 친구의 생일 선물이에요.

남 이것은 어떠세요?

여 좋네요. 제 친구가 좋아할 것 같아요. 얼마죠?

남 40달러입니다. 10퍼센트 할인한 가격입니다.

여 알겠어요. 두 개 살게요. 하나는 제 거고요. 다른 하나는 친구 거로요.

남 이 두 스카프요? 그밖에는요?

여 없어요. 그게 전부예요. 여기 백 달러예요.

남 감사합니다. 여기 잔돈 있습니다. 좋은 하루 보내세요.

해설

여자는 40달러짜리 스카프를 두 개 사고 백 달러를 냈으므로 20달러를 거슬러 받을 것이다.

어휘

scarf[skɑːrf] 스카프 / change[tʃeindʒ] 잔돈

18 ②
Script

① W Look at these paintings! Aren't they fantastic?
   M Yes. They're my favorites.

② W Don't sit on the bench. The paint hasn't dried yet.
   M Thank you. I was going to sit down.

③ W I can't reach the upper part. What should I do?
   M Why don't you use this? You can step on it.

④ W Can you show me how to draw this picture?
   M I'm sorry, but I didn't do that one.

⑤ W I'm looking for paint and brushes.

M We have a wide selection. Come this way.

해석

① 여 이 그림들 좀 봐! 멋있지 않니?

남 응. 그것들은 내가 제일 좋아하는 것들이야.

② 여 벤치에 앉지 마, 페인트가 아직 마르지 않았어.

남 고마워. 앉으려고 했었어.

③ 여 윗부분에 손이 닿지 않아요. 어떻게 해야 하죠?

남 이것을 사용하지 그러니? 그 위에 올라서면 돼.

④ 여 이 그림을 어떻게 그리는지 보여 주시겠어요?

남 미안하지만, 그것은 제가 그린 것이 아니에요.

⑤ 여 나는 페인트와 붓이 필요해요.

남 우리는 다양한 상품이 있습니다. 이리로 오십시오.

해설

벤치에 칠이 마르지 않아서 앉지 못하도록 말리는 상황이다.

어휘

favorite[féivərit] 매우 좋아하는 것; 매우 좋아하는 / dry[drai] 마르다 / reach[riːtʃ] ~에 닿다 / upper[ʌ́pər] 위쪽의, 높은 쪽의 / step on ~을 밟다 / draw[drɔː] ~을 그리다 / wide[waid] 넓은, 광범위한 / selection[silékʃən] 선택

19 ①

Script

M Amanda, are you looking for something?

W I left my purse and a few books here.

M And?

W They disappeared when I came back from the restroom.

M Was anyone else here?

W No, nobody.

M What did you have in your purse?

W I had 200 dollars and my student ID card.

M What a shame!

해석

남 Amanda, 뭔가를 찾고 있니?

여 내 지갑과 책 몇 권을 여기에 두었는데.

남 그런데?

여 화장실에 갔다 오니까 사라졌어.

남 여기에 다른 사람이 있었니?

여 아니, 아무도 없었어.

남 너의 지갑에 뭐가 들어 있었는데?

여 2백 달러하고 학생증이 있었어.

남 그거 안 됐구나!

해설

2백 달러와 학생증을 잃어버렸다는 말에 "그거 안 됐구나!"라는 응답이 가장 적절하다.

② 그것들 둘 다 잃은 것 같아서 걱정이야.

③ 걱정하지 마. 내 생각에 그거면 충분해.

④ 현금은 약간 있는데 학생증은 없어.

⑤ 분실물 센터에서 그것들을 찾았다니 다행이다.

어휘

purse[pəːrs] 지갑 / disappear[dìsəpíər] 사라지다 / restroom[réstrùːm] 화장실 / ID card (=identity card) 신분증

20 ⑤

Script

W You don't look good. Are you okay, Brian?

M Well, not really. I've got a sore throat, and I think I have a fever, too.

W You may be catching a cold. Why don't you go home and take a rest?

M I want to, but I can't. You know we're going to have a test on Friday.

W Yeah, right. But we still have 5 days to prepare for the test.

M I know, but I haven't studied at all. I'm so worried.

W Is there anything I can do for you?

M Yes. Can you lend me your notebook?

해석

여 너 안 좋아 보인다. 괜찮니, Brian?

남 음, 별로야. 목이 아프고, 열도 있는 것 같아.

여 감기에 걸렸나 보다. 집에 가서 좀 쉬는 게 어때?

남 나도 그러고 싶지만, 그럴 수 없어. 우리가 금요일에 시험을 본다는 것을 너도 알잖아.

여 응, 맞아. 하지만, 시험까지는 아직 5일이나 준비할 시간이 있잖아.

남 알아. 하지만 공부를 하나도 하지 않았어. 정말 걱정돼.

여 내가 너를 위해서 뭐 해 줄 거라도 있니?

남 응. 네 공책을 나에게 빌려 줄 수 있니?

해설

도와줄 것이 있느냐는 말에 "응. 네 공책을 나에게 빌려 줄 수 있니?"라는 응답이 가장 적절하다.

① 아니. 내가 너 공부하는 걸 도와줄게.

② 그렇게 하기에 너무 빠른 것 같지 않니?

③ 알았어, 네 조언을 받아들일게.

④ 응. 너는 시험을 준비해야 해.

어휘

sore throat 인후염, 목의 통증 / fever[fíːvər] 열 / catch a cold 감기에 걸리다 / take a rest 휴식을 취하다 / have a test 시험을 보다 / prepare for ~을 준비하다 / worried[wə́ːrid] 걱정하는, 걱정스러운 / lend[lend] 빌려 주다

2회 실전모의고사

p.140~143

01 ②	02 ①	03 ④	04 ③	05 ⑤
06 ④	07 ①	08 ③	09 ②	10 ②
11 ②	12 ④	13 ②	14 ③	15 ⑤
16 ⑤	17 ①	18 ④	19 ②	20 ⑤

01 ②

Script

M Excuse me, I'd like to buy an electronic pencil sharpener for my child.

W Okay. Why don't you come over here, please?

M Okay. I like the house-shaped one over there.

W But that's not an electronic pencil sharpener.

M I see. Then what about the racing car-shaped one?

W It's very cute, and boys usually like that one. Is your child a boy or a girl?

M My child is a girl.

W Then, how about the one with a panda on the front? Girls usually like animal-shaped ones.

M But I'll buy the non animal-shaped one. My daughter likes automobiles.

해석

남 실례합니다. 제 아이를 위한 자동연필 깎기를 사고 싶은데요.

여 알았습니다. 이리로 오시겠어요?

남 네. 저기 집 모양 연필 깎기가 마음에 드네요.

여 하지만 저것은 자동연필 깎기가 아니에요.

남 그렇군요. 그러면 경주용 자동차 모양은 어떤가요?

여 그것은 매우 귀여워요. 그리고 일반적으로 남자아이들이 좋아하고요. 자녀분이 아들인가요, 딸인가요?

남 제 아이는 딸이에요.

여 그럼 앞에 판다가 그려져 있는 건 어떠세요? 일반적으로 여자아이들은 동물 모양을 좋아해요.

남 하지만, 동물 모양이 아닌 걸로 살게요. 제 딸은 자동차를 좋아하거든요.

해설

남자는 동물 모양이 아니라 딸이 좋아하는 자동차 모양을 사려고 한다.

어휘

electronic[ilèktránik] 전기의, 전자의 / pencil sharpener 연필깎기 / shaped[ʃeipt] 모양의, 형체의 / racing car 경주용 자동차 / automobile[ɔ́ːtəməbìːl] 자동차

02 ①

Script

W Have you met our new English teacher? She's from the USA.

M No, I haven't. How is she?

W She seems nice, but I feel a little strange when she is trying to call me by waving her hand towards herself.

M What's wrong with that?

W I mean she was waving her hand with her palm upward like she was calling a dog!

M Aha, I know what you mean. That is what they do. It's the opposite of how we do it.

해석

여 너 새로 온 우리 영어 선생님을 만나 보았니? 그녀는 미국에서 왔어.

남 아니, 못 만나 봤어. 어때?

여 좋은 사람 같은데, 그녀가 자기 쪽을 향해 손을 흔들면서 나를 부를 때 기분이 좀 이상했어.

남 그게 뭐가 잘못되었는데?

여 내 말은 그녀가 마치 강아지를 부르는 것처럼 손바닥을 위로 하고 손을 흔들었다고!

남 아, 네가 무슨 말을 하는지 알겠다. 그게 그들의 방식이야. 우리가 하는 것의 반대지.

해설

손바닥이 위로 가고 부르는 사람 쪽을 향해 손을 흔드는 동작은 ①번이다.

어휘

wave one's hand 손을 흔들다 / toward[tɔːrd] ~을 향하여 / palm[pɑːm] 손바닥 / upward[ʌ́pwərd] 위로 향한 / opposite[ápəzit] 반대

03 ④

Script

M Please have a seat.

W Thank you.

M Can you tell me why I have to hire you?

W Well, I'm very creative and good at teamwork.

M I see. We have many foreign customers here. Do you speak any foreign languages?

W Yes, I'm good at Japanese and Chinese. My father teaches Japanese at a high school, and my mother is Chinese.

M That's amazing. You also have some job experience, right?

W Yes, I used to work at an Italian restaurant.

M Perfect.

해석

남 자리에 앉으세요.

여 감사합니다.

남 제가 왜 당신을 고용해야 하는지 말씀해 보세요?

여 네, 저는 매우 창의적이며 협동심이 강합니다.

남 그렇군요. 우리는 외국인 손님들이 많은데요. 외국어를 하실 줄 압니까?

여 네, 저는 일본어와 중국어에 능합니다. 저의 아버지가 고등학교에서 일본어를 가르치시고, 어머니는 중국인이십니다.

남 놀랍군요. 경력도 있으시죠, 그렇죠?

여 네. 이탈리아 음식점에서 일했습니다.

남 완벽하군요.

해설

남자는 지원자를 인터뷰하는 면접관이고, 여자는 면접을 보고 있는 지원자이다.

어휘

have a seat 자리에 앉다 / hire[háiər] ~을 고용하다 / foreign[fɔ́(:)rin] 외국의 / customer[kʌ́stəmər] 고객, 손님 / job experience 경력 / used to+동사원형 ~하곤 했다

04 ③

Script

[Telephone rings.]

W Hi, Michael. This is Yvette.

M How are you doing, Yvette?

W Not very well. I sprained my left ankle.

M Really? Are you all right? Did you see a doctor?

W Yes, I did. The doctor said I shouldn't walk for a couple of days. So, Michael, will you be able to hand in my homework?

M Sure, I'll stop by your house to pick it up on my way to school tomorrow morning. I hope you feel better soon.

W Thank you, Michael.

해설

여 안녕, Michael. 나 Yvette이야.

남 잘 지내니, Yvette?

여 좋지 않아. 나 왼쪽 발목을 다쳤어.

남 정말? 괜찮아? 병원에는 갔니?

여 응, 갔었어. 의사가 이틀 정도 걸으면 안 된대. 그래서 Michael, 내 숙제를 좀 제출해 줄 수 있니?

남 물론, 내일 아침 학교 가는 길에 숙제를 가지러 너의 집에 들를게. 곧 나아지길 바라.

여 고마워, Michael.

해설

여자는 과제물을 대신 제출해 달라고 부탁하고 있다.

어휘

sprain[sprein] ~을 삐다 / ankle[ǽŋkl] 발목 / hand in ~을 제출하다 / stop by ~에 들르다

05 ⑤

Script

M Janet, I have something to tell you.

W What is it?

M Luke told me to tell you that he has no choice but to refuse your offer.

W Why?

M He said his parents wouldn't let him do that.

W That's too bad. I mean it could be a great opportunity for him.

M I know. You two could bring a better result if you worked together.

W That's what I'm saying.

해설

남 Janet, 너에게 할 말이 있어.

여 뭔데?

남 Luke가 너의 제안을 받아들일 수 없다고 전해 달래.

여 왜?

남 그의 부모님이 그가 그것을 하도록 허락하지 않으셨대.

여 그거참 안 됐다. 내 말은 그에게 좋은 기회가 될 수도 있었을 텐데.

남 알아. 너희 둘이서 함께 일하면 더 좋은 결과를 가져올 수 있을 텐데.

여 그게 내 말이야.

해설

여자는 Luke가 자신의 제안을 받아들일 수 없게 되어 실망했을 것이다.

어휘

have no choice but to+동사원형 ~하지 않을 수 없다 / refuse[rifjúːz] ~을 거절하다 / offer[ɔ́(:)fər] 제안 / let[let] ~하게 시키다 / opportunity[àpərtjúːnəti] 기회 / result[rizʌ́lt] 결과

06 ④

Script

W I didn't expect to see you at the library.

M I know. I have no reason to be here.

W Then what brought you here?

M I came here to help my mom find some books. She said she needs some material for a cooking contest.

W I guess she wants to get some recipes from the cookbooks.

M I guess so. Now I'm looking for some cooking magazines.

W I think the magazines are downstairs.

해설

여 너를 도서관에서 보리라고는 예상하지 못했어.

남 알아. 나는 여기에 올 이유가 없어.

여 그런데 왜 왔어?

남 우리 엄마가 책을 찾는 것을 도와주러 왔어. 요리 대회를 위한 자료가 좀 필요하다고 하셔서.

여 요리책에서 조리법을 얻기를 원하시는 것 같구나.

남 그런 것 같아. 지금은 요리 잡지를 찾는 중이야.

여 잡지는 아래층에 있는 것 같아.

해설

남자는 엄마가 요리책을 찾는 데 도움을 주려고 도서관에 오게 되었다.

어휘

expect[ikspékt] ~을 예상하다, 기대하다 / material[mətíəriəl] 자료 / recipe[résəpiː] 요리법 / downstairs[dàunstέərz] 아래층에

07 ①

Script

M Hello, Catherine? It's me, Jeremy.

W Oh, hi Jeremy. What's up?

M I got free tickets for a movie tonight. I was thinking that we could go together.

W I'm really sorry, but I have a quiz tomorrow.

M I know. Don't you remember we are in the same class?

W Since you mentioned that, don't you think we have to study for the quiz?

M It's just a quiz. This is a good chance to watch a movie for free. I don't want to miss it. What do you think?

W I'd like to take a rain check.

해석

남 여보세요, Catherine? 나야, Jeremy.

여 어, 안녕, Jeremy. 웬일이야?

남 오늘 밤 공짜 영화표가 생겨서. 우리가 함께 갈 수 있을까 하고.

여 정말 미안하지만, 내일 쪽지 시험이 있어.

남 알아. 우리가 같은 반이라는 것을 잊었니?

여 네가 먼저 말을 꺼냈으니까 말인데, 쪽지 시험공부를 해야 한다고 생각하지 않니?

남 겨우 쪽지시험일 뿐이잖아. 영화를 공짜로 볼 좋은 기회란 말이야. 놓치고 싶지 않아. 어떻게 생각해?

여 다음 기회에 할게.

해설

rain check(초대나 제안에 응할 수 없을 때 하는)은 다음 기회를 기약하는 뜻이므로 거절의 의미라는 것을 알 수 있다.

어휘

mention[ménʃən] 언급하다 / for free 공짜로 /
rain check (초대나 제안에 응할 수 없을 때 하는) 다음 기회, 후일의 약속

08 ③
Script

W Would you like to drink something, sir?

M Yes. I'm a little thirsty. May I have some cold water?

W Here you go, sir.

M Thank you. And one more thing. I think I'm kind of hungry. Will you be serving lunch soon?

W Yes. We're almost done with the beverage service. Right after this, we'll be serving lunch.

M Great. What is being offered?

W We have a choice of beef or chicken today.

M Sounds okay!

해석

여 마실 것 좀 드릴까요, 손님?

남 네. 목이 약간 마르네요. 찬물을 좀 주시겠어요?

여 여기 있습니다, 손님.

남 감사합니다. 그리고 한 가지 더요. 배가 약간 고픈 것 같아요. 곧 점심을 주실 건가요?

여 네. 음료 제공이 거의 다 끝나가거든요. 음료 제공 후에 바로 점심을 드릴 거예요.

남 잘됐네요. 어떤 음식을 선택할 수 있죠?

여 오늘은 쇠고기와 닭고기 중에서 선택할 수 있으세요.

남 괜찮네요!

해설

여자가 남자가 자는 것을 깨운 것은 아니다.

어휘

thirsty[θə́ːrsti] 목마른 / beverage[bévəridʒ] 음료 / offer[ɔ́(ː)fər] ~을 제공하다 / beef[biːf] 쇠고기

09 ②
Script

W Are you ready to cross the river?

M Sure, I've practiced it for a long time.

W That's true. I've seen you swim every day.

M I feel very confident.

W I see. Before swimming, let me ask you one thing. Is there any life guard around here?

M Why? I don't need one.

W I understand how good you are, but you need to prepare in case of an emergency.

M Okay, I got it.

해석

여 너는 강을 건널 준비가 되었니?

남 물론, 나는 오랫동안 연습을 해 왔잖아.

여 맞아. 나는 네가 매일 수영하는 것을 보았어.

남 나는 정말 자신 있어.

여 알았어. 수영하기 전에 한 가지 물어볼게. 이 주변에 안전 요원은 있니?

남 왜? 나는 안전 요원은 필요 없어.

여 네 실력이 좋은 줄은 알지만, 비상사태에 대비해야 해.

남 알았어. 무슨 말인지 이해했어.

해설

강을 건너기 전에 비상사태에 대비하자는 내용이므로 "돌다리도 두드려 보고 건너라."라는 속담이 가장 적절하다.

① 부전자전

③ 무소식이 희소식이다.

④ 시작이 반이다.

⑤ 겉을 보고 속을 판단하지 마라.

어휘

cross[krɔːs] 건너다 / confident[kánfidənt] 자신만만한 / life guard 안전 요원 / prepare[pripέər] 준비하다 / in case of ~에 대비하여 / emergency[imə́ːrdʒənsi] 비상사태

10 ②
Script

① **M** Keep going straight.

W Where do I make a left turn?

② M Keep pedaling and try to control it.

W OK. Hold tightly, please.

③ M How do you go to school every day?

W I go to school by bike.

④ M Do you think you can go alone?

W Sure, there is nothing to be afraid of.

⑤ M When and where do I have to get off?

W Don't worry. I'll tell you later.

해석

① 남 계속 똑바로 가세요.
여 어디서 좌회전을 하나요?

② 남 페달을 계속 밟으면서 균형을 잡도록 해 봐.
여 알았어요, 꽉 잡아 주세요.

③ 남 학교에 매일 어떻게 가나요?
여 저는 자전거를 타고 가요.

④ 남 네 생각에 너는 혼자 갈 수 있을 것 같니?
여 그럼요, 무서울 것 없어요.

⑤ 남 제가 언제, 어디서 내려야 하나요?
여 걱정하지 마세요. 제가 나중에 얘기해 줄게요.

해설

아버지가 딸의 자전거를 밀어주면서 자전거 타는 것을 가르쳐 주는 상황이다.

어휘

keep[kiːp] 계속 ~하다 / straight[streit] 똑바로 / make a left turn 좌회전하다 / hold tightly 꽉 잡다 / get off 내리다

11 ②

Script

W David, why didn't you wear your helmet? How many times have I told you to wear one?

M Sorry, but it's too hot and humid to wear one.

W I understand what you mean, but imagine if some heavy tools or objects fell on you. You might get seriously injured or even lose your life. You have to follow the safety rules.

M I know. However, it's not comfortable at all.

W Okay, David. If you want to feel comfortable, you don't need to come to work.

M That's not what I mean. I know safety comes first.

해석

여 David, 너는 왜 안전모를 착용하지 않았니? 내가 도대체 너에게 안전모를 쓰라고 몇 번이나 말을 했니?

남 죄송합니다만, 모자를 쓰면 너무 덥고 습해서요.

여 네가 무슨 말을 하는지 이해는 하지만, 무거운 공구나 물체가 너에게 떨어지는 것을 상상해 봐. 너는 심하게 부상을 당하거나 심지어 목숨을 잃을 수도 있어. 너는 안전 규정을 따라야 해.

남 알아요. 하지만, 전혀 편하지가 않아서요.

여 알았다, David. 네가 편하기를 바란다면, 너는 일을 하러 오지 않아도 된다.

남 제 말은 그것이 아니에요. 저도 안전이 우선이라는 것은 알아요.

해설

두 사람은 안전모를 착용해야 하는 건설 현장에 있다.

어휘

humid[hjúːmid] 습한 / tool[tuːl] 공구, 연장 / seriously[síəriəsli] 심각하게 / injured[índʒərd] 다친 / follow[fálou] ~을 따르다 / safety rule 안전 수칙 / comfortable[kʌ́mfərtəbəl] 편안한 / come first 우선하다

12 ④

Script

W Mr. Smith, can I have a few days off next week?

M How many days?

W The whole week.

M Can you tell me why?

W My mother is sick, and I need to take care of her until she gets well.

M Hum... Do you think a week will be enough?

W As a matter of fact, I'm not sure. I need to talk to the doctor first.

M Okay, but if anything happens, you should let me know. I can give you another week.

W I really appreciate that.

해석

여 Smith 씨, 다음 주에 며칠 휴가를 낼 수 있을까요?

남 며칠이나요?

여 일주일이요.

남 이유를 말해 줄 수 있어요?

여 어머니가 아프셔서 나아지실 때까지 돌봐 드려야 해요.

남 음……. 일주일이면 충분할 것 같아요?

여 사실, 잘 모르겠어요. 의사하고 먼저 얘기를 해봐야 해요.

남 알았어요, 무슨 일이 있으면 나에게 알려 주세요. 일주일의 휴가를 더 줄게요.

여 정말 감사합니다.

해설

여자는 일주일의 휴가를 내고, 일주일의 휴가를 더 받을 수 있으므로 여자가 휴가를 갈 수 있는 최장 기간은 이주일이다.

어휘

day off 휴가 / take care of ~을 돌보다 / as a matter of fact 사실 / happen[hǽpən] 발생하다, 일어나다 / appreciate[əpríːʃièit] 감사하다, 고마워하다

13 ②

Script

M Jessica, what do you want to do next?

W How about going on the roller coaster?

M Roller coaster? I don't like riding it because I get so dizzy.

W Then let's join the Dance Party. There will be some dancers from Brazil.

M That sounds good. By the way, aren't there any fireworks?

W I don't think we can see it since we have to leave here before 6.

M That's right. The tickets to the Character Parade were sold out. Let's just do a few things instead before we leave.

해석

남 Jessica, 다음엔 무엇을 하고 싶어?

여 롤러코스터를 타는 것은 어때?

남 롤러코스터? 나는 현기증이 나서 그런 거 타는 것을 좋아하지 않아.

여 그러면 댄스파티에 참가하자. 브라질에서 온 댄서들이 있을 거야.

남 좋아. 그런데 불꽃놀이를 하지 않니?

여 우리는 여기에서 6시 전에 떠나야 하니까 그것을 볼 수 있을 것 같지 않아.

남 그렇구나. 만화영화 주인공 퍼레이드 표가 매진되었네. 떠나기 전에 대신 몇 가지만 더 하고 가자.

해설

두 사람이 참여할 수 있는 것은 6시 이전에 할 수 있는 일이어야 하므로 Dance Party와 Acrobatic이다.

어휘

roller coaster 롤러코스터 / dizzy[dízi] 어지러운, 현기증 나는 / Brazil[brəzíl] 브라질 / firework[fáiərwə̀ːrk] 불꽃놀이 / sold out 매진된 / instead[instéd] 대신에

14 ③

Script

[Telephone rings.]

W Stewart's restaurant. May I help you?

M I just had dinner there with my family. When I came home, I checked the bill, but I think I was short-changed.

W Really? That can't be.

M You charged us drinks that we didn't even order.

W Okay. Please tell me the number on the bottom of the receipt so that I can check it out.

M Sure, it's 7569.

W Thank you. I'll call you back when I'm done checking. Can I have your number?

M Sure. It's 786-6131.

W Thank you.

해석

여 Stewart 식당입니다. 도와드릴까요?

남 제가 방금 제 가족과 그곳에서 식사했는데요. 집에 와서 계산서를 확인해 보니 거스름돈을 덜 받은 것 같습니다.

여 정말요? 그럴 리가 없는데요.

남 우리가 주문하지도 않은 음료 값을 부과했더군요.

여 알았습니다. 제가 확인할 수 있도록 영수증의 밑에 있는 번호를 말씀해 주세요.

남 네, 7569입니다.

여 감사합니다. 제가 확인해보고 전화 드리죠. 전화번호 좀 주실래요?

남 네, 786-6131입니다.

여 감사합니다.

해설

남자는 지불한 음식값이 잘못 계산된 것 같아서 식당에 전화했다.

어휘

bill[bil] 계산서, 영수증 / short-change ~에게 거스름돈을 덜 주다 / charge[tʃɑːrdʒ] ~을 부과하다 / order[ɔ́ːrdər] 주문하다 / bottom[bátəm] 밑, 바닥 / receipt[risíːt] 영수증 / check out ~을 확인하다, 조회하다

15 ⑤

Script

M I'm at the center of the Olympic complex. The most important event today was certainly the men's two-hundred-meter freestyle competition. An American swimmer, Mike Phelps, won the gold medal in the competition He swam the 200 meters in a new world's record of four minutes twelve seconds. So in the first 3 days of the Olympic Games the American team has won 9 gold medals and Phelps has got 8 of them. Isn't that amazing?

해석

남 저는 올림픽 경기장에 나와 있습니다. 오늘의 가장 중요한 경기는 분명히 남자 200미터 자유형 시합이었습니다. 미국인 수영 선수인 Mike Phelps가 시합에서 금메달을 획득했습니다. 그는 200미터를 4분 12초의 기록으로 수영하여 세계 신기록을 수립했습니다. 이로써 올림픽 경기의 처음 사흘 동안에 미국 팀은 아홉 개의 금메달을 획득했는데 그 중에서 8개가 Phelps가 획득한 것입니다. 놀랍지 않습니까?

해설

미국 팀은 총 8개가 아니라 9개의 금메달을 획득했다.

어휘

complex[kəmpléks] (건물들의) 집합체, 단지 / certainly[sə́ːrtənli] 확실히 / freestyle[fríːstàil] 자유형(의) / competition[kàmpətíʃən] 경기, 시합

16 ⑤

Script

M What's wrong with you?

W My baby brother tore up my notebook.

M Oh, really? That's a shame. I know how it feels.

W The problem is that my teacher will check student notebooks tomorrow.

M Oh, no. Why don't you start copying it right now?

W I can't. There are too many pages to cover.

M I see. Then, just tell the teacher what happened.

W It will be no use. He will scold me, anyway.

해석

남 무슨 문제가 있는 거야?

여 나의 막냇동생이 내 공책을 찢어버렸어.

남 어, 정말? 안 됐다. 네 기분이 어떤지 알아.

여　문제는 우리 선생님이 내일 공책 검사를 할 거라는 거야.

남　저런. 지금 당장 공책을 베껴 쓰기 시작하는 게 어때?

여　할 수 없어. 베껴야 할 쪽수가 너무 많아.

남　그렇구나. 그러면, 그냥 무슨 일이 있었는지 선생님께 말씀드려.

여　소용없을 거야. 어쨌든 나를 꾸짖으실 거야.

해설
여자는 남동생이 공책을 찢어서 화가 났다.

어휘
tear up 갈가리 찢다 / be no use 소용없다 / scold[skould] 꾸짖다

17 ①
Script

M　I need to get some information on this.

W　I think you need to borrow an encyclopedia from Edward.

M　What is that?

W　It's a book containing many facts about many different subjects.

M　I see what you mean, but do I really need it?

W　Yes. That's the best way you can get your information.

M　Is it possible for me to find it on the Internet?

W　Yes, you can. But it might take longer, and you might have to pay for it.

M　I see. Then I'd better borrow it.

해석
남　나는 이것에 대한 정보가 좀 필요해.

여　내 생각에 너는 Edward에게 백과사전을 빌려야 할 것 같아.

남　그게 뭔데?

여　백과사전은 여러 가지 다른 주제에 대해서 많은 사실을 담은 책이지.

남　무슨 말인지 알았는데 나에게 그것이 정말 필요할까?

여　응. 그것이 네가 정보를 얻을 수 있는 최고의 방법이야.

남　인터넷을 통해서 정보를 좀 얻는 것이 가능할까?

여　응, 그럴 수 있어. 하지만 시간이 더 오래 걸릴지도 모르고, 돈을 지불해야 할지도 몰라.

남　알았어. 그럼 빌리는 게 낫겠다.

해설
남자는 백과사전을 빌리려고 하고 있다.

어휘
borrow[bɔ́(:)rou] ~을 빌리다 / encyclopedia[ensàikloupíːdiə] 백과사전 / contain[kəntéin] ~을 포함하다 / subject[sʌ́bdʒikt] 주제, 대상

18 ④
Script

M　Jake lost his camera. He had to find it because it had some important film in it. His best friend, Jessica called the Lost and Found office. She tried to help him, but she couldn't. She did her best to help Jake find his camera.

In this situation, what might Jake say to Jessica?

해석
남　Jake는 카메라를 잃어버렸다. 그 안에 중요한 필름이 있기 때문에 카메라를 찾아야만 했다. 그의 가장 친한 친구인 Jessica가 분실물 센터에 전화를 했다. 그녀가 그를 도우려고 애썼지만, 도울 수 없었다. 그녀는 Jake가 사진기를 찾도록 도와주려고 최선을 다했다.

　　이러한 경우에 Jake는 Jessica에게 무엇이라고 말을 하겠는가?

해설
카메라를 찾지는 못했지만, 자신을 도와주려고 애쓴 사람에게 할 말은 "내 카메라를 나와 함께 찾아 주어서 고마워."이다.

① 식은 죽 먹기야.

② 괜찮아. 어쨌든 그것은 낡은 거였어.

③ 나는 내 카메라를 분실물 센터에서 찾았어.

⑤ 그 카메라 정말 비싼 거였어. 어떻게 해야 할지 모르겠어.

어휘
the Lost and Found 분실물 센터 / do one's best 최선을 다하다

19 ②
Script

M　Hello, may I help you?

W　Yes, my name is Jennifer Walker, and I have a reservation at 7.

M　OK. Let me check the list. Ma'am, I can't find your name on the list.

W　That can't be. I even called here last night to make sure.

M　That's pretty strange.

W　So do I have to wait?

M　Sorry, ma'am. We are fully booked today, and we can't take any more customers.

W　This is unacceptable.

해석
남　안녕하세요, 도와드릴까요?

여　네, 제 이름은 Jennifer Walker이고, 7시에 예약이 되어 있습니다.

남　알았습니다. 명단을 확인을 해보겠습니다. 손님, 명단에서 성함을 못 찾겠네요.

여　그럴 리가요. 확실히 하려고 어젯밤에 이곳에 전화도 했는데요.

남　그것참 이상하군요.

여　그러면 기다려야 하나요?

남　죄송합니다, 손님. 저희는 오늘 예약이 다 차서 더는 손님을 받을 수가 없습니다.

여　이것은 받아들일 수가 없네요.

해설
예약까지 확인했는데 손님을 받을 수가 없다고 했으므로 "이것은 받아들일 수가 없네요."라는 응답이 가장 적절하다.

① 훌륭하네요!

③ 괜찮아요. 기다릴게요.

④ 물론, 진정하지요.

⑤ 걱정해줘서 고마워요.

reservation[rèzərvéiʃən] 예약 / make sure 확실히 하다 / fully[fúli]
완전히, 충분히 / book[buk] 예약하다 / customer[kʌ́stəmər] 손님 /
unacceptable[ʌ̀nəkséptəbəl] 받아들이기 어려운

20 ⑤

Script

M Excuse me, but you seem pretty familiar to me.

W Sorry, but I've never seen you before.

M I got it. Aren't you Sarah Pearson, the famous opera singer?

W That's right.

M I want to be a great performer like you. Can you give me some tips?

W Try to practice every day as much as possible.

해석

남 실례합니다만, 당신이 꽤 낯이 익어 보여서요.

여 죄송하지만, 저는 전에 당신을 본 적이 없는데요.

남 알았어요. 당신은 Sarah Pearson 아닌가요, 그 유명한 오페라 가수?

여 맞아요.

남 저는 당신과 같은 훌륭한 공연가가 되고 싶어요. 저에게 조언을 좀 해 주실 수 있으세요?

여 매일 가능한 한 많이 연습을 하도록 노력하세요.

해설

조언을 해 달라고 했으므로 "매일 가능한 한 많이 연습을 하도록 노력하세요."
라는 응답이 가장 적절하다.

① 훌륭하군요. 감사합니다.

② 저를 알아봐 주시다니 좋네요.

③ 미안하지만, 지금은 돈이 한 푼도 없어요.

④ 감사합니다. 사인을 해 드릴게요.

어휘

familiar[fəmíljər] 낯익은, 익숙한 / famous[féiməs] 유명한 /
performer[pərfɔ́ːrmər] 공연가 / tip[tip] 조언, 정보 /
practice[prǽktis] 연습하다; 연습

중학 영어듣기

MP3
www.nexusEDU.kr
MP3 무료 다운로드

AFTER SCHOOL Listening

시·도 교육청 공동 주관 중학교 영어듣기능력평가 기출 문제 완전 분석

최신 듣기평가 기출 유형이 100% 반영된 모의고사 16회분과 실전 영어듣기평가 2회분

잘 들리지 않았던 부분을 확실히 확인할 수 있도록 도와주는 회별 Dictation Test

기출 문제 유형 분석과 각종 핵심 표현을 총정리한 실전 대비 학습

NEXUS makes your next day

www.nexusEDU.kr | 책에 대해 궁금한 사항은 넥서스에듀 홈페이지 1:1 고객상담 게시판을 이용하세요.

	초1	초2	초3	초4	초5	초6	중1	중2	중3	고1	고2	고3

Writing

공감 영문법+쓰기 1~2

도전만점 중등내신 서술형 1~4

영어일기 영작패턴 1-A, B · 2-A, B

Smart Writing 1~2

Reading

Reading 101 1~3

Reading 공감 1~3

This Is Reading Starter 1~3

This Is Reading 전면 개정판 1~4

원서 술술 읽는 Smart Reading Basic 1~2

원서 술술 읽는 Smart Reading 1~2

[특급 단기 특강] 구문독해 · 독해유형

[앱솔루트 수능대비 영어독해 기출분석] 2019~2021학년도

Listening

Listening 공감 1~3

The Listening 1~4

After School Listening 1~3

도전! 만점 중학 영어듣기 모의고사 1~3

만점 적중 수능 듣기 모의고사 20회 · 35회

TEPS

NEW TEPS 입문편 실전 250⁺ 청해 · 문법 · 독해

NEW TEPS 기본편 실전 300⁺ 청해 · 문법 · 독해

NEW TEPS 실력편 실전 400⁺ 청해 · 문법 · 독해

NEW TEPS 마스터편 실전 500⁺ 청해 · 문법 · 독해

중학 영어듣기
한 방에 끝낸다

AFTER SCHOOL Listening

애프터스쿨
리스닝
level 3

유형별 학습

NEXUS Edu

중학 영어듣기
한 방에 끝낸다

AFTER
SCHOOL
Listening
애프터스쿨
리스닝
level 3

유형별 학습

NEXUS Edu

Part 1 그림묘사 - 인물, 사물, 표지판, 인물의 행동 등

🔍 기출엿보기

Type 1 그림 보고, 사물 고르기

대화를 듣고, 학급 문집의 표지로 가장 알맞은 것을 고르세요.

①  ② 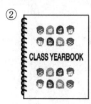 ③   ④   ⑤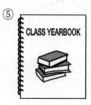

Script

M Our job is to design our class yearbook cover. **How about putting the title on the top center?** It's quite common, you know.

W Well, we can make it a little different, like **placing it in the very middle.**

M Then we won't have space for our picture.

W We can **use the picture as a background.**

M Oh, that's a good idea. Then what kind of picture do you like?

W Hmm. What about using the school picture?

M Well, it's for our class, so I think it's **better to use our class picture.**

W Great. Let's go for it!

해석

남 우리 반 학급 문집의 표지를 디자인하는 것이 우리의 일이야. 제목을 맨 위쪽 가운데 놓는 것이 어때? 너도 알듯이, 그게 꽤 흔한 방법이잖아.

여 글쎄. 우리는 약간 다르게 할 수 있지 않을까, 한가운데 제목을 놓는 것처럼 말이야.

남 그러면 우리 사진을 놓을 공간이 없어질거야.

여 사진을 배경으로 이용할 수 있잖아.

남 아, 그거 좋은 생각이야. 그러면 너는 어떤 종류의 사진이 좋아?

여 음. 학교 사진을 사용하는 건 어때?

남 글쎄. 이건 우리 반을 위한 거잖아. 내 생각엔 우리 반 사진을 사용하는 것이 더 좋은 것 같아.

여 좋아. 그렇게 하자!

정답 ②

해설 제목 글씨가 한가운데 위치하며, 배경 그림으로 학급 급우들의 사진이 있는 표지를 찾는다. "How about putting the title on the top center?"라는 말에 대해 "Well, we can make it a little different, like placing it in the very middle."이라고 거절을 했으므로 이 문장으로 인해 함정에 빠지지 않도록 주의한다.

Tip 🌿 사물을 묘사할 때 사용하는 표현

- There is/are ~. ~이 있다.
- What does it look like? 그것은 어떻게 생겼나요?
- It's one of the biggest+복수명사. 그것은 ~ 중에서 가장 ~하다.
- It's shaped like ~. 그것은 ~처럼 생겼다.

다음을 듣고, 그림과 일치하지 않는 것을 고르세요.

①   ②   ③   ④   ⑤

Script		해석

Script

W **Number 1**   M There's a tree **in** the tiger's area.

W **Number 2**   M The zebra lives **next to** the monkey.

W **Number 3**   M The elephant lives **between** the tiger **and** the lion.

W **Number 4**   M There is a table **in front of** the food court.

W **Number 5**   M There are fish **in** the dolphin's pool.

해석

여 1번   남 호랑이 우리에 나무가 한 그루 있다.

여 2번   남 얼룩말은 원숭이 옆에 산다.

여 3번   남 코끼리는 호랑이와 사자 사이에서 산다.

여 4번   남 식당가 앞에 테이블이 하나 있다.

여 5번   남 돌고래풀에 물고기가 있다.

정답 ③

해설   호랑이와 사자 사이에는 동물이 없다.

① 나무(tree)가 호랑이 우리(tiger's area) 안(in)에 있는지 확인한다.

② 얼룩말(zebra)이 원숭이(monkey) 옆(next to)에 있는지 위치를 확인한다.

③ 코끼리(elephant)가 호랑이(tiger)와 사자(lion) 사이(between)에 있는지 확인한다.

④ 테이블(table)이 식당가(food court) 앞(in front of)에 있는지 확인한다.

⑤ 물고기(fish)가 돌고래풀(dolphin's pool) 안(in)에 있는지 확인한다.

Tip 위치를 묘사할 때 사용하는 표현

- be north/south/east/west of ~의 북/남/동/서에 있다
- live in/on ~에 살다
- lie in/on ~에 눕다, ~에 놓여 있다
- be located in/on/near ~에/가까이에 위치해 있다

1 대화를 듣고, 남자의 친구를 고르시오.

① ② ③ ④ ⑤

2 다음을 듣고, 그림에 대한 설명으로 알맞은 것을 고르세요.

① ② ③ ④ ⑤

3 대화를 듣고, 남자가 지금 하고 있는 일을 고르세요.

① ② ③ ④ ⑤

4 아래의 지도를 보고 잘못 설명된 것을 고르세요.

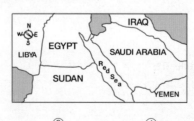

① ② ③ ④ ⑤

🔍 기출엿보기

Type 1 어색한 대화 고르기

다음을 듣고, 두 사람의 대화가 어색한 것을 고르시오.

①   ②   ③   ④   ⑤

Script

① W Our speech contest is tomorrow, isn't it?

   M Yes, it is. I'm so nervous.

② W Your car looks great. When did you buy it?

   M Oh, last month. But it's not brand-new. It's a used car.

③ W What are you doing tonight?

   M Nothing special. Why?

④ W What kind of **movie** would you like to see?

   M I don't like **moving** here and there.

⑤ W Oh, my! It's already five. I have a meeting at five thirty. I need to go right now.

   M Oh, I'm not sure you can make it in time.

해석

① 여 우리 말하기 시합이 내일이지, 그렇지 않니?

   남 응, 그래. 나는 너무 긴장돼.

② 여 너 차 좋아 보인다. 언제 샀어?

   남 어, 지난달에. 하지만 새 차는 아니야. 중고차야.

③ 여 오늘 밤에 뭐 할 거야?

   남 특별한 것 없는데. 왜?

④ 여 어떤 종류의 영화를 보고 싶니?

   남 나는 여기 저기 이사 다니는 게 싫어.

⑤ 여 이럴 수가! 벌써 5시야. 5시 30분에 회의가 있어. 지금 당장 가야겠어.

   남 이런, 네가 제 시간에 도착할 수 있을지 모르겠다.

정답 ④

해설 movie와 moving은 발음은 비슷하지만, 의미적으로 자연스러운 대화가 아니다. 이 대화에서처럼 비슷한 발음 (movie, moving)이 나는 단어를 사용해서 어색한 대화를 만들기도 하므로 비슷한 발음이 나올 경우 특히 주의 깊게 들어야 한다.

Tip 🌿 어색한 대화

◉ W Would you like some more pizza? 피자를 좀 더 드실래요?

  M Sure, help yourself. 물론이죠, 마음껏 드세요.

    해설 더 먹고 싶으냐고 물었는데 마음껏 먹으라고 대답을 하는 것은 어색하다. "Help yourself.(마음껏 드세요)"의 의미를 잘 암기해 두는 것이 중요하다.

◉ W What's the matter with you? 무슨 일이야?

  M It couldn't be better. 이보다 더 좋을 수 없어.

    해설 무슨 일이냐고 묻는 경우는 대개 상대방이 안 좋아 보일 때이므로 대답으로는 주로 부정적인 내용이 나온다. "이보다 더 좋을 수 없어." 라는 말은 안부를 묻는 경우에 답할 수 있는 말이다.

◉ M How have you been? 어떻게 지냈어?

  W I have been there by bus. 나는 그곳에 버스를 타고 갔어.

    해설 how로 시작한다고 해서 무조건 수단이나 방법을 묻는 것이 아니다. 안부를 묻는 질문이므로 버스로 그곳에 갔다는 대답은 어색하다.

다음을 듣고, 그림의 상황에 가장 잘 어울리는 대화를 고르시오.

①   ②   ③   ④   ⑤

Script

① W Can I help you?

   M I would like to buy some **roses**.

② W What are you doing?

   M I'm **helping** my mom.

③ W How much is this watch?

   M It's not expensive.

④ W Thanks for the flowers.

   M You're welcome. I hope you'll get well soon.

⑤ W I need some pictures to decorate my **room**.

   M Let's go find some.

해석

① 여 도와드릴까요?

   남 장미를 좀 사고 싶습니다.

② 여 뭐 하니?

   남 우리 엄마를 돕고 있어.

③ 여 이 시계는 얼마인가요?

   남 그것은 비싸지 않아요.

④ 여 꽃 고마워.

   남 천만에. 빨리 나아지기를 바라.

⑤ 여 내 방을 꾸밀 사진이 좀 필요해.

   남 가서 좀 찾아보자.

정답 ④

해설 병원에 입원해 있는 여자에게 남자가 꽃을 사 들고 병문안을 온 상황이다. 그림에 등장하는 단어(roses)나, 그림을 보고 연상할 수 있는 단어(helping, room)를 이용하여 오답이 되는 대화를 만들기도 하므로 함정에 빠지지 않도록 주의한다.

Tip 상황에 어울리는 대화

● M Can I try this on? 이 옷을 입 어봐도 되나요?

  W Sure. The fitting room is over there. 그럼요. 옷 갈아입는 곳은 저기예요.

  해설 옷 가게, 백화점 등에서 할 수 있는 대화이다.

● W Here you are. There is no sugar in it. 여기 있어요. 설탕은 들어있지 않아요.

  M Thanks. I like my coffee black. 고마워요. 저는 블랙커피를 좋아해요.

  해설 음식점이나 커피숍 등에서 할 수 있는 대화

● M I got a poor grade in English. 영어에서 안 좋은 성적을 받았어요.

  W Cheer up. You'll do better next time. 기운 내. 다음번에는 잘할 거야.

  해설 집이나 학교에서 친구나 가족, 교사가 시험을 잘 보지 못한 학생을 위로할 때 할 수 있는 대화이다.

1 다음을 듣고, 두 사람의 대화가 <u>어색한</u> 것을 고르시오.

①   ②   ③   ④   ⑤

2 다음을 듣고, 두 사람의 대화가 <u>어색한</u> 것을 고르시오.

①   ②   ③   ④   ⑤

3 다음을 듣고, 그림의 상황에 가장 어울리는 대화를 고르시오.

①   ②   ③   ④   ⑤

4 다음을 듣고, 그림의 상황에 가장 어울리는 대화를 고르시오.

①   ②   ③   ④   ⑤

Part 3 관계, 직업

🔍 기출엿보기

Type 1 직업 고르기

대화를 듣고, 남자의 직업을 고르세요.

① nurse   ② dentist   ③ teacher

④ businessman   ⑤ hotel manager

Script

W White Dental Clinic. How may I help you?

M This is Tom Smith. I have an appointment with Dr. Robinson this Friday.

W Let me check... Here you are. Tom Smith at five o'clock Friday afternoon.

M Can I change it to Thursday at five o'clock? **I have an important meeting with my students' parents.**

W Five o'clock is booked. How about three o'clock?

M No problem. **I have no class at three.**

W OK. See you on Thursday.

해석

여 White Dental Clinic입니다. 무엇을 도와 드릴까요?

남 저는 Tom Smith입니다. Robinson 선생님과 이번 금요일에 진료약속이 있습니다.

여 확인해 볼게요⋯⋯. 여기 있군요. Tom Smith 씨 금요일 오후 다섯 시네요.

남 그것을 목요일 다섯 시로 변경할 수 있을까요? 학부모와 중요한 모임이 있어서요.

여 다섯 시는 예약이 있습니다. 세 시는 어떠세요?

남 괜찮아요. 세 시에는 수업이 없어요.

여 알겠습니다. 목요일에 뵙겠습니다.

정답 ③

해설 학부모와 모임이 있다고 했으므로 남자의 직업은 교사임을 알 수 있다. 대화에 등장하는 단어를 듣고 연상할 수 있는 직업을 오답으로 출제하므로 함정에 빠지지 않도록 주의한다. 내가 골라야 하는 사람이 여자인지 남자인지를 먼저 인지하는 것이 중요하며, 남자나 여자가 제공하는 특정 정보를 주의 깊게 들어야 한다.

함정어구와 오답: White Dental Clinic - dentist, nurse / appointment, important meeting - businessman / is booked - hotel manager

---

 Tip 직업 관련 표현

cook

• Now it's time to cook with Jim. 자, Jim과 함께하는 요리 시간이에요.

• Welcome to Jim's Kitchen! 'Jim의 키친'에 오신 걸 환영합니다.

• I'd like to make "Mushroom Stew." '버섯전골'을 만들겠습니다.

• I'll use only the finest and freshest ingredients. 가장 좋고 가장 신선한 재료만을 사용할 거예요.

police officer

• The most difficult part is that people don't always follow the traffic rules.
가장 힘든 것은 사람들이 항상 교통규칙을 지키는 것은 아니라는 거예요.

• Most often, they are drivers. They don't obey the speed limit, so I have to give them speeding tickets.
대부분은 운전자들이에요. 그들은 제한 속도를 지키지 않아서 제가 그들에게 속도위반 딱지를 부과해야 하죠.

flight attendant

• I work on a plane looking after passengers and serving meals to them.
나는 비행기에서 승객들을 돌보고 식사를 제공하는 일을 해요.

• I love it because I can travel a lot. 나는 여행을 많이 할 수 있어서 이 일이 좋아요.

대화를 듣고, 두 사람의 관계로 가장 알맞은 것을 고르세요.

① 교사 – 학부모　　　② 의사 – 환자　　　③ 엄마 – 아들

④ 상담사 – 학생　　　⑤ 교사 – 학생

Script

M Please have a seat, Mrs. Brown.

W Thank you.

M How's Amy doing at home?

W She seems to be doing fine. Is she in trouble?

M Well, **she's very shy and doesn't get along well with other classmates.**

W I didn't know that.

M **She's also having trouble focusing on her studies. That's why her scores are getting lower.**

W What should I do with her?

M Why don't you take her to a counselor? She can get some help.

해석

남 Brown 부인 앉으세요.

여 감사합니다.

남 Amy는 집에서 어떤가요?

여 괜찮은 거 같아요. 무슨 문제가 있나요?

남 음. Amy는 매우 소극적이고 반 친구들과 잘 지내지 못해요.

여 몰랐어요.

남 공부에 집중도 잘 못하고요. 그래서 성적이 점점 떨어지고 있어요.

여 제가 Amy를 어떻게 해야 할까요?

남 상담교사에서 데려가 보시는 게 어때요? 도움을 받을 수 있을 거예요.

정답 ①

해설 학생의 학교생활에 관해 상담을 하고 있는 상황이므로 교사와 학부모의 관계라는 것을 알 수 있다. other classmates, studies, scores 등의 단어에서 학생과 관련된 상황이라는 것을 짐작할 수 있다. 대화에 사용된 단어(counselor)를 사용하여 오답을 만들기도 하므로 함정에 빠지지 않도록 주의한다.

Tip 관계 관련 표현

면접관과 지원자의 관계

면접관 We're looking for someone with computer skills. 우리는 컴퓨터를 다룰 줄 아는 사람을 찾고 있습니다.

Thank you for coming in for today's interview. 오늘 면접에 와 주셔서 감사합니다.

지원자 I used them a lot in my previous job. 저는 전 직장에서 그것들을 많이 사용했었어요.

손님과 약사의 관계

손님 Here's the prescription the doctor gave me. 여기 의사가 준 처방전이요.

약사 Here's your medicine. Take this every eight hours. 여기 약이 있어요. 여덟 시간마다 한 번씩 드세요.

1 대화를 듣고, 여자의 직업으로 알맞은 것을 고르세요.

① 선생님

② 교통경찰관

③ 소방관

④ 의사

⑤ 점원

2 대화를 듣고, 남자의 직업을 고르세요.

① Cook

② Waiter

③ Reporter

④ Announcer

⑤ Traveler

3 대화를 듣고, 두 사람의 관계를 고르시오.

① reader - writer

② director - actress

③ actress - fan

④ singer - composer

⑤ photographer - actor

4 다음을 듣고, 누가 누구에게 하는 말인지 고르세요.

① 교사 → 학생

② 면접관 → 지원자

③ 후보자 → 유권자

④ 사회자 → 방청객

⑤ 아나운서 → 시청자

Part 4   목적

🔍 기출엿보기

Type 1 전화를 건 목적 고르기

대화를 듣고, 여자가 전화를 건 목적을 고르세요.

① to go to a concert   ② to get Min-ji's address   ③ to go to an orphanage

④ to go to a festival   ⑤ to say hello

Script

[Telephone rings.]

W Hello, can I speak to Minho?

M Speaking. Who's calling, please?

W It's me, Betty. It's been a long time. How's it going?

M Not so bad, thanks. What's up?

W **Would you like to go to a rock concert this Sunday?** I have two tickets.

M I'm afraid I can't. I am planning to volunteer at an orphanage.

W Isn't it hard taking care of the children?

M Not at all. About the concert, why don't you call Minji? I think she likes rock music.

W That's a good idea. I'll call her.

해석

여 여보세요, 민호와 얘기할 수 있을까요?

남 전데요. 누구 시죠?

여 나 Betty야. 오랜만이야. 어떻게 지내?

남 나쁘지 않아. 고마워. 무슨 일이야?

여 이번 일요일에 록콘서트에 갈래? 표가 두 장 있거든.

남 미안하지만 갈 수 없어. 나는 고아원에 자원 봉사를 갈 계획이거든.

여 아이들을 돌보는 것이 힘들지 않니?

남 전혀. 콘서트는, 민지에게 전화해 보는 게 어때? 그녀가 록음악을 좋아하는 거 같아.

여 좋은 생각이야. 그녀에게 전화해 볼게.

정답   ①

해설   여자는 남자에게 콘서트에 함께 가자고 말하려고 전화를 했다. 제안, 요구, 요청, 부탁, 초대 등의 의미를 담은 문장은 주로 조동사로 시작하므로 조동사로 시작하는 문장을 주의 깊게 듣는다.

> **Tip** 🖋 전화 관련 표현
>
> • Would you like to leave a message? 메모를 남기시겠어요?
> • No, thanks. I'll call her back. 아니오, 감사합니다. 제가 다시 그녀에게 전화할게요.
> • I'm afraid you have the wrong number. 죄송하지만 전화를 잘못 거신 것 같군요.
> • May I speak to Mary? Mary와 통화할 수 있을까요?
> • This is she speaking. 전데요.
> • There's no one here by that name. 그런 사람 없습니다.
> • Hold on, please. 잠시만 기다리세요.
> • Her line is busy. 그녀는 통화 중입니다.

다음을 듣고, 방송을 하는 목적이 무엇인지 고르세요.

① 경기 안내

② 선수 모집

③ 축하 행사 안내

④ 훈련 일정 안내

⑤ 동아리 회원 모집

Script

W Good morning, everyone! I'm very excited to let you know that our school basketball team won the national championship yesterday. To celebrate this victory, **we are planning to have a party. Please stop by the front lobby after school.** You can talk to the players in person while having free snacks and drinks. **Come and join us!**

해석

여 좋은 아침입니다. 여러분! 어제 있었던 전국 대회에서 우리 학교 농구팀이 우승을 했다는 것을 알리게 되어 매우 기쁩니다. 우승을 축하하기 위해 파티를 개최할 예정입니다. 방과 후에 로비에 들러주세요. 무료로 제공되는 간식과 음료를 드시면서 선수들과 개별적으로 이야기를 나눌 수 있습니다. 와서 우리와 함께하세요!

정답 ③

해설 축하파티 개최를 알리는 것이 이 글의 목적이다. 대화와 담화의 주제가 주로 목적이 되므로 주제가 되는 문장을 놓치지 않고 듣는 것이 중요하다.

Tip 🌿 **목적 관련 표현**

요구 / 부탁

• I'm looking for a detective novel. 나는 탐정 소설을 찾고 있어요.

• I'm having a problem with my new washing machine. 새로 산 세탁기에 문제가 있어요.

• Can I use your printer tonight? 내가 오늘 밤에 네 프린터를 사용해도 될까?

초대 / 제안

• Can you come to my house for dinner? 저녁 식사하러 우리 집에 올 수 있니?

• I'd like to go for a bike ride with you. 나는 너와 함께 자전거를 타러 가고 싶어.

질문

• When does the library open? 도서관이 언제 여나요?

• Are you open on weekends? 주말에도 문을 여나요?

1 대화를 듣고, 남자가 전화를 건 목적으로 가장 알맞은 것을 고르세요.

① 컴퓨터 성능을 시험하려고

② 백신 프로그램을 설치하려고

③ 컴퓨터 구입 안내를 받으려고

④ 인터넷 사용 요금을 문의하려고

⑤ 컴퓨터 고장에 대해 도움을 청하려고

2 대화를 듣고, 남자가 전화를 한 목적으로 알맞은 것을 고르세요.

① 안부 묻기

② 약속 변경

③ 숙제 묻기

④ 결석 알림

⑤ 진료 예약

3 대화를 듣고, 남자가 전화를 한 목적을 고르세요.

① 파티를 취소하려고

② 파티에 초대하려고

③ 장소를 바꾸려고

④ 주소를 물어보려고

⑤ 우체국에 함께 가려고

4 대화를 듣고, Tom이 전화를 건 목적을 고르세요.

① 시험공부를 방해하려고

② 시험범위를 정정해 주려고

③ 숙제가 무엇인지 물어보려고

④ 시험 공부한 것을 자랑하려고

⑤ 영어숙제를 하지 않아도 된다고 말하려고

Part 5   심정

Type 1 대화 듣고, 심정 고르기

대화를 듣고, 남자의 심정으로 가장 적절한 것을 고르시오.

① proud

② angry

③ sad

④ bored

⑤ disappointed

Script

W What did you do yesterday?

M Jaemin and I visited an orphanage in my neighborhood.

W What did you do there?

M We played sports with the children and helped them clean their rooms. I think it's a good thing to do and **I take pride in the work I did.**

정답 ①

해설 남자는 보육원에서 봉사를 하고 자신이 한 일을 자랑스러워하고 있다.

해석

여 너 어제 뭐했어?

남 재민이와 나는 이웃에 있는 고아원을 방문했어.

여 거기에서 무엇을 했는데?

남 아이들하고 운동을 하고 아이들이 방을 청소하는 것을 도와줬어. 좋은 일을 한 것 같아. 그리고 내가 한 일이 자랑스러워.

Tip 긍정적 감정과 관련 표현

긍정적 감정

comfortable 편안한	curious 호기심이 많은	excited 신이 난	happy 행복한	joy 기쁨
pleasant 유쾌한	proud 자랑스러운	satisfied 만족한	thankful 감사하는	proud 자랑스러운

관련 표현

- I'll give you a ride. I think you can make it then. 내가 태워 줄게. 그러면 시간 안에 도착할 수 있을 것 같아.
- I jumped for joy. 나는 기뻐서 펄쩍 뛰었어.
- I can't wait for the next game against the USA. 미국과 하는 다음 경기를 빨리 보고 싶어.

다음을 듣고, 남자의 심경을 가장 잘 나타낸 것을 고르세요.

① proud

② happy

③ lonely

④ nervous

⑤ relaxed

Script

M I happened to get two free tickets for the musical. I didn't want to miss such a good chance, so I asked Sally to see it with me. It starts at seven o'clock tonight, and we were supposed to meet at 6:30 in front of the theater. However, it's already 6:45 and Sally hasn't come yet. She called me to say she is coming, but **I'm afraid that she will not be here in time.**

해석

남 나에게 우연히 공짜 뮤지컬 표 두 장이 생겼습니다. 나는 이렇게 좋은 기회를 놓치기 싫어서 Sally에게 함께 보자고 했습니다. 뮤지컬은 오늘 밤 7시에 시작합니다. 우리는 6시 30분에 극장 앞에서 만나기로 했습니다. 하지만, 벌써 6시 45분인데 Sally는 아직 오지 않았습니다. 그녀가 오고 있다고 전화를 했지만, 나는 그녀가 시간 안에 도착할 수 없을 것 같아 걱정입니다.

정답 ④

해설 남자는 Sally가 만나기로 한 시간이 지났는데도 도착하지 않아서, 그녀가 제 시간에 도착할 수 없을 것 같아 불안해하고 있다.

Tip 부정적 감정과 관련 표현

부정적 감정

afraid 두려운	angry 화가 난	ashamed 수치스러운	bored 지루한
disappointed 실망한	frustrated 좌절한	jealous 시기하는	lonely 외로운
nervous 불안한	sad 슬픈	scared 겁이 난	tired 피곤한
upset 화가 난	worried 걱정하는		

관련 표현

- What's wrong? 무엇이 문제야?
- I'm afraid I have to stay home all day then. 하루 종일 집에 있어야 할 것 같아서 걱정돼.
- I wish I had seen it. 봤으면 좋았을 텐데.
- It seems like I lost everything. 모든 것을 다 잃은 것 같아.
- My neighbors upstairs make a lot of noise every night. 우리 위층에서 매일 밤 시끄럽게 해.
- That's a shame. 그거 유감이야.
- I was really upset. 나 정말 화났어.
- I don't know why she was so careless. 나는 그녀가 왜 그렇게 부주의한지 모르겠어.
- I won't talk to my sister for a while! 나는 한동안 내 동생과 말하지 않을 거야!
- His singing makes me crazy. 그의 노래가 나를 미치게 해.

1 다음을 듣고, Andy의 심경으로 가장 알맞은 것을 고르세요.

① scared

② angry

③ tired

④ happy

⑤ excited

2 대화를 듣고, 여자의 심정을 가장 잘 나타낸 것을 고르세요.

① angry

② ashamed

③ pleasant

④ happy

⑤ satisfied

3 대화를 듣고, 남자의 심정으로 알맞은 것을 고르세요.

① 지루함

② 우울함

③ 초조함

④ 불쾌함

⑤ 아쉬움

4 대화를 듣고, 남자의 기분으로 알맞은 것을 고르세요.

① bored

② lonely

③ excited

④ satisfied

⑤ frustrated

Part 6   장소

🔍 기출엿보기

Type 1   대화하는 장소 고르기

대화를 듣고, 두 사람이 대화하는 장소를 고르세요.

① bank

② hotel

③ airport

④ train station

⑤ travel agency

Script

M   Hi, Janet! What a surprise! I didn't expect to see you here. What are you doing?

W   Hi, David. I'm waiting for my sister, Kate. **She's coming back from New York today.** What are you doing?

M   **I'm leaving for Japan.** My uncle in Tokyo wants me to visit him.

W   Oh, does he? **When does your flight leave?**

M   I only have ten minutes. I have to go now.

W   Okay. Have a nice trip, David.

M   Thanks. I'll call you when I get home. Take care.

해석

남   안녕, Janet! 뜻밖인걸! 너를 여기서 보리라고는 생각하지 못했어. 무엇을 하고 있는 거야?

여   안녕, David. 내 동생 Kate를 기다리고 있어. 오늘 뉴욕에서 돌아오거든. 너는 무엇을 하고 있는 거야?

남   나는 일본으로 떠날 거야. 도쿄에 있는 삼촌이 내가 오길 바라셔서.

여   아, 그래? 비행기는 언제 출발하니?

남   10분밖에 안 남았어. 지금 가야 해.

여   알았어. 여행 잘해, David.

남   고마워. 집에 돌아오면 전화할게. 잘 지내.

정답   ③

해설   여자는 뉴욕에서 돌아오는 동생을 마중 나왔고, 남자는 삼촌을 방문하러 일본에 가는 길이므로 공항(airport)이라는 것을 알 수 있다.

Tip 🌿 비행 관련 표현

- I'd like to make a reservation for a round-trip ticket to L.A. L.A.행 왕복표를 예약하고 싶어요.
- When would you like to leave? 언제 출발하고 싶으세요?
- All flights are booked. 모든 비행편이 다 예약되었습니다.
- Which class would you like? 어떤 등급의 좌석을 원하세요?
- Economy class and a window seat, please. 이코노미에 창가 좌석으로 주세요.
- How much does it cost? 얼마인가요?
- Would that be one-way or round-trip? 편도인가요, 아니면 왕복인가요?

대화를 듣고, 남자가 지난 주말에 간 장소를 고르시오.

① Theater

② Library

③ Museum

④ Swimming pool

⑤ Amusement park

Script

W Did you have a good time last weekend?

M Yes, I did.

W What did you do?

M I rode a roller coaster and a merry-go-round with my brother. I also enjoyed water rides and train rides.

W What else?

M Then I saw a dolphin show and ate hamburgers and lots of ice cream.

정답 ⑤

해설 남자와 남동생이 롤러코스터와 회전목마 등의 놀이기구를 탄 것으로 보아 그들은 놀이동산(amusement park)에 다녀온 것임을 알 수 있다.

해석

여 지난 주말에 좋은 시간을 보냈니?

남 응.

여 무엇을 했어?

남 남동생과 롤러코스터와 회전목마를 탔어. 물 위로 다니는 놀이기구랑 트랙 위로 다니는 놀이기구도 재미있었어.

여 그 밖에는?

남 그러고 나서 돌고래 쇼를 보고 햄버거를 먹었어. 아이스크림도 많이 먹었어.

Tip 장소 관련 표현

bus
- I have to get off at the next stop. 다음 정류장에서 내려야 해요.
- Please take my seat. 제 자리에 앉으세요.

bank
- I want to put some money in my savings account. 제 저축 계좌에 돈을 좀 넣고 싶어요.
- I'd like to open an account. 계좌를 하나 개설하고 싶어요.
- How much money would you like to deposit? 얼마나 저축하시겠어요?
- How much interest do you offer? 이자율이 얼마나 되나요?

restaurant
- I'd like to reserve a table for dinner tomorrow. 내일 저녁 식사 예약을 하고 싶어요.

library
- Where can I find books about world culture? 세계 문화에 관련된 책을 어디에서 찾을 수 있을까요?
- How many books can I check out? 책을 몇 권이나 대출할 수 있나요?
- How long can I keep them? 며칠 동안 대출할 수 있나요?

1 다음을 듣고, 두 사람이 대화하는 장소로 알맞은 것을 고르세요.

① 학교

② 병원

③ 놀이방

④ 우체국

⑤ 헬스클럽

2 다음을 듣고, 대화가 이루어지는 장소를 고르세요.

① 학교

② 식당

③ 극장

④ 터미널

⑤ 비행기

3 대화를 듣고, 두 사람이 대화하는 장소를 고르세요.

① 공항

② 은행

③ 우체국

④ 여행사

⑤ 경찰서

4 다음을 듣고, 대화가 일어나고 있는 장소로 가장 알맞은 것을 고르세요.

① fitness club

② concert hall

③ travel agency

④ computer class

⑤ information center

Part 7   수치 계산

🔍 기출엿보기

Type 1 지불해야 할 금액 고르기 Ⅰ

대화를 듣고, 남자가 지불해야 할 총 금액을 고르세요.

① $2   ② $3   ③ $4   ④ $5   ⑤ $6

Script

M   I want to rent this DVD.

W   Do you have a membership card?

M   Yes. Here it is. How much is it?

W   This is a new movie, so **it's four dollars**. Just a moment.
You didn't pay the late fee last time. **That's two more dollars.**

M   Oh, really? Here you go.

해석

남 이 DVD를 빌리고 싶어요.

여 회원 카드가 있으세요?

남 네. 여기요. 얼마죠?

여 이것은 새로 나온 영화라서 4달러예요. 잠깐만요. 지난번에 연체료를 내지 않으셨네요. 2달러 더 내셔야 해요.

남 아, 정말요? 여기 있어요.

정답 ⑤

해설   새로 나온 영화 DVD를 빌리는 돈이 4달러, 연체료가 2달러이므로 총 6달러를 내야 한다. 수치를 계산하는 문제는 주로 들리는 숫자가 답이 되는 경우보다 두 수치를 더하거나 빼는 등 계산을 해야 하는 문제가 주로 출제되므로 주의해야 한다.

Tip ✄ 수치 관련 표현

❖ M That's 100 dollars. I can't afford to buy it. 그것은 100달러예요. 나는 그것을 살 만한 여유가 없어요.
    W I know. But it's forty percent off. 알아요. 하지만, 40퍼센트 할인이에요.
     해설 100달러에서 40퍼센트를 할인한다고 했으므로 60달러이다.

❖ W It was 400 dollars, but it's on sale now for 10% off. 그것은 400달러지만 지금은 10퍼센트 할인을 해.
     해설 400달러에서 10퍼센트 할인한다고 했으므로 360달러이다.

❖ M That'll be 30 dollars. 그것은 30달러입니다.
    W Oh, it's too expensive. 아, 너무 비싸네요.
    M You can send it at half the price by regular parcel service. 일반 소포로 보내면 반값에 보내실 수 있어요.
     해설 일반 소포는 반값이므로 15달러이다.

❖ M He was 155 centimeters. 그는 155센티미터였어.
    W How much taller did he get? 그가 얼마나 더 컸니?
    M Ten centimeters in only two months. 겨우 두 달이었는데 10센티미터나 컸어.
     해설 155센티미터에서 10센티미터 더 컸으므로 남자는 165센티미터이다.

대화를 듣고, 이어서 들려주는 질문에 대한 알맞은 답을 고르세요.

FOOD		DRINKS	
Pizza	$3	Milk	$1
Chicken	$4	Soda	$1
Spaghetti	$5	Shake	$2

① $7   ② $8   ③ $9   ④ $10   ⑤ $11

Script

M Are you ready to order?

W Yes. **We'll both have the chicken.**

M Would you like something to drink?

W We'll have **a soda** and **a shake**, please.

M **Two chicken, a soda and a shake.**

W Right.

질문입니다. **How much does the woman have to pay?**

해석

남 주문하시겠어요?

여 네. 우리 둘 다 치킨으로 할게요.

남 음료는 무엇으로 하시겠어요?

여 소다 하나하고 셰이크 하나 주세요.

남 치킨 두 개, 소다 하나, 셰이크 하나입니다.

여 맞아요.

질문입니다. 여자는 얼마를 지불해야 합니까?

정답 ⑤

해설 치킨 두 개가 8달러, 소다 하나가 1달러, 셰이크 하나가 2달러이므로 총 11달러를 지불해야 한다.

Tip 수치 관련 표현

◉ W He made 3,000 won for washing his father's car, and he received another 2,000 won from his mother for doing the dishes. But he needs 5,000 won more to buy the CD.
아버지의 차를 세차하고 삼천 원을 벌었고, 설거지를 하고 어머니에게 이천 원을 받았다. 하지만 CD를 사려면 아직도 오천 원이 더 필요하다.
질문입니다. **How much is the CD?** CD는 얼마입니까?
해설 아버지에게 삼천 원, 어머니에게 이천 원을 받았는데 아직도 오천 원이 부족하므로 CD는 만 원이다.

◉ M They are 10,000 won per box, but we're selling them at 20% off to celebrate our grand opening.
한 상자에 만 원이지만, 개업 축하를 기념해서 20퍼센트 할인해서 팔고 있어요.
W That's great. I'll take one box, please. 좋네요. 한 상자 주세요.
질문입니다. **How much will the woman pay for the tomatoes?** 여자는 토마토 값으로 얼마를 지불할까요?
해설 한 상자에 만 원이지만 20퍼센트 할인한다고 했으므로 팔천 원을 지불할 것이다.

1 대화를 듣고, 여자가 주문할 구두의 가격을 고르세요.

① $50

② $70

③ $85

④ $100

⑤ $115

2 대화를 듣고, 여자가 지불해야 할 금액을 고르세요.

Regular Mail		Express Mail	
Weight	Cost	Weight	Cost
Up to 1 kg	$5	Up to 1 kg	$15
Up to 2 kg	$10	Up to 2 kg	$20
Up to 3 kg	$15	Up to 3 kg	$25

① $5　　② $10　　③ $15　　④ $20　　⑤ $25

3 다음을 듣고, 두 사람이 토요일 공연에 가고자 할 때 지불해야 할 비용을 고르세요.

① $40

② $50

③ $60

④ $70

⑤ $80

4 대화를 듣고, 남자가 지불할 금액을 고르세요.

① 20,000원

② 30,000원

③ 40,000원

④ 50,000원

⑤ 60,000원

Part 8 날짜, 시간

🔍 기출엿보기

`Type 1` 행사나 사건이 있었던 날짜 고르기

대화를 듣고, 영어 팝송 대회 날짜를 고르세요.

SEPTEMBER, 2006

SUN	MON	TUE	WED	THU	FRI	SAT
					1	2
3	4	5	6	7	8	9
10	11	12	13	14	15	16
17	18	19	20	21	22	23
24	25	26	27	28	29	30

① September 6   ② September 13   ③ September 20

④ September 23   ⑤ September 27

Script

W Hey, Jimmy. I heard your school will hold an English Pop Song Contest this month.

M Yes. It will be a very big contest. We've practiced a lot.

W That sounds very interesting. I really want to see it. When will it be?

M Today is Wednesday, September 13th. It will be two weeks from today.

정답 ⑤

해설 오늘이 9월 13일 수요일이고 오늘부터 두 주 후니까 9월 27일 수요일에 영어 팝송 대회가 있을 것이다.

해석

여 안녕, Jimmy. 너희 학교에서 이번 달에 영어 팝송 대회가 있을 거라고 들었어.

남 응. 정말 큰 대회가 될 거야. 우리는 연습을 많이 하고 있어.

여 정말 재미있을 것 같구나. 나도 정말 보고 싶어. 언제야?

남 오늘이 9월 13일 수요일이지. 오늘부터 두 주 후에 있을 거야.

Tip 🌿 날짜 표현

❖ W It's April seventh, but the party will be four days later, on Saturday, April eleventh.
4월 7일이지만, 파티는 4일 후인 4월 11일 토요일에 있을 거야.
해설 파티가 열릴 날은 4월 11일이다.

❖ W Next Friday is her last day at this school. How about seventh period this Friday?
다음 주 금요일이 그녀가 이 학교에서 지내는 마지막 날이야. 이번 금요일 7교시에 하는 게 어때?

❖ M That's too soon. I think next Thursday is better because we also need some time to prepare.
그건 너무 빨라. 우리가 준비하는 데도 시간이 좀 필요할 테니까 내 생각엔 다음 목요일이 더 나을 것 같아.
해설 송별회는 다음 목요일에 있을 것이다.

대화를 듣고, 현재의 시각을 고르세요.

① 2:40

② 2:50

③ 3:00

④ 3:10

⑤ 3:20

Script

W Excuse me, but may I ask you a question?

M Sure. What is it?

W How often does the bus come here?

M **Every twenty minutes.**

W **What time was the last bus?**

M **It was at 2:50.**

W Thank you. **I only have ten more minutes to wait.**

해석

여 실례지만, 뭐 하나만 물어봐도 될까요?

남 물론이죠. 뭐죠?

여 여기 버스가 얼마나 자주 오나요?

남 20분마다 와요.

여 마지막 버스가 몇 시에 왔어요?

남 2시 50분이었어요.

여 감사합니다. 10분만 더 기다리면 되겠군요.

정답 ③

해설 마지막 버스가 2시 50분이었고, 버스는 20분마다 오는 데 10분만 더 기다리면 된다고 했으므로 지금은 3시이다.

Tip 시간 표현

• Ten to nine? You mean eight fifty. 9시 10분전이라고? 8시 50분이라는 말이구나.

• Let's meet at 4:30. 4시 30분에 보자.

• It's exactly twenty minutes to six. 정확히 6시 20분전이야.

• How about thirty minutes later? I have to finish my homework first. 30분 더 후에 보는 게 어때? 숙제를 먼저 끝내야 하거든.
    해설 4시 30분에서 30분 후에 보자고 했으므로 5시에 만날 것이다.

시간 읽는 방법

• ten forty five = a quarter to[before] eleven : 10시 45분

• eleven fifteen = a quarter past[after] eleven : 11시 15분

• seven thirty = half past seven : 7시 30분

1 대화를 듣고, 오늘이 무슨 요일인지 고르세요.

Science Expo

Day	Open	Closed
Mon	Closed	
Tue~Fri	9:00 a.m.	6:00 a.m.
Sat	10:00 a.m.	3:00 a.m.
Sun	10:00 a.m.	2:00 a.m.

① 월요일　　② 화요일　　③ 목요일　　④ 토요일　　⑤ 일요일

2 대화를 듣고, 남자가 한국을 떠나는 날짜를 고르세요.

① July 1st

② July 25th

③ July 31st

④ August 1st

⑤ August 2nd

3 대화를 듣고, 두 사람이 보려고 하는 영화의 시작 시각을 고르세요.

① 6시

② 6시 30분

③ 7시

④ 7시 30분

⑤ 8시

4 다음을 듣고, 비행기의 도착 시간을 고르세요.

① 10:20 a.m.

② 10:30 p.m.

③ 10:50 a.m.

④ 11:00 a.m.

⑤ 12:00 p.m.

Part 9 이유, 의도

🔍 기출엿보기

Type 1 이유 고르기

대화를 듣고, 남자가 우표를 수집하는 이유를 고르세요.

① 해외여행을 할 수 있기 때문에
② 우표는 값이 비싸지 않기 때문에
③ 외국친구를 사귈 수 있기 때문에
④ 우표를 통해서 문화를 알 수 있기 때문에
⑤ 인터넷에서 우표를 구입할 수 있기 때문에

Script

W Students, today we're going to talk about hobbies.

M Let me go first. I collect stamps.

W **Do you have any special reasons for that?**

M Yes. **It is because stamps show cultures and traditions of different countries.**

W Where and how do you get them?

M I buy some over the Internet and I also get them from my pen pals.

W I hope you become a world famous stamp collector some day.

해석

여 여러분. 오늘은 취미에 대해서 이야기해 볼 거예요.

남 제가 먼저 할게요. 저는 우표를 모아요.

여 우표를 모으는 특별한 이유가 있나요?

남 네. 우표가 다른 나라의 문화와 전통을 보여 주기 때문이에요.

여 어디서, 어떻게 우표를 얻나요?

남 인터넷으로 사기도 하고, 펜팔 친구들에게 서 얻기도 해요.

여 언젠가 세계적으로 유명한 우표 수집가가 되기를 바라요.

정답 ④

해설 남자는 우표를 통해서 다른 나라의 문화와 전통을 알 수 있어서 우표를 모은다고 했다.

> **Tip** 🌿 이유 관련 표현
>
> ◉ M Is there a problem? 무슨 문제가 있나요?
>   W Yes. We can only give you a refund within 30 days. 네. 저희는 30일 안에만 환불을 해 드리거든요.
>   해설 환불기간이 지나서
>
> ◉ M Why did you do that? 왜 그랬어?
>   W Well, I started to write about mountain climbing, but I didn't think it was very interesting.
>   음. 등산에 관해 글을 쓰기 시작했는데 별로 재미가 없는 것 같아서.
>   해설 흥미롭지 못해서
>
> ◉ W Why? 왜?
>   M I'll be competing in the Golden Bell Quiz Show during the school festival. I'll be representing my homeroom class. So, I want to check out some science books.
>   학교 축제 기간에 골든벨 퀴즈쇼에 나갈 거야. 내가 우리 반 대표거든. 그래서 과학책을 좀 대출하려고.
>   해설 과학책을 대출하려고
>
> ◉ M What's wrong with it, ma'am? 무슨 문제라도 있나요, 부인?
>   W This shirt is nice, but one button is missing. Can I exchange it for another one?
>   이 셔츠는 좋은데, 단추가 하나 없어졌어요. 다른 것으로 교환할 수 있을까요?
>   해설 셔츠를 교환하려고

대화를 듣고, 남자가 여자에게 말하는 의도를 고르세요.

① 기원

② 조언

③ 칭찬

④ 요청

⑤ 주문

Script

W You're in pretty good shape. What do you do for exercise?

M Well, I start with a warm-up that stretches my muscles. Then, I usually jog for one hour, and then, I lift weights for thirty minutes.

W Wow! You really like to stay in shape.

M Sure. How about you?

W I don't exercise at all. I just watch TV.

M That's not good. **If I were you, I would exercise more.** A good workout will improve your health.

정답 ②

해설 "내가 너라면 운동을 더 하겠다."라는 가정법 문장을 이용하여 상대방에게 조언을 하고 있다.

해석

여 너 몸매가 꽤 좋아 보인다. 무슨 운동을 해?

남 음. 근육을 이완시켜 주는 준비운동으로 시작해서 보통 한 시간 동안 달리기를 해. 그러고 나서 30분 동안 역기 들기를 해.

여 와! 너 정말로 몸매를 유지하고 싶구나.

남 물론이지. 너는 어때?

여 나는 운동을 전혀 안 해. 나는 그냥 텔레비전을 봐.

남 그건 좋지 않아. 내가 너라면 운동을 더 하겠다. 충분한 운동이 건강을 좋아지게 해 줄 거야.

Tip 의도 표현

충고

• You'd better place the computer in the living room where you can keep an eye on them.
그들을 잘 살펴볼 수 있도록 컴퓨터를 거실에 놓는 것이 좋겠어.

• I'm afraid it may have harmful effects. I think it's better to drink a lot of fresh water.
해로운 영향을 끼칠 것 같아 걱정돼. 내 생각에 신선한 물을 많이 마시는 것이 더 좋을 것 같아.

감사

• Thanks a million. You're a life saver. 정말 고마워. 너는 생명의 은인이야.

용서

• Don't worry about it. I'm glad you made it. 걱정하지 마. 네가 와서 기뻐.

1 대화를 듣고, 남자가 어머니를 도우려는 이유를 고르세요.

① 칭찬을 들으려고

② 필요한 돈을 얻으려고

③ MP3 플레이어를 사려고

④ 숙제를 하지 않으려고

⑤ 엄마를 놀라게 해 주려고

2 대화를 듣고, 남자가 늦은 이유를 고르세요.

① He got on the wrong bus.

② He walked all the way from his house.

③ He had trouble reading maps.

④ He forgot about the appointment.

⑤ He missed his stop.

3 대화를 듣고 남자의 마지막 말에 담긴 의도를 고르세요.

① 사과

② 용서

③ 주의

④ 칭찬

⑤ 변명

4 대화를 듣고 여자가 하는 말의 의도를 고르세요.

① 거절

② 충고

③ 지시

④ 소개

⑤ 감사

Part 10 할일, 한일

🔍 기출엿보기

Type 1 할 일 고르기

대화를 듣고, 남자가 일요일에 할 일을 고르세요.

① 등산하는 시각장애인 안내   ② 가난한 사람 돕기

③ 간호사 시험공부   ④ 노벨 수상자 조사

⑤ 테레사 수녀에 대한 조사

Script

W Are you interested in helping people?

M Sure. I respect Mother Teresa. She spent her whole life helping the poor.

W Wasn't she the nun who received the Nobel Peace Prize?

M Yes, she was. I think she was one of the greatest heroines of our day.

W Did you know that I'm a volunteer for the Eyes for the Blind Club? **Some blind students will go hiking this Sunday. Can you volunteer to guide them?**

M I'd love to. It sounds great.

해석

여 너는 사람들을 돕는 데 관심이 있니?

남 물론이지. 나는 테레사 수녀님을 존경해. 자신의 일생을 가난한 사람들을 도우면서 보내셨잖아.

여 노벨 평화상을 받은 수녀님이 아니니?

남 맞아. 요즘 세상에 가장 훌륭한 영웅 중 한 명이었다고 생각해.

여 너 내가 The Eyes for the Blind Club (맹인들의 눈이 되어 주는 모임)에서 자원봉사를 한다는 것을 알고 있니? 이번 일요일에 시각 장애가 있는 학생들이 등산을 할 거야. 그들을 안내해 주는 자원봉사를 해 줄 수 있니?

남 하고 싶어. 좋을 것 같아.

정답 ①

해설 시각 장애가 있는 학생들이 도보 여행을 가는 데 안내를 해 줄 것이다.

Tip 🌿 할 일 관련 표현

◈ M Do you mind if I help you practice? I love that play. I can be your partner, the prince.
내가 너의 연습을 도와주면 어때? 나는 그 연극을 정말 좋아해. 내가 너의 상대역인 왕자 역할을 해 줄 수 있어.

W Sure. That will be a great help. 그래. 그러면 정말 도움이 될 거야.
해설 연극 연습을 할 것이다.

◈ M Mom, I don't feel well today. I have a sore throat. 엄마, 오늘 몸이 안 좋아요. 목이 아파요.

W Let's see. Oh, you have a fever. You need to see a doctor. I'll make an appointment for you. But first, I'd better call your homeroom teacher.
어디 보자. 이런, 열이 있구나. 병원에 가야겠다. 내가 예약을 할게. 하지만 먼저 담임 선생님께 전화를 걸어야겠다.
해설 엄마는 담임 선생님께 전화를 걸 것이다.

◈ W I'll make you an extra big dinner this evening, OK? 너를 위해 저녁을 거하게 준비할게, 알았지?

M Wonderful. 좋아요.
해설 저녁 식사 준비를 할 것이다.

대화를 듣고, 여자가 주말에 한 일을 순서대로 나열한 것을 고르세요.

(A)   (B)   (C)

① (A)-(B)-(C)

② (A)-(C)-(B)

③ (C)-(A)-(B)

④ (C)-(B)-(A)

⑤ (B)-(A)-(C)

Script

M How was your weekend?

W It was great.

M What did you do?

W On Saturday morning I **went hiking** in the mountains with my dad. After that, we **had a great dinner** at a Chinese restaurant. On Sunday I stayed home and **watched television**.

M Mountain, dinner, and television? Sounds great!

정답 ③

해설 산에 올라가는 그림(C) – 저녁을 먹는 그림(A) – 텔레비전을 보는 그림(B) 순서이다.

해석

남 주말은 어땠어?

여 좋았어.

남 무엇을 했어?

여 토요일 아침에 아빠와 산으로 도보여행을 갔어. 그 후에는 중국집에서 맛있는 저녁을 먹었고, 일요일에는 집에서 텔레비전을 봤어.

남 산에, 저녁에, 텔레비전까지? 굉장하다!

Tip 한 일 관련 표현

◈ M What did you do over the weekend? 주말에 뭐했니?

W I visited a nursing home. I helped elderly people clean their beds. 양로원에 갔었어. 어르신들의 이부자리 청소를 도와드렸어.

해설 여자는 주말에 봉사활동을 했다.

◈ W Did you enjoy yourself at the baseball game on Saturday? 토요일에 야구 경기는 재미있었니?

M Unfortunately, I couldn't go to the game. I had to plant trees. 운이 나쁘게도 경기에 갈 수 없었어. 나무를 심어야 했거든.

해설 남자는 토요일에 나무를 심었다.

1 대화를 듣고, 남자가 여자에게 부탁한 일을 고르세요.

①   ②   ③

④   ⑤

2 대화를 듣고, 남자가 다음에 할 행동으로 가장 알맞은 것을 고르세요.

① 친구에게 연락한다.

② 다음 주까지 기다린다.

③ 다른 서점으로 간다.

④ 전화번호부를 찾아본다.

⑤ 이름과 전화번호를 남긴다.

3 대화를 듣고, 여자가 내일 할 일이 <u>아닌</u> 것을 고르세요.

① 집 청소

② 치과 방문

③ 숙제 도와주기

④ 피아노 연습

⑤ 인터넷 게임

4 대화를 듣고, 두 사람이 제일 먼저 할 일로 알맞은 것을 고르세요.

① 영화를 본다.

② 극장 입장권을 산다.

③ 서점에 간다.

④ 아버지 선물을 산다.

⑤ 백화점에 쇼핑을 간다.

Part II 주제, 화제, 속담

🔍 기출엿보기

Type 1 무엇에 대한 설명인지 고르기

다음을 듣고, 무엇에 대한 설명인지 고르시오.

① 냉면   ② 잡채   ③ 식혜   ④ 불고기   ⑤ 비빔밥

Script

M This is considered to be one of the most popular Korean dishes. Its name means **cold noodles**. It is a summer favorite for many Koreans. Thin noodles are served in a **cold beef broth** with **green onions, radishes, pears, cucumbers and boiled egg.** Most Koreans like to add **hot mustard** before eating it. What is this?

해석

남 이것은 한국에서 가장 인기 있는 음식 중 하나로 여겨진다. 이것의 이름은 차가운 면이라는 의미이다. 많은 한국 사람들의 여름철 별미이다. 가느다란 면이 차가운 쇠고기 국물과 파, 무, 배, 오이, 삶은 달걀과 함께 제공된다. 한국 사람들 대부분이 이것을 먹기 전에 겨자를 넣는 좋아한다. 이것은 무엇일까?

정답 ①

해설 차가운 면으로 소고기 국물에, 무, 배, 오이, 삶은 달걀을 곁들여 먹는 여름 음식은 냉면이다. 주제나 화제를 고르는 문제는 전반적인 정보를 모두 듣고 설명하는 바를 이해해야 한다.

Tip 주제, 화제, 소재, 글의 유형

두괄식

W Welcome to the Royal Museum. **I'd like to announce some rules.**
로얄 박물관에 오신 걸 환영합니다. 몇 가지 규칙을 안내해 드리겠습니다.
해설 박물관 이용 규칙을 이야기할 것이다.

소재 파악

W **Yellow dust** from China will hit Korea for the first time this year. **Yellow dust** is carried by strong winds from the Yellow River region and the Gobi desert in China. **The yellow dust** may cause many health problems.
중국에서 온 황사가 올해 처음으로 한국에 나타났습니다. 황사는 중국에 있는 황하와 고비 사막에서 강한 바람에 실려 옵니다. 황사는 많은 건강 문제를 일으킬 수 있습니다.
해설 황사가 직접 언급되어 황사가 소재임을 알 수 있다.

주장

M **We should not drink coffee** because it makes us jittery and we will have trouble studying.
커피는 우리의 신경을 예민하게 만들고, 학습을 방해하므로 마시지 말아야 합니다.
해설 커피를 마시지 말자는 주장이다.

뉴스

M Four bombs rocked London's subway stations and a double-decker bus during the morning rush hour on Thursday. It began at 8:51 a.m. London time. Eyewitnesses say the bombings were so powerful that survivors would be seriously hurt. **This is John Williams, EBS.**
목요일 아침 러시아워 시간에 폭탄 네 개가 영국의 지하철역과 이층 버스를 뒤흔들었습니다. 런던 시간으로 아침 8시 51분에 시작되었습니다. 목격자들은 폭탄이 너무 강력해서 생존자들이 심하게 다쳤을 거라고 말하고 있습니다. EBS, John Williams였습니다
해설 사건에 대해 보고하는 형식으로 어느 방송에 누구라는 정보를 확인함으로써 글의 종류가 뉴스라는 것을 알 수 있다.

대화를 듣고, 남자의 충고를 가장 잘 표현한 속담을 고르세요.

① Walls have ears.

② Like father, like son.

③ Better late than never.

④ Out of sight, out of mind.

⑤ Kill two birds with one stone.

Script

W Mike, **I give up on my science report.**

M Do you mean the report due this Friday?

W Yes. The topic is too difficult for me and I only have two days left.

M Come on! **Give it a try** and you will at least get a C. **If you don't even try, you will fail for sure.**

W But it's too late.

M Don't say that. I'll help you. Let's start right now.

해석

여 Mike. 나 과학 보고서 쓰는 것을 포기했어.

남 이번 금요일까지 해야 하는 보고서를 말하는 거야?

여 응. 나한테는 주제가 너무 어려워. 그리고 이제 겨우 이틀 밖에 안 남았잖아.

남 그러지마! 한 번 해 봐. 최소한 C는 받을 거야. 시도도 하지 않으면 분명 낙제를 할 거야.

여 하지만 너무 늦었어.

남 그런 말 하지 마. 내가 도와줄게. 지금 당장 시작하자.

정답 ③

해설 하지 않는 것보다 늦게라도 하는 것이 낫다는 의미의 속담은 "Better late than never."이다.

Tip 속담

- Pie in the sky. 그림의 떡
- It's a piece of cake. 식은 죽 먹기다.
- Time heals all wounds. 시간이 약이다.
- Well begun is half done. 시작이 반이다.
- Kill two birds with one stone. 일석이조
- Like father, like son. 그 아버지에 그 아들이다.
- Blood is thicker than water. 피는 물보다 진하다.
- Out of sight, out of mind. 눈에서 멀어지면 마음도 멀어진다.
- One picture is worth a thousand words. 백문이 불여일견
- A little knowledge is a dangerous thing. 선무당이 사람 잡는다.
- Don't judge a book by its cover. 겉모습으로 속을 판단하지 마라.
- Too many cooks spoil the broth. 사공이 많으면 배가 산으로 간다.
- Better late than never. 아예 안 하는 것보다 늦게라도 하는 것이 낫다.
- The early bird catches the worm. 일찍 일어나는 새가 벌레를 잡는다.
- Time and tide wait for no man. 시간과 파도는 사람을 기다려주지 않는다.

- Time flies. 세월은 유수와 같다.
- Clothes make the man. 옷이 날개다.
- Seeing is believing. 보는 것이 믿는 것이다.
- Hunger is the best sauce. 시장이 반찬이다.
- Every dog has his day. 쥐구멍에도 볕 들 날이 있다.
- Walls have ears. 낮말은 새가 듣고, 밤말은 쥐가 듣는다.

1 대화를 듣고, 무엇에 관한 내용인지 알맞은 것을 고르세요.

① 독서
② 자연보호
③ 화재예방
④ 에너지절약
⑤ 금연캠페인

2 다음을 듣고, this가 가리키는 것이 무엇인지 고르세요.

① money
② sleep
③ grade
④ health
⑤ beauty

3 대화를 듣고, 상황에 가장 어울리는 속담을 고르세요.

① It's a piece of cake.
② Every dog has his day.
③ Well begun is half done.
④ Too many cooks spoil the broth.
⑤ The early bird catches the worm.

4 다음을 듣고, 내용과 가장 관련 있는 속담을 고르세요.

① Time flies.
② Walls have ears.
③ Clothes make the man.
④ Kill two birds with one stone.
⑤ A little knowledge is a dangerous thing.

Part 12 이어질 응답

🔍 기출엿보기

Type 1 상황 파악 후, 할 말 고르기

다음을 듣고, Peter가 여자에게 할 말로 가장 적절한 것을 고르세요.

① Is anyone sitting here?

② Will you take an exam?

③ Do you like this library?

④ What time shall we make it?

⑤ How long will you stay here?

Script

W Peter went to the library to prepare for his mid-term exam. There were so many people that he couldn't find an empty seat. After he looked around the library for five minutes, he finally found a seat next to a girl. **Peter wanted to make sure that there was no one in that seat. In this situation, what would Peter say to her?**

해석

여 Peter는 중간고사를 준비하러 도서관에 갔다. 사람이 너무 많아서 그는 빈자리를 찾을 수 없었다. 도서관을 5분 동안 돌아다니고 나서, 마침내 한 소녀 옆에 빈자리를 발견했다. Peter는 그 자리가 빈자리인지 확인하고 싶었다. 이 상황에서, Peter는 소녀에게 무엇이라고 말을 할까?

정답 ①

해설 자리 주인이 있는지 물어봐야 하므로 "여기 누구 앉은 사람이 있어요?"라고 묻는 것이 가장 자연스럽다. 비슷한 표현으로 Is this seat taken?(이 자리 주인 있어요?)이 있다.

Tip 🌿 상황 응대 표현

상대방의 말이 잘 들리지 않을 때

• I can't hear you. 잘 안 들려요.

• Can you speak louder? 좀 더 크게 말씀해 주시겠어요?

• Could you say that again? 다시 한 번 말해 주시겠어요?

쇼핑할 때

• I'm just looking around. 그냥 둘러보는 중이에요.

• I'm just browsing. 그냥 구경하는 중이에요.

대화를 듣고, 여자의 말에 이어질 남자의 대답으로 가장 적절한 것을 고르시오.

① Help yourself.

② Where is the restaurant?

③ The prices are good too.

④ It's fifteen minutes away.

⑤ OK. When shall we make it?

Script

W I'm hungry. Are there any nice restaurants nearby?

M What kind of restaurant are you looking for?

W A restaurant with good food and good service.

M There's a very nice restaurant near here called Napoli's.

W What kind of food do they have?

M Italian food. Their food is delicious.

W **How are the prices?**

M _____

해석

여 나 배고파. 근처에 괜찮은 식당이 있니?

남 어떤 식당을 찾는데?

여 음식도 좋고, 서비스도 좋은 식당.

남 이 근처에 Napoli's라는 정말 좋은 식당이 있어.

여 무슨 음식을 파는데?

남 이탈리아 요리. 음식 맛이 좋아.

여 가격은 어때?

남 _____

정답 ③

해설 "가격은 어때?"라고 물었으므로 "가격도 괜찮아."라는 대답이 가장 자연스럽다.

Tip 자연스러운 응답

◈ W OK. I'll help you. 알았어. 내가 도와줄게.
  M I appreciate it. 고마워.
  해설 도와주겠다고 했으므로 고맙다는 응답이 자연스럽다.

◈ W I was ten minutes late because there was a car accident, so I didn't have enough time to finish the exam.
  차 사고가 나서 10분 늦었고, 그래서 기말시험은 보는 데 시간이 충분하지 않았어.
  M Sorry to hear that. 그렇게 됐다니 안 됐다.
  해설 안 좋은 상황을 겪었다는 이야기를 들었으므로 그렇게 되서 안됐다는 응답이 자연스럽다.

◈ M How long is the flight? 비행은 얼마나 걸려?
  W It's about 45 minutes. 약 45분 정도야.
  해설 비행이 얼마나 걸리는지 물었으므로 걸리는 시간을 응답해 주는 것이 가장 자연스럽다. 의문사를 주의 깊게 들어야 한다.

◈ W Can I get you something to drink before you order? 주문하시기 전에 마실 것을 가져다드릴까요?
  M Coke, please. Thanks. 콜라 주세요. 감사합니다.
  해설 음료를 주문하겠냐고 물을 때 주로 쓰는 표현으로 응답으로는 음료의 이름을 대거나, 또는 No, thanks.(아니오. 고마워요.) 등 거절의 의사를 표현하는 것이 자연스러운 응답이 된다.

1 다음을 듣고, 여자가 소년에게 할 수 있는 알맞은 표현을 고르세요.

① You bet.

② Don't be too sure.

③ That's all my fault.

④ You can count on me.

⑤ Go to the back of the line.

2 다음을 듣고, Sally가 할 말로 가장 알맞은 것을 고르세요.

Sally: _____

① I will buy some more.

② I want my money back.

③ Sorry, but I don't like the color.

④ I'm sorry, but these are too big.

⑤ Excuse me, I'm looking for some bed linen.

3 대화를 듣고, 남자의 마지막 말에 대한 여자의 응답으로 가장 적절한 것을 고르시오.

① Of course you can.

② At the library.

③ I like English writing.

④ I'm good at English.

⑤ OK, that's a good idea.

4 대화를 듣고, 여자의 마지막 말에 대한 남자의 응답으로 가장 적절한 것을 고르시오.

① Yes, I do a lot.

② No, I'm just trying.

③ I don't use paper cups.

④ Nature is very important.

⑤ I want many people to do so.

1 ②

Script

W Is your friend flying in from Tokyo?

M Yeah, can you pick her up at the airport this afternoon?

W I don't know if I'll recognize her. What does she look like?

M Well, she's tall and slim. She has long curly hair.

W How old is she?

M She's twenty. I'm sure you'll recognize her.

해석

여 도쿄에서 오는 네 친구가 비행기로 도착하니?

남 응. 오늘 오후에 공항으로 그녀를 데리러 갈 수 있니?

여 내가 그녀를 알아볼 수 있을지 모르겠어. 그녀는 어떻게 생겼니?

남 글쎄, 키가 크고 날씬해. 긴 곱슬머리를 하고 있어.

여 몇 살이야?

남 스무 살이야. 너는 분명히 그녀를 알아볼 수 있을 거야.

2 ⑤

Script

① W The boy is lying in the bathtub.

② W The alarm is set for 9 o'clock.

③ W The boy has short and straight hair.

④ W The pillow has flower prints.

⑤ W The boy is wearing long-sleeved pajamas.

해석

① 여 소년은 욕조 안에 누워 있다.

② 여 알람이 9시 정각에 맞춰져 있다.

③ 여 소년은 짧은 생머리를 하고 있다.

④ 여 베게는 꽃무늬이다.

⑤ 여 소년은 긴팔 잠옷을 입고 있다.

3 ①

Script

[Telephone rings.]

M Hello.

W Hello, Min-ho, what are you doing now?

M Oh, hi, Yoon-jee. I'm watching a football game on TV. It's a great final game.

W Sounds fun. I heard that England and Korea have a big match this afternoon on channel 9. Are you watching that game now?

M Yes, I am.

W By the way, do you have free time tomorrow?

M For what?

W I'd like to go to a concert with you.

M Sure. That sounds great.

해석

남 여보세요.

여 여보세요. 민호야, 너 지금 뭐하니?

남 어, 안녕, 윤지야. 나 텔레비전에서 하는 미식축구를 보고 있어. 대단한 결승전이야.

여 재밌겠다. 영국하고 대한민국하고 오늘 오후에 9번에서 큰 시합이 있을 거라고 들었는데. 너 지금 그 경기를 보고 있는 거야?

남 응. 그래.

여 그런데 너 내일 시간 있니?

남 뭐하게?

여 너랑 콘서트에 가고 싶어서.

남 그래. 재미있겠다.

4 ①

Script

① W Libya is west of Egypt.

② W Egypt is north of Sudan.

③ W Sudan is south of Egypt.

④ W Saudi Arabia is between the Red Sea and Iraq.

⑤ W Yemen is east of Saudi Arabia.

해석

① 여 리비아는 이집트의 동쪽에 있다.

② 여 이집트는 수단의 북쪽에 있다.

③ 여 수단은 이집트의 남쪽에 있다.

④ 여 사우디아라비아는 홍해와 이라크 사이에 있다.

⑤ 여 예멘은 사우디아라비아의 동쪽에 있다.

Part 2

1 ④

Script

① M These cookies are delicious!

  W I'm glad you like them.

② M You're the best friend in the world.

W How nice of you to say so!

③ M Smoking is not good for your health.

W I know, but it's hard to quit.

④ M How often do you watch TV?

W I watch TV in the living room.

⑤ M Can you tell me how to get to the 63 Building?

W Sure. Go straight for three blocks and turn left.

해석

① 남 이 쿠키 맛있다!
여 네가 좋다니 기뻐.

② 남 너는 세상에서 제일 좋은 친구야.
여 그렇게 말해 주니 참 고마워!

③ 남 흡연은 건강에 좋지 않아.
여 나도 알지만 끊기가 힘들어.

④ 남 얼마나 자주 텔레비전을 보니?
여 나는 거실에서 텔레비전을 봐.

⑤ 남 63빌딩에 어떻게 가는지 알려 주시겠어요?
여 물론이죠. 세 블록을 곧장 가셔서 왼쪽으로 도세요.

2 ③

Script

① W How often do you go shopping?

M Once a week.

② W Do you have a stomachache?

M Yes, I ate too much.

③ W When do you get home?

M I get up around six in the morning.

④ W How many hours do you sleep?

M Seven or eight.

⑤ W What do you want to be when you grow up?

M I want to be a scientist.

해석

① 여 얼마나 자주 쇼핑을 가니?
남 일주일에 한 번.

② 여 너 배가 아프니?
남 응. 너무 많이 먹었나 봐.

③ 여 집에 언제 도착해?
남 나는 아침 6시 정도에 일어나.

④ 여 잠을 몇 시간이나 자니?
남 일곱에서 여덟 시간.

⑤ 여 커서 뭐가 되고 싶어?
남 나는 과학자가 되고 싶어.

3 ④

Script

① M What is your favorite hobby?

W I love swimming.

② M Can I try on this shirt?

W Sure, go ahead.

③ M Does this bus go to City Hall?

W No, you should take bus number 301.

④ M How would you like to pay?

W I'll pay with cash.

⑤ M Excuse me, is there a restroom nearby?

W Yes, it's just around the corner.

해석

① 남 가장 좋아하는 취미가 뭐야?
여 나는 수영을 좋아해.

② 남 이 셔츠를 입어 봐도 될까요?
여 그럼요. 입어 보세요.

③ 남 이 버스가 시청에 가나요?
여 아니오. 301번 버스를 타셔야 해요.

④ 남 어떻게 지불하시겠어요?
여 현금으로 낼게요.

⑤ 남 실례지만, 이 근처에 화장실이 있나요?
여 네. 모퉁이를 돌면 바로 있어요.

4

Script

① W How much is the fee?

M It's five dollars for an adult.

② W Where can I find travel books?

M They're on the next shelf.

③ W May I help you?

M I'd like to send this package to Canada.

④ W What's the purpose of your visit?

M I'm here on holiday.

⑤ W How often should I take this medicine?

M Three times a day after meals.

해석

① 여 요금이 얼마예요?
남 성인은 5달러입니다.

② 여 여행 책자를 어디서 찾을 수 있나요?
남 다음 서가에 있습니다.

③ 여 도와드릴까요?
남 캐나다로 이 소포를 보내고 싶어요.

④ 여 이번 방문의 목적이 무엇인가요?
남 휴가차 왔어요.

⑤ 여 이 약을 몇 번 먹어야 하나요?
남 하루에 세 번 식후에 드세요.

Part 3

1 ②

Script

M What is the most difficult part of your job?

W Well, the most difficult part is that people don't always follow the traffic rules.

M What kind of people are they?

W Most often, they are drivers. They don't obey the speed limit, so I have to give them speeding tickets.

해석

남 당신의 일에서 가장 힘든 부분이 무엇입니까?

여 글쎄요. 가장 힘든 것은 사람들이 항상 교통 규칙을 잘 지키는 것은 아니라는 거예요.

남 그 사람들은 어떤 사람들이죠?

여 대부분은 운전자들이죠. 제한 속도를 지키지 않아서 속도위반 딱지를 부과해야 해요.

2 ①

Script

W Good evening! Now it's time to cook with Jim. Hi, Jim!

M Good evening! Welcome to Jim's Kitchen!

W What are you going to make today?

M I'd like to make "Mushroom Stew."

W Let's start.

M Today I'll use only the finest and freshest ingredients.

해석

여 안녕하세요! 자, Jim과의 요리 시간입니다. 안녕하세요, Jim!

남 안녕하세요! Jim's Kitchen에 오신 걸 환영합니다.

여 오늘은 무엇을 만들어 볼까요?

남 '버섯전골'을 만들어 보겠습니다.

여 시작하시죠.

남 오늘은 가장 좋고, 가장 신선한 재료만을 사용할 거예요.

3 ③

Script

M You are Sori Kim, aren't you?

W Yes, I am.

M Wow! This is unbelievable. I'm so pleased to see you. I'm your biggest fan.

W Thanks a lot.

M I've seen all of your movies. You're even prettier in person than in the movies. Can I take a picture with you?

W Of course. My pleasure.

해석

남 당신이 김소리 씨인가요, 그렇죠?

여 네, 맞아요.

남 와! 믿을 수가 없군요. 당신을 만나게 되어 정말 기쁩니다. 저는 당신의 열렬한 팬이에요.

여 정말 감사합니다.

남 당신의 영화는 다 봤어요. 영화보다 실물이 훨씬 예쁘시네요. 함께 사진을 찍어도 될까요?

여 물론이죠. 기꺼이.

4 ③

Script

M Ladies and gentlemen, please look around our city. Are you satisfied with what you see? Don't you want a healthier and safer environment? There is an answer! On this coming election day, vote for me. Please remember my name! I'm John Smith. The future of our city depends on your decision.

해석

남 신사, 숙녀 여러분, 우리 도시를 좀 둘러보십시오. 지금 보고 계신 것에 만족하십니까? 더 건강하고 더 안전한 환경을 원하지는 않으십니까? 해결책이 있습니다! 다가오는 이번 선거에서 저를 뽑아 주십시오. 제 이름을 기억해 주십시오! 저는 John Smith입니다. 우리 도시의 미래가 여러분의 결정에 달려 있습니다.

Part 4

1 ⑤

Script

[Telephone rings.]

W Customer Service Center, how can I help you?

M My computer is frozen.

W I'm sorry to hear that. Have you tried rebooting your computer?

M Yes, I have tried, but it still keeps freezing.

W Your computer may have a virus. I will send someone to check it. When are you available?

M Tomorrow morning.

해석

여 고객 서비스 센터입니다. 무엇을 도와드릴까요?

남 제 컴퓨터가 멈췄어요.

여 그렇게 됐다니 죄송합니다. 컴퓨터를 다시 켜 보셨나요?

남 네, 해 봤어요. 하지만 계속 멈춰요.

여 컴퓨터에 바이러스가 있을 수도 있어요. 확인해보도록 사람을 보내겠습니다. 언제 가능하세요?

남 내일 아침이요.

2 ④

Script

[Telephone rings.]

W Hello.

M Hello. May I speak to Mrs. Baker?

W This is she. Who's calling, please?

M This is Tom's father. Tom has been sick since last night. He has a high fever and a runny nose, too.

W It sounds like he has a bad cold.

M I think so, too. I think he'd better stay home today.

W Okay. I hope he gets well soon.

해석

여 여보세요.

남 여보세요. Baker 부인과 통화할 수 있을까요?

여 전데요. 누구 시죠?

남 저는 Tom의 아버지입니다. Tom이 어젯밤부터 아파서요. 고열이 있고 콧물도 계속 나고 있어요.

여 감기가 심한 것 같네요.

남 저도 그렇게 생각해요. 오늘은 집에서 쉬는 게 나을 것 같아서요.

여 알겠습니다. 곧 낫기를 바랄게요.

3 ④

Script

[Telephone rings.]

M Hello. May I speak to Mary?

W Mary speaking.

M Hello, Mary. This is Tom.

W Hi, Tom! Are you coming to my party Friday night?

M Sure. That's why I'm calling. I forgot your address.

W I'm at 38 Washington Road.

M Where is that?

W It's near the Central Post Office.

M Oh, I see. Thanks. See you on Friday.

W Bye.

해석

남 여보세요. Mary와 통화할 수 있을까요?

여 전데요.

남 안녕, Mary. 나 Tom이야.

여 안녕, Tom! 너 금요일 밤 파티에 올 거니?

남 물론이지. 그래서 전화한 거야. 네 주소를 잊어버렸거든.

여 나는 워싱턴 가 38번지에 살아.

남 그게 어디지?

여 중앙 우체국 근처야.

남 아, 알겠어. 고마워. 금요일에 보자.

여 안녕.

4 ②

Script

[Telephone rings.]

W Hello.

M Hello. This is Tom. May I speak to Jane?

W This is Jane. What's up?

M Did you finish studying for the English final exam?

W No, I'm in the middle of doing it now. Why?

M I got a phone call from John and he told me that we don't have to study lessons 1 and 2. We should only study lessons 3 to 5.

W Oh, no! I've just finished studying lessons 1 and 2. You should have called me earlier.

해석

여 여보세요.

남 여보세요. 전 Tom인데요. Jane이랑 통화할 수 있을까요?

여 나 Jane이야. 무슨 일이야?

남 영어 기말 고사 공부를 다 했니?

여 아니. 지금 하는 중이야. 왜?

남 John한테 전화를 받았는데, 1과와 2과는 공부하지 않아도 된다고 그랬어. 3과에서 5과까지만 공부하면 된대.

여 이런! 나 지금 막 1, 2과 공부를 끝냈단 말이야. 네가 좀 더 일찍 전화를 했으면 좋았을 텐데.

Part 5

1 ①

Script

W Andy was sitting in a chair looking around the room. After a while, the dentist came in and sat down next to him. She asked Andy to open his mouth. She looked very kind, so Andy thought it would not hurt much. However, as soon as the dentist pushed something into his mouth, he nearly jumped out of his seat. He held on tightly to the arms of the chair and kept his eyes closed.

해석

여 Andy는 의자에 앉아서 방을 둘러보고 있었다. 잠시 후, 치과의사가 들어와서 그의 옆에 앉았다. 그녀는 Andy에게 입을 벌리라고 했다.

그녀는 매우 친절해 보여서 Andy는 많이 아프지 않을 거라고 생각
했다. 하지만, 의사가 무엇인가를 그의 입안으로 밀어 넣자마자 그
는 거의 의자 밖으로 튀어나갈 뻔했다. 그는 팔걸이를 꼭 잡고 눈을
감고 있었다.

2 ①

Script

M I heard you moved last weekend. How's your
new home?

W I thought it was a quiet place, but it isn't.

M Are there any problems?

W Yeah, my neighbors upstairs make a lot of noise
every night.

M What kind of noise?

W Their daughter plays the piano until 10 p.m. and
her little brother runs around all the time.

해석

남 네가 지난 주말에 이사했다고 들었어. 새집은 어때?
여 조용한 곳인 줄 알았는데 아니야.
남 무슨 문제라도 있니?
여 응. 윗집 사람들이 매일 밤마다 너무 시끄러워.
남 뭐가 그렇게 시끄러운데?
여 딸은 밤 열 시까지 피아노를 치고, 그 애의 남동생은 항상 뛰어다녀.

3 ⑤

Script

W Did you see the Seoul International Marathon
yesterday?

M No, I didn't. I usually get up late on Sundays, so
I missed it.

W Yi Bong-ju took first place in the race.

M That's amazing for a thirty-eight year old man.

W It's because he trains hard all the time.

M Oh, I wish I had seen it.

해석

여 너 어제 서울 국제 마라톤 대회를 봤니?
남 아니, 못 봤어. 나는 대개 일요일에는 늦잠을 자서 못 봤어.
여 이봉주가 일등을 했어.
남 서른여덟 살의 노장에게 있어서 대단한 일인데.
여 그가 항상 열심히 훈련을 하기 때문이지.
남 아, 봤으면 좋았을 텐데.

4 ⑤

Script

M Oh, no!

W What's the matter?

M My computer just broke down while I was
working on my project.

W Did you save the files?

M No, I did not think of it. It seems like I lost
everything, and I have to finish this project by
Friday. What am I going to do?

해석

남 이런, 안 돼!
여 무슨 일이야?
남 프로젝트 관련 작업을 하고 있었는데 컴퓨터가 갑자기 고장 났어.
여 파일을 저장했니?
남 아니, 이렇게 될 줄은 몰랐어. 모두 잃어버린 것 같아. 게다가 금요일
까지 이 프로젝트를 끝내야 하는데. 어떻게 해야 하지?

Part 6

1 ②

Script

M When are you expecting the baby?

W Next month. I'm very nervous.

M Don't worry. Everything will be okay.

W Thanks.

M So... what can I do for you? Any problems?

W I want to have a health check-up before I have
my baby.

M Okay. Let's see.

해석

남 아기의 출산 예정일이 언제죠?
여 다음 달이요. 너무 긴장돼요.
남 걱정하지 마세요. 모든 것이 다 잘 될 거예요.
여 고마워요.
남 그럼…… 무엇을 도와드릴까요? 무슨 문제라도 있으신가요?
여 아기를 낳기 전에 건강검진을 받았으면 해서요.
남 알겠습니다. 어디 보죠.

2 ②

Script

M Good evening. How many are there in your
party?

W Six, two adults and four children.

M Then, may I suggest the non-smoking section?

W Sure. I think it will be good to have dinner in
non-smoking environment.

M Please give me a minute to check to see if
there's a table available for you.

W Thanks.

해석

남 안녕하세요. 일행이 몇 분이시죠?
여 여섯 명이요. 어른 둘에 아이 넷이요.
남 그러면, 금연 구역을 권해 드릴까요?
여 네. 금연 환경에서 저녁을 먹는 것이 좋을 것 같네요.
남 제가 테이블이 있는지 확인해 볼 동안 잠시만 기다려 주세요.
여 감사합니다.

3 ③

Script

M Good morning. I want to send a parcel to Australia.

W OK. Do you want to send it by express mail or by standard mail?

M I think I'll send it by express mail. I want it to get there quickly. How much does it cost?

W To Australia by express mail? That will be 9 dollars.

M Here you are.

W Here are your stamps and your change.

M Thank you very much.

해석

남 안녕하세요. 호주로 소포를 보내고 싶어요.
여 알겠습니다. 빠른우편으로 보내시겠어요, 일반 우편으로 보내시겠어요?
남 빠른우편으로 보낼게요. 빨리 도착했으면 좋겠거든요. 얼마인가요?
여 호주로 가는 빠른우편이지요? 9달러입니다.
남 여기 있어요.
여 여기 우표하고 거스름돈입니다.
남 정말 감사합니다.

4 ④

Script

W Hi, everybody. Today we will learn how to use a word processor. Please turn on your computers first. Can you see the Hangeul icon?

M Uh-oh, hold on please. I cannot find it! Where is it?

W Don't worry. Click the start menu and find the Hangeul program.

M OK. Let me see.

W Did you find it?

M Oh, I'm sorry. Could you show me where it is?

W Sure. Let me show you.

해석

여 안녕하세요 여러분. 오늘은 워드 프로세서 사용법을 배울 거예요.

우선 컴퓨터를 켜세요. 한글 아이콘이 보이죠?
남 어, 잠깐만요. 아이콘을 찾을 수가 없어요! 어디에 있죠?
여 걱정 마세요. 시작 메뉴를 클릭하고 한글 프로그램을 찾아보세요.
남 알겠어요. 어디 볼게요.
여 찾았나요?
남 아. 죄송해요. 어디에 있는지 알려 주시겠어요?
여 물론이죠. 제가 찾아 줄게요.

Part 7

1 ③

Script

W Look at this website. I've found the shoes I liked so much.

M Really? Which ones?

W The same shoes we saw at the department store.

M Oh, right. As far as I remember, they were one hundred dollars there.

W Yeah, but they're 15 dollars cheaper on-line!

M Do they have your size?

W Yes, they have them in size 7.

M Then you should buy them.

W Okay. I'll order them right now.

해석

여 이 웹사이트를 좀 봐봐. 내가 정말 마음에 들어 했던 신발을 발견했어.
남 정말? 어떤 건데?
여 우리가 백화점에서 봤던 것과 같은 신발이야.
남 아, 그러네. 내가 기억하기로 백화점에서는 백 달러였어.
여 맞아. 하지만 온라인에서는 15달러가 더 싸!
남 네 사이즈가 있어?
여 응. 7사이즈가 있어.
남 그러면 신발을 사는 게 좋겠다.
여 그래. 지금 당장 주문할 거야.

2 ⑤

Script

M May I help you?

W I'd like to send this box to Chicago.

M Let me check the weight. It's three kilograms.

W Three kilograms!

M Would you like to send it by regular or express mail?

W Express, please.

해석

남 도와드릴까요?

여 이 상자를 시카고로 보내고 싶은데요.
남 무게를 재 볼게요. 3킬로그램이네요.
여 3킬로그램이군요!
남 일반 우편으로 하시겠어요, 아니면 빠른우편으로 하시겠어요?
여 빠른우편으로 해 주세요.

여 오늘 운이 좋으시네요. 두 개를 사시면, 처음 한 개는 사만 원이지만, 두 개째는 50퍼센트 할인해 드려요.
남 알았어요. 잘됐네요! 그러면 두 개 주세요.

3 ③

Script

W Thank you for calling Macquarie Ticketing System. Our automated telephone service is designed to answer your questions quickly and easily. Ticket prices for the musical *Peter Pan* are as follows:

General Admission: Thursday $20, Friday $25, Saturday $30, and Sunday $35. There are no refunds or exchanges.

해석

여 맥쿼리 티켓팅 시스템에 전화를 주셔서 감사합니다. 저희 자동 응답 서비스는 여러분의 질문에 빠르고 쉽게 대답을 하도록 고안되었습니다. 뮤지컬 「피터 팬」의 티켓 가격은 다음과 같습니다.
일반 입장료: 목요일 20달러, 금요일 25달러, 토요일 30달러, 일요일 35달러입니다. 환불과 교환은 불가합니다.

4 ⑤

Script

W May I help you?

M Do you sell computer games?

W Yes, what kind of game are you looking for?

M I'm looking for a soccer game.

W This game is a new one that's very popular right now.

M How much is it?

W 40,000 won.

M 40,000 won? That's too expensive. I need to buy two — one for me and one for my cousin.

W Today is your lucky day. If you buy two, the first one is 40,000 won and the second one is 50% off.

M OK, great! Then I'll take two.

해석

여 도와드릴까요?
남 컴퓨터 게임을 판매하나요?
여 네. 어떤 종류의 컴퓨터 게임을 찾으세요?
남 축구 게임을 찾고 있어요.
여 이 게임은 새로 나온 건데 요새 매우 인기가 있어요.
남 얼마죠?
여 사만 원입니다.
남 사만 원이요? 너무 비싸네요. 제 것과 사촌 것으로 두 개를 사야 하거든요.

Part 8

1 ④

Script

M Where are you going?

W I'm going to the Science Expo to write a paper about it.

M That's cool. But, Jane, it's two-twenty. I think the Expo is closed now.

W Don't worry. I already checked the time. It closes at three o'clock today.

해석

남 어디에 가니?
여 과학 엑스포에 대해 글을 써야 해서 과학 엑스포에 가.
남 멋진데. 하지만 Jane, 지금 2시 20분이야. 내 생각엔 지금쯤이면 엑스포가 끝났을 것 같은데.
여 걱정하지 마. 내가 벌써 시간은 확인했어. 오늘은 3시에 문을 닫아.

2 ④

Script

W When did you come to Korea?

M I came here on the first day of July.

W What is your impression of Korea?

M It is very beautiful and the people are really nice.

W How much longer will you stay?

M I was thinking of staying for twenty days, but my friend's birthday is on July 25th. So, I won't leave until the end of this month.

W You mean you will stay here until July 31st?

M Yes. I'll leave the next day.

해석

여 한국에 언제 오셨나요?
남 저는 이곳에 7월 1일에 왔어요.
여 한국에 대한 인상이 어떠세요?
남 매우 아름답고, 사람들이 정말 친절해요.
여 얼마나 머무르실 건가요?
남 20일 머무를 생각이었지만, 친구 생일이 7월 25일이라서 이번 달 말까지 떠나지 않을 거예요.
여 7월 31일까지 여기 있을 거라는 말이죠?
남 네. 그 다음날 떠날 거예요.

3 ⑤

Script

M If you're free tonight, how about getting together and seeing the new movie, *Finding Neverland*?

W That's a great idea. When does the movie start?

M There are two showings; one at 6 and the other at 8.

W Let's go to the later show.

M Okay. I'll pick you up at 7:30.

해석

남 오늘 밤에 시간 있으면 함께 「네버랜드를 찾아서」라는 새로 나온 영화 보러 갈래?

여 좋은 생각이야. 영화가 언제 시작하는데?

남 하나는 6시, 다른 거는 8시 이렇게 2회 상영해.

여 더 나중에 상영하는 거 보자.

남 알았어. 7시 30분에 데리러 갈게.

4 ④

Script

M Good morning, ladies and gentlemen. This is your captain speaking. Please fasten your seat belts. In ten minutes, we'll be arriving at JFK International Airport. The local time is now 10:50 in the morning. We hope that you enjoyed your flight and hope to see you again soon. Thank you and have a nice day.

해석

남 좋은 아침입니다. 승객 여러분. 저는 여러분의 기장입니다. 안전벨트를 매 주십시오. 우리 비행기는 10분 후에 JKF 국제공항에 도착할 예정입니다. 지금 현지 시간은 아침 10시 50분입니다. 즐거운 비행 하셨기를 바라며 또 다시 뵙기를 바랍니다. 감사합니다. 좋은 하루 보내십시오.

Part 9

1 ②

Script

W I'm so tired of all this housework.

M Mom, you should rest. I'll take care of everything.

W Really? I'm surprised. You're usually so lazy.

M Not anymore. I want to be a good son.

W Hmm. You're up to something, right? What is it?

M Well, I've spent all my money on an MP3 player, but I need to buy a birthday gift for my friend. And...

W OK. I get it.

해석

여 이 모든 집안일이 정말 힘이 드는구나.

남 엄마, 좀 쉬세요. 제가 모든 것을 알아서 할게요.

여 정말? 놀랍구나. 너는 대개 매우 게으른 편이잖아.

남 더 이상은 아니에요. 착한 아들이 되고 싶어요.

여 음. 너 뭔가 있구나. 맞지? 뭔데 그러니?

남 있잖아요. 제가 MP3 플레이어를 사는 데 제 돈을 다 써버렸는데 친구 생일 선물을 사야 해서요. 그래서……

여 알았다. 이해했어.

2 ⑤

Script

M I'm sorry I'm late.

W Why are you late? Did you have any trouble finding this place?

M No. I didn't push the buzzer and the bus passed by my stop. I had to get off at the next stop and walk back.

W That's too bad.

해석

남 늦어서 미안해.

여 왜 늦었어? 여기 찾기가 힘들었니?

남 아니. 벨을 누르지 않아서 버스가 내려야 할 정류장을 지나쳤어. 다음 정류장에서 내려서 걸어 돌아와야 했어.

여 저런.

3 ②

Script

W Hi, Mike. Have you been waiting long?

M Only about ten minutes.

W I'm sorry, but the traffic was terrible.

M Don't worry about it. I'm glad you made it.

해석

여 안녕, Mike. 오래 기다린 거야?

남 약 10분 정도야.

여 미안해. 교통이 나빴었어.

남 걱정 마. 네가 와서 기뻐.

4 ②

Script

W Are you drinking another coffee?

M I love coffee.

W You drink too much coffee. You'd better not drink it.

M Why not? I think coffee is the best when you feel tired.

W I'm afraid it may have harmful effects.
  I think it's better to drink a lot of fresh water.

해석

여 또 커피를 마시는 거야?

남 나는 커피가 정말 좋아.

여 너는 커피를 너무 많이 마시는 것 같아. 지금 그 잔은 마시지 않는 게 좋겠어.

남 왜 마시지 말라는 거야? 피곤할 때는 커피가 제일 좋은 것 같은데.

여 네 건강에 해를 입힐까봐 걱정이 돼서 그래. 내 생각엔 신선한 물을 많이 마시는 것이 더 좋을 것 같아.

Part 10

1 ③

Script

W Hi, honey. Welcome home! How was your camping trip?

M It was great. We took a lot of pictures.

W By the way, what are you going to wear to the concert this evening?

M My new shirt, but I forgot to iron it. Can you please do that for me?

W Well, okay. Let me warm up the iron first. And while I'm waiting, I am going to read today's newspaper.

M Thanks.

해석

여 어서 와요. 여보. 집에 돌아온 것을 환영해요! 캠프는 어땠어요?

남 좋았어요. 사진을 많이 찍었어요.

여 그런데 오늘 저녁 콘서트에는 무엇을 입고 갈 거예요?

남 새로 산 셔츠요. 하지만 깜빡 잊고 다리미질을 하지 않았네요. 다리미질을 좀 해 줄 수 있어요?

여 음. 알았어요. 우선 다리미 예열을 해야겠어요. 그리고 기다리는 동안 오늘 신문을 읽어야겠어요.

남 고마워요.

2 ③

Script

M Excuse me, do you have the social studies textbook?

W I'm sorry. That book is sold out.

M Oh, no. I need that book before the class begins.

W If you leave your name and number, we'll contact you as soon as we get more in.

M When will that be?

W We're expecting more books to come in next week.

M Next week? That will be too late.

W Well, some copies may still be available in another store.

M All right. I'll try another store.

해석

남 실례합니다. 사회 교과서 있나요?

여 죄송합니다. 그 책은 다 팔렸어요.

남 어, 이런. 수업이 시작하기 전에 그 책이 필요한데요.

여 이름하고 전화번호를 남겨주시면 사회 교과서가 더 들어오는 대로 연락드릴게요.

남 그게 언제쯤일 거 같나요?

여 다음 주에 책이 더 들어올 거라고 예상하고 있어요.

남 다음 주요? 그러면 너무 늦을 텐데요.

여 그럼. 다른 가게에 가시면 아직 팔고 있을지도 몰라요.

남 알겠습니다. 다른 가게에 가 볼게요.

3 ⑤

Script

M Do you have any plans for tomorrow?

W Well, I'm going to be really busy all day.

M What are you going to do?

W First, my mom asked me to help her clean the house in the morning, and then I have a dentist appointment at 11:30. After that, I need to meet Jennifer at 3 to help her with her science homework.

M Wow, you are really going to be busy.

W That's not all. I also have to practice the piano.

M Well, do you think you'll have time in the evening to play some online computer games?

W That would be great, but my computer is broken.

M Oh, no! That's too bad.

해석

남 내일 무슨 계획이 있니?

여 글쎄. 하루 종일 정말 바쁠 것 같아.

남 무엇을 할 건데?

여 우선 우리 엄마가 아침에 집 청소하는 것을 도와달라고 하셨고, 11시 30분에는 치과에 가야 해. 그 후 3시에는 과학숙제를 도우러 Jennifer를 만날 거야.

남 와. 너 정말 바쁘겠다.

여 그게 다가 아니야. 피아노 연습도 해야 해.

남 음. 저녁에 온라인 게임을 할 시간이 있을 거 같니?

여 그러면 좋겠지만 내 컴퓨터는 고장 났어.

남 저런. 안됐구나.

4 ②

Script

M Oh, no. They only have tickets for after 5 p.m.

W What time is it now?

M It's only two o'clock. Do you still want to see the movie?

W Of course.

M What do you want to do for three hours?

W How about going shopping? My father's birthday is just around the corner. It would be nice if you could help me find some gifts.

M Okay. But first, let's buy the tickets.

해석

남 이런. 오후 5시 이후 표만 남았어.

여 지금 몇 시야?

남 겨우 2시야. 너 아직도 영화 보고 싶어?

여 물론이지.

남 세 시간 동안 뭐하고 싶어?

여 쇼핑을 하는 건 어때? 곧 우리 아버지의 생신이야. 내가 선물을 사는 걸 네가 도와주면 좋겠는데.

남 알았어. 하지만 먼저 표를 사자.

Part II

1 ④

Script

M It's getting colder and colder. Can we turn on the heater?

W No, I'm afraid we can't. Electricity is too expensive.

M But I can't study when I'm cold.

W How about putting on another sweater? It will keep you warm, and we can save energy.

해석

남 점점 추워지고 있어. 히터를 켜도 될까?

여 안 돼. 미안하지만 그럴 수 없어. 전기료가 너무 비싸.

남 하지만 난 추우면 공부를 할 수가 없단 말이야.

여 스웨터를 하나 더 입는 게 어때? 그게 널 따뜻하게 해 주고, 에너지도 절약할 수 있어.

2 ②

M If you want this, make yourself busy during the day. If you are tired, you will get this more easily. Avoid coffee. Drink warm milk. Try reading a boring book. These will work.

해석

남 당신이 이것을 원한다면 낮 동안 바쁘게 생활하세요. 피곤하면 더 쉽게 이것을 얻을 수 있습니다. 커피를 피하세요. 따뜻한 우유를 마셔보세요. 지루한 책을 읽어 보세요. 이러한 방법들이 효과가 있을 거예요.

3 ④

Script

W Have you thought about where we should go for a picnic?

M Yeah. I'd like to go to a park.

W But Su-mi said she would rather go swimming.

M What do you think?

W Well, I want to go camping in the forest and get some fresh air.

M It's hard to make a decision when everyone has different ideas.

W I don't know what to do. It's driving me crazy.

해석

여 소풍을 어디로 갈지 생각해 봤니?

남 응. 나는 공원에 가고 싶어.

여 하지만 수미는 수영하러 가는 게 낫겠다고 했는데.

남 너는 어떻게 생각해?

여 글쎄. 나는 숲으로 캠핑을 가서 신선한 공기를 좀 마시고 싶어.

남 모두 다른 의견을 가지고 있으니 결정을 하기가 어렵네.

여 어떻게 해야 할지 모르겠다. 미치겠다.

4 ⑤

Script

W Yesterday Jack called me. His computer wasn't working well. I said to Jack "I know a lot about computers," and I went to his house to fix his computer. I took the computer apart and tried to fix it but I made it worse. To make a long story short, we had to call the computer repair shop.

해석

여 어제 Jack이 나에게 전화를 했다. 그의 컴퓨터가 잘 작동하지 않고 있었다. 나는 Jack에게 "내가 컴퓨터에 대해 많이 알아."라고 말했다. 그리고 컴퓨터를 고쳐 주려고 Jack의 집으로 갔다. 나는 컴퓨터를 분해해서 고치려고 애를 썼지만, 점점 나빠졌다. 간단히 말해서 우리는 컴퓨터 수리점에 전화를 해야 했다.

Part 12

1 ⑤

Script

W I didn't have any breakfast because I woke up late this morning. I was very hungry. As soon as the bell rang after the fourth class, I ran to the cafeteria as fast as I could. There were already several students in line. While I was waiting, a boy cut in line in front of me. I was angry. And I stared at him but he did not move.

해석

여 나는 오늘 아침에 늦게 일어나서 아침을 먹지 못했다. 나는 배가 몹시 고프다. 4교시 수업이 끝나는 종이 울리자마자 나는 가능한 빨리 학교 구내식당으로 달려갔다. 이미 몇 명의 학생들이 줄을 서 있었다. 내가 기다리는 데 한 소년이 내 앞에서 새치기를 했다. 나는 화가 났다. 그리고 그를 빤히 쳐다보았지만 그는 움직이지 않았다.

2 ②

Script

W The other day, Sally bought some bed sheets at a small store near her home. But when she got home and examined the sheets, Sally was shocked. One of them had a big hole in the middle and the others were very dirty. Sally was very angry and went back immediately to complain. In this situation, what would Sally most likely say to the salesperson?

해석

여 며칠 전에 Sally는 집 근처의 작은 가게에서 침대보를 몇 개 샀다. 하지만 집에 와서 침대보를 자세히 살펴보고는 충격을 받았다. 침대보 중 하나에는 중간에 큰 구멍이 나 있었고, 나머지는 매우 더러웠다. Sally는 너무 화가 나서 항의를 하려고 즉시 그 가게로 돌아갔다. 이 상황에서 Sally는 판매원에게 뭐라고 이야기하겠는가?

3 ⑤

Script

M Hi, Su-mi. Where are you going?

W I'm going to the library. I need some books for my English writing homework.

M What are you going to write about?

W I haven't decided yet. Have you?

M Yes, I'm going to write about the people who have changed our history. Why don't you write about the same topic as me?

W _____

해석

남 안녕 수미? 어디 가는 길이니?

여 도서관에 가는 길이야. 영어 작문 숙제를 하려면 책이 좀 필요해.

남 무엇에 대해서 쓸 건데?

여 아직 결정을 못했어. 너는 결정했어?

남 응, 나는 역사를 바꾼 사람들에 대해 쓸 거야. 너도 나와 같은 주제로 글을 써 보는 건 어때?

여 _____

4 ③

Script

W What are you doing, Steve?

M I'm picking up some trash. People don't care about the environment these days. They're just destroying the environment.

W Right. I recycle and ride my bike instead of driving.

M Good for you! We need to do more to save the earth.

W What else do you do?

M _____

해석

여 무엇을 하고 있니, Steve?

남 쓰레기를 좀 줍고 있어. 요즘 사람들은 환경에 대해 신경을 쓰지 않아. 사람들은 환경을 파괴하고만 있을 뿐이야.

여 맞아. 나는 재활용을 하고, 운전하는 대신에 자전거를 타고 다녀.

남 잘 했어! 지구를 살리려면 더 많은 일을 해야 해.

여 너는 그 밖에 무슨 일을 하고 있어?

남 _____

중학 영어듣기

AFTER SCHOOL Listening

- 시·도 교육청 공동 주관 중학교 영어듣기능력평가 기출 문제 완전 분석
- 최신 듣기평가 기출 유형이 100% 반영된 모의고사 16회분과 실전 영어듣기평가 2회분
- 잘 들리지 않았던 부분을 확실히 확인할 수 있도록 도와주는 회별 Dictation Test
- 기출 문제 유형 분석과 각종 핵심 표현을 총정리한 실전 대비 학습

NEXUS makes your next day

www.nexusEDU.kr | 책에 대해 궁금한 사항은 넥서스에듀 홈페이지 1:1 **고객상담 게시판**을 이용하세요.